Understanding & Sharing:

An Introduction to
Speech Communication

Sixth Edition

Judy Cornelia Pearson
Ohio University, Athens

Paul Edward Nelson
Ohio University, Athens

WCB Brown &
Benchmark
PUBLISHERS

Madison, Wisconsin • Dubuque, Iowa

Book Team

Editor *Stan Stoga*
Developmental Editor *Steve Lehman*
Production Editor *Marlys Nekola*
Designer *Kristyn A. Kalnes*
Art Editor/Art Processor *Joseph P. O'Connell*
Permissions Editor *Mavis M. Oeth*
Publishing Services Specialist *Sherry Padden*
Marketing Manager *Pamela S. Cooper*
Advertising Manager *Jodi Rymer*

Brown & Benchmark

A Division of Wm. C. Brown Communications, Inc.

Executive Vice President/General Manager *Thomas E. Doran*
Vice President/Editor in chief *Edgar J. Laube*
Vice President/Sales and Marketing *Eric Ziegler*
Director of Production *Vickie Putman Caughron*
Director of Custom and Electronic Publishing *Chris Rogers*

Wm. C. Brown Communications, Inc.

President and Chief Executive Officer *G. Franklin Lewis*
Corporate Senior Vice President and Chief Financial Officer *Robert Chesterman*
Corporate Senior Vice President and President of Manufacturing *Roger Meyer*

Joan Miro, *CIFFRES ET CONSTELLATIONS EN AMOUREUX DE SA FEMME,* 1941, gouache on paper, 45.8 × 38.2 cm, Gift of Mrs. Gilbert W. Chapman, © 1993 The Art Institute of Chicago. All Rights Reserved.

Dedicated to our parents:

Sophia and J. D.
Ferne and H. B.

Brief Contents

part 1

Elements of the Communication Process   1

part 2

Interpersonal Communication   155

part 3

Public Communication   233

Contents

 part 1

Elements of the Communication Process   1

chapter 1

The Nature of Communication   2

part 2

Interpersonal Communication   155

chapter 8

Interpersonal Relationships: Close Encounters   156

chapter 9

Intercultural and Co-cultural Communication   186

chapter 10

Small Group Communication, Leadership, and Conflict Resolution 208

part 3

Public Communication 233

chapter 13

Finding Information 284

chapter 14

Organizing Your Speech 314

chapter 15

Delivery and Visual Aids 350

Chapter Activities

Preface

You are about to begin a course that can make an important difference in your life. The book is about you. It is about the way you communicate with yourself, with other individuals, with small groups, and with larger audiences. The ideas you learn in this course can be applied at once in your daily life, and you can keep on using them for a lifetime.

Understanding and Sharing is now in its sixth edition because so many students like it and so many professors adopt it for their courses. Perhaps they like the book because it instructs in an attractive manner. As one of the professors who reviewed this text said, ". . . I am really uncomfortable with textbooks which are dominated by 'flash and sizzle,' particularly flash and sizzle for flash and sizzle's sake. *This text does a good job of balancing substance and sizzle.*"

This book is an introduction to speech communication. Intended for beginning students of any age; the text is for majors and nonmajors alike. It does not assume prior knowledge of the field, and it is written in a conversational, easy-to-read, style. Above all, this book is practical and applicable. You may never dissect another frog or do another physics experiment in your entire life, but you will have to communicate. This book is written so you can learn to do it effectively.

Helping You to Learn

Each chapter begins with questions that the chapter will answer. If you use them as a guide before you read the chapter, you will be able to focus better on the main points and remember them. Every concept is defined when introduced and then defined again in the end of chapter Key Terms. Distributed in the chapters are exercises, checklists, cartoons, applications, photos, and line drawings to sustain interest and to encourage immediate application. Correct answers for the exercises appear at the end of the chapters.

How is the Book Organized?

Partitioned by communication contexts, the book has three parts. Part 1, "Elements of the Communication Process," introduces concepts useful in any context. The seven chapters in this section cover communication process; perception; self-awareness and self-concept; active and empathic listening; critical listening and critical thinking; and nonverbal and verbal codes.

Part 2, "Interpersonal Communication," has three chapters that cover material on interpersonal relationships; intercultural and co-cultural communication; and small group communication, leadership, and conflict resolution.

Part 3, "Public Communication," includes seven chapters including information about topic selection and audience analysis; communication apprehension and speaker credibility; finding information; organizing the speech; delivery and visual aids; informative speaking; and persuasive speaking.

What is New?

Professors who have been using this text for fourteen years are always curious about changes. A major change is the addition of chapter 9, "Intercultural and Co-cultural Communication." Authored by Mark Orbe, a Ph.D. candidate who has a Filipino parent and an African-American spouse, this chapter is designed to meet the new demand for more formal instruction on diversity. Many disciplines remain silent on this issue, but the field of speech communication should be in the forefront in facing the issue. This chapter will help start the discussion.

The most innovative chapter in the last edition was the one on critical thinking, another topic that was rarely discussed at the time. After praising the authors for including chapter 5 and after stressing that universities liked the inclusion of critical thinking in an introductory course, users admitted that the symbolic logic and the nine rules of inference were difficult to teach and to learn. This edition provides a different and more palatable approach to critical thinking.

Some material has been moved or deleted from this edition. The chapters on small group communication and leadership have been combined into a chapter on group communication, leadership, and conflict resolution. Instruction on interviewing for information has been retained in chapter 13, "Finding Information," and a new appendix has been added to cover basic guidelines and information about interviewing for jobs. Chapter 8, "Interpersonal Relationships: Close Encounters," continues to carry the concepts ordinarily studied in that context, but the particular application to family and friends has been dropped.

Finally, the entire text has been judiciously pruned. Books tend to grow larger and more expensive with each new edition, but this sixth edition had five professor-reviewers help us trim the size without reducing the quality of the text.

What Accompanies the Book?

Experienced professors and new teachers alike will find the ancillary materials highly useful. They include the following:

- An Instructor's Manual with a detailed summary of each chapter, semester and quarter sample schedules, classroom exercises for every chapter, and over 900 essay, true or false, and multiple-choice questions. The latter have been classroom tested and rated for difficulty level, and they are available as a computerized test bank.

- Transparencies of the introductory questions and illustrations to help the teacher preview the chapters and discuss the concepts.

- A wide variety of videotapes dealing with public speaking, small group communication, and interpersonal communication that can be used by teachers in the classroom.

- An annotated instructor's edition expertly prepared by Jon Hess of the University of Minnesota to further assist the teacher in effectively using this text.

Who Are the Authors?

The authors of *Understanding and Sharing* have spent their entire professional lives writing books for basic speech communication courses. They have written five editions of *Confidence in Public Speaking* and six editions of *Understanding and Sharing*. The books grew out of their many years of directing basic courses and teaching them at many different universities. Both have won awards from the professional associations as outstanding teachers.

The first author is Judy C. Pearson, a professor and Director of Graduate Studies in the School of Interpersonal Communication at Ohio University. After earning her bachelor's degree from St. Cloud State University in Minnesota, she earned M.A. and Ph.D. degrees from Indiana University. She was a basic course director at Bradley University, at Indiana-Purdue University in Ft. Wayne, Indiana, and at Iowa State University. She has authored or co-authored sixteen textbooks and is working on her second trade book.

The second author is her spouse, Paul E. Nelson. He earned his B.S., B.A., M.A. and Ph.D. degrees from the University of Minnesota. A basic course director at the University of Missouri, he was also Director of that university's Honors College. He chaired the department at Iowa State University and has been Dean of the College of Communication at Ohio University for twelve years. His greatest pleasure is teaching nearly 800 students each year in 101, "Introduction to Human Communication," a course that uses *Understanding and Sharing*. These students provide ample feedback about what they like and dislike about the book, and they provide considerable incentive for writing the book well.

Who Helped with the Sixth Edition?

Top students who earned an A in both "Introduction to Human Communication" and "Fundamentals of Public Speaking" were invited to critically evaluate every sentence in the book. They suggested ways to make the book more interesting to our end users, the students. They were Jon Ohlinger, Jen Moore, Amy Musyt, Dana Harrington, and Lori Anderson. Their comments were particularly insightful because after they earned their As in the basic courses, they served as tutors for the students in the 101 course.

Professional colleagues also critically evaluated the sixth edition and made constructive suggestions for improvement. They are not to be blamed for any shortcomings of the book. The authors always did as suggested when at least two of the critics agreed, but occasionally, they took the author's option of doing what they felt was right regardless of the critic's comments. The colleagues who provided these helpful suggestions follow:

Carol Armbrecht	*North Central College, Naperville, Illinois*
George Bradley	*Sul Ross State University, Alpine, Texas*
Maresa Brassil	*University of Montgomery, Montgomery, Alabama*
Carol Stringer Cawyer	*University of Oklahoma, Norman, Oklahoma*
Betsy Gordon	*McKendree College, Lebanon, Illinois*
Chris R. Kasch	*Bradley University, Peoria, Illinois*
Albert Katz	*University of Wisconsin–Superior, Superior, Wisconsin*
Kathie Leeper	*Northwest Missouri State University, Maryville, Missouri*
Marie Liberace	*Rockland Community College, Suffern, New York*
Kathleen Valdetero	*University of Southwestern Louisiana, Lafayette, Louisiana*

We also acknowledge the assistance of the following colleagues, who took time out of their busy schedules to respond to a survey on the fifth edition:

Harlene Adams
*California State University–
  Sacramento*

Vicki Anderson
Southwestern Community College

Robert Becker
Standing Rock Community College

George Bradley
Sul Ross State University

Suzanne Calvert
Mississippi State University for Women

Mary Darling
Spring Arbor College

Diane Gorcyca
Missouri Western State College

Julie Johnson
South Plains College

Albert Katz
University of Wisconsin–Superior

Terry Lawrence
Bethel College

Janet Mays
Oklahoma Christian University

Barry McCauliff
Clarion University of Pennsylvania

Juanita Palmerhal
New Mexico State University

Sage Platt
Southern Utah University

Roger Smitter
North Central College

Linda Strasma
Bradley University

Ronald Subeck
Wilbur Wright College

Richard Sweeney
Pennsylvania College of Technology

Keith Titus
Alpena Community College

Kathleen Valdeterro
University of Southwestern Louisiana

Tom Walton
West Arkansas Community College

If you have suggestions for improving the book, you should call the authors at the following numbers:

Judy C. Pearson   *614-593-4831*
Paul E. Nelson   *614-593-4884*

part 1

Elements of the
Communication Process

What do you need to know first? In college education, the first concepts you need to learn are in the general education courses. In a discipline or field of study there are core ideas, basic concepts you need to understand in order to comprehend the rest. We call them the elements of the communication process.

Chapter 1, "The Nature of Communication," defines *communication,* explains a model, and compares the contexts: intrapersonal, interpersonal (pairs and groups), and public communication. Chapter 2, "The Role of Perception in Communication," shows how your perception shapes communication. Chapter 3, "Understanding through Self-Awareness and Self-Concept," shows the importance of you in communication. Chapter 4, "Listening in Communication," explores you as a receiver of messages. Chapter 5, "Critical Listening and Thinking," shows how to analyze information. Chapter 6, "Nonverbal Communication," includes use of body, face, space, touch, voice, and clothing in communication. Chapter 7, "Language and Communication," explores the role of words, vocabulary, and thought in communication.

You begin these six chapters on the fundamentals, the core ideas, by learning what communication is and how it works.

chapter 1

The Nature of Communication

To begin your understanding of communication, you need to know what it is. This chapter defines the term, shows how it begins with you and extends to other people, reveals its seven components—people, messages, channels, feedback, codes, encoding, decoding, and noise, and shows differences and similarities among its three contexts—intrapersonal, interpersonal, and public. We start by learning the answer to the question: Why should I study communication?

What will you learn?

When you have read and thought about this chapter, you will be able to answer the following questions:

1. Why should you study communication?

2. What is the definition of communication?

3. What are two ways that communication begins with self?

4. How does communication involve other people?

5. What are the differences among action, interaction, and transactional models of communication?

6. What are the seven components of communication?

7. What are five ways that intrapersonal, interpersonal, and public communication differ from each other?

Effective loving calls for knowledge of the object. . . . How can I love a person whom I do not know? How can the other person love me if he [she] does not know me?

Sidney M. Jourard

Americans report that their greatest fear is the fear of speaking in front of a group.

Bruskin Report

Speech is civilization itself. The word, even the most contradictory word, preserves contact—it is silence which isolates.

Thomas Mann

T hink about how much time we spend communicating. Experts say we spend more time talking and listening than any other activity.[1] Even though we spend much of our life communicating, many of us realize that we need improvement. We need improved communication skills in our personal lives and on the job.[2] Some adults are poor at giving directions or listening to instructions. Others have poor relationships with friends and loved ones because they don't talk or don't listen. Thousands of people are afraid to speak to large groups or even small groups. Let us consider why we should study communication.

Why Should We Study Communication?

Although there are many others, here are a few of the reasons why you need to know more about communication.

1. By understanding the nature of communication and how it works, you will see more clearly why one communication is successful and why another is not successful. It helps to have definitions, know components, and see models for a theoretical understanding of communication.
2. By knowing how communication changes in different contexts, you increase your flexibility as a communicator.
3. By understanding how your own perceptions shape what you say and how you listen, you increase your own effectiveness.
4. By becoming more aware of yourself and how you assess yourself, you learn how self-awareness influences your communication.
5. By understanding why and how you listen, you can improve your capacity to learn from and respond to others.
6. By learning how to think critically, you improve your analytical skills as a consumer of ideas.
7. By studying verbal and nonverbal communication, you discover how both kinds of communication combine in the sending and receiving of messages.
8. By learning more about human relationships, you find out how they develop and how they disintegrate and how problems can be resolved.
9. By studying how language functions between and among cultures and co-cultures, you can facilitate understanding among diverse people.
10. By understanding small group communication, you can learn more about how human groups solve problems and make decisions.
11. By exploring leadership, you can discover why some people become leaders and why many do not.
12. By studying public speaking, you can learn all the research, organization, and delivery skills that lead to effective, informative, and persuasive speeches.

The importance of learning about communication goes well beyond the personal gains you might make through better human relations. Indeed, our society is in considerable trouble because the melting pot is no longer the metaphor for our nation. As usual, the arts sense the tempo first and depict it in film and literature. The movie, *Bladerunner*[3] shows a society run by the elite over and around brutish metropolitan masses. The novel *The Pelican Brief*[4] by John Grisham pictures a society dominated by hate groups, and the brilliant analysis of American culture entitled *The Good Society*[5] points out that most Americans now live and work in cultural enclaves of people just like themselves, intentionally isolated from others. Any American can mentally construct a list of who hates whom from the daily newscasts. The United States almost self-destructed in the Civil War, which cost more American lives than any war since, including World War II. Now our country seems less committed to a common purpose and more determined to self-destruct by pitting neighbor against neighbor because of their political party, religion, nationality, color, or economic status.

Fictional accounts do not have to be self-fulfilling prophecies. Many people were relieved when the details of Orwell's book *1984* never occurred. Literary accounts of a dismal future can be used as a way to avoid or prevent a destructive future. Communication plays a major role in reunification efforts because principles of communication, effective human relations, and civility are prerequisites to the common purposes that make the modern democratic country.

This book, if you think about and practice what it says, can improve your communication skills and make your life more satisfying. Besides improving life on the personal front and in the work place, its principles can help mend a fractured nation. Applied internationally, the ideas espoused in this book can be used to keep us from killing each other in endless conflicts. The sooner you learn the important precepts of communication, the sooner you can apply them. Let's move on to discover what communication is.

A Definition of Communication

Communication: The Process of Understanding and Sharing Meaning

The word *communication* is used in a variety of ways. Before we use the term any further, we should establish a common understanding of its definition. Communication comes from the Latin *communicare,* which means "to make common." This original definition of the word is consistent with the definition of communication used in this text.

Communication is an activity in which we participate.

In this text, **communication** is defined as the process of understanding and sharing meaning. Communication is considered a **process** because it is an activity, exchange, or set of behaviors—not an unchanging, static product. Communication is not an object we can hold in our hand—it is an activity in which we participate. David Berlo, a well-known communication figure, probably provides the clearest statement about communication as a process. Berlo writes:

> If we accept the concept of process, we view events and relationships as dynamic, ongoing, ever-changing, continuous. When we label something as a process, we also mean that it does not have a beginning, an end, a fixed sequence of events. It is not static, at rest. It is moving. The ingredients within a process interact; each affects all of the others.[6]

What is an example of how a process operates in everyday communication? Picture two students passing on the sidewalk between classes and exchanging a few sentences. Did this very tiny communication episode really begin and end with their first and last word? Do we have to consider that both of them spoke to each other in English, that they must have had some prior encounter, or that they would not have stopped to exchange messages. If they have common understanding of what was said, then they must share some

Human communication involves understanding and sharing among people.

experiences that shape their perceptions similarly. Didn't their message go beyond the words to how they looked, if they smiled, and how much volume they used? Did the episode end with the last word and look or was it used to solidify their relationship? Was their brief conversation thought about later that day and the next, and did it lead to another meeting that night? Communication is a complicated process. It is variable, active, and dynamic. It starts long before the words begin to flow and can last long after the words stop.

Communication is a process that requires **understanding.** Your professor asks, "What is the ontogeny of your misogeny?" You hear the words, but you may not be able to understand or interpret them. An Asian student who has to struggle with English as a second language may have the same trouble with words that most Americans regard as easy to understand. Understanding, or grasping, the meaning of another person's message does not occur unless the two communicators can elicit common meanings for words, phrases, and non-verbal codes. The importance of this kind of understanding was emphasized by humanistic psychologist Carl Rogers in his book *On Becoming a Person.* He wrote, "I have found it of enormous value when I can *permit* myself to understand another person."[7]

In addition to understanding, communication involves **sharing.** Consider the popular use of the word *sharing*. We share a meal, we share an event, we share a sunset. Sharing is a gift that people exchange. We can also share with ourselves when we allow ourselves time to relax and daydream, time to consider who we are and what our goals are. We share with others when we talk to them alone or in larger groups. Regardless of the context, communication involves sharing.

What exactly is understood and shared in the communication process? When you use language for expression, **meaning** is the shared understanding of your feelings. When you use language for pragmatic purposes, meaning is the appropriate response that indicates the message was understood. For example, you ask for a drink, and the other person gives you one. Meaning is the message you construct in your mind as you interpret the message sent.

An example of how meaning operates is the Rodney King incident in which people around the world saw an African American being beaten by Los Angeles police. The meaning of the videotaped event was whatever interpretation people developed in their own minds. Most people perceived the incident as police power gone awry. When the jury acquitted the police, many people interpreted the decision as a miscarriage of justice. Everyone who saw the videotapes or who read about the verdict constructed their own meaning, their own interpretation of the incident. The meaning attributed to the incident fashioned responses from agreement, to disbelief, to violence.

Communication Within, Between, and Among People

The term *communication* may be used broadly to refer to the understanding and sharing that occurs among animals other than humans.[8] In this text, we limit our discussion to human communication, the communication that occurs within, between, and among humans. As such, we observe that communication begins with the self and involves others.

Communication Begins with the Self

Our communication is viewed from the perspective of self. As Carl Rogers wrote, "Every individual exists in a continually changing world of experience of which he [or she] is the center."[9] Consider, for example, the case of Magic Johnson, the African-American professional basketball star who was diagnosed HIV positive for AIDS. Before he contracted the disease, it was not perceived as a threat by most Americans because the disease was thought to be limited to Haitians, homosexuals, and habitual drug users. Magic Johnson clearly did not fit this profile. Newly married, about to have his first child, and one of the most admired people in America, Johnson looked within himself and decided he must use his example to save others. Communication was initiated by Magic Johnson's internal assessment of himself as a star, a victim, and a crusader.

Figure 1.1 Barnlund's "six people" involved in every two-person communication.

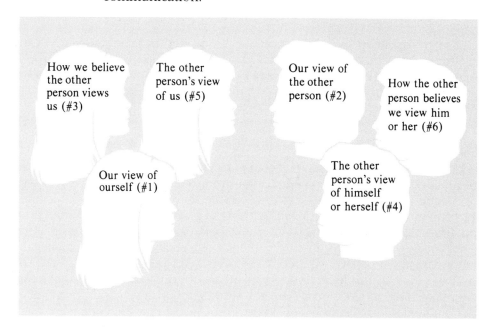

Dean Barnlund, a communication theorist, introduced the idea that communication is viewed from one's own perspective in his discussion of the "six persons" involved in every two-person communication situation (figure 1.1)[10] These six persons emerge in the following ways:

1. How you view yourself
2. How you view the other person
3. How you believe the other person views you
4. How the other person views himself or herself
5. How the other person views you
6. How the other person believes you view him or her.

Barnlund believes that we "construct" ourselves, as well as other persons, through the relationships that we have, wish to have, or perceive ourselves as having. He encourages us to consider the various perspectives involved in communication and to recognize the centrality of the self in communication.

An example may clarify Barnlund's six people. Suppose you see yourself as an enthusiastic, highly-motivated student (1). You perceive your best friend as a very intelligent, yet judgmental, underclassperson (2). She sees you as fun-loving and achievement-oriented (5) and views herself as of moderate intelligence but a good conversationalist (4). You, therefore, respect her and ask her opinion on academic matters, yet discount her negative messages concerning other areas.

She, in turn, offers frequent advice but fails to share her opinions (6). She, in addition, sees you not as "driven" but as energetic and funny. Your tendency, therefore, may be to downplay your accomplishments and emphasize your sense of humor (3).

As participants in communication, we are limited by our own view of the situation. A student, for instance, may describe a conflict with an instructor as unfair treatment. "My professor doesn't like me and, therefore, grades me more harshly." The instructor, conversely, might remark, "The student is unfamiliar with class policy."

Communication Involves Other People

Even when we "talk to ourselves," communication involves other people. How does this occur? We view communication from our own perspective and with our unique perceptual processes; however, the self we know is largely learned from others. George Herbert Mead explains that self originates in communication. The child, through verbal and nonverbal symbols, learns to accept roles in response to the expectations of others.[11] We establish our self-image, the sort of person we believe we are, by the ways other people categorize us. The positive, negative, and neutral messages others offer us enable us to determine who we are. Our self-definition, then, arises through our interactions with others.

Communication also involves others in the sense that the competent communicator considers the other person's needs and expectations as he or she selects appropriate and effective messages to share. The competent communicator understands that a large number of messages can be shared at any time, but sensitivity and responsiveness to the other communicator are essential. Thus, we observe that communication begins with the self, as defined largely by others, and involves others, as defined largely by the self.

Communication Models

Barnlund's six persons rendition of communication is a model, a kind of pictorial depiction of how communication looks if we diagram it. A model's relationship to reality is like that of a wiring diagram to the actual wiring of an apartment, or a dress pattern to the actual construction of a dress. A model is a simplification, but it is also a predictor of how communication might occur.

Three more communication models show communication as action, interaction, and transaction. In the past, people believed that communication could be viewed as **action,** that is, one person sends a message and another receives it. This view, depicted in figure 1.2, can be compared to the situation in which one person holds a basketball and throws it to another. The second person does not return the ball, but only catches (or fumbles) it. Using this model of communication, the speaker sends the message to the audience as a kind of innoculation in which the message is a shot that may or may not take effect.

Figure 1.2
Communication as
action.

Figure 1.3
Communication as
interaction.

Figure 1.4
Communication as
transaction.

S = Sender

S = Sender

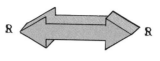

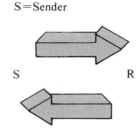

S ⟶ R

S   R

R̄ = Sender and receiver

R = Receiver

A second view evolved in which communication is viewed as **interaction.** One person sends a message to a second person, who receives it and responds with another message. The communicators take turns sending and receiving messages. This point of view is pictured in figure 1.3. To continue with our basketball analogy, this perspective would be similar to a game of catch. Each person catches (or drops) the ball, and each person throws the ball. However, the ball cannot be thrown until it is caught. Using this model of communication, the speaker and receiver take turns being speaker and listener in a linear fashion.

Viewing communication as a **transaction** means we believe communicators simultaneously send and receive messages rather than identifying people as senders or receivers (figure 1.4). Thus, speaking and listening are not separate activities, nor do they occur one at a time. According to the transactional view (accepted in this text), people are continually sending and receiving messages; they cannot avoid communication. We view communication as a confusing ball game in which a person catches and throws an unlimited number of balls at any time, in any direction, to any other person. An individual's throwing a ball is not dependent on an ability to catch one first. He or she does not always "take turns" in this game. The game has some rules and some predictability, but from time to time, balls fly through the air without preplanning or preparation. Under this model messages are everywhere. The person talking to you on the sidewalk, nodding to a passerby while stating agreement with you, is in a transactional situation with multiple messages. How you look, what you say, how receptive you are, and what is happening around you all become part of the transactional model.

In some settings, one person may serve as the primary transmitter of messages, while another person or persons serve(s) primarily as receiver(s) of messages. For example, in public speaking, we can identify a speaker and an audience of listeners. In interpersonal communication, such a distinction frequently cannot be made. In those situations in which one person is perceived as the initiator of messages, or as the speaker, we refer to the listeners' transmission of verbal and nonverbal messages as feedback. Feedback will be defined more fully later in this chapter.

Components of Communication

You know communication is understanding and sharing meaning and you know several models of communication. Now you will discover the components of communication.

People

People are involved in the human communication process in two ways. They serve as the *sources* and the *receivers* of messages. The **source** is the component that initiates a message. The **receiver** is the component that absorbs, or takes in, the message. Individuals do not perform these two roles independently. Instead, they are the source and the receiver of messages simultaneously and continually.

As you know, people are not like programmed computers or machines. They do not respond in a uniform way to all messages, nor do they provide the same messages in exactly the same way. Individual characteristics of people, including their race, gender, age, culture, values, and attitudes affect both their sending and receiving qualities. Intercultural communication and gender and communication have both become increasingly important topics during the past three decades. Throughout this text you will find examples that illustrate that an individual's membership in a culture or co-culture affects his or her communication behavior.

Message

The **message** is the verbal and nonverbal form of the idea, thought, or feeling that one person (the source) wishes to communicate to another person or group of persons (the receivers). It is the content of the interaction. The message includes the words and phrases we use to communicate our ideas as well as our facial expressions, bodily movements, gestures, touch, tone of voice, and other nonverbal codes. The message may be relatively brief and easy to understand, or it may be long and complex. Some messages are intentional, while others are accidental.

Channel

The **channel** provides the mode by which a message moves from the source of the message to the receiver of the message. Both light waves and sound waves are major channels when we interact with another person, and we can see and hear him or her. Similarly, if we are watching television or a movie, we rely on both light waves and sound waves. Some forms of communication require only one channel. For instance, we rely on sound waves alone when we listen to the radio or are plugged into an "audio-only" conference call. We rely exclusively on light waves when we read a book or when we read the print on a computer monitor.

Feedback

Feedback is the receiver's verbal and nonverbal response to the source's message. Let us say you need to find a restroom in an unfamiliar building. You say to a person passing quickly past, "Excuse me, can you. . . ," but the person keeps on going without acknowledging your inquiry. This is zero feedback, a case in which the intended receiver did not acknowledge your message. What if the person turns before you finish your question and says, "What did you say?" That is feedback indicating the receiver did not fully understand your inquiry. The best feedback in this situation would be an answer to your question concerning the location of the restroom.

The previous example is an interpersonal situation, but feedback is part of any communication situation. Silence and hesitation on the telephone is feedback. Restive behavior and quizzical looks in the lecture hall are examples of feedback for a public speaker. High fidelity communication occurs when the source is sensitive to feedback and responds appropriately to verbal and nonverbal messages sent by the receiver or audience.

Code

People have ideas or thoughts they wish to express, and they express them in the form of messages. How do our thoughts become messages? We use codes to share our ideas with others. We typically use the word *code* to describe the secret language that children use or to refer to specialized, stylized, or shortened languages, such as Morse code. For our purposes, however, a **code** is any systematic arrangement or comprehensive collection of symbols, letters, or words that have arbitrary meanings and are used for communication.

Two major types of codes are used in communication: verbal codes and nonverbal codes. **Verbal codes** consist of words and their grammatical arrangement. It is easier to think of the German or French language as a code than it is to realize that our own language is a code. All language are codes. The English symbols, letters, and words we use are arbitrary. We have no more reason to call a heavy outer garment by the word *overcoat* than a German does to call it *der Mantel*. Nature does not provide a rationale for any particular language. Chapter 7 discusses the importance and role of verbal codes in communication.

Nonverbal codes consist of all symbols that are not words, including our bodily movements, our use of space and time, our clothing and other adornments, and sounds other than words. Nonverbal codes should not be confused with non-oral codes. All non-oral codes—such as bodily movement—are nonverbal codes. Nonverbal codes also include oral codes, such as pitch, duration, and rate of speech, as well as sounds like *eh* and *ah*. Nonverbal codes refer to *all* codes that do not consist of words. Chapter 6 discusses the nature and role of nonverbal codes in communication.

Encoding and Decoding

If communication involves the use of codes, the process of communicating can be viewed as one of encoding and decoding. **Encoding** is defined as the act of putting an idea or thought into a code. **Decoding** is assigning meaning to that idea or thought. For instance, suppose you are interested in purchasing a new car, and you are trying to describe a compact model to your father who wants to help you buy a car. You might visualize the car that belongs to your best friend, picturing the black leather interior, red racing stripe, and sporty design. Putting this vision into words, you might say a compact car is small and well-designed. You encode your perceptions of a particular car into words that describe the model. Your father, on hearing this, decodes your words and develops his own picture. His encounters with larger cars affect this process. As a result of your definition, he envisions a sedan. As we can see, misunderstanding often occurs because of the limitations of our language and the inadequacy of our descriptions. Nonetheless, encoding and decoding are essential in sharing our thoughts, ideas, and feelings with other people.

Noise

Noise is any factor that hinders your reception of messages. It can be physical noise, such as loud sounds; distracting sights, such as a bit of food on someone's face; or unusual behavior, such as a person standing too close. Noise also can be mental, psychological, or semantic, such as daydreaming about a loved one, worry about the bills, pain from a tooth, or uncertainty about what another person's words are supposed to mean.

Contexts of Communication

Communication does not occur in a vacuum. Communication occurs in a **context,** a set of circumstances or a situation. Communication occurs between two friends, among five business acquaintances in a small group setting, and between a lecturer and her audience that fills an auditorium. The importance of the context is less obtrusive in some situations and of greater importance in other situations. The number of people involved in communication affects the

Intrapersonal communication is the process of understanding and sharing meaning within the self.

kind of communication that occurs. We may communicate with ourselves, with another person, or with a large number of others. The differences among these situations affect our choices of the verbal and nonverbal codes we will most appropriately use.

This text is organized around the contexts of communication. These contexts are defined in terms of our definition of communication as the process of understanding and sharing meaning. Let us preview the contexts covered in the text. Each is examined in more detail in upcoming chapters.

Intrapersonal Communication

Intrapersonal communication is the process of understanding and sharing meaning within the self. Why would we need to communicate with ourselves? Suppose you and your dating partner of two years share the same attitude toward education and a future career. You plan to attend graduate school together next year and later operate your own business. One day, your friend informs you that he or she intends to work after graduation this year—in the family's business. This action, in your opinion, will seriously limit your future together. When you begin to share your feelings with your friend, your friend becomes angry with you and replies it is just one more example of your narrow-mindedness. You probably feel a certain amount of psychological discomfort.

What is likely to occur? (1) You could dismiss your friend's remark and the change of plans as irrelevant and act as though nothing has happened to alter your friendship. (2) You could dismiss your friend from any interactions with you. (3) You could decide you were wrong to prejudge your friend's change of plans and that she or he is right in pointing it out to you. None of these outcomes is immediately likely, however. Instead, you are more apt to consider these alternatives—and others—as you try to understand what has occurred. In a sense, you are examining alternative explanations for what has happened and attempting to gain some consistency or coherence among the events and beliefs that you have held. You are engaged in communication within yourself.

Intrapersonal communication occurs, as this example suggests, when we evaluate or examine the interaction that occurs between ourselves and others. Intrapersonal communication is not limited to such times, however. This form of communication occurs prior to, and during, other forms of communication as well. For instance, you argue with yourself during a conversation in which someone asks you to do something you don't really wish to do.

Intrapersonal communication is far more complex than it may appear. Intrapersonal communication involves our central nervous system, our brain hemispheres, and our ability to think. Professor Blaine Goss, from New Mexico State University, states that intrapersonal communication involves the gathering, storing, and retrieving of information and is surrounded by three components: (1) the cognitive component, which includes meanings and language; (2) the affective component, which contains attitudes and self-concept; and (3) the operational component, which includes listening and speaking.[12]

Intrapersonal communication is not restricted to "talking to ourselves"; it also includes such activities as internal problem solving, resolution of internal conflict, planning for the future, emotional catharsis, evaluations of ourselves and others, and the relationships between ourselves and others. Intrapersonal communication involves only the self, and it must be clearly understood by the self because it constitutes the basis for all other communication.

We are engaged in intrapersonal communication almost continually. We might become more easily absorbed in talking to ourselves when we are alone—walking to class, driving to work, taking a shower—but most of us are involved in this form of communication in the most crowded circumstances as well—during a lecture, at a party, or when visiting friends. Think about the last time you looked at yourself in a mirror. What were your thoughts? Intrapersonal communication is almost continuous, yet we seldom focus on our communication with ourselves.

Interpersonal Communication

Interpersonal communication is the personal process of understanding and sharing meaning between ourselves and at least one other person when relatively mutual opportunities for speaking and listening occur. Interpersonal, like intrapersonal, communication occurs for a variety of reasons: to solve problems,

The Case of Sharon Black

Sharon Black, a sophomore at an extension university, worked thirty hours a week at a local department store—a very busy schedule. Sharon wanted to spend more time with her coworkers, but her college work interfered. The other workers usually ate lunch together, but Sharon had a class that started at 12:30 P.M. four days a week. She usually couldn't attend parties because she had homework to do.

Sharon became increasingly quiet at work and felt more alienated as time passed. Her coworkers began to suspect that "the college girl" was avoiding them because she felt superior. They began to plan activities that excluded Sharon.

Sharon's work was exemplary, and she became eligible for promotion to supervisor. Her boss told her that a lot depended on whether the other workers would accept her leadership and cooperate with her. Sharon's coworkers were resentful of the possible promotion of a person who had so little experience at the store. They also felt that she was being "pushed ahead" because she was a college student. At lunch that day, they decided that Sharon would not get the promotion if they had anything to say about it. One of the women offered to tell the boss how they felt.

Sharon was called into the office two days later. Her boss explained that she wasn't going to be promoted because she didn't seem to be getting along well with the others, and it did not look as if they would cooperate with her. Sharon broke into tears and ran from the office.

1. What made Sharon's coworkers feel that Sharon thought she was superior to them?

2. Explain the intrapersonal communication that may have occurred for Sharon. What kinds of internal conflicts was she likely to have been experiencing?

3. Why did the misunderstanding between Sharon and the others grow to this level? Why did they not discuss their differences?

4. Write a dialogue in which Sharon and her coworkers discuss their perceptions.

5. Is Sharon's situation realistic? Identify a similar experience in which you had a misunderstanding with another person or with other people. How did you resolve it?

6. What conclusions can you draw about communication problems with others?

to resolve conflicts, to share information, to improve our perception of ourselves, or to fulfill such social needs as the need to belong or to be loved. Through our interpersonal communication, we are able to establish relationships with others that include friendships and romantic relationships. In chapter 8, interpersonal relationships will be considered.

Dyadic communication, a subset of interpersonal communication, simply refers to two-person communication and includes interviews with an employer or teacher; talks with a parent, spouse, or child; and interactions among strangers, acquaintances, and friends. **Small group communication,** another subset of interpersonal communication, refers to communication involving three or more people. Small group communication occurs in social organizations, such as clubs, civic groups, and church groups and in business settings for the purpose of problem solving or decision making.

The addition of another person complicates communication greatly. Although each of us holds conflicting perceptions, beliefs, values, and attitudes (indeed, a great deal of our intrapersonal communication concerns these conflicts), the differences between two people are generally far greater than those within an individual. In addition, we all have different ways of expressing what we feel. Consequently, the possibility of successful communication decreases.

Next to intrapersonal communication, interpersonal communication is generally considered the most influential form of communication and the most satisfying to the individuals involved in it. Interpersonal communication typically occurs in an informal setting and generally involves face-to-face verbal and nonverbal exchanges and a sharing of the roles of source (speaker) and receiver (listener).

Public Communication

Public communication is the process of understanding and sharing meaning with a number of other people when one person is generally identified as the source (speaker), and others are recognized as receivers (listeners). The speaker adapts his or her message to the audience in an attempt to gain maximum understanding. Sometimes, virtually everyone in the audience understands the speaker's message; at other times, many people fail to understand the speaker. A variety of factors contribute to the level of understanding the speaker achieves. We discuss these factors in part 3.

Public communication, or public speaking, is recognized by its formality, structure, and planning. We are frequently the listeners to public communication in lecture classes, at convocations, and in church. Sometimes, we are speakers: when we speak with a group, when we try to convince other voters of the merits of a particular candidate for office, or when we introduce a guest speaker to a large audience. Public communication most often has the purpose

Table 1.1

Differences in Communication Contexts

	Intrapersonal Communication	Interpersonal Communication		Public Communication
		Dyadic Communication	Small Group Communication	
The number of people involved	One	Two	Usually three to ten; maybe more	Usually more than ten
The degree of formality or intimacy	Most intimate	Generally intimate; interview would be formal	Intimate or formal	Generally formal
The opportunities for feedback	Complete feedback	A great deal of feedback	Less than in intrapersonal communication, but more than in public communication	Less than in small group communication, but more than in mass communication
The need for prestructuring messages	None	Some	Some	A great deal
The degree of stability of the roles of speaker and listener	The individual serves as both speaker and listener	Speaker and listener alternate; unstable	Speakers and listeners alternate; unstable	Highly stable; one speaker with many listeners

of informing or persuading, but it can also have the intent of entertaining, introducing, announcing, welcoming, or paying tribute. We will consider public communication in chapters 11 through 17.

The various contexts—intrapersonal, interpersonal, and public—in which communication can occur can be categorized on the basis of the number of people involved, the degree of formality or intimacy, the opportunities for feedback, the need for prestructuring messages, and the degree of stability of the roles of speaker and listener.

Table 1.1 summarizes the differences among the communication contexts considered in this text. Table 1.1 indicates that, as more and more people are added to the communicative context, the degree of formality increases, the degree of intimacy decreases, the opportunities for feedback decrease, the need for prestructuring messages increases, and the roles of speaker and listener become increasingly stable.

This text proceeds from the most basic context in which communication occurs (intrapersonal communication), moves to interpersonal communication, and concludes with public communication. In each context, we examine the roles of self and others and how individuals attempt to establish understanding and sharing.

Summary

Communication is a relevant topic for the contemporary college student. In this chapter, you were introduced to the basic terminology and some of the essential concepts that will guide your understanding in the rest of the text. You learned that communication is the process of understanding and sharing meaning. In this book, we limit our discussion to human communication. Human communication begins with the self and involves others. Communication involves people, messages, channels, feedback, codes, encoding and decoding, and noise. People are the sources and receivers of messages. Messages include ideas, thoughts, and feelings that one individual wishes to communicate to another person or group of people. Channels are the modes by which messages move from the source of the message to the receiver of the message. Feedback includes the verbal and nonverbal responses provided by the receiver to the source. Codes are systematic arrangements of symbols, letters, and words that have an arbitrary meaning and are used for communication. Encoding occurs when we put a thought or idea into a code. Decoding occurs when we assign meaning to that thought or idea. Any factor that intervenes between encoding and decoding is known as noise.

Communication occurs in differing contexts, including the intrapersonal, interpersonal, and public. The number of people involved, the degree of formality or intimacy, the opportunities for feedback, the need for prestructuring messages, and the degree of stability of the roles of speaker and listener all vary as a result of the communication context. This text is organized on a contextual basis with a consideration of self and others in each context.

While you may spend a great deal of your time engaged in communication, you may find that you do not communicate as successfully as you might wish. This text will assist you in improving your ability to communicate with other people.

Key Terms

action The view of communication that suggests that one person sends a message and the other person receives it.

channel The mode by which a message moves from the source of the message to the receiver of the message; both light waves and sound waves are major channels when we interact and can see and hear the other communicators.

code Any systematic arrangement or comprehensive collection of symbols, letters, or words that have arbitrary meanings and are used for communication.

communication Making common; the process of understanding and sharing meaning.

context A set of circumstances or a situation.

decoding To assign meaning to a verbal code we receive.

dyadic communication Communication between two persons.

encoding To put an idea or thought into a code.

feedback The receiver's verbal and nonverbal responses to the source's messages.

interaction The view of communication that suggests that communicators take turns sending and receiving messages.

interpersonal communication The personal process of sharing and understanding meaning between ourselves and at least one other person.

intrapersonal communication The process of sharing and understanding meaning within ourselves.

meaning What we share and understand in the process of communication; that which is felt to be the significance of something; a more accurate and useful descriptor of the object of communication than the words, message, or thought.

message A unit containing verbal and nonverbal symbols, but in which meaning is not inherent.

noise Any interference in the encoding and decoding processes that lessens the clarity of the message.

nonverbal codes A code consisting of any symbols that are not words, including nonword vocalizations.

process Action, change, exchange, and movement; not an unchanging, static product.

public communication The process of understanding and sharing meaning with a number of other people when one person is generally identified as the source or speaker, and others are recognized as receivers or listeners.

receiver The component of the communication process that receives the message.

sharing Interaction between ourselves and others to exchange meaning.

small group communication Communication that consists of a relatively small number of persons who have a mutually interdependent purpose and a sense of belonging, demonstrate behavior based on norms and values, use procedures accepted by the group, and interact orally.

source The component of the communication process that initiates a message.

transaction The view of communication that describes communicators as continually sending and receiving messages at the same time.

understanding The perception and comprehension of the meaning of incoming stimuli, usually the verbal and nonverbal behavior of others.

verbal codes A code consisting of words and their grammatical arrangement.

chapter 2

Perception:

The Process of Understanding

Y ou see the world from your own unique perspective. Your perceptions are shaped by your family, neighborhood, ethnicity, and many other factors. In this chapter on perception, you will learn why people's perceptions vary through selection, organization, and interpretation. After reading this chapter, you should emerge with a better understanding of why people see the world differently and the impact differences and similarities have on their communication. First, you will discover what perception is.

The three quoted descriptions at the start of the chapter concern the same accident. They can be recognized as descriptions of a similar event, but they vary in all other details. The first description, from the police report, is factual and objective. The second report, from a student, is embellished and more interesting. The dean offers an explanation for the accident and gives more details.

In none of the descriptions does the speaker claim to have witnessed the accident, but eyewitness accounts can also vary greatly. Accident reports are filled with conflicting evidence. People who have seen an automobile accident, for example, will disagree about who was at fault; the number of people involved; and the year, the make, and even the color of the vehicles.

Differences in perception, in the way people see, hear, smell, taste, or feel a specific stimulus, are common. Whether we are describing an event (an automobile accident), an idea (how communication occurs), or something about ourselves (how we feel about our own bodies), we encounter differences in perception. Individual experiences are not identical. Neither are individual perceptions, even of the same event. Perceptions are personal constructs of the perceiver.

W hat will you learn?

When you have read and thought about chapter 2, you should be able to answer the following questions:

1. What is the difference for communicators between the passive and the active views of perception?

2. What are three causes for differences in perception?

3. What are three activities that occur in perception?

4. What is an example from your own life in which you and another person interpreted the same event differently?

5. How does your race, culture, role, and co-culture affect your perceptions?

6. What are some examples that illustrate how figure and ground, proximity, closure, similarity, and perceptual constancy function in communication situations?

At 8:07 P.M. on March 7, 1987, a late-model blue sedan was involved in a collision with a lightweight ten-speed bicycle at 2200 College Drive. No one was injured, but the bicycle was damaged.

Police report

Did you hear what happened last night? I didn't get all the details, but some instructor ran into a student on a bicycle. It's bad enough that those guys have to flunk us—now they're running over us!

College student

I am sorry to report that an unfortunate accident occurred last evening. As a result of our inadequate street lighting, an automobile driven by a student was hit in the rear bumper by a faculty member on a bicycle. Luckily, no one was injured, but the front fender on the bicycle was bent.

Dean of the college

How Does Communication Involve Perception?

Perception is the mental process through which we interpret that which we sense. You sit next to an international student in the library. Your perceptions of yourself and of him or her will decide whether you talk, what you talk about, and how you feel about the episode later.

Your perception of yourself might be that you are a friendly person who treats others as fellow human beings. If so, you are likely to initiate a conversation and feel fulfilled in doing so. Your own perception of yourself will make a difference.

Your perception of others also is a factor. Even though you see yourself as friendly, you may or may not be comfortable talking to someone from another culture. We make judgments about others within a few seconds of meeting them.[1] Our perception of others determines if we communicate, how we communicate, and how we feel about the experience before, during, and after the event.

What is Perception?

At one time, even the experts tended to see perception as passive. **Passive perception** means that people were like video recorders who tended to receive what they sensed in the same way. Reception was **objective;** receivers did not add to or change what they sensed. The things they sensed had **inherent meaning:** a chair was a chair, and that is all there was to it.

Now perception is considered more active. **Active perception** means that we are all different video cameras. We aim the camera differently and at different things, our lenses are different, we see different colors, and our sound systems pick up different sounds. Perception is **subjective** and **creative:** we interpret what we sense; we make it our own; and we add to and subtract from what we see, hear, smell, and touch. As depicted in figure 2.1, our perception of the apple is not the same as anyone else's perception of it. If you like apples and you are hungry, you will interpret differently if you spot a worm hole.

Consider how much your inner state affects your perceptions. If you have a bad headache, it probably will affect the way you treat your children, the way you respond to your employer's request for some extra work, and even the way you see yourself in the mirror. Consider also how complicated communication becomes when you know that everyone has his or her own view, uniquely developed and varying both by what is happening outside and inside his or her own head. Finally, consider what happens to Barnlund's six-persons model when you add to the equation all the variations that can and will occur

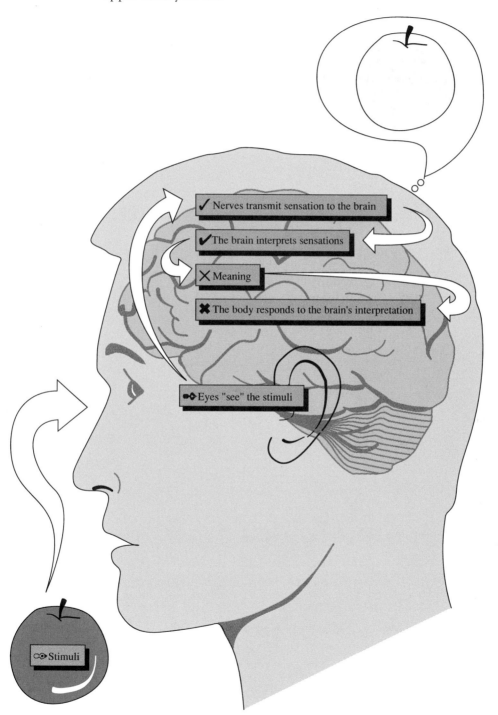

Figure 2.1 Perception is far more complex than merely sensing stimuli. For example, this color blind individual "sees" a different apple than you do.

25

when perception is taken into account. Perception is just one of the many reasons communication gets complicated, differences invite conflict, and commonality of view is hard to achieve.

Why Do Differences in Perception Occur?

We have just demonstrated a common phenomenon—different people perceiving the same event in different ways. Moreover, perception is subjective, active, and creative. Differences occur in perception because of physiological factors, different past experiences, and differences in present feelings and circumstances.

Physiological Factors

None of us is physiologically identical to anyone else. We vary in height, weight, body type, sex, and in our senses. People can be tall or short, have less than perfect vision, or suffer from impaired hearing. They can be particularly sensitive or insensitive to smells or odors. Sensitivity to temperature similarly varies from one individual to another.

Gender may be an important physiological difference to be considered in perception. Some authors have suggested that hemispheric differences in the cerebral cortex of the brain are sex-linked. These differences are said to account for females' language facility and fine hand control and males' spatial and mathematical abilities, as well as their increased likelihood of suffering with dyslexia, stuttering, delayed speech, autism, and hyperactivity.[2] However, conclusive evidence has not been established for an anatomic difference between the brain structures of human females and males.

Differences in perception also arise from temporary conditions. A headache, fatigue, or an injured finger can cause you to perceive a critical comment when a friendly one is being offered. You sometimes may not see a stop sign if your thoughts are elsewhere. Your health may affect your ability to perceive sensory stimuli. Similarly, if you are tired, you may perceive stimuli differently than when you are well-rested. Other physiological needs like hunger or thirst may also affect your perceptive skills.

Past Experiences

If our size, gender, and physical needs affect our perceptions, so do our past experiences, role, culture, and co-culture.

A concept called **perceptual constancy** refers to the idea that our past experiences lead us to see the world in a way that is difficult to change. At your age you already have certain ways that your perceptions invite you to respond to wealthy people, professors, Latinos, white people, clean air, and foreign cars. Your perceptual constancy, the tendency to keep seeing the world in the future the way you saw it in the past, is influenced by such factors as your roles, culture, and co-culture.

You are a student, a worker, a son or daughter. You might also be a student leader, a single mother, a divorced father, a political independent, or a business major. All these roles affect your perceptions. All roles also affect your communication: who you talk to, how you talk to them, the language you use, and the way you respond to their feedback. A good example of how perceptional constancy and role are related is how parents treat their children. Even after children have become adults, they are often still treated as children. A friend in his late forties went to his thirtieth high school reunion, returned from the party in the wee hours of the morning, only to find that his mother had waited up for him, unable to sleep until he returned safely home.

Another basic factor in perception is culture. Marshal R. Singer, an intercultural communication researcher, maintains that what we see, hear, taste, touch, and smell is conditioned by our cultures. He postulates that our perceptions are largely learned; and the greater the experiential differences among people, the greater the disparity in their perceptions. Conversely, the more similar their backgrounds, the more similarly they perceive the world.[3]

People of color in America have anxieties that never enter the minds of the predominant white culture. White people rarely worry about how they will be treated by a salesclerk, barber, beautician, banker, or realtor. A New York taxi driver may not take you to your home in Harlem, even if you are dressed in a suit. White people do not worry much about being hassled by the police, treated poorly by service personnel, or getting equal treatment when seeking a job. People of color find themselves always having to adapt to the dominant culture, which has so far made few adaptations and concessions to them.

To complicate matters further, your co-culture affects your perceptions of the world as well. Male or female, gay or straight, Christian or Jew, single or married, young or old—all these co-cultures influence perceptions. Rural children are more apprehensive about communicating with others than are urban children.[4] Women and men tend to see the world differently, communicate about it differently, and even practice and perceive communication itself differently.[5] Women, for example, tend to see talk as relational, as a way to share and understand feelings. Men, on the other hand, tend to see talk as instrumental, as a way to achieve some task. Roles, cultures, and co-cultures are just a few features of ourselves that affect our perceptions of the world.

Present Feelings and Circumstances

Your daily, monthly, or yearly cycle may affect how you perceive stimuli. If you are an "evening person," you might not be able to discriminate among multiple-choice answers on an exam at 8:00 A.M. as well as you could later in the day. If you are having a bad week, you might be offended by the humor

Our cultural background affects our perceptions and our interactions with others.

of one of your friends; later in the month, you might find the same remark very humorous. Accordingly, you might perceive stimuli more acutely in the cooler months of winter than you do in the warmer summer months.

If you have ever spent a night alone in a large house, a deserted dormitory, or an unfamiliar residence, you probably understand that perceptions are altered by circumstances. Most people experience a remarkable change in their hearing at night when they are alone. Creaking, whining, scraping, cracking sounds are heard, although none was heard in the daytime. The lack of other stimuli—including light, other sounds, and other people with whom to talk—coupled with a slight feeling of anxiety, provide circumstances that result in more acute hearing.

Similar circumstances may account, in part, for the mirages seen by lonely travelers. Commander Robert Peary encountered massive snowy pinnacles that appeared to rise thousands of feet above the plain of solid ice deep inside the Arctic Circle in 1906. Seven years later, Donald MacMillan, another explorer, verified his discovery. However, when MacMillan asked his Eskimo guide to choose a course toward the peaks, the guide explained that the spectacle was *poo-jok* (mist). Meteorologists have explained the existence of such mirages but have hastened to add that they are "reported infrequently because people aren't looking for them."[6] The variance in the feelings and circumstances of the many explorers may account for the differences in sighting or not sighting specific illusions.

What Occurs in Perception?

According to the most recent information, people engage in three separate activities during perception. None of us is aware of these separate processes because they occur quickly and almost simultaneously. Nonetheless, each activity is involved in our perceptions. The three activities include **selection** (we neglect some of the stimuli in our environment and focus on a few), **organization** (we group the stimuli in our environment into units or wholes), and **interpretation** (we give particular meanings to stimuli).

Selection

None of us perceives all the stimuli in our environment. For example, if you drove to school today, you were bombarded with sights, sounds, smells, and other sensations during your ride. At the time, you elected to perceive some of the stimuli, and you chose to disregard others. Now, you can recall some of the stimuli you perceived, but you have forgotten others. In the future, you will also expose yourself to some sensations and ignore others.

Our selectivity is of at least two types. First, we are selective in the stimuli to which we attend. **Selective attention** means we focus on certain cues and ignore others. In class, we might notice the earring worn by the man three seats ahead of us but fail to notice the new outfit worn by our best friend seated next to us. We might be tuned in to the low music piped in on an elevator but not notice the conversation held by the couple standing nearby.

Second, we select the stimuli we will recall or remember. **Selective retention** means we categorize, store, and retrieve certain information, but we discard other information. If you played the car radio on your way to school, try to remember one of the songs, commercials, or public-service announcements you heard. Although your attention may have been drawn to a particular song or message this morning, you may find that you cannot remember anything you heard. Your mind has discarded the sounds you heard from your radio. You may recall a criticism your date offered last night but have forgotten that your mother made a similar comment two days ago.

The relationship between selection and communication can be clarified by the concept of stereotyping. **Stereotyping** is the process of placing people and things into established categories, or of basing judgments about people or things on the categories into which they fit, rather than on their individual characteristics. Stereotyping has a negative connotation because we sometimes exhibit "hardening of the categories," placing items in inappropriate categories,

Figure 2.2 The unorganized figure.

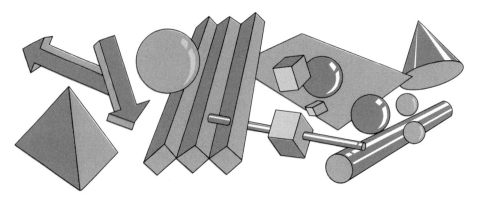

or we do not recognize that others categorize differently than we do. All of us stereotype to a certain extent, but particular stereotypes vary from person to person. Stereotyping involves selective attention and selection retention.

Still another way of looking at selective attention is to consider it **filtering.** Filtering is the many ways that our development screens and changes what we perceive. Think of yourself as a camcorder with a lens and microphone. One filter for your camcorder is education. It allows you to see a tree as an example of photosynthesis, to understand terms that others can't interpret, and to understand another language. Another filter is your I.Q., which might allow considerable understanding or much less. Still another filter is your personal circumstance. If you are fighting for a degree so you can get a job and feed your hungry family, you have a different filter than if your parents are paying for your education.

Our perception is selective, and our perception can invite us to see others in stereotypical fashion and hinder our ability to understand and share with others through communication. Our development also can provide filters that enhance the images we see to improve our understanding.

Organization

All of us tend to organize the stimuli in our environment. The unorganized figure 2.2 is difficult to describe if we only glance at it for a minute. When we attempt to describe it, we do so by organizing the lines we see. We might say it consists of straight and squiggly lines, or it has a rectangle, a triangle, and a square, or we may categorize the stimuli in some other way. The important point is we attempt to organize the figure as we describe it.

We organize stimuli in a number of ways. One method of organizing is to distinguish between **figure and ground.** In figure 2.3, some people perceive a vase or a candlestick, while others perceive twins facing each other. People

Figure 2.3 An example of figure and ground: a vase or twins?

Figure 2.4 An example of figure and ground: ink blobs or a bearded man?

who see a vase identify the center of the drawing as the figure and the area on the right and left as the ground, or background. Conversely, people who see twins facing each other see the center as the background and the area on the right and left as the figure.

Figure 2.4 is another illustration of the principle of figure and ground. As we first glance at the drawing, we perceive only ink blobs—nothing is clearly distinguishable as either the figure or the ground. If we continue to look at the drawing, however, we perceive the face of Christ, or of a bearded man, at the top center of the picture. When we see the face, it becomes the figure; the rest of the drawing becomes the ground.

Let us look at some examples of how figure and ground work in communication encounters. A man whose spouse was famous found that whenever they were together at a public occasion, people flocked to talk with his spouse and ignored him. She was figure, he was ground. When my boss talked to me this morning I missed most of what he said because of the fresh shaving cut that was spotting his collar. The cut was figure, the message was ground. During job evaluation, my employer talked about my weaknesses and strengths, but the so-called weaknesses made me so angry that I don't even remember the strengths. The messages about weaknesses were figure, and the messages about strengths were ground. Because of who and what we are and because of our own unique perceptual processes, our attention focuses and fades, and we choose the figure or ground of what we see, hear, smell, touch, and taste.

Another way of organizing stimuli is described as **closure.** We engage in closure every time we fill in information that does not exist. If someone showed us figure 2.5 and asked us what we perceived, we would probably say that it was a picture of a cat. As we can clearly see, however, the figure is incomplete. We can see a cat only if we are willing to fill in the blank areas. Additional examples of closure are given in figures 2.6 and 2.7. Most of us would identify figure 2.6 as a triangle and figure 2.7 as a circle, rather than claiming that both are simply short lines.

Figure 2.5 An example of closure: ink blobs or a cat?

Figure 2.6 An example of closure: triangle or straight lines?

Closure functions in our communication interactions. You see two people standing face to face and looking deep into each other's eyes, and you "fill in" your inference that they are lovers. Someone tells you, "My roommate, Mary Jo, went out with her new boyfriend last night and didn't return until 4:30 in the morning," and you assume they did more than go to the video store. A public speaker says, "We need to preserve our neighborhoods," and you assume he is against the proposed low-income housing. Your professor says with a total lack of interest, "My door is always open," and you conclude that you are not really welcome in that office. Visual closure might be completing the circle or seeing the cat, but mental closure means "filling in" the meaning of what you hear and observe.

We also organize stimuli according to their **proximity.** The principle of proximity, or nearness, operates whenever we group two or more things that happen to be close to each other. When we group according to proximity, our assumption is "birds of a feather flock together," even though we know this is not always true. Other clichés that illustrate this phenomenon are the contradictory "out of sight, out of mind" and "absence makes the heart grow fonder." In figure 2.8, we tend to perceive three groups of lines with three lines in each group, rather than nine separate lines, because of the principle of proximity.

You use proximity when you communicate. Two people enter the room together, and you assume they have a relationship. At the courthouse, you might assume that the well-dressed people with bulging briefcases are lawyers, but when you see a person standing behind a counter in the store you assume he or she is a salesperson. When your boss says, "We are going to have to lay off some people," and a couple of minutes later says, "I want to see you in my office" the proximity of the messages invites you to think he or she means you.

Similarity also helps us to organize stimuli. We sometimes group elements together because they resemble each other in size, color, shape, or other attributes. For instance, there is a tendency to believe that people within the same income range enjoy the same sort of life-style. We may assume a fellow

Figure 2.7 An example of closure: a circle or straight lines?

Figure 2.8 An example of proximity: three groups of lines or nine separate lines?

Figure 2.9 An example of similarity: squares and circles or a group of geometric shapes?

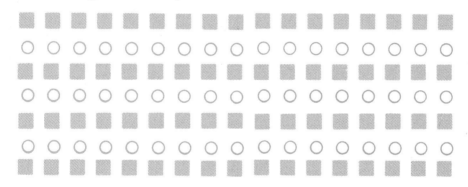

Republican or Democrat takes the same stance on defense spending. In figure 2.9, we perceive squares and circles, rather than a group of geometric shapes, because of the principle of similarity.

Similarity is useful as you organize messages. An African American woman, the principal of a private academy for African American children, pointed out to her audience of African American alumni that they needed to be more sensitive to how they treated brothers and sisters who had not experienced their privileged education, good jobs, and healthy incomes. She recounted their graduation from the same university, their race, and their success to demonstrate commonality of background and purpose.

To understand the relationship between the organizing of stimuli and communication, let us consider a classroom setting. When you enter the room, your tendency is to organize the stimuli, or people there, into specific groups. Your primary focus in on acquaintances and friends—the *figure*—rather than on the strangers, who function as the *ground*. You talk to friends sitting near

Figure 2.10 An example of interpretation: the inkblot.

the doorway as you enter, due to their *proximity*. You then seat yourself near a group of students you perceive as having interests identical to yours, thus illustrating *similarity*. Lastly, you notice your instructor arrive with another professor of communication; they are conversing enthusiastically, laughing, and smiling. *Closure* is a result of your assumption that they have a social relationship outside of the classroom.

Interpretation

Interpretative perception means that you determine what stimuli mean, that perception is a blend of internal states and external stimuli. The more ambiguous the stimuli, the more room we have for interpretation. The basis for the well-known inkblot test lies in the principle of interpretation of stimuli. Figure 2.10 shows three inkblots a psychologist might ask you to interpret. The ambiguity of the figures is typical.

In our interpretation of stimuli, we frequently rely on the context in which we perceive the stimuli, or we compare the stimuli to other stimuli. Sometimes, there are helpful clues. In figure 2.11, for example, the letters and numbers are useful to us as we attempt to interpret the middle figure. The contexts indicate that, in the top diagram, the middle figure is two number ones with a dash between them, while in the bottom diagram, the middle figure is an H.

Nonetheless, comparisons and the use of context can be confusing. All of us are familiar with figures like 2.12 and 2.13. In these figures, we perceive differences in the lengths of the lines, and in the height of the candle and the width of the candle holder, although no differences exist.

You can become so accustomed to seeing people, places, and situations in a certain way that your senses do not pick up on the obvious. Many people who read the following sentence will miss seeing the problem with the sentence.

The cop saw the man standing on the the street corner.

They achieve closure on the sentence, interpret its meaning, without consciousness of the details, and miss the repeated word, *the*.

Figure 2.11 An example of the usefulness of context in the interpretation of stimuli.

Figure 2.12 An example of interpretation: Which line is longer?

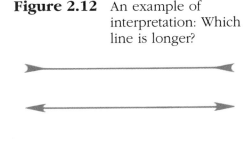

Figure 2.13 An example of interpretation: Is the width of the holder the same length as the candle?

Context provides cues for how an action, object, or situation is to be interpreted or perceived. Not seeing the double *the* in the sentence would be no problem for a reader who was trying to comprehend meaning, but a proofreader would be in jeopardy if it were missed.

Individuals will never see the world identically, but gaining commonality in perceptions comes mainly through sharing. Korean grocers and their black and Hispanic clientele need to reach accommodation, a unifying of their perceptual worlds, if they are to live together as do African Americans and whites, developers and environmentalists, management and labor, and hundreds of other groups. Understanding perception and its role in communication is key to both the problems and the solutions in our contemporary society.

Summary

In this chapter, we examined the role of perception. Perception is the process by which we come to understand ourselves and others, and understanding is an activity basic to communication. The older view of perception suggested it

Differences in Perception

Jack can see he sees
what he can see Jill can't see,
and he can see
that Jill can't see that she can't see,
but he can't see WHY
Jill can't see that Jill can't see. . . .
Jill can see Jack can't see
and can't see he can't see.
Jill can see WHY
Jack can't see,
but Jill cannot see WHY
Jack can't see he can't see. . . .
Jack can't see he can't see
and can't see
Jill can't see Jill can't see it,
and vice versa.

Differences in perception can be overcome in our interaction with others.

From R.D. Laing, "Differences in Perception," in ***Knots.*** © 1970 R.D. Laing. Reprinted by permission of Pantheon Books, Div. of Random House, Inc.

The poem captures the complexity of perception and the difficulty of establishing common perceptions.

Discuss an experience in which you and another person attempted to reach an agreement but could not. Identify the differences in perception, suggest reasons for those differences, and list the methods you used to validate your perceptions.

was passive and objective, and that meaning was inherent in the stimuli perceived. The contemporary view of perception is that it is a subjective, active, and creative process.

Differences in perceptions arise among people. Physiological features of the individual, including height, weight, body type, gender, and differences in our senses, contribute to those differences in perceptions. Past experiences, including those dependent on our cultures and co-cultures, also affect our perceptions. Finally, our current circumstances and our present feelings affect our perceptions.

While we are unaware of the separate processes that occur in perception, we engage in selection, organization, and interpretation. Each of these processes was examined in detail in this chapter. In chapter 3, we will consider a related topic, understanding oneself.

Key Terms

active perception   The view that people add to or subtract from the stimuli to which they are exposed.

closure   The organization of stimuli so missing information in the original is filled in by the perceiver to provide the appearance of a complete or whole unit.

creative perception   The view that meaning is imparted to stimuli by the perceiver, rather than being an inherent property of the thing perceived.

figure and ground   The organization of perception so some stimuli are brought into focus while other stimuli form the background.

filtering   The developmental features of our existence that alter and change the way we perceive the world (e.g., education, religion, occupation, status).

inherent meaning   The view that meaning is inherent in stimuli; hence, that perception is passive.

interpretation   The assignment of meaning to stimuli.

interpretive perception   The view that perception is a blend of internal states and external stimuli.

objective perception   The view of the perceiver as a nonevaluative recorder of stimuli.

organization   The structuring of stimuli into meaningful units or wholes.

passive perception   The view that perceivers are mere recorders of stimuli.

perception   What a person sees, hears, smells, feels, or tastes; the process by which we come to understand the phenomena in the world.

perceptual constancy   The invariable nature of the perception of a stimulus once it has been selected, organized, and interpreted by the perceiver.

proximity   The organization of stimuli into meaningful units or wholes according to their perceived physical or psychological distance from each other.

selection   Neglecting some stimuli in our environment to focus on other stimuli.

selective attention   A focus on particular stimuli so that other stimuli are ignored.

selective retention   The recollection of information after selection, organization, and interpretation have occurred; the mental categorization, storage, and retrieval of selected information.

similarity   A basis for organizing stimuli into meaningful units by perceiving the similarities among them.

stereotyping   The process of placing people and things into established categories, or of basing judgments about people or things on the categories into which they fit, rather than on their individual characteristics.

subjective perception   The view that perception is based on the physiological and psychological characteristics of the perceiver.

chapter 3

Self-Awareness and Self-Concept:

Understanding Yourself

H ow does self-awareness affect communication? You will learn the answer to this question in the beginning of this chapter. Our self-concept originates and changes as we interact with others. We may find we are confirmed, rejected, or disconfirmed in these interactions. The components of self-concept—self-image and self-esteem—are detailed in the chapter. As we will determine, our self-concept is in process and specific steps for improving self-concept will be discussed. Gender affects one's self-concept and the improvement of that self-concept. Let us begin our discussion by defining self-awareness.

What will you learn?

After reading and thinking about this chapter, you should be able to answer the following questions:

1. How is self-awareness related to communication?

2. What are the differences between self-concept and self-esteem?

3. What does your Johari Window look like in your relationship with your professor? Your parents? Your best friend?

4. What are some examples of confirmation, rejection, and disconfirmation?

5. How has your self-concept changed over the last five years?

6. What steps can you take to improve your self-concept?

7. What is the relationship between gender differences and self-concept?

I have to live with myself, and so I want to be fit for myself to know; I want to be able as days go by, Always to look myself straight in the eye.
Edgar A. Guest, Myself

Know thyself
Attributed to Thales

To love oneself is the beginning of a life-long romance
Oscar Wilde, An Ideal Husband, III

How well do you know yourself? What is your potential? How does what you think of yourself affect your communication with others? The introductory quotations suggest that the concept of the self has existed for thousands of years, but now this awareness of self, this assessment of self, is something that you have to consider as you explore yourself as a communicator.

Self-Awareness

In chapter 2 you learned about perception, but in this chapter you are going to look at your self-perception under a microscope. You will start with the basic concept of self-awareness, move to self-concept with its components of self-image and self-esteem, and conclude with gender differences and improving your self-concept.

How you perceive yourself plays a central role in communication, regardless of whether the communication is in a daydream, a journal, a small group, or at a podium. An early step in considering yourself as a communicator is to contemplate your own **self-awareness,** your sense of self, your accommodation with your past, your plans for your future, and all the prejudices, potentialities, and possibilities that are you.

Let us explore the notion of self-awareness in a chronological fashion by looking at your past, your present, and your future. Your past goes all the way back to how you were reared, or the way your family taught you to think, believe, and behave. You began as a spontaneous creature who rolled into a ball and cried when hungry, angry, or frustrated; who lashed out at others when angry; and who laughed loudly and beamed when happy. Over time, your elders took some of that spontaneity out of you until you behaved like an adult: you ate at meal times, held you anger in check with your teachers, laughed when appropriate, and cried little if at all. Your emotions as well as your physical responses were altered to make you responsible for your own behavior.

Once you mastered language, **symbolic interactionism**—the messages and feedback you received from family, friends, peers, teachers, police, neighbors, and the organizations to which you belonged, such as church, scouts, and sports—shaped you in ways that made you what you are today. You may have been punished for acting up in class, rewarded for athletic skill, punished for talking too much, or ignored for saying too little. The net result, is the person you see in the mirror each day, a person molded by your past into someone with loves and hates, talents and limitations, and useful and debilitating experiences.

The ancients said "know thyself" because they, like people today, believe that self-knowledge or self-awareness is a discovery worth making about yourself. It tells you in the present which choices are open to you and which are not. If you are bad at math, you will not have a future as an accountant. If you hate chemistry, you should not become a physician or a druggist. If you like to write and are good at it, you may have a future as a journalist. If you are skillful at athletics, perhaps you can exploit that talent with scholarships, varsity sports, and professional teams. What you learned about yourself in high school and since affects your future.

Will Schutz wrote about the importance of self-awareness in his book *Here Comes Everybody:*

> Every thought, gesture, muscle tension, feeling, stomach gurgle, nose scratch, fart, hummed tune, slip of the tongue, illness—everything is significant and meaningful and related to the now. It is possible to know and understand oneself on all these levels, and the more one knows the more he [or she] is free to determine his [or her] own life.
>
> If I know what my body tells me, I know my deepest feelings and I can choose what to do. . . . Given a complete knowledge of myself, I can determine my life; lacking that mastery, I am controlled in ways that are often undesirable, unproductive, worrisome, and confusing.[1]

Yes, in the here and now, you should be aware what kind of a person you are. Are you timid, shy, and unassertive? Are you healthy, vigorous and energetic? Do you welcome change, adventure, and risk? Do you see yourself as capable, unstoppable, and hard-driving? The answers to these questions and many more are the key to your self-awareness.

Warren Doyle, a professor from Connecticut, approached self-awareness more dramatically. He went backpacking alone, and he set two records for hiking the 2,040-mile Appalachian Trail. Doyle reported:

> There's a theory that most people have high self-concepts that crumble in situations of crisis or adversity. Many of us never have a chance to find out who we really are. . . . I was alone for sixty-six days. I lost my physical fat and my emotional fat as well. I saw myself as I really was.[2]

You may not be able to do as Doyle did, but you can focus on your body, your emotions, and the present. You can discover yourself by testing yourself in mastering courses of study, in succeeding on the job, and in improving your relationships.

Your self-awareness also considers your potential, your future prospects. Abraham Maslow called this concept **self-actualization** and saw it as the highest order in his hierarchy of human needs.[3] Carl Rogers labeled the self-actualized person as "the fully functioning person"; Sidney Jourard called it the "disclosed self"; Charles Morris identified it as the "open self"; and Theodore Landman wrote of the "beautiful and noble person." An army recruiter might express it today by telling a potential volunteer to "be all you can be." All of these writers held an optimistic, empirically based view that recognized that self-awareness leads to self-actualization.

You too have a future, and the seeds of it are in what you are today. The more you know yourself and become self-aware, the more you can get in touch with yourself and with what you think of yourself, and how and why you communicate with others.

Self-awareness is essential to communication, but too much self-control can result in avoidance of communication.

Self-Concept

Self-concept is each person's consciousness of his or her total, essential, and particular being. Included in self-concept are all of our physical, social, and psychological perceptions about ourselves. These perceptions are a result of our past, present, projected experiences, and interactions with our environment—including the people in our environment.

The importance of others in determining self-concept cannot be overemphasized. We do not move from the spontaneous beings we are as children to complex adults without the intervention of countless other people. Our self originates in interactions with others. Our communicative exchanges tell us what our roles are and encourage, or discourage, us from internalizing specific predispositions.

One way to understand the influence of others on our self-concept is through the **Johari Window,** depicted in figure 3.1. The Johari Window is a square divided into four areas. Each of these areas, or quadrants, contains a different picture of self.

The **open self** in the first quadrant represents information about yourself known both to you and others. Included in this quadrant might be your name, nickname, gender, age, and religious affiliation or membership.

Figure 3.1 The Johari Window. (From *Group Processes: An Introduction to Group Dynamics* by Joseph Luft, by permission of Mayfield Publishing Company. Copyright © 1984, 1970, and 1969 by Joseph Luft.)

	Known to self	Not known to self
Known to others	Open self	Blind self
Not known to others	Hidden self	Unknown self

The second quadrant, the **blind self,** consists of information known to others but not known to you. Included here would be your behaviors of which you are unaware, such as blinking frequently when you feel threatened, interrupting others when they talk to you, or bragging about your grade point average. Also included in this quadrant are occurrences no one has told you about—you were adopted, you nearly died in infancy, or your grandfather was a thief.

The third quadrant, the **hidden self,** includes information you are aware of about yourself but you have not shared with others. You might have done something about which you are embarrassed or ashamed—stolen merchandise from a department store, had an abortion, or cheated on a test—or about which you are proud—made the Dean's list, received a scholarship, or were chosen for an important award.

The **unknown self** in the fourth quadrant includes information that no one—neither you nor anyone else—knows. The junior high school student who pumps iron every day may emerge someday as an olympic athlete. Many traditional college students do not know if they will marry or if they will have children in the future. People who will win the lottery in the future don't know that they will be rich, and some people who are wealthy today will die poor. Grandma Moses became a famous painter even though she did not begin painting until she was older than most people are when they retire. Our lives are a script with characters and plot changes of which we are currently unaware. Until they are played out, these potentialities remain part of our unknown self.

This examination of the Johari Window allows us to see why others may respond to us differently than we expect. For example, when your friends and family fail to point out your mistakes due to the fear of arousing your heated temper, this may confuse you—particularly if you consider yourself a mild-mannered individual. They may very well be responding to information in the blind area of your self. On the other hand, these same people may not understand your overly cautious behavior while driving because you never told them of a near collision with a semitrailer that occurred while you were driving alone—an aspect of your hidden self.

Watzlawick, Beavin, and Jackson, the authors of a classic communication book, have suggested other people respond to us in three distinct ways.[4] These responses include confirmation, rejection, and disconfirmation. **Confirmation** occurs when others treat us consistently with who we believe we are. For instance, if we see ourselves as a philosopher who is knowledgeable about rhetoric, we are confirmed when others ask our opinion on Plato's *Phaedrus* or on Aristotle's *Rhetoric*. Confirmation is not only satisfying, it strengthens our established self-concept.

Rejection occurs when others treat us inconsistently with our self-definition. Consider people who mistakenly believe they have unusual insight into solving problems. These individuals believe their ideas are generally excellent and that others can benefit from them. In group meetings, these people offer their ideas freely, but they observe that no one seems to respond positively to their ideas. Their ideas are ignored or discarded as unworkable. The result is that individuals' definitions of self are rejected. These people's self-concepts may be altered over time if they continue to receive messages that reject their previously established perception of self.

Disconfirmation occurs when others fail to respond to our notion of self, or when others respond in a neutral way. Neutrality may not sound disconfirming, but consider small children who make continual attempts to gain responses to their notions of self from their parents. Consider marital partners who have spouses who rarely offer personal comments. Think about grandparents who are the recipients of little conversation and even less conversation about how they are seen by others. These individuals are disconfirmed, and their self-concept may be altered as a result of such interactions. Disconfirmation suggests to people they do not exist, or they are irrelevant to others. People who are disconfirmed may experience loneliness and alienation.

Two Components of Self-Concept

Self-Image

Self-concept is composed of two parts. *Self-image* is the descriptive part of self, while *self-esteem* is the evaluative part of self.[5] Your **self-image** is the picture you have of yourself, the sort of person you believe you are. Included in your self-image are the categories in which you place yourself, the roles you play, and other similar descriptors you use to identify yourself. If you tell an acquaintance that you are a grandfather of three who just lost his wife and does volunteer work on the weekends, several elements of your self-image are brought to light—the roles of grandparent, widower, and conscientious citizen.

Consider how you identify yourself as a student. Do you tell people you are a part-time student, a Phi Delta, a senior, a nontraditional student, a fifth year undergraduate, a community college student, or a resident assistant? The label you use to identify yourself reflects your self-image and, in turn, affects your communication with others.

Our self-image is originally based on categorization by others. Other people categorize us by role: husband, mother, boss. Others categorize us by personality traits—intelligent, enthusiastic, neurotic, superstitious—or by physical characteristics—tall, beautiful, wiry. Family roles are used most often in the categorization of other people, followed by occupation, marital status, and religious affiliation.[6]

The roles we play directly influence the way we communicate. The role of parent calls for a kind of communication that is different from a student's. What you say, how you say it, to whom you speak, and how frequently you speak are largely determined by the roles you play.

Self-Esteem

Our self-image is *descriptive,* while our self-esteem includes *evaluative feelings* that bear some relationship to our self-image. **Self-esteem** is how we feel about ourselves, how well we like ourselves. A first-time mother shares her self-esteem when she explains how excited she is to be a parent but how anxious she is that it will interfere with her job. You may share your own self-esteem when you explain your joy about your recent marriage and eagerness that it succeed in spite of the fact that you are still in school and your parents are divorced.

Self-esteem is usually based on perceptions of our own successes or failures. If you have a favorable attitude toward yourself, you are said to have high self-esteem. If you have unfavorable or negative attitudes toward yourself, you have low self-esteem. Self-esteem—whether high or low—affects our perceptions and our communication. For example, people with high self-esteem tend to view others who are motivated as bright people and those who are not motivated as less bright. In other words, they feel that people who put forth great effort also have great ability. People with low self-esteem do not make this distinction. This lack of discrimination may prevent people with low self-esteem from understanding the prerequisite behaviors for succeeding.[7]

Both low and high self-esteem become a self-fulfilling prophecy, as we shall determine later in this chapter. We communicate in a variety of ways, whether or not we value ourselves. Similarly, other people's communication to us affects our self-esteem. The role of self-esteem in our perceptions and our communication is important to understand.

Excessive concern over self-esteem, however, is often associated with **self-consciousness.** People who are self-conscious are usually shy, easily embarrassed, and anxious in the presence of other people. Most of us are sometimes shy, embarrassed, or anxious. Nearly all public speakers experience stage fright from time to time. A self-conscious person, however, suffers stage fright in all situations, to the point of being unwilling to even try to speak before any group. Self-conscious people experience shyness, embarrassment, and anxiety regularly.

Self-Concept in Process

If someone asks you who you are, you might respond in a variety of ways—depending on the situation, the other person, and the way you feel at the moment. If you are applying for a job and the person requesting information is the prospective employer, you might identify yourself in terms of specific work experience or educational background. If the situation involves an intimate friend or spouse, you would probably respond with far different information—perhaps with more emphasis on your feelings than on your specific experiences.

When we say our self-concept is *in process,* we mean our self-concept is not the same in all situations, with all people, and at all times. Indeed, the situations, people, and times have a direct impact on how we see ourselves. We selectively attend to some parts of who we are, and we ignore other parts. As was observed earlier, the importance of others and events outside of ourselves in determining our self-concept cannot be overemphasized. Since our self originates in interactions with others, the view of ourself we share in class is different from the view of ourself we share at a party. The verbal and nonverbal symbols offered by others encourage us to play different roles for our employer and for our family. By placing ourselves in the positions of others and attempting to view ourselves as we imagine others see us, we change from inexperienced adolescents into competent young adults.

In considering the idea that self-concept changes, we should also consider how self-concept was originally formed. In essence, our self-concept is determined by the treatment we receive from others and the relationships we have with them. Our self-image, as we have stated, occurs as a result of our being categorized by others. Our self-esteem depends on whether we have been rewarded or punished by them.

From the moment we are born, and some researchers believe even earlier, the treatment we receive from others influences who we believe we are. As babies, we respond to the nonverbal messages of hugging, kissing, cuddling, and touching. As we begin to understand language, we respond to verbal

Our self-concepts originate in our interactions with significant others.

messages as well. Early verbal messages—"Big boys don't cry," "Little ladies don't make messes," and "Daddy thinks you're the best baby in the whole world"—influence our self-concept, as well as shape our self-control and self-expression.

Small children are trusting, and they have little experience on which to draw; consequently, they believe what other people tell them. Parental evaluation—verbal and nonverbal—has a particularly strong effect on the development of the child's self-concept. What the parents believe about the child has a tendency to become a self-fulfilling prophecy.

The **self-fulfilling prophecy** is the tendency to become what people expect you to become. In the book *Pygmalion in the Classroom: Teacher Expectation and Pupils' Intellectual Development,* authors Rosenthal and

Jacobson speak of the importance of the self-fulfilling prophecy. These two researchers summarize a number of studies of academic performance that show that students who are expected to do well actually do perform better. Rosenthal and Jacobson conclude:

> To a great extent, our expectations for another person's behavior are accurate because we know his [or her] past behavior. But there is now good reason to believe that another factor increased our accuracy of interpersonal predictions or prophecies. Our prediction or prophecy may in itself be a factor in determining the behavior of other people.[8]

The self-fulfilling prophecy is relevant to self-concept. Our concept of ourselves originated in the responses we received when we were young, and, to some extent, self-fulfilling prophecies help to maintain our self-concept. In many ways, we attempt to behave consistently with other people's expectations, regardless of whether those expectations are positive or negative. Suppose a young boy is reprimanded by his parents for crying when hurt, scolded by his teachers for embracing a playmate, and labeled by classmates as a "sissy" for playing with dolls. The result may be a frustrated young man who is afraid to display his emotions. Conversely, suppose the boy is praised for playing nicely with his sister and her dollhouse, encouraged to hug his friends, and allowed to cry when he is upset or in pain. The result may be a very sensitive, compassionate young man.

The self-fulfilling prophecy is not quite so simple. We do not simply and routinely behave in the ways other people expect. A transaction occurs between other people's expectations and our expectations for ourselves. For some people, other people's expectations play a more important role than their own expectations. For others, their own expectations are more relevant than are the messages they receive through interaction. This caveat helps us to understand why Rosenthal and Jacobson's study has been questioned in more recent investigations.

In his insightful, though somewhat depressing book titled *Lost in the Cosmos: The Last Self-Help Book,* Walker Percy discusses the idea that we continue to gain more and more information about a number of things, including the cosmos, but that we know increasingly less about ourselves. Percy identifies some of the unique features of the self that appear to apply to most people in our culture.

One of the characteristics of the self Percy identifies as particularly relevant here is how the self feels misplaced. Percy describes our situation of attempting to be the person we believe others want us to be, while encouraging others to be the self that they believe we want them to be. He provides the following example:

> Imagine you are walking down Madison Avenue behind Al Pacino, whom you have seen frequently in the movies but never in the flesh. He is shorter than you thought. His raincoat is thrown over his shoulder. Hands in pockets, he

stops to look in the window of Abercrombie & Fitch. His face takes on a characteristic expression, jaws clenched, eyes dark and luminous, like young Corleone in *The Godfather*. The sight of Pacino in the flesh acting like Pacino on the screen gives you a peculiar pleasure. Then you become aware that, though Pacino is looking at the articles in the window display, he is also checking his own reflection in the glass. This, too, gives you pleasure, though of a different sort. Explain the difference. (Hint: The aesthetic pleasure of seeing an instance of a symbol, Pacino in the flesh at Abercrombie's, measure up and conform to the symbol itself, Pacino on the screen, and the different pleasure of seeing the instance, Pacino, rescued from the symbol and restored to human creatureliness, the self in all its vagary, individuality, and folly. The first case: Ah, there is Pacino acting just like Corleone! The second case: Ah, there is Pacino acting like me!)[9]

As Percy illustrates in his book, the complicated, multifaceted individuals we become are not only a result of other people's responses and reactions to us, but also our perception of the meaningfulness of those responses and reactions. Each of us receives unique and individual responses from others; moreover, we react to the responses in specialized and individualistic ways. Percy illustrates Barnlund's six-persons model presented in chapter 1.

Gender Differences in Self-Concept

We also observed in chapter 1 that gender differences in communicative behavior have been widely studied in the past three decades, and our discussion of self-concept is incomplete without our consideration of gender. In this section, we will share some of the important findings relative to gender and self-concept.

Earlier in this chapter, we noted one's integrated self tends toward the behaviors others encouraged and tends away from behaviors others discouraged. From the time we are born, we are treated differently because of our biological gender. We dress male and female babies in different kinds and colors of clothing. Parents respond differently to male and female infants.[10] We describe male and female babies with different adjectives: boys are strong, solid, and independent, while girls are loving, cute, and sweet. People describe identical behavior on the part of infants differently if they are told the infant is a boy or a girl.[11] Preschool children observe commercials and cartoons on television, are read books, and play with toys in which "appropriate" gender roles are depicted. In many ways, people are treated differently because of their biological gender.

Since the messages about gender roles are abundant, we may be surprised children do not develop specific gender role conceptions earlier than they currently do. Before the age of three, children have little notion of their gender role, but between the ages of three and five, gender roles develop.[12] Between the ages of five and seven, gender constancy, or the tendency to see oneself consistently as a male or female, develops in most people.[13] Role models, educational institutions, games and toys, and children's literature all reinforce different male/female roles.

Females are encouraged to behave in a feminine manner, and males are encouraged to behave in a masculine manner. How are femininity and masculinity expressed in our culture? Table 3.1 depicts the personality characteristics that have been validated in a well-known masculinity-femininity measure.[14] Although recent evidence demonstrates that all women are not feminine and all men are not masculine, a strong relationship exists between being a man and masculine and being a woman and feminine.[15]

Our culture tends to be masculinist, that is, masculine attitudes, predispositions, and characteristics are more highly valued than are those associated with femininity. For example, our dominant culture is more likely to reward men or women who are independent, assertive, confident, dominant, forceful, industrious, inventive, shrewd, strong, and tough than it is to reward people who are considerate, contented, cooperative, dependent, emotional, forgiving, friendly, helpful, modest, sensitive, sentimental, sincere, submissive, sympathetic, timid, and warm. Since men are more likely to possess masculine characteristics and women are more likely to possess feminine characteristics, we should not be surprised that men rise to leadership positions in both government and industry. Even feminine occupations, such as elementary teaching, often have men at their heads in the form of principals or superintendents.

The tendency of women to act in a feminine manner within our culture, which may be perceived as being biased toward men, often causes women to report lower self-esteem than men do. Although some studies have not reported differences between women and men,[16] most research provides evidence of lower self-esteem in women than in men.[17]

Other specific factors alter the relationship between one's biological gender and one's self-concept. For instance, a woman's sense of being home- or career-oriented makes some difference in how she defines her self-esteem. Women who are home-oriented base their self-esteem more on friendships and social abilities and less on intellectual and technical abilities, while career-oriented women tend to base their self-esteem on intellectual and technical abilities rather than on friendships and social abilities.[18]

Single women also tend to be higher in self-esteem than married women. Their higher esteem may be based on their paid employment, on spending less time at home, or on other differences. Single women value personal growth and achievement, stating they are self-determined, while married women value personal relationships and describe themselves with associated characteristics, kinship roles, and household activities.[19]

Although this information on gender differences in self-esteem may be depressing, particularly if you are a woman, you should keep in mind that the self-concept is not an unchanging commodity. In the next section, we will consider how the self-concept is in process, and we will offer some specific information on the changing self-concepts of both women and men.

Improving Self-Concept

Numerous people have made dramatic changes in their life-style, behavior, and, in turn, their self-concept. Our news is filled with stories of ex-cons who become responsible members of the community, alcoholics who are able to abstain from drinking, and highly-paid television, movie, and rock stars who are able to overcome their fame and have fairly normal family lives. Dramatic changes occur in people. While we might not choose to follow the paths of those in the news, they do provide evidence that people can change.

Barriers to Improving Self-Concept

Altering our self-concept is not a simple matter, however. One of the factors that makes change difficult is that people who know us expect us to behave in a certain way. In fact, they helped to create and maintain the self-concept we have. These people will continue to insist we maintain a particular self-concept, even when we are attempting to change. For instance, eliminating negative statements from your conversational patterns may be difficult because they are anticipated by others and anything you say might be interpreted as pessimistic.

Sometimes, we work against ourselves when we try to change our self-concept. For example, you might label yourself as "passive." Even when others voice opinions contrary to yours or attack values you hold, you say nothing in defense. This may be due to the fact that other aspects of your self-concept include "open-minded" and "non-argumentative." We can alter one aspect of our self-concept only to the extent that it does not contradict other aspects. If your nonassertiveness fits with your self-concept of being warm and supportive of others, you may find it difficult to become more assertive unless you are also willing to be less supportive on some occasions.

Another problem in altering our self-concept occurs even when we have changed and others recognize we have changed. Sometimes, we hamper the development of our self-concept. For instance, if you changed the "passive" label to "assertive," you could very well defend your views. Others may respond positively. Still you are concerned about being perceived as weak.

Steps to Improving Self-Concept

If we wish to change our self-concept to improve our ability to communicate with others, at least two steps are essential. First, we need to *become aware* of ourselves; second, we need to *establish a positive attitude* toward ourselves and toward others. The first step is not an automatic, natural process. We are conditioned to be out of touch with ourselves. We need to develop sensitivity to our own feelings and our own thoughts.

It is essential we acknowledge *all* of our feelings. We are all more familiar with certain aspects of ourselves than others. If we have low self-esteem, we probably focus on those aspects of ourselves that we see as problems or deficiencies. If we have high self-esteem, we probably ignore our liabilities and focus on our assets. All of us have negative as well as positive characteristics, and it is important we recognize both of these aspects of ourselves.

Take the study of communication as an example. Two groups of people may feel that studying communication is a waste of time. One group feels it is unnecessary because they are experienced public speakers, because they have been successful in small group discussions, or because they can successfully communicate with one other person at a time. A second group dismisses studying communication because they suffer from communication apprehension. They feel they simply cannot give a speech, or they cannot talk to a member of the opposite sex and never will, or that communication is just frustrating to them, regardless of the communication situation.

The second group, people who suffer from low self-esteem, generalize from one type of communication situation, in which they feel they fail, to all other communication situations. The first group, people who enjoy high self-esteem, generalize from specific communication successes to all other communication situations. It is essential to our understanding of ourselves that we acknowledge all of our abilities and failings and not make the error of generalizing from one or two specific cases. Few people are competent in every communication situation; fewer still are incompetent in all communication situations.

To become more aware of ourselves, it is also necessary that we *focus* on ourselves, rather than on others. Instead of using your parents' perception of you, try to establish your own view. Rather than deciding "who you are" on the basis of cultural standards and norms, attempt to make your assessment on the basis of your own standards and norms. No one else knows you as well as you do—it is important you use yourself, the best source available to you.

One woman, Amy, can illustrate the importance of focusing on ourselves instead of on others. She attended an assertiveness training workshop because she was unable to talk with her husband about family finances. She was certain her husband felt he should be the family financial expert, but during their ten-year marriage, Amy had experienced countless financial crises. Every time she tried to talk with her husband, he acted sullen and withdrawn. His responses encouraged her to keep her ideas about the family budget to herself. Amy found herself in a vicious cycle. She believed him to be incompetent with money, but she was unable to talk with him about the problem.

As Amy worked through her communication problem, she made a number of discoveries. Confronting her husband with the situation, Amy found that he did not really like to handle the money and preferred that she do it. He had only seemed sullen and withdrawn because he was embarrassed by his distaste for keeping the checkbook and paying the bills. He thought that it was "the man's job" to handle the finances. Amy found she was better at balancing the checkbook, budgeting the family resources, and investigating investments. She finally realized that she had been taking her cues from her husband, rather than from herself. Focusing on ourselves, rather than on others, is essential to becoming aware of who we are.

The second step in changing our self-concept—establishing a positive attitude toward ourselves and others—is more difficult than increasing self-awareness. If we are to alter our self-concept, we must strive for the situation in which we believe that we, and other people also, are worthy of liking and acceptance. We need to reject highly critical attitudes about both ourselves and others. We need to develop the belief that we, and others, have potentialities worthy of respect. We need to free ourselves of anxiety, insecurity, cynicism, defensiveness, and the tendency to be highly evaluative. Our goal should be to free ourselves so we can establish meaningful relationships with ourselves and with others.

It was important that Amy did not verbally attack her husband for his nonverbal behavior. When she approached him about the problem, she did so in a clear and straightforward manner. She did not criticize his inability to handle the checkbook or his reluctance to talk with her about his problem. Instead, she tried to communicate her respect for him while discussing the problem. She showed her concern about their family's problem while maintaining her love for her husband.

Amy exemplifies the kind of respect we should feel for everyone. We may not accept another person's behavior, but we need to maintain an appreciation for his or her potentialities that goes beyond the immediate situation. This kind of respect or appreciation of other people allows us to become the kind of person we truly wish to become.

Gender Differences in Improving Self-Concept

Earlier we noted women and men do not develop similar self-concepts. We explained that because men are viewed more positively in our culture than are women in most places, they develop a more positive self-concept. Here we will observe that other factors interact with gender and they suggest some ways for improving one's self-concept.

In the album notes for *Sharepickers,* Mason Williams wrote the following:

Here I Am Again

One night after a concert with a symphony orchestra, I was sitting by myself in my room, wondering what a super-duper love star like me is doing all alone, and I began to feel sorry for myself. I started thinking about where I was and how I had got here. I felt like I was going to cry, so naturally I grabbed my guitar to catch the tears and wrote this song, which is about living a way of life and writing songs off to it beyond the need to.

I realized I was just another blues singer with nothing to be blue about except being stuck having to sing the blues, trapped by the truth— it's not what you don't do that holds you back, it's what you do well that gets you. It seems like if you're successful at something and it comes easy, you always try to free ride it past the right point. I've met a lot of people who are stuck in spiritual ruts because they'd latched onto a magic and tried to ride it too far. Good luck turns bad on you after awhile; you have to learn where to get off. I realized I'd missed my stop. Here I was alone again writing another lonely song about being alone again, instead of really being with a friend. I had used music, God bless it, just to get to the top. It was only a ticket, and here I was fondling my ticket in a hotel room in Hartford, Connecticut, way off the track.

I realized that all my life I'd been afraid—afraid to ask for what I wanted—because of what I wanted. I realized that I had become rich and famous, a star, just so everything would come to me—even more than I could use—and I could take my pick from it without risking rejection. Suddenly it struck me that that's probably why most successful people are unhappy. They get themselves into a position where they don't have to

One's locus of control affects self-concept. The placement of locus of control allows women to perceive themselves as favorably as men. Sixth grade girls who had high **internal locus of control** (they perceived themselves, rather than outside forces, as responsible for the events in their lives) viewed themselves as favorably as did sixth grade boys. Sixth grade females with a strong **external locus of control** (they perceived people and events outside of themselves controlled their lives) viewed themselves significantly lower on measures of self-esteem.[20] Girls who have an external locus of control may be more susceptible to the debilitating effects of the sex-biased culture than are girls who look within for control of the events of their lives.

The results of a national study of successful female professors lend support to this conclusion. Women who were successful in gaining promotion and tenure in the field of speech communication were asked to offer their advice ask for things, without realizing that if they don't practice asking for what they want from others, they're not good at asking for what they want from themselves—which means they don't know what they want. And you know, you never can satisfy somebody who doesn't know what he wants.

You have to practice asking to be a good asker. What's more, you have to practice *true* asking. You've got to ask for what you really want and not what somebody else wants you to ask for or what you think is right to want. Practice doesn't make perfect unless you practice perfectly.

That's what praying is all about, my friends. To pray is to practice asking, and if you're not really asking, you're not really practicing. A person could spend the rest of his life afraid to ask for what he wants, because of what he wants, whether he really wants it or not.

Williams lends support to the idea that it is essential to know ourselves, and our needs, to be satisfied. Suggest needs of your own that must be fulfilled for you to be satisfied. Is it necessary for you to alter your behavior to meet these needs? Have you been avoiding this? Do you need to enlist the help of others? Write down one or two needs you have not been meeting. Resolve to change your behavior and enlist any necessary help from others to meet your needs. If you feel comfortable doing so, report the results to your classmates. You may be able to help others find the courage to make changes, too.

Is it necessary for you to alter your self-concept to meet your needs? For instance, if you feel you need a full-time career in teaching to satisfy your desire to serve others, you might have to change your view of yourself as someone who is too busy with a family to pursue a career. If you need a certain amount of time alone each day, you may have to alter your view of yourself as a person who always has time for everybody.

"Here I Am Again," by Mason Williams. Album liner notes from *Sharepickers*.

on success to others. These women suggested that others should (1) exhibit **androgynous** (a combination of traditional masculine and traditional feminine) and flexible behavior, (2) do their jobs well, (3) develop internal locus of control, and (4) gain the support of others. The third point is particularly relevant to the importance of developing one's own standards rather than relying on the perceptions of others.[21]

Although women may have some unique problems in establishing positive self-esteem, they can do so. The female sex role may encourage low self-esteem and depression insofar as it teaches women they are weak and not in control of their own fate. However, women can alter their self-perception by participating in self-help groups. Women who participate in such groups tend to overcome low self-esteem, reduce depression in their lives, decrease their tendency to blame others, and feel that they are more in control of their own lives.

Both women and men can change their self-concepts. We are not saddled with an unchanging sense of self that will limit our opportunities or negatively affect our communicative opportunities with others. The available research suggests means by which we can more positively view ourselves, and in turn, those with whom we interact.

Summary

In this chapter, we examined how we come to understand ourselves. Self-awareness plays a central role in communication. Parental and social conditioning reinforces our lack of self-awareness. Self-awareness is essential to our mental health and to our ability to communicate competently.

Self-concept is each person's consciousness of his or her total, essential, and particular being. Our self-concept is affected by our interactions with others. Other people may confirm, reject, or disconfirm our self-concept.

Self-concept consists of self-image and self-esteem. Our self-image is the picture we have of ourselves, the sort of person we believe we are. Included in our self-image are the categories in which we place ourselves, the roles we play, and the other ways we identify ourselves.

Self-esteem is how we feel about ourselves. To have high self-esteem is to have a favorable attitude toward yourself. To have low self-esteem is to have an unfavorable attitude toward yourself. Self-consciousness is excessive concern about self-esteem. It is characterized by shyness, embarrassment, and anxiety in the presence of others.

Self-concept is in process. Our self-concepts change with the situation, the other person or people involved, and our own moods. Our self-concept is originally formed by the treatment we receive from others and our relationships with them. It is maintained largely through our interactions with others.

Gender differences affect self-concept. People are treated differently from the time they are born on the basis of their biological gender. Furthermore, the culture tends to be masculinist. As a result, women tend to have lower self-esteem than do men. These findings are consistent with studies that have shown members of minority groups often suffer from negative self-esteem because they have responded to the evaluations of the dominant culture.

Self-concept can be improved, but the process is not a simple matter. The two essential steps in changing self-concept are becoming aware of ourselves and establishing a positive attitude toward ourselves and others. Both women and men can improve their self-concepts.

Key Terms

androgynous   The term used to describe an individual who possesses both female and male traits.

blind self   The quadrant of the Johari Window that illustrates the proportion of information about ourselves known to others but not to us.

confirmation   The feeling that occurs when others treat us in a manner consistent with our self-definition.

disconfirmation   The feeling that occurs when others fail to respond to our self-definition or when others respond in a neutral way.

external locus of control   Perceiving others, rather than yourself, as responsible for the events in your life.

hidden self   The quadrant of the Johari Window that illustrates the proportion of information about ourselves that is known to us but not to others.

internal locus of control   Perceiving yourself, rather than others, as responsible for the events in your life.

Johari Window   A model of self-disclosure that indicates the proportion of information about ourselves that is known and/or unknown to ourselves, others, and both.

open self   The quadrant of the Johari Window that illustrates the proportion of information about ourselves that is known to ourselves and others.

rejection   The feeling that occurs when others treat us in a manner inconsistent with our self-definition.

self-actualization   Maslow's term for fulfilling your potential as a person.

self awareness   The ability to consciously distinguish between our self-image and our self-esteem.

self-concept   Our consciousness of our total, essential, and particular being; composed of self-image and self-esteem.

self-consciousness   An excessive concern about self-esteem.

self-esteem   Our attitudes and feelings toward our self-image; how well we like ourselves.

self-fulfilling prophecy   The self-image and self-esteem expected of us by others; the tendency to become what others expect us to become.

self-image   The sort of person we think we are; our own description of who we are and what we do.

symbolic interactionism   A theory that suggests the self develops through interplay or interaction with others.

unknown self   The quadrant of the Johari Window that illustrates the proportion of information about ourselves that is unknown to ourselves and others.

chapter 4

Active and Empathic Listening:

Understanding Another

W hat will you learn about listening in this chapter? First, you will learn about the listening process and determine that listening and hearing are not the same phenomenon. Second, you will read about two types of listening: active listening and empathic listening. Most of us have difficulty listening effectively. Why? Interference comes from the message and occasion, ourselves, and our perceptions of other people. You will be able to distinguish various specific distractions in each of these categories. We can improve our ability to listen, and nine suggestions are provided. Finally, we will identify verbal and nonverbal behaviors associated with effective listening. Let us begin by distinguishing between listening and hearing.

What will you learn?

When you have read and thought about this chapter, you should be able to answer the following questions:

1. What is the difference between hearing and listening?

2. What are two kinds of listening?

3. What are some examples of things that tend to interfere with effective listening?

4. Can you explain with examples self-focus, defensiveness, and experiential superiority?

5. How do status and stereotypes interfere with effective listening?

6. What are some suggestions for improving your listening?

7. What verbal and nonverbal behaviors are associated with effective listening?

8. Can you cite examples of effective and ineffective listening from your own experience?

It is the province of knowledge to speak and it is the privilege of wisdom to listen.

Oliver Wendell Holmes

I like to listen. I have learned a great deal from listening. Most people never listen.

Ernest Hemingway

I know that you believe you understand what you think I said, but I am not sure you realize that what you heard is not what I meant.

Anonymous

H aving learned the role of perception and the importance of self in communication, you can now consider how you learn to understand others. Perhaps the most important way that we learn to understand others is through a skill called listening.

Listening is the process of receiving and interpreting aural stimuli. In other words, it is figuring out what you heard. Hearing and listening are different, however. **Hearing** is simply the act of receiving sound. You can avoid seeing by closing your eyes, touch by avoidance, and smell by breathing through your nose. Hearing you cannot avoid because you have no ear flaps. Listening means that you have to apply your brain to the sounds you hear by interpreting them or by giving them meaning. You hear with your ears; you listen with your brain.

The Listening Process

What is involved in the listening process? Current investigators are attempting to determine the specific steps involved in listening.[1] Figure 4.1 summarizes some of these steps. The process of listening includes, at minimum, stimuli that we hear with our ears. Nerves transmit these sensations to our brain. We then determine if we will attend to the stimulus or ignore it, which of several meanings we may assign to it, and whether we will store it in short-term or long-term memory.[2]

Let us consider an example. Suppose you are reading one of your textbooks. Loud voices can be heard outside your window. You might not "listen" to the voices because you are engrossed in your book. Although you can hear the conversation, listening is not occurring. After some time, you begin to listen and realize that two of your friends are arguing. You sit very quietly, attempting to hear their exact words and determine that one is accusing the other of plagiarizing a paper. You have suspected this friend of cheating before and you decide, with no other evidence, that he is guilty. Not only do you convict your friend without a trial, you remember this conversation long after you have eavesdropped.

Although listening and hearing are different activities, most of us have been in situations where people assumed they were the same.

We may recall embarrassing moments when we were not even aware that a friend had asked us a question, even though they thought they were being heard. Another time, we might have been confronted by an angry girlfriend or boyfriend, "What do you mean you don't feel like going out tonight? I know you heard me yesterday when I told you how important this party is to me!" Many people incorrectly assume listening and hearing are the same.

Similarly, many people incorrectly believe they listen well. Most of the evidence, however, is in the other direction. In general, when tested immediately after being presented with a message, people recall about half of what they have heard, even when they have been informed they will be tested on the

Figure 4.1 Listening is more than simply hearing a message.

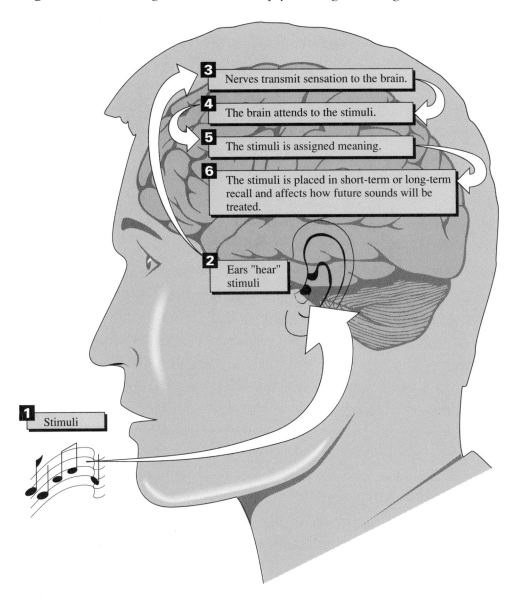

3 Nerves transmit sensation to the brain.

4 The brain attends to the stimuli.

5 The stimuli is assigned meaning.

6 The stimuli is placed in short-term or long-term recall and affects how future sounds will be treated.

2 Ears "hear" stimuli

1 Stimuli

We listen more than we talk, write, or read.

information. When they are tested two months later, they recall only about a quarter of the information.[3] However, students do recall more information if they have been told that they will be tested and graded on the information.[4]

Can you improve your ability to recall information? Can you become a better listener? Indeed, you can. After you have completed this chapter, you should be more effective in this essential communicative activity.

Listening is a fundamental component of communication, and we spend a great deal of time engaged in the activity. A classic study showed that we spend more than 40 percent of our time engaged in listening.[5] Similarly, contemporary studies demonstrate we listen to a greater extent than we engage in any other form of verbal communication. Weinrauch and Swanda found that business personnel, including those with and without managerial responsibilities, spent nearly 33 percent of their time listening, almost 26 percent of their time speaking, nearly 23 percent of their time writing, and almost 19 percent of their time reading.[6] When Werner investigated the communication activities of high school and college students, homemakers, and employees in a variety of other occupations, he determined they spent 55 percent of their time listening, 13 percent reading, and 8 percent writing.[7] Many other studies have documented the great amount of time people spend listening.[8]

Figure 4.2 Proportions of communication activities.

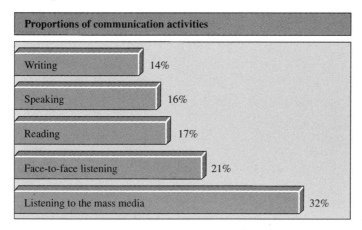

How much time do you spend listening each day? Researchers have determined the relative proportion of time spent in various communication activities by college students. Each day, you spend 32 percent of your time listening to the mass media, 21 percent in face-to-face listening, 17 percent reading, 16 percent speaking, and 14 percent writing.[9] Over half of your time (53 percent) is spent listening to either the mass media or to other people. These communication activities are depicted in the bar graph in figure 4.2

If these investigations were to be repeated in the 1990s, perhaps an even larger percentage of our time would be shown to be devoted to listening. Today, as in the past, we spend time listening to people in social situations, in the classroom, and at work. The developments in mass communication and technological advancements, however, have encouraged additional modes of listening. Today we listen to radio, television, records, cassette tapes, movies, cable programs, word synthesizers, and people brought to us by teleconference calls.

Types of Listening

We engage in listening for a variety of reasons—for appreciation, discrimination, comprehension, evaluation, empathy, and therapy.[10] Listening also can be distinguished in terms of purpose, behavior of the listener, nature of the information under discussion, communication setting, and many other categories. Here, for reasons of clarity, we consider two kinds of listening: active listening and empathic listening. In chapter 5, we will consider critical listening.

Active Listening

Active listening is "involved listening with a purpose."[11] Over twenty-five years ago, active listening was distinguished from passive listening:

> In the former, the individual listens with more or less his or her total self—including his [or her] special senses, attitudes, beliefs, feelings, and intuitions. In the latter, the listener becomes mainly an organ for the passive reception of sound, with little self-perception, personal involvement, . . .or alive curiosity.[12]

Active listening is desirable in both interpersonal communication and public speaking. Active listening requires activity on the part of the listener. The listener does not lethargically sit or stand while another speaks; instead, active listening is characterized by movement, change, and responsiveness on the part of the listener.

Active listening implies feedback is offered to the speaker. **Feedback** was defined in chapter 1 as the listener's verbal and nonverbal responses to the speaker's messages. The responses must be received and interpreted by the speaker. Feedback allows us to monitor our communication with others and to avoid many misunderstandings. For example, speakers can alter, correct, or enforce their original messages as they observe and interpret the feedback offered to them. They may add additional examples or speak more concretely if the listener does not appear to understand the point being made. They may retract what they have said or apologize for their position if they believe the listener is disagreeing with them. Finally, they may embellish their message and even take a more radical stand if they recognize agreement coming from the listener.

Feedback can be distinguished along a number of lines, but the discussion in this chapter is limited to the difference between positive and negative feedback. **Positive feedback** includes such nonverbal behaviors as positive facial expression, smiling, laughing, a forward body lean, increased touching, and movement toward the other person. Verbal examples of positive feedback are statements like, "I hear what you're saying," "I know where you're coming from," "Of course," and "That's interesting. What happened then?" Positive feedback results in speakers increasing the length of their messages, decreasing linguistic errors and nonfluencies, and decreasing feelings of **defensiveness** (the tendency to protect ourselves against danger or intimacy).

Negative feedback is characterized by frowns and other negative facial expressions, movement away from the speaker, decreased touching, a focus on people other than the communicator, decreased eye contact, and general nonresponsiveness. Statements such as, "I don't see your point," "You seem to be really uninformed," "Let's change the subject," or just "So what?" are extreme examples of negative verbal feedback. Negative feedback results in a message of decreasing length, an increasing number of linguistic errors and nonfluencies, and increasing feelings of defensiveness on the part of the speaker.

You may have observed that not all feedback is clear, nor is all feedback useful. For feedback to be effective, the speaker needs to be able to understand a listener's response, the speaker must be able and willing to accept the information, and the speaker must be able to act on the information.

First, if you are a listener and want to provide effective feedback, you must carefully choose any words you intend to use so the other communicator will understand what you mean. Is the other person likely to understand the language you have chosen? Will the other person be aware of what you are describing? Can you place your feedback in a context in which the meaning will be more easily understood? Should you preface your feedback with explanations, observations, or other information?

Second, to help the other communicator accept the information you are providing, you need to consider his or her feelings, attitudes, and values. Avoid "loaded" terms that might produce emotional reactions. Attempt to be descriptive, rather than evaluative. For example, instead of "I don't know why you let things others say bother you!" or "You never put any energy into your work!" you might offer "I see that you're hurt by the comment she made," or "I understand that you're very tired by all your coursework this year."

State your perceptions as opinions and reactions, rather than as absolute and indisputable facts. Refer to specific, observable behavior, rather than general or global issues. Discuss the relevant behavior, rather than the person. Communicate acceptance of the other person and his or her right to view the world in a manner different from your own.

Third, to help the other communicator act on your feedback, you may need to examine the content of your response. Do not provide feedback to individuals about things over which they have no control. Consider how improvement may occur once the other individual has received your feedback. Suggest specific outcomes, rather than leaving the person bombarded with general information. Provide possible means of altering behavior.

An example may clarify these suggestions. Suppose you and your roommate are debating the consequences of changing the grade point scale. Your roommate is in favor of changing the scale to include an A+ point, thus altering the A range. You listen attentively to the detailed reasoning expressed; you then could say, "I see that you would like the grade point scale to be changed to accommodate an A+. As the scale now stands, you feel that exceptional students are not rewarded for their efforts. I do not think that such a change is necessary, and there are some strong arguments to support my view. Would you take the time to hear me out?"

This example illustrates clear and useful feedback. In your feedback, you have used clear language so your partner should understand what you are stating. You have helped your friend to accept the information by first considering his or her feelings and attitudes before stating your own. You have not used evaluative language, but you have remained highly descriptive. You have stated the two positions as though reasonable individuals could hold either point of view. You have relied upon the other individual's words, rather than

Table 4.1

Active Listening and Empathic Listening are Similar, but Empathic Listening Adds the Attempt to Understand the Other Person

Active Listening	Empathic Listening
Involved listening	Involved listening
Has a purpose	Has a purpose
	Attempt to understand another person

on issues or matters that go far beyond the current discussion. Finally, you have helped the other person to act on your feedback. You have clearly stated that you would appreciate having your friend listen to arguments on the other side of the issue as well. You did not provide feedback over an issue about which he or she has no control, and you suggested a specific behavior the person could exhibit.

Do not be discouraged if you find it is easier to read about effective feedback than to provide it. Providing appropriate feedback is particularly difficult when the topic is one about which the two communicators have strongly divergent opinions. With practice, however, you can improve your ability to offer feedback that is clear and useful to others with whom you communicate.

Empathic Listening

Empathic listening is a second kind of listening. Empathic listening, like active listening, is involved listening with a purpose. Empathic listening has the additional characteristic, however, of attempting to understand another person (table 4.1). **Empathy** is the ability to perceive the other person's view of the world as though it were our own. Clark elaborates on this definition by stating that empathy is

> "the capacity of an individual to feel the needs, the aspirations, the frustrations, the joy, the sorrows, the anxieties, the hurt, indeed, the hunger of others as if they were his [or her] own."[13]

Empathic listening is the type of listening that has total understanding of the other person as its goal.

Most of us assume that other people perceive things the way we do. As we said in chapter 2, however, great variations in perceptions exist. If we wish to be more understanding of others, we need to recognize that such differences occur, and we should attempt to determine what other people's experiences

DENNIS the MENACE

"IT WAS NICE TO HEAR FROM YOU, DEAR."

"THANK YOU. IT WAS NICE TO HAVE SOMEBODY LISTEN TO ME."

are. Bochner and Kelly, two communication scholars, described empathy as "the essence of all communicative processes."[14] Howell observed that "empathic skills are central to competence in human interaction."[15]

Empathy is distinct from neutrality. We exhibit **neutrality** when we show indifference to another person. Neutrality is harmful because it indicates that we do not have respect or positive regard for the other person.

When we listen with empathy to others, we do not need to feel the same emotions they are experiencing. What we communicate to them is an awareness, appreciation, and acceptance of their emotions. Empathic listening requires sensitivity to others and an ability to demonstrate this sensitivity. We should strive to communicate to others that we are with them, not because we are sharing their emotions, but because we understand and accept their feelings.

If we fail to empathize with others, we fail to understand them. In a very real sense, we are hurting ourselves. To the extent that we do not empathize with others, we restrict ourselves to our personal experiences and feelings. As Howell observed,

"Empathy enables us to engage in true joint ventures, giving weight to the interests of others as well as promoting our own."[16]

Feedback, which demonstrates active listening, may be verbal or nonverbal, positive or negative, immediate or delayed.

Empathic listening is not easy to achieve. We need to empathize with others precisely when it is most difficult for us to do so. When we disagree most with others, it is then that we most need to show them that we understand them and their point of view. Our tendency in such situations is to spend a great deal of time and energy defending our own position and finding fault with others' points of view. We feel a need to prove that we are right and that other people are wrong.

Empathic listening allows us to enter another person's world as though it were our own. Empathy implies understanding, rather than judgment. Carl Rogers has expressed the importance of empathy in the statement that

> "a person who is loved appreciatively, not possessively, blooms, and develops his or her own unique self. The person who loves nonpossessively is himself or herself enriched."[17]

Empathic listening is satisfying and enriching to both parties in an interpersonal relationship.

We have just discussed feedback in active listening. Appropriate feedback when we are engaged in empathic listening takes different forms. Carl Rogers determined that feedback can be classified into five categories: evaluative, interpretive, supportive, probing, and understanding. *Evaluative feedback,* which occurs most frequently in conversations, includes those responses that make a judgment about the worth, goodness, or appropriateness of the other person's statement. *Interpretive feedback,* which occurs with the next most frequency, includes responses in which we attempt to explain to the other person how his or her statements have been interpreted by us. When we offer *supportive feedback,* we are attempting to assist or bolster the other communicator. *Probing feedback* includes those responses in which we attempt to gain additional information, to continue the discussion, or to clarify a point that has been made. Finally, *understanding feedback,* which occurs least frequently in everyday conversations, attempts to discover completely what the other communicator means by his or her statements.

It may be interesting for you to note that the frequency of these kinds of responses probably occurs in an inverse order of appropriateness for the length of relationship and its usefulness to the communicators. For example, evaluative feedback occurs most frequently, yet few individuals can accept evaluation from others until they have experienced a relationship of some duration and have come to trust the other person. Similarly, supportive, probing, and understanding responses are less frequently relied upon by communicators. None of these response styles are inherently incorrect. We must examine the situation, the relationship with the other person, and other variables in order to determine an appropriate response. To improve your understanding, complete the accompanying exercise on response styles on page 70.

Interference with Our Ability to Listen

Studies cited earlier show that we do not listen well. Understanding another by listening requires that we hear both verbal and nonverbal messages; that we understand the content, the intent, and the accompanying emotions; and that we communicate our understanding. A number of difficulties and breakdowns in communication can occur on the way to understanding. Let us consider some of the factors that may interfere with our ability to listen.

Noise

In chapter 1, the term *noise* was introduced to refer to interference in the communication process from external and internal sources. The first of these distractions is external in that it is something outside the self, incidental to the message, that keeps you from listening.

Response Styles

In order to determine if you understand the various response styles identified by Rogers, complete the following exercise. For each of the statements, provide the kind of response requested. After you have provided the specified response, indicate which response you would probably use and which response would probably result in the most satisfactory communication for both persons.

1. "I can't believe the job market this year. I've never had a problem getting a summer job before, and I have references from three different places. I spent all day looking for something that begins in June, and so far, I've had absolutely no luck!"

   Evaluative feedback: _____

   _____

   Interpretive feedback: _____

   _____

   Probing feedback: _____

   _____

2. "My mom just called me and said that she and my dad were thinking about separating for a while. I can't believe it—they don't fight like my friends' parents, and they've been married for over twenty years."

   Interpretive feedback: _____

   _____

   Supportive feedback: _____

   _____

   Understanding feedback: _____

   _____

3. "I've had it with Bill. We've gone together for almost two years, and he has never even said that he cares about me. I thought that by now we'd be engaged. If he wants to play around, I can too!"

Evaluative feedback: _____

_____

Supportive feedback: _____

_____

Probing feedback: _____

_____

4. "I've been living with Donna for over two years, and I really thought that I knew her, but last night she told me that she was homosexual. I really didn't know what to say to her, and I feel strange living with her now."

Supportive feedback: _____

_____

Probing feedback: _____

_____

Understanding feedback: _____

_____

5. "I just got my grade report for this term. I knew I wasn't doing very well, but I never expected to find myself on academic probation."

Evaluation feedback: _____

_____

Interpretive feedback: _____

_____

Supportive feedback: _____

_____

Listeners are sometimes distracted by noise and cannot listen to the speaker's message. Careful attention to the speaker allows listeners to avoid distractions.

Physical distractions, then, are all of the stimuli in the environment that keep you from focusing on the other person and the message. It could be actual sounds (loud music, two people talking during a lecture), sights (a blinking light, an outrageous tie), or smells (too much perfume or too little deodorant).

The other three distractors that interfere with effective listening are internal and are more a function of what is going on in your mind than what is going on in your environment. **Mental distractions** are the mental side trips, fantasies, and daydreaming that occur when you are supposed to be listening. These distractions might be inspired by how the speaker looks or what she says, but they are not part of the intended message. An example of a mental distraction would be thinking about your lover when you are supposed to be discussing taxes with your accountant.

Factual distractions occur when you get so wrapped up in individual facts that you miss the main point. The history professor is reciting the particular battles, but you don't know what war he is talking about.

Semantic distractions, also inspired by the message, occur when we overrespond to an emotion-laden word or concept. The professor seems to be hinting that women are inferior, and the very thought makes you so angry that you don't listen any more.

Ourselves

Other factors that interfere with our ability to listen are related to ourselves. Self-focus, defensiveness, experiential superiority, and egocentrism all interfere with our ability to understand another.

Self-focus, or a preoccupation with thoughts about ourselves, hampers listening and empathy. We need to develop positive feelings about ourselves and about other people. Self-focus suggests we have developed regard for ourselves, but we have failed to develop the same feeling toward others. In the conversation that follows, Tom is unable to empathize with Karen because he allows his personal concerns to dominate his thinking and his communication.

Karen has just received word that her grandmother has died. Tom is the counselor at the company where she works. Karen is extremely upset and goes to Tom because she needs to talk to someone. She has talked with him only casually in the past, but she feels he will understand because he is a trained counselor.

Karen: *Tom, do you have a minute?*
Tom: *Sure, Karen, come on in.*
Karen: *I wanted to talk to someone for a little while.*
Tom: *Fine. What would you like to talk about?*
Karen: *Well, I just got a phone call from home saying that my grandmother died, and I guess I just needed someone to talk to.*
Tom: *Yeah, I know how you feel. I had a grandmother who died about eight years ago. She was the neatest lady I have ever known. Why, when I was a kid she used to bake cookies for me every Saturday. We used to go to the park on weekends for picnics. She sure was fun to be with.*
Karen: *I'm sure you had a good time, but I sort of wanted to talk about my grandmother.*
Tom: *Oh sure. Well, what was she like?*
Karen: *Well, she was really a good person, but . . .*
Tom: *Yeah, I guess all grandmothers are pretty good.*
Karen: *I guess so, but . . .*
Tom: *You know, it's been a long time since I thought about my grandmother. I'm really glad you came in today.*
Karen: *Yes, well, I guess my break is about over, so I'd better get back to work.*
Tom: *Okay. It's been nice talking to you. Stop by anytime.*
Karen: *Sure.*

A number of factors may account for a person's focus on him- or herself, rather than on the other person. Defensiveness, which was mentioned as an outcome of negative feedback, is a common reason. People who feel they must defend their position usually feel threatened. They feel that, in general, people are attacking them and their ideas, and they develop the habit of defending themselves. Sometimes, people who are championing a specific cause—such as the CIA, the Democratic-Socialist party, the Ku Klux Klan, or supporters of the ERA—develop this attitude. They stand ready to respond to the least provocation, and they tend to find fault with other people.

In the interview that follows from the organizational setting, the supervisor demonstrates a defensive attitude and is consequently unable to listen to the employee. The supervisor is the director of operations in a social service agency. She has arranged this appraisal interview with the employee because she is evaluating his performance as a community organizer.

Supervisor: *As you know, after sixty days, we evaluate each new employee. That's why I've asked you to come here today. Here is the evaluation form I have filled out. Please read it.*

Employee: *(after reading) I don't understand why you have marked me so low in dependability.*

Supervisor: *Because you always ask so many questions whenever I tell you to do something.*

Employee: *But the reason I ask questions is that I don't understand exactly what you want me to do. If I didn't ask the questions, I wouldn't be able to perform the task because your instructions usually are not clear to me.*

Supervisor: *I marked you low in that area because you require so much supervision.*

Employee: *It's not supervision I need, it's clear instruction, and I don't feel it's fair for you to mark me low in this area when I am not.*

Supervisor: *It doesn't really matter what you think because I'm doing the evaluation.*

Employee: *Don't I have anything to say about it?*

Supervisor: *No. Now that you've read it, will you please sign here?*

Employee: *Definitely not. I feel that it is unfair and inaccurate.*

Supervisor: *Then check the box that indicates that you are not in agreement with the evaluation. All your signature means is that you have read it, not that you agree with it.*

Employee: *This is the most ridiculous evaluation I have ever had in my entire life.*

Supervisor: *That's unimportant at this point. If you don't have anything else to say, that will be all.*

The defensive verbal behavior by the supervisor clearly interfered with her ability to listen to her employee. Defensiveness usually interferes with our ability to listen.

Another reason for self-focus is known as **experiential superiority.** People who have lived through a variety of experiences sometimes express this attitude toward people who have had less experience. Professors often cannot listen or empathize with a student who is explaining why an assignment was not completed on time; they assume the student is offering an excuse they have heard before. Parents sometimes fail to listen to their children's problems or to empathize with them; they feel, from their own experience with a similar problem, they can just give a pat answer.

A variation of experiential superiority occurs in long-term relationships, when people have a good deal of experience in the relationship and feel they can predict the other person's statements. Husbands may respond with an occasional "uh-huh" over the newspaper at breakfast; wives may repeat, "Sure, honey," while daydreaming about other matters. The characters in the "Hägar" cartoon typify people who no longer listen to each other—probably as a result of a long relationship.

Another reason people focus on themselves is simple egocentrism. **Egocentrism** is self-focus carried to an extreme. It is the tendency to view the self as the center of any activity. An egocentric person is overly concerned with self and pays little attention to others. This person appears to be constantly asking, "How do I look?" or "How do I sound?" instead of responding to the other person.

One place you can observe egocentric people is at a party. Egocentric people usually make a number of attention-getting moves that place them at the center of the stage. They may arrive late, talk loudly, dress flamboyantly, and stand in the center of the room to make others focus on them. They also move from person to person or group to group, but they do not give their full attention to the people with whom they are talking. They look around the room, glancing from one person to another. Rarely do they focus on anyone for more than a moment, and even then they do not concentrate on the other person's message.

Our Perception of the Other Person

Other factors that interfere with our ability to listen involve our perception of the other person and preconceived attitudes, such as status or stereotypes.

If we believe other people have **status,** we accept what they say easily, rather than listening carefully and critically. We usually do not listen carefully or critically when the speaker is an M.D., a Supreme Court justice, or a visiting expert. If we think other people have low status, we often do not listen to their statements at all, nor do we retain their messages. Adults rarely seek advice from youngsters on career options, and intelligent people seldom listen to those they consider unintelligent. We dismiss statements made by people of lesser status; thus, we tend not to listen carefully to persons whom we perceive to have either a higher or lower status than ourselves. We tend to listen more critically and respond more argumentively with people we consider our peers.

Our **stereotypes** also affect our ability to listen. Each of us places people into groups we respect and groups we do not respect. When people are within our respected groups, we tend to believe what they say. When they belong to a group for whom we have little regard, we tend to reject their messages. If we look up to Democrats, teachers, or 4.0 students, we are more likely to listen to someone who fits into one of those categories than to someone who belongs to another political party, holds a different occupation, or has lower grades.

Improving Our Ability to Listen

Just as we can identify factors that interfere with our ability to listen, so can we identify ways of improving our listening ability. Let us reconsider the three sets of factors that interfere with our listening—noise, ourselves, and our perception of the other person—and suggest ways of overcoming each.

As we mentioned earlier, noise distracts. It can be external or internal noise: physical, mental, factual, or semantic.

1. *Moving to another location* is a simple way to solve the problem of external, physical noise, such as loud sounds, bright lights, or odors. Since it is not possible to move to another location in a public speaking situation, the speaker needs to reduce distractions (teachers make talking students be quiet), or the speaker needs to apply extra focus and concentration.

2. *Identifying the other person's central idea and placing the information in our own conceptual framework* is a way to reduce mental side trips. Because Americans speak at an average rate of 125 words per minute but can receive about 800 words per minute, you have time to think about how ideas translate into your framework.

3. *Focusing on main ideas,* instead of getting caught up in all the details, is the key to avoiding factual distractions. After all, it is less offensive to others to ask for specifics than to ask, "What in the world are you talking about?"

4. *Remembering that words are arbitrary symbols* helps to reduce semantic distractions. Words have no inherent or natural meaning shared by all. There is nothing wrong about asking what someone means by a word, and you can explain negative connotations to another person if they unwittingly use a term that angers you.

We also examined distractions that result from ourselves: self-focus, defensiveness, experiential superiority, and egocentrism. Here are some suggestions for overcoming these distractions to effective listening.

1. *Focusing on other people as sources of feelings, thoughts, ideas, and information* is a way to avoid self-focus. Because everyone has different experience, they know something you do not. Learn from them by listening to them instead of dismissing them.

2. *Focusing on the meaning and experiences we share* is a helpful way to avoid defensiveness. In the face of apparent disagreement, seek common ground. Republicans want to reduce capital gains taxes Democrats oppose, but both want to reduce the deficit. Honest disagreement on issues is fine, but neither party needs to be defensive by not listening to the other.

3. *Giving the other person a full hearing and suspending judgment* are two ways to defuse experiential superiority. Instead of assuming that a high school dropout cannot know as much as you do, hear him or her out and

see if he or she has a good idea. Many ideas, such as the earth is round, humans can defy gravity, and people should have social security, were first dismissed as unworthy of consideration.

4. *Concentrating on the other person* helps to overcome egocentrism. Listening to another person when he or she speaks invites them to listen to you. Others think more highly of someone who is an active and empathic listener. No center stage activity, clothing, makeup, or jewelry will make you as attractive to others as your ability to listen.

Now that you know how to avoid distractions to effective listening, review by reading the "Checklist for Effective Listening" in the exercise on page 79.

Behaviors Associated with Effective Listening

Along with the general guidelines for improving our ability to listen, there are specific verbal and nonverbal behaviors associated with effective listening. Joseph N. Capella, a professor at the University of Wisconsin at Madison, identified some of these behaviors. He named eye gaze, posture, gestures, distance, dominance, involvement, the regulation of speaking turns, language choices, and the use of intimate questions.[18] Let us consider these behaviors and others associated with effective listening. You may wish to consider your own listening behavior to determine which of these behaviors you regularly demonstrate and which of these skills you may want to add to your repertoire.

Verbal Skills of Effective Listening

The notion of verbal components in listening may seem strange to you. You may reason that if you are engaged in listening, you cannot also be speaking. As you will recall from chapter 1, however, people encode and decode simultaneously, and you can make verbal responses while you are deeply involved in listening. The verbal components of active listening are identified below and on the following pages. In order to determine your current competence in this area, consider those skills that you regularly practice.

1. *Invite additional comments.* Suggest that the speaker add more details or give additional information. Phrases like "Go on," "What else," "How did you feel about that?" and "Did anything else occur?" encourage the speaker to say more and to continue to share ideas and information.
2. *Ask questions.* One method of inviting the speaker to continue is to ask direct questions. The questions you ask may request more in-depth details, definitions, or clarification.

Checklist for Effective Listening

To determine how effectively you listen to others, complete the following exercise after you have engaged in a conversation with another person:

_____ 1. Did you focus on the main ideas the other person was presenting, rather than on specific facts and details?

_____ 2. Did you avoid being distracted by an unusual word, by a word that offended you, or by a word used in an unusual manner?

_____ 3. Did you focus on the intent, as well as the content, of the other person's message?

_____ 4. Did you engage in the conversation in a place that was free of physical distractions, or did you move to such a place if your original setting was distracting?

_____ 5. Did you focus on the meaning and experiences that you shared with the other person, rather than on the meaning and experiences that are different?

_____ 6. Did you give the other person a full hearing, rather than exhibiting impatience with him or her?

_____ 7. Did you concentrate on the other person, rather than on yourself?

_____ 8. Did you suspend judgment until the other individual was finished speaking, rather than jumping to premature conclusions?

_____ 9. Did you focus on the other person as a valuable source of ideas and information, rather than categorizing and dismissing him or her?

3. *Identify areas of agreement or common experience.* Briefly relate similar past experiences, or briefly explain a similar point of view that you hold. Sharing common ideas, attitudes, values, and beliefs are the basis of communication. In addition, such comments demonstrate your understanding.
4. *Vary verbal responses.* Use a variety of responses such as "Yes," "I see," "Go on," and "Right" instead of relying on one standard unaltering response such as, "Yes," "Yes," "Yes."
5. *Provide clear verbal responses.* Use specific and unambiguous words and phrases in your feedback to the speaker. Misunderstandings can occur if you do not provide easily understood responses. In the following example, the farmer's ambiguous responses to his wife's questions confuse the issue. The student who supplied this dialogue stated that it provides a typical example of his parents' communication behavior.

Mom:	*What time do you want dinner?*
Dad:	*Well, I have to grind feed and do chores up north and vaccinate a sick steer.*
Mom:	*The meat loaf and potatoes will take about an hour to bake.*
Dad:	*What time will Dan be home? Do you think he will have time to help me when he gets home?*
Mom:	*I don't know if Dan can help you, but I would like to know what time you want to eat.*
Dad:	*It will have to wait until I get all my work done.*
Mom:	*I guess I will have to figure it out for myself.*

The father in the preceding dialogue offered vague, general answers to the mother's questions. In the following dialogue, two roommates are discussing the end of a relationship, but the listener offers little clear feedback. The overused and ambiguous words are too general to supply the speaker with satisfaction.

Charlie:	*I've just broken up with my girlfriend.*
Fred:	*Oh.*
Charlie:	*We've gone together for the past three-and-a-half years, and she just cut it off.*
Fred:	*That's something.*

In both dialogues, the listeners fail to supply clear responses to the other communicator. If the father in the first dialogue had answered his wife's questions directly and if Fred had offered more specific comments, these conversations would have been greatly improved and active listening would have been demonstrated.

6. *Use descriptive, nonevaluative responses.* Use responses such as, "Yes," "I understand your explanation," "Your perspective is clear," and "I agree," rather than judgmental or negative statements such as "No," "That's not what I think," "I don't agree," or "I don't think so." Trivializing or joking about serious disclosures will suggest a negative evaluation of the speaker.

Similarly, derogatory remarks or put-downs will be seen as offensive. Attempting to be superior to the speaker by stating that your believe you have a more advanced understanding will suggest an evaluative tone. The conversation between Charlie and Fred that was begun earlier became worse as it continued. Not only did Fred respond with ambiguous comments, but he also appeared to act superior to Charlie. The dialogue continues:

Charlie: *Hasn't this ever happened to you?*
Fred: *No.*
Charlie: *I thought you broke up with Jane.*
Fred: *Yes, but that was different. You see, I broke it up, not her!*

Charlie probably felt defensive because of Fred's act of superiority and demonstrated his frustration with the somewhat aggressive question about one of Fred's earlier relationships.

7. *Provide affirmative and affirming statements.* Comments like "Yes," "I see," "I understand," and "I know" provide affirmation. Offering praise and specific positive statements demonstrate concern.

8. *Avoid complete silence.* The lack of any response suggests that you are not listening to the speaker. The "silent treatment" induced by sleepiness or lack of concern may result in defensiveness or anger on the part of the speaker. Appropriate verbal feedback demonstrates your active listening.

9. *Allow the other person the opportunity of a complete hearing.* When you discuss common feelings or experiences, avoid dominating the conversation. Allow the other person to go into depth and detail; allow the other person the option of changing the topic under discussion; allow the other person to talk without being interrupted. Silence is frequently appropriate when the other person is talking. One woman reported the following conversation that she'd had with her roommate's brother. She stated that she felt very frustrated because she was unable to complete any of her thoughts, and Jerry had not listened to her.

Jerry: *So you and Maggie are going to move out of the house?*
Char: *Yeah, we're thinking about . . .*
Jerry: *Well, I think it's wrong. Have you talked with your folks about it?*
Char: *Yes, I talked to . . .*
Jerry: *Is it what they want?*
Char: *Yes . . .*
Jerry: *How do you know?*
Char: *Well, my mom said . . .*
Jerry: *What?*
Char: *(Hesitating because of the continuing frustration she is feeling): That is was up to me to make my own decisions about where I live.*

Verbal Demonstrations of Effective Listening

In each of the examples listed, one person is making an assertion or asking a question. For each comment, provide the requested response. After you have completed the exercise, identify the response you would probably offer. Would your response differ depending on the other speaker? Would the age or sex of the other speaker alter your response? Offer examples of how your response would differ depending upon personality characteristics of the other communicator or circumstances within the environment.

1. "Would you close the door?"

    Ask Question: _____

    Provide Affirmative Statement: _____

    Restate Content: _____

2. "Jerry and I are breaking up—after five years."

    Invite Additional Comments: _____

    _____

    Ask Questions: _____

    _____

    Use Descriptive, Nonevaluative Response: _____

    _____

3. "Anorexia nervosa is a special problem for young women between the ages of 13 and 19 who are high achievers."

    Provide Clear Verbal Responses: _____

    _____

    Allow the Other Person the Opportunity of a Complete Hearing:

    _____

    Paraphrase Intent: _____

    _____

4. "I understood from your newspaper ad that you had blazers on sale— where are they?"

    Ask Questions: _____

    Provide Clear Verbal Responses: _____

    _____

    Paraphrase Content: _____

    _____

Jerry:	*Well, that's not what she wants at all. She's just saying that because she knows that you are so headstrong and won't do what she wants anyway.*
Char:	*I can't talk to you anymore about this now. I'll see you later.*

Char said that she felt a great deal of frustration in this conversation, and the net effect was to lower her concern for Jerry. After a number of similar conversations, she began to avoid him completely.

10. *Restate the content of the speaker's message.* Use repetition of key words, phrases, and ideas to demonstrate your understanding of the conversation. Such restatements should be brief.
11. *Paraphrase the content of the speaker's message.* Restate the speaker's message in your own words to determine if you understand the content of the message. Your goal in paraphrasing should be to completely understand the other person, rather than to disagree or to state your own point of view.
12. *Paraphrase the intent of the speaker's message.* People generally have a reason for making statements or disclosing information. Demonstrate your understanding of the speaker's intention by attempting to state it in your own words. Paraphrases of content and intent should be concise.

Now that you know twelve verbal demonstrations of effective listening, you can practice them by completing the exercise on "Verbal Demonstrations of Effective Listening."

Nonverbal Skills of Effective Listening

While we demonstrate active listening through the verbal skills previously listed, the majority of our active listening ability is shown through nonverbal communication. The following nonverbal components are essential in our ability to demonstrate active listening. Have a friend observe your nonverbal behavior as you listen to another person to determine if you are practicing these skills.

1. *Demonstrate bodily responsiveness.* Use movement and gestures to show your awareness of the speaker's message. Shaking your head in disbelief, checking the measurements of an object by indicating the size with your hands, and moving toward a person who is disclosing negative information would demonstrate appropriate bodily responsiveness. Large or exaggerated movements, such as walking around the room and sweeping arm gestures are generally inappropriate.
2. *Lean forward.* By leaning toward the speaker, a good listener will demonstrate his or her interest in the speaker. A forward lean suggests responsiveness as well as interest. In addition, it places you in a physical state of readiness to listen to the speaker.

3. *Use direct body orientation.* Do not angle yourself away from the speaker; instead, sit or stand so you are directly facing him or her. Parallel body position allows the greatest possibility for observing and listening to the speaker's verbal and nonverbal messages. When you stand or sit at an angle to the speaker, you may be creating the impression that you are attempting to get away or that you are moving away from the speaker. It also blocks your vision and allows you to be distracted by other stimuli in the environment.

4. *Use relaxed, but alert, posture.* Your posture should not be tense or "proper," but neither should it be so relaxed that you appear to be resting. Slouching suggests unresponsiveness, a tense body position suggests nervousness or discomfort, and a relaxed position that is accompanied by crossed arms and legs, a backward lean in a chair, and a confident facial expression suggest arrogance. Your posture should suggest to other persons that you are interested and that you are comfortable talking with them.

5. *Establish an open body position.* Sit or stand with your body open to the other person. Crossing your arms or legs may be more comfortable for you because of habit, but it frequently suggests that you are closed off psychologically, as well as physically. In order to maximize your nonverbal message to the other person that you are "open" to him or her, you will want to sit or stand without crossing your arms or legs.

6. *Use positive, responsive facial expression and head movement.* Your face and head will be the primary focus of the speaker. He or she will be observing you, and the expression of your face and the movement of your head will be the key. You can demonstrate your concern by nodding your head to show interest or agreement. You can use positive and responsive facial expression, such as smiling and raising your eyebrows.

7. *Establish direct eye contact.* The other person will be watching your eyes for interest. One of the first signs of a lack of interest is the listener's tendency to be distracted by other stimuli in the environment. Examples include the instructor who continually glances out of the door of her office, the parent who looks at a pot boiling on the stove, the roommate who glances at the television program that is playing, or the business executive who regularly looks at his or her watch. Try to focus and direct your gaze at the speaker. When you begin to look around the room you may find any number of other stimuli to distract your attention from the speaker and from his or her message.

A football player at a "Big Eight" university reported this conversation in which poor eye contact contributed to his feeling that the coach was not interested in him. Interestingly, the reason he was quitting the team was because he had not felt that anyone on the coaching staff had taken an interest in him.

WEE PALS

Player: *Coach, got a minute?*

Coach: *(Absorbed in paper work): Yeah, sure, what do you want? Have a seat.*

Player: *I want to talk about the team.*

Coach: *(Not looking up): Go on, kid.*

Player: *I'm going to turn in my gear.*

Coach: *(Turning around to his filing cabinet): Go on.*

Player: *I just don't feel . . .*

Coach: *(Interrupting): Lewis, I want to see you after you are dressed.*

Player: *. . . feel like I'm of value around here.*

Coach: *(With his back to the player, digging through the filing cabinet): Uh-huh, go on.*

Player: *My gear is in my locker, goodbye, Coach.*

The player stated that if the coach had finished his work and then devoted his full attention to him, the conversation would have been quite different. Eye contact could have made a great deal of difference in this case.

8. *Sit or stand close to the speaker.* Establishing close proximity to the speaker has two benefits. First, you put yourself in a position that allows you to hear the other person and that minimizes the distracting noises, sights, and other stimuli. Second, you demonstrate your concern or your positive feelings for the other person. We typically do not stand or sit close to persons we do not like, do not respect, or with whom we do not have common experiences. <u>Close physical proximity allows active listening to occur.</u>

9. *Use vocal responsiveness.* <u>Change your pitch, rate, inflection, and volume as you respond to the speaker.</u> Appropriate changes and choices will suggest that you are actually listening rather than responding in a standard, patterned manner that suggests that you are only appearing to listen. The stereotypical picture of the husband and wife at the breakfast table with the husband, hidden behind a newspaper, responding, "Yes, yes, yes" in a monotone voice while the wife tells him that their son has shaved the cat,

that she is running off with the mail carrier, and that the house is on fire, provides a familiar example of the appearance of listening while you are actually far away from the speaker's message.

10. *Provide supportive utterances.* Sometimes you can demonstrate more concern through nonverbal sounds like "Mmm," "Mmm-hmm," and "uh-huh" than you can by stating "Yes, I understand." You can easily provide supportive utterances while other persons are talking or when they pause. You are suggesting to them that you are listening, but you do not want to interrupt with a statement or verbalization of your own at this particular time. Such sounds will encourage them to continue without interruption.

Active listening requires a great deal of energy and sensitivity to the other person, but it is a reachable goal. The skills previously outlined should assist you in listening more actively to others. As you can see, nonverbal communication is important. Chapter 6 will provide even more ideas on how to use the speaker's nonverbal cues.

Summary

In this chapter, we considered the importance of understanding other people when we communicate with them. We can increase our understanding of other people by improving our ability to listen. Listening is the process of receiving and interpreting aural stimuli. It is far more complicated than simply hearing another person. We spend more time engaged in listening than we do in speaking, reading, or writing.

Active listening occurs when we are involved and when we have a purpose in listening. Empathic listening has the total understanding of the other person as its goal. A number of factors interfere with our ability to listen and to empathize. These factors fall into three categories—those related to the message and the occasion, such as factual, semantic, mental, and physical distractions; those related to ourselves, such as self-focus, defensiveness, experiential superiority, and egocentrism; and those related to the other person, such as status and stereotypes.

We can overcome these obstacles, however, and improve our ability to listen to others by focusing on the main ideas, keeping in mind that words are arbitrary symbols, identifying the other person's central idea and determining how the information fits into our personal conceptual framework, moving when physical distractions interfere, focusing on shared meaning and experiences, giving the other person a full hearing, concentrating on the other person, suspending judgment, and focusing on the other person as a source of feelings, thoughts, ideas, and information.

What verbal and nonverbal behaviors are associated with effective listening? The verbal behaviors include inviting additional comments; asking questions; identifying areas of agreement or common experience; varying verbal responses; providing clear verbal responses; using descriptive, nonevaluative responses; providing affirmative and affirming statements; avoiding complete silence; allowing the other person the opportunity of a complete hearing; restating the content of the speaker's message; paraphrasing the content of the speaker's message; and paraphrasing the intent of the speaker's message. Nonverbal behaviors are demonstrating bodily responsiveness; leaning forward; using direct body orientation; using a relaxed but alert posture; establishing an open body position, using positive, responsive facial expressions and head movement; establishing direct eye contact; sitting or standing close to the speaker; using vocal responsiveness; and providing supportive utterances.

Key Terms

active listening Involved listening with a purpose.

defensiveness Protecting and supporting our ideas and attitudes against attack by others; induced by the feeling that the self and the validity of self-expression are threatened.

egocentrism The tendency to view ourselves as the center of any exchange or activity; an overconcern with the presentation of ourselves to others.

empathic listening The type of listening that has total understanding of the other person as its goal.

empathy The ability to perceive the other person's view of the world as though it were our own.

experiential superiority The attitude that our experiences are more important and valid than the experiences of others.

factual distractions The tendency to listen to facts rather than to main ideas; a barrier to listening.

feedback The receiver's verbal and nonverbal responses to the source's messages; the responses must be received and interpreted by the source.

hearing The physiological process by which sound is received by the ear.

listening The process of receiving and interpreting aural stimuli.

mental distractions Occur when we communicate with ourselves while we are engaged in communication with others; a barrier to listening.

negative feedback Negative responses to the speaker's messages including frowns and other negative facial expressions, movement away from the speaker, decreased touching and eye contact, and statements such as, "No," "I don't agree," and "I don't understand."

neutrality Indifference to another person.

physical distractions Environmental stimuli that interfere with our focus on another person's message; a barrier to listening.

positive feedback Positive responses to the speaker's messages including positive facial expression, forward lean, smiling, increased touching, and such statements as "I understand," "Yes," and "I agree."

self-focus Developing a view of ourselves from our own perspective, rather than through the eyes of others; a preoccupation with thoughts about ourselves.

semantic distraction Bits or units of information in the message that interfere with understanding the main ideas or the total meaning of the entire message; a barrier to listening.

status The relative social position, reputation, or importance of another person.

stereotypes Conventional, oversimplified generalizations about a group, event, or issue.

chapter 5

Critical Listening and Thinking:

Using Your Mind

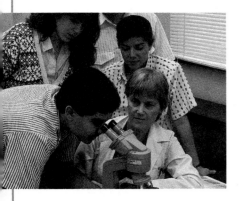

I n this chapter, you will be introduced to the topics of critical listening and critical thinking. First, the nature and definition of critical listening will be offered. Then, you will learn the steps to critical listening including capturing the information, establishing standards of appraisal, and applying those standards to messages. An added bonus in this section of the chapter is that you will learn to take more effective notes, which will have immediate application to your other college courses.

Next, we will turn our attention to critical thinking and consider the nature and definition of this ability. What are the attitudes of critical thinking? You will discover them in this chapter. You will also determine the abilities related to critical thinking, including distinguishing between observation and inferences; categorizing evidence or proof as emotional, logical, or personal; and understanding types of arguments. Finally, we will consider errors that are sometimes made in critical thinking. We begin with a consideration of critical listening.

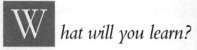

What will you learn?

When you have read and thought about this chapter, you should be able to answer the following questions:

1. What are three basic steps involved in critical listening?
2. What are the primary errors made by poor note takers?
3. How can you take effective notes to improve your listening?
4. Why should you learn how to think critically when listening?
5. What is the difference between observation and inferences?
6. Can you identify logical, emotional, and personal proofs when you hear them?
7. What is the difference between truth and validity?
8. Do you know what questions to ask in determining if someone is speaking or writing logically?
9. Can you identify a logical fallacy when you hear it?

You ain't learnin' nothing when you're talkin'.

Lyndon B. Johnson

My mind is made up—I don't want to be confused with the facts.

Anonymous

It is better to stir up a question without deciding it than decide it without stirring it up.

Joseph Joarbut

ritical listening and critical thinking are central to the communication process. In chapter 4, we considered the importance of listening and focused on active and empathic listening. Listening allows us to understand other people and their intended messages. Critical thinking is essential, too. We use critical thinking in both the sending and receiving aspects of communication. We must be able to make critical distinctions as we attempt to understand the messages of others and as we plan our own messages.

Critical listening and critical thinking are viewed as increasingly important. For example, in 1989, a survey of nearly 5,500 faculty members at over 300 colleges and universities of all sizes across the country was conducted by the Carnegie Foundation. The survey showed that over 70 percent of the faculty members believed that a goal of undergraduate education is enhancing students' abilities to think. Just five years before, in 1984, less than 50 percent held that belief.[1]

Critical listening and critical thinking go hand-in-hand. Some people use the terms synonymously. In this text we distinguish between the two, although we recognize the common elements in each. Both include three essential steps: gathering information, ideas, or arguments; establishing a basis for evaluation; and applying those standards to the information or ideas we have gathered.

How are critical listening and critical thinking distinct from each other? First, critical listening requires more than one communicator. It involves at least one speaker and one listener; thus, it is an interpersonal process—it occurs between people. Critical thinking occurs within a single individual and is, therefore, an intrapersonal process.

Second, critical listening is generally focused on one message while critical thinking often extends to several. You are involved in critical listening when you hear a speech in your class on the importance of recycling. You are engaged in critical thinking when you consider all the arguments you have gathered on the advantages and disadvantages of recycling and make a decision about how recycling will, or will not, become part of your life-style.

Critical Listening

The Nature of Critical Listening

In the last chapter, we considered two kinds of listening. We defined active listening as "involved listening with a purpose."[2] We defined empathic listening as listening that has total understanding of the other person as its goal. **Critical listening** may be defined as listening that challenges the speaker's message and evaluates its accuracy, meaningfulness, and utility. Critical listening results

Critical listening occurs frequently in the public speaking context.

in the total, or partial, acceptance or rejection of another person's oral message. Active listening is marked by involvement; empathic listening is marked by understanding; critical listening is marked by judgment.

Critical listening occurs often in an interpersonal context as well. A telemarketer encourages you to contribute to the disabled firefighter's children fund; your spouse wants you to move to a better apartment; your insurance person says you need more life insurance; and your physician claims that you need to run five miles per day and avoid red meat. Television and radio present you with advertising and opinions that you need to assess. Life is full of opportunities for critical listening.

Three Steps to Critical Listening

What is involved in critical listening? Essentially, critical listening depends on three steps: capturing the information, establishing standards of appraisal, and applying the standards to the materials. Let us consider each of these steps.

Step One: Capturing the Information by Taking Notes

The first step toward becoming a more critical listener is note taking. You have been taking notes all through your academic career, and you may feel you need no instruction in this area. However, many college students are unable to take effective notes. In this section, we consider some tips that may make you more proficient at notetaking.

What errors do people who take poor notes make? They can be summarized as (1) attempting to write too much, (2) writing too little, and (3) becoming distracted by the message and occasion, ourselves, or our perception of the other person. Because we considered a variety of distractions in chapter 4, we will focus here on the first two errors and how to correct them.

Attempting to write too much. Have you ever met someone who is badly overweight and always dieting? People often fail at dieting because they attempt to overdo. Instead of determining a reasonable level of caloric intake, they cut their calories beyond the level that could reasonably be expected. Soon they begin to overeat and the diet fails, primarily because their expectations were unreasonable.

In the same way, poor students often make resolutions to become more effective by attempting too much. They attend class and try to capture every adjective and adverb offered by the teacher. After a few minutes they become frustrated because no one can take complete notes at the rate most people speak. While we can listen more quickly than others speak, we cannot write more quickly. If you want to be successful at notetaking, do not expect to capture every word.

Writing too little. At the other end of the continuum is the person who takes too few notes. Perhaps because of some of the distractions mentioned in chapter 4, this individual drifts in and out of the material and captures only bits of the speaker's message. He or she may feel that a word or two here and there will be all that is needed to recall the information. Unfortunately, the sparse notes make no sense weeks later. Typically, listeners lose 50 percent of the content immediately after hearing it—unless they take the precaution of writing down reminders.

Effective note taking. What does the effective note-taker do? He or she does not try to capture every word and nuance of meaning; nor does he or she leave a one-hour lecture with five or six words scrawled on a single sheet. The most effective note-takers use key words and phrases, and they attempt to organize the information they hear as they write it down.

Key words and phrases are used rather than complete sentences. Most sentences include a subject, a verb, and several modifiers. In most instances, the subject and verb provide the essential meaning. Sometimes one or two of the modifiers are necessary to capture the precise meaning offered by a speaker. Never is every word necessary to understand the speaker.

Effective note-takers try to organize the information they hear as they write it down. Some people use formal outlines, others indent to indicate main ideas and subordinate ideas. Still others use headings and "bullets," or phrases with a dash or dot before them. People skilled at note-taking know that they must understand the relationship among the ideas presented by a speaker as well as the ideas themselves. To refine your note-taking skill, read the exercise, "Effective Note Taking," on pages 96–97.

Step Two: Establishing Standards of Appraisal

The second step toward becoming a more critical listener is to establish standards of appraisal. When someone tells you to vote for Jane Doe, you do not automatically do it. Instead, whether you are conscious of it or not, you apply standards to evaluate your decision. Your standards might include: Does she belong to the same political party which I support? Is she experienced in politics? Will she fight for causes that I believe in? Will my friends respect me after the election?

Step Three: Applying Standards to Messages

The third step in critical listening is to apply your standards of appraisal to the messages you receive. You are likely to value some of your standards more than others. In weighing your criteria, you might decide that Jane Doe's political party and experience are less important than how closely her platform fits with your own ideas. You might decide that you don't have to tell your friends how you voted. In any case, you are using standards of appraisal just as you would if you were buying a new television, watching an advertisement on cable, considering an opinion by a radio commentator, or selecting a vacation destination with the family.

Critical Thinking

The Nature of Critical Thinking

Critical thinking has its roots in rhetoric, philosophy, and psychology. Plato, for instance, felt that scientific and rational skills were critical to those seeking leadership roles in the ideal state. Socrates emphasized several concepts that are viewed today as elements of the critical thinking process, including stating

Do you take effective notes? The following is from a speech delivered by Laurie Sheridan, an Ohio University student in the Future Farmers of America Speech Contest, 1988.

Biotechology: Benefits for Our Future

How many people in this audience feel that they know what biotechnology is and how it can be applied to food production, nonfood products, and our environment? Raise your hands. Ten years ago, biotechnology sounded like a frightening science fiction scenario: cell fusers and gene splicers producing plants never before seen on earth, laboratory-designed animals, and obedient microbes. At that time, the agricultural sector could see little significance in the advantages biotechnology would give to food production. Even today, many of us have no real concept of what biotechnology is or what it can do for us.

Today I want to tell you about biotechnology: what it is, how it works, and how it will provide food and products for use in years to come. My interest in biotechnology came from my own experience in agriculture, from interviews with experts in biotechnology, and from my own research on the subject.

We will consider this interesting subject together by examining the positive impact of biotechnology on food production, on useful products, and on our environment.

What is biotechnology? It can be defined as the natural use of biological systems to create substances and products too complex and expensive to make by traditional chemical means.

How would the note-taker who tries to write too much respond to this speech? Here is an example:

How many people in this audience . . .

Ten years ago . . .

At that time . . .advantages biotechnology

Even today . . . no real concept . . .

Today, I want to tell you . . .

My interest in biotechnology . . .

We will examine this . . .

Notice that the person was able to capture the beginning of most sentences, but actually gained little of the central message.

How did the person who took too few notes do? Here is an example:

biotechnology
food production

agricultural sector

what it is
examining the impact

Both of these note-takers failed to capture the essence of the introduction to the speech. Few people could grasp the central ideas by looking at these brief words and phrases.

The person who used key words and phrases and attempted to organize the material as he or she took notes might have produced something like the following:

Biotechnology: Benefits for future
  10 years ago,
   frightening
   few advantages
today,
    no real concept
    don't know what it can do
purpose of speech
    what biotec. is
    how it works
    how it will provide food and products
impact of b. on
    food production
    useful products
    environment

The individual who wrote these notes can recall the speaker's main points and can determine the relationship among her ideas.

To determine if you understand how to take effective notes, read the conclusion to Ms. Sheridan's speech. In the space provided, write the key words or phrases that would capture the essence of this conclusion.

As I have illustrated, environmental problems caused by agricultural practices can be reduced with the use of biotechnology. Presently, technology isn't the only issue: product quality, profitability, and ecology also play significant roles in this process. With biotechnology the agricultural picture can once again be a bright and profitable one. Biotechnology can answer challenges facing our society by focusing on the production of higher quality edible and nonedible agricultural products and by altering environmental imbalances.

How many of you now feel that you have a better understanding of biotechnology? Raise your hands. Biotechnology is not science fiction nor is it something that we should fear. Instead, your increased knowledge of what it is, how it works, and what it can produce may help you look forward to our challenging future with biotechnology.

propositions and testing their validity through the extension of their consequences. Aristotle described how people discern truth through their rational thought, and he viewed reason as a benchmark of correct behavior.

During the mid-nineteenth century, people began to view the human mind as a "working mechanism with underlying operations that could be scientifically studied."[3] Biologists, such as Darwin and Spencer; a Gestalt psychologist such as Wertheimer; behavioral psychologists, such as Thorndike and Skinner; and information processing theorists, such as Newell, Abelson, and Papert have all considered the role of thinking from their distinctive viewpoints.

What is critical thinking? The term may be defined narrowly or globally. Robert H. Ennis, who is well known for his comprehensive analysis of **critical thinking,** defined the term very broadly as the "correct" assessment of statements.[4] More recently he qualified the definition as "reasonable, reflective thinking that is focused on deciding what to believe or do."[5] He defined "reasonable" in a functional way as occurring when a person attempts to analyze arguments carefully, seeks valid evidence, and reaches sound conclusions.

Is critical thinking the logical opposite of creative thinking? The authors of *Dimensions of Thinking: A Framework for Curriculum and Instruction* observe that critical thinking is primarily evaluative, while creative thinking is more constructive, but the two are not opposites. Indeed, they argue that the two kinds of thinking often complement each other and suggest that they may share some qualities.[6]

Is critical thinking the same as problem solving? This may be another misconception. Critical thinking consists of more skills and abilities than does problem solving, but problem solving is clearly a component of critical thinking. Problem-solving techniques, such as the one suggested by John Dewey and presented in chapter 10, can be taught. Critical thinking cannot be taught in the same way. The educator T. G. Devine notes:

> We cannot teach critical thinking as a process in itself. We can teach about critical thinking. We can select abilities which seem to be associated with critical thinking and we can discuss these abilities with our [students]. But we cannot teach these abilities as such.[7]

Critical thinking is essential for all of us. If we do not develop the ability to engage in reasonable and reflective thinking about all the messages presented to us each day, we will become robots. We will relinquish our free will, and our lives will largely be determined by those in control of governments and industry. Critical thinking allows us the freedom and choice to determine what we will believe and what we will do.

Critical thinking is important to you as a student and it will continue to be essential throughout your life. Educators have stressed the role of critical thinking. For example, the well-known educator Benjamin Bloom proposed a hierarchy of kinds of learning. He placed problem solving and thinking at the top of his hierarchy.[8] Similarly, educational theorist Jean Piaget asserted that when

Critical thinking is basic to true education.

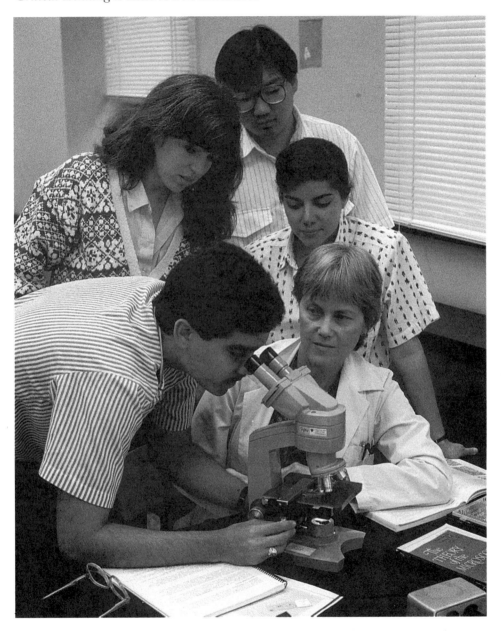

people acquire knowledge by memorization, they do not have true knowledge. For him, real knowledge was acquired when people constructed ideas.[9] Lauren B. Resnick and Leopold E. Klopfer observe:

> Cognitive scientists today share with Piagetians a constructivist view of learning, asserting that people are not recorders of information but builders of knowledge structures. To know something is not just to have received information but also to have interpreted it and related it to other knowledge. To be skilled is not just to know how to perform some action but also to know when to perform it and to adapt the performance to varied circumstances.[10]

Critical thinking is thus basic to true education. It is also consistent with the contemporary view of perception discussed in chapter 2. You will also discover that critical thinking encourages behavioral flexibility, which is considered in chapter 8.

Critical thinking is important to people who will find their life's work within business and industry. In *The Proactive Manager: A Complete Book of Problem Solving and Decision Making,* authors Plunkett and Hale identify the skills necessary for the successful manager. They include two primary skill areas: cause analysis and decision making. First, cause analysis is the description of the problem and involves determining the identity, location, timing, and magnitude of the problem. Second, decision making involves stating the purpose of the decision, establishing criteria, considering the limitations and desirability of the criteria, identifying alternatives, comparing alternatives, considering risks, assessing the risks, and making a decision.[11]

Principles of Critical Thinking

Although there are dozens of principles you should observe as a critical thinker—intellectual curiosity, objectivity, flexibility, intellectual honesty, systematic thinking, persistence, and decisiveness, to name a few—we will focus on five principles that seem most important.[12]

1. *The critical thinker should explore issues and ideas.* This principle means that you need to know about matters that concern you so you are not fooled. Let us say you are going to buy a car. For thirty dollars and ten hours of your time you can save hundreds of dollars, make a correct choice, and not regret your decision. You can read magazines that analyze cars' features; you can read consumer books that show dealer price, low and high price, as well as maintenance records for every model; and you can consult with friends who know more about cars than you do. No salesperson will be able to fool you about paint sealant, rust protection, maintenance agreements, or loan payments.

2. *The critical thinker is open-minded.* What you firmly believe to be true today may prove false tomorrow. Norman Thomas was unsuccessful as a socialist politician, but thirty years after he espoused his views, most of his ideas were social policy. Among his ideas were unemployment insurance, minimum wages, old age pensions, and health insurance. Your position on issues can grow and change as you learn more. The critical thinker seeks information and ideas as contributions to intellectual development

3. *The critical thinker is skeptical.* This principle means that you raise questions, seek answers, and desire proof and evidence for what you believe. If a physician recommends surgery, you seek a second opinion. If a politician says it is in our best interest to raise taxes, you ask why. If a professor claims that her favorite poet is the greatest literary figure of all time, you want to know why she thinks so.

4. *The critical thinker is intellectually honest.* This principle means that you know what you think and why you think it. You know the basis, the support for your beliefs and positions on the issues. Why do you belong to a particular political party? Is it mainly because your family and friends support it or because you truly embrace its platform? Why do you believe in your religion, why are you majoring in a certain field, and why are you planning a particular career? To be honest with others, you have to begin by being honest with yourself.

5. *The critical thinker respects other viewpoints.*[13] One of the most difficult principles to live by, this one means that you have to respect people with divergent views. You have a right to question and be skeptical about the positions others take on issues, but you do not have the right to reject them as people just because they do not believe the same things you do. The critical thinker actually enjoys exploring the views of people who have a different set of beliefs and different positions on issues.

Learning to live by these principles may take time and practice, but eventually, they can become what one book calls "highly general operating principles that govern behavior."[14] Further, they become part of your intrapersonal communication. A recent text suggests:

> . . .[W]hen thinking about a topic or interacting with others about it, a person with these dispositions would probably engage in self-talk like the following:
> Let's see, am I clear about what we're discussing here? Why would he be trying to persuade me to take that position? I don't have all of the facts; I'd better clarify the issue. Am I being open-minded about what he is saying to me, or have I already concluded that he can't be right? I'm starting to be convinced; I'd better modify my original opinion.[15]

Critical thinking results in more carefully determined conclusions. It can also help us better understand ourselves and others.

Abilities Related to Critical Thinking

What are some of the subsets of critical thinking behavior? The individual who thinks critically must distinguish between observations and inferences; must categorize evidence or proof as emotional, logical, or personal; and must understand types of arguments. Let us consider each of these abilities.

Distinguish between Observations and Inferences

Observations are descriptions based on phenomena that can be sensed—seen, heard, tasted, smelled, or felt. **Inferences** occur when we draw a conclusion from, or about, information we have received through our senses. For instance, if you see a small child playing alone near a busy street, the observation is that a small child is playing alone near a busy street. The inferences vary: the child is in a dangerous situation, the child is an orphan, the child is not loved nor cared for, the child will be injured or killed, or the child should be legally removed from his or her parents.

Observations and inferences can be distinguished in a number of ways. While inferences can be made before, during, or after an observation, observations can only occur when something is viewed. While inferences go beyond that which is seen, observations do not. *Interpretation* is the goal of inferences, while *reporting* is the goal of observation. Finally, while observations are more likely to be agreed upon by observers, inferences vary widely in the agreement they elicit from individuals.[16]

Categorize Emotional, Logical, or Personal Proofs

Arguments consist of propositions and their justification.[17] The **proposition** states what you believe, while the **justification** is all of the evidence, or proof, you have gathered that supports the proposition. People who try to persuade others use three types of proof: dealing with logic, dealing with emotion, and dealing with themselves as competent and trustworthy sources of messages. You will learn more about these kinds of proof in chapter 17. You will also determine that the most effective persuasive messages combine logical, emotional, and personal proof.

When we engage in critical thinking it is important, however, that we distinguish between these forms of evidence. Sometimes arguments combine elements of all three, but most proofs may be categorized as primarily emotional, primarily logical, and primarily personal. These have been referred to traditionally as pathos, logos, and ethos. An **emotional proof** is based on feelings or emotions. An example would be a roommate who says, "I'm hungry; let's go have a pizza." A **logical proof** shows reasoning and use of evidence or proof. An example would be someone who says, "Yes, you should landscape with eastern white pine because they grow fast, grow tall, will grow anywhere, and are resistant to disease." A **personal proof** accepts the authority and knowledge of a credible source. An example would be the interior decorator who says, "You should use imported English polished cotton for your drapes."

As with any kind of proof, you as the critical thinker have to decide the merit of the claims in the message. Let us turn next to some types of arguments that you might receive.

Understand Types of Arguments

People engaged in critical thinking must also understand types of arguments. While proofs, the building blocks of arguments, can be distinguished as logical, emotional, or personal, arguments consist of these proofs and propositions. Arguments can be classified as inductive or deductive. **Inductive arguments** are those that move from specific instances to some general conclusions. Professors Anita Taylor, Arthur Meyer, Teresa Rosegrant, and B. Thomas Samples suggest that "Inductive thinking may also be called generalization."[18] An inductive argument concerning aerobics would be:

> Jane is in great shape, and she does aerobics. (Observation)
> Bill looks terrific, and he does aerobics too. (Observation)
> Kim's great muscle definition is from aerobics. (Observation)
> (Inference)
> Therefore, people who do aerobics look good. (Generalization)

You critically evaluate inductive reasoning by deciding if the observations are accurate and if there are enough observations to justify the generalization. The person who says, "I was treated badly by a teller at Bank One so they provide poor service." Is one instance, one observation, enough to justify the generalization? A critical thinker would discount one instance as insufficient to infer the generalization.

Deductive arguments move from a general proposition to a specific instance. The entire three-part form is called a **syllogism.** The first part of the syllogism is called a major premise, the specific instance is called a minor premise, and the link between the two premises is called the conclusion. It might look like this:

> If you do aerobics, you will look thin. (Major premise)
> Jane does aerobics. (Minor premise)
> Therefore, Janes looks thin. (Conclusion)

Deductive arguments are evaluated in two ways. One way is to judge the **accuracy** of the major and minor premise. The major premise in the example is worth questioning because some people who do aerobics do not look thin. The minor premise is verifiable, but the truth of the conclusion is in jeopardy because Jane might have looked thin before she ever tried aerobics. The second way to judge a deductive argument is to examine its structure, or arrangement. If

Distinguishing between Logical, Emotional, and Personal Proofs

Do you understand the differences between logical, emotional, and personal proofs? To test your understanding, complete this exercise. The beginning of a persuasive speech given by Mark Dupont in *Fundamentals of Public Speaking,* Iowa State University, which encourages people to participate in aerobics follows. Identify each of the arguments as *L* for logical, *E* for emotional, or *P* for personal.

Aerobics
Mark Dupont

"The way I look at it, my heart is only going to beat a certain number of times, and I'm not going to waste some of my valuable heartbeats on aerobics."

1._____

"Well, I just can't afford aerobic exercise. I mean, it just takes too long. I've got to study and go to work, and I have an eight o'clock every morning. I just don't have the time."

2._____

"Hey, I'm only eighteen. My heart and lungs are in great shape. I don't need aerobics; that's for old people, and I'm nowhere near thirty yet."

3._____

Why should we care about aerobic exercise? We're either too young, can't afford it, or don't want to "waste those valuable heartbeats." Too young? Autopsies done on American soldiers killed in the Vietnam War, young men whose average age was 22.1 years, revealed that 55% of them showed evidence of arteriosclerosis, a hardening of the arteries. Maybe we're not so young. Can't afford aerobics? Well, a program of aerobics does demand that we make time in our busy schedules to exercise regularly, but the time we devote to our bodies is an inexpensive

4._____

the conclusion can be logically derived from its propositions, then it is said to be **valid.** Accuracy and validity are the two means of evaluating a deductive argument, but perhaps an example of each would clarify the concept.

Most of us would agree with the following deductive argument, which is both accurate and valid:

People who drive while they are intoxicated are more likely to have accidents than are those who only drive when they are not intoxicated.

Jack regularly drives while he is intoxicated.

Therefore, Jack is more likely to have an accident than are those who do not drive while intoxicated.

alternative to spiraling medical costs we might have to face because of an unhealthy heart, circulatory system, and lungs. Insurance companies are now recognizing this fact in the form of discounts to policyholders who participate in exercise programs like aerobics. Maybe we can afford it after all, but what about those heartbeats? Well, there is no evidence that the number of times our hearts will beat is limited. What there is evidence of is that by strengthening the heart and improving the lungs and blood vessels, aerobic exercise can improve your health and perhaps increase your life span. Maybe it's time we learn something more about aerobics.

5.____

When Dr. Kenneth Cooper published his book, *Aerobics,* he introduced to America an exercise program which has become so popular that aerobics is well on its way to becoming a household word. As America becomes more interested in physical fitness and preventive medicine, more of us are being urged to participate in aerobic exercise. Ultimately, the decision on whether to do so is up to each of us. To make such a decision, we need to have a general knowledge of what aerobics is.

6.____

Today, I'd like to acquaint you with what I call the three Ps of aerobics—its purpose, its program, and its profit, which I have learned through research on exercise. What you do with this knowledge is up to you, but knowing the purpose, the program, and the profit of aerobics will enable you to make a well-informed judgment of it and make you familiar with a program millions of Americans have made a part of their lives.

Answers: 1. E, 2. E, 3. E, 4. L, 5. P, 6. P.

The following argument, based on the same idea, includes propositions that are not true.

People who drive while they are not intoxicated are more likely to have accidents than are those who only drive when they are intoxicated.

Jill drives only while she is not intoxicated.

Therefore, Jill is more likely to have an accident than are those who drive while intoxicated.

Most of us would not accept the generalization, that people who drive when they are not intoxicated are more likely to have an accident than are those who drive when they are intoxicated. The falsity of this premise renders the entire argument false, or not true. However, the argument is a valid one in that it follows the valid form for an argument, symbolically represented as:

A is more likely than B.
Jill is an example of A.
Therefore, Jill is more likely than B.

Unfortunately, speakers practically never provide listeners with the structure of their thought. Rarely will you receive a list of observations and inferred generalizations, nor are you likely to hear a syllogism. Instead, you are likely to hear someone say, "You ought to go to Florida over spring break," a generalization with all of the observations missing. To find out whether the generalization is worth heeding, you need to ask, why? Then the speaker has to supply the observations with which you may or may not agree: "Florida is warm in the Spring," "The trip is inexpensive if we go together," and "Lots of students go to Florida during break." Then, you can decide if you agree with the observation, the inferential leap, and the generalization.

Deductive arguments, too, are rarely heard in their full form. Instead, people tend to talk in **enthymemes,** or part of the entire argument, such as a premise or just the conclusion. An example of an enthymeme (en-thi-mēm) would be: "Taxes are unjust" (the major premise of a deductive argument) or "This new 1 percent increase is unjust" (the conclusion of a deductive argument). If you can mentally lay out the argument like this:

Sales taxes are unjust. (Major premise)
The 1 percent increase is a sales tax. (Minor premise)
Therefore, the 1 percent increase is unjust. (Conclusion)

The syllogism is correctly arranged, so it is valid, but you certainly could question the accuracy of the major premise that sales taxes are unjust.

The main point is that you have to seek more information about a speaker's inductive and deductive arguments if you are a critical thinker. Speakers in both public and interpersonal communication often assume receiver agreement with the unstated parts of their argument, and the receiver mentally fills in the rest of the argument using his or her own observations or premises, which may or may not be what the sender has in mind. Don't be afraid to inquire about a speaker's intended meaning, because it may not be what you thought, and it may make a difference in its acceptability.

Errors in Critical Thinking

Perhaps you have heard someone say, "That is a fallacious argument," but you were unsure what the term meant. A **fallacy** is an argument that is flawed, that does not follow the rules of logic, and is, therefore, not to be believed. Actually, we use fallacies all the time, but as a critical thinker you need to know how to recognize them and why you should discount them.

There are hundreds of fallacies, many of them with fancy Latin names, but we are going to provide ten of the most common ones to help you become a better critical thinker and listener. Each will be named and followed by at least one example. To help you remember them, they will be placed in two categories: **fallacies of relevance** which are flawed because the conclusion is based on irrelevant premises and **fallacies of ambiguity** which are flawed because the argument has multiple meanings. We will begin with the fallacies of relevance.

Fallacies of Relevance

1. **Argument against the person.** This fallacy, called *argumentum ad hominem* in Latin, means literally "argument to the man" instead of to the issue. It is also a propaganda device called name calling. When you say, "Beth is a jerk" in response to an argument with her about an issue, you are using this "argument against the person." It is a fallacy, or a flawed argument, because it is irrelevant to the issue. It is a sidetrack that does not logically follow from the argument. You can probably think of many examples, but "he's just a racist," "she's a man hater," and "they're just rich snobs," are a few examples of how we sidestep arguing an issue.

2. **Appeal to the people.** Also known as the bandwagon effect in the propaganda literature, this fallacy invites you to join the group and do something because "everyone is doing it." Buy white zinfandel wine because the in-crowd is drinking it; eat at the country club because that's where the wealthy group gathers; and get a convertible so you too can attract beautiful people. Remember that what "everyone is doing" can sometimes be unwise, so you should think critically about following this appeal whether you hear it from your friends, the politicians, or the advertisers.

3. **Appeal to authority.** Sometimes an appeal to authority can be legitimate, such as when you ask a physician about your health, a mechanic about your car, or an old salt about fishing. This appeal becomes fallacious, however, when the person is outside his or her area of expertise. A sports figure selling cars, an actor selling windows, or a chemist commenting on race relations are examples. Another variation is the "plain folks" approach of acting as if the person is just an ordinary person whose advice should be followed. In either case, the flaw is that the authority outside his or her field of expertise or the ordinary person is no expert on this particular subject.

4. **Hasty generalization.** This fallacy could be called a premature generalization because you draw the inference before you have enough observations to justify it. The generalization is inferred before you have enough evidence to justify it, or it is drawn about one dramatic instance. A white man mugged me, so I distrust and dislike white men; I was bit once by a dog, so all dogs are mistrusted; and a woman once jilted me, so I'll never go out with one again—all of these statements are instances of drawing an inference with insufficient evidence.

5. **False cause.** Called *post hoc ergo propter hoc* in Latin, this fallacy literally means "after this; therefore, because of this." The problem with this kind of thinking is that sometimes one thing follows another without being caused by it. For example, I smoked a cigar, and my wife is pregnant; staying up late must cause headaches because I stayed up drinking and had a headache the next day; and I went out without a sweater and caught a cold. Causal links are tough to make. Consider how many people still disbelieve the long established casual link between smoking and cancer. A false cause means no connection between the alleged cause and the apparent effect.

6. **Begging the question.** Also called a circular argument, this fallacy is based on using a conclusion that is also your premise. For example, all educated people can speak competently in public. How do I know? I know this because all competent public speakers are educated. You are arguing that if all A=B, then all B=A. It sounds rights, but it is circular, and your system is closed to outside inspection.

7. **Irrelevant conclusion.** This fallacy occurs when your evidence supports one conclusion, but you make another. For example, suppose you are in a particular organization, and you are attempting to make the group less racist. You suggest some measures that would open the group up to greater black membership. After you have argued in favor of these measures for some time, you could conclude that racism is a heinous crime against society. Most people might agree with this conclusion, but it is not drawn from your arguments for specific measures that would decrease racism in your group. While your conclusion is applauded, it remains irrelevant to your arguments or premises.

8. **False alternatives.** This fallacy is committed when we rely on "either-or" thinking. It suggests that only two alternatives are possible and often hints that one of the two is disastrous or to be avoided. For instance, if you are campaigning for the presidency of one of your clubs or organizations, you might assert that people are either for you or they are against you. Actually, many people may support some of your positions and some of the positions of your opponents. This fallacy may be viewed more broadly as oversimplification. Generally, more than two alternatives exist in considering any matter.

Identifying Fallacies

Do you think you can recognize the ten common fallacies discussed in this chapter? In order to determine your understanding, complete the following exercise. For each argument, identify it as true or name the fallacy that is committed by using the number it was listed in the text.

_____ 1. Good lamb is rare today. Don't err by ordering it medium-well!

_____ 2. The bald eagle is nearly extinct. The bird in that tree is a bald eagle; therefore, it must be nearly extinct.

_____ 3. Successful businessmen tend to marry only one time. If I marry only one time, I will be a successful businessman.

_____ 4. Successful women wear expensive clothing. If I wish to be successful, I should wear expensive clothing.

_____ 5. The great psychologist Sigmund Freud asserted that educated people cannot accept religious values.

_____ 6. You cannot believe Bill Clinton. His brother was a dope addict.

_____ 7. Communism did not work for Russia and it did not work for several other countries. Therefore, we should work for peace in the world.

_____ 8. I have eaten Wheaties all my life. Today, I am taller and stronger than when I was ten years old. Therefore, Wheaties has made me strong and tall.

_____ 9. President Clinton endorses Pepsi Cola.

_____ 10. This university is known for its excellent communication majors. Margaret Riley is a communication major at this university. Therefore, Margaret Riley is an excellent communication major.

_____ 11. Freedom of speech is an essential feature of a democratic society because a democratic society is dependent on such freedoms.

_____ 12. We have only two choices. Either we befriend Russia in this time of change or we enter another world war.

_____ 13. Everyone smokes marijuana. Don't you want to try some?

_____ 14. Two people cheated on the last exam. This proves that you cannot trust college students.

_____ 15. No one who is anyone buys clothes at K-Mart!

_____ 16. I have had a cold for ten days and I have tried everything to cure it. Last night, I drank honey, lemon, and brandy before I went to bed. Today, my cold is gone. Nothing cures a cold like honey, lemon, and brandy.

See page 112 for answers.

Fallacies of Ambiguity

9. **Equivocation.** The fallacy of equivocation occurs when people purposefully use the ambiguous qualities of language to their advantage or when they use two different meanings of the same word within a single context. Some words are relative. For instance, the words "good," "small," "better," "thin," "big," "worse," and "tall" all need to be qualified or considered in a context. Let us consider some examples. A college professor may be the oldest person in his or her classroom, but far from the oldest person at a family reunion. A member of Weight Watchers who has achieved his or her goal may be the thinnest person in the weekly meetings, but not the thinnest person in his or her work setting. A person who is 5'10" tall could be the tallest person in his or her family, but not in a group of friends. We equivocate when we note that someone is the oldest, the thinnest, or the tallest without specifying the context.

10. **Division.** Two forms of the fallacy of division exist: (1) arguing that what is true of the parts must be true of the whole and (2) arguing that what is true of the whole must be true of the parts. An example of the first form is when we observe that one of the students in a particular section of a class is highly motivated and conclude that everyone in that section is similarly motivated. An example of the second form is when we note that a certain class has a particularly high accumulated grade point average and assume that everyone in the class has similarly high grades. Both conclusions are fallacious. The ten common fallacies are summarized in the activity "Identifying Fallacies. on page 109.

Summary

In this chapter you learned about critical listening and critical thinking. Both are extremely important to the communication process, because we must be able to make critical distinctions when we are receiving and when we are sending messages. Critical listening is defined as the type of listening that challenges the speaker's message and that evaluates its accuracy, meaningfulness, and utility. Critical listening involves capturing the information, establishing standards of appraisal, and applying the standards to the materials. Effective note taking will assist you in capturing the information you hear.

Critical thinking is "reasonable, reflective thinking that is focused on deciding what to believe or do." Critical thinking is important to you now as a student, and it will continue to be of value throughout your life. A number of attitudes that encourage critical thinking were presented in the chapter. Some of the activities related to critical thinking include distinguishing between observations and inferences, categorizing emotional, logical, and personal proofs, and understanding types of arguments. We concluded this section by considering ten common errors, or fallacies, in critical thinking.

Key Terms

accuracy A term used to describe the truthfulness of the premises in a deductive argument or syllogism.

appeal to authority A fallacy that involves appealing to an authority.

appeal to the people A fallacy that involves stirring people up, exciting them, or stimulating the public.

argument against the person A fallacy that directs the argument against the person rather than at the issues.

arguments Propositions and their justification.

begging the question A fallacy in which the conclusion of the argument is used as one of the premises in the argument.

critical listening The type of listening that challenges the speaker's message and evaluates its accuracy, meaningfulness, and utility.

critical thinking "Reasonable, reflective thinking that is focused on deciding what to believe or do."

deductive arguments Arguments that move from a general proposition to a specific instance; includes three parts—a generalization, a specific instance of the general phenomena, and a conclusion that links the specific instance to the generalization.

division A fallacy in which it is argued that what is true of the parts must be true of the whole or that what is true of the whole must be true of the parts.

emotional proof A proof based on feelings or emotions.

enthymeme A truncated syllogism; it is part of a deductive argument.

equivocation A fallacy that results when people purposefully use the ambiguous qualities of language to use two different meanings of the same word within a single context.

fallacies of ambiguity Incorrect arguments that occur because the conclusions are based on terms that have more than one meaning.

fallacies of relevance Incorrect arguments that occur because the conclusions are based on irrelevant propositions.

false alternatives A fallacy that relies on "either-or" thinking and suggests that only two alternatives are possible.

false cause A fallacy in which something that occurs before another event is viewed as the cause of it.

hasty generalization A fallacy that occurs when generalization occurs from only a few cases or from exceptional cases to all cases.

inductive arguments Arguments that move from specific instances to some general conclusions.

inferences Conclusions from, or about, things we have received through our senses.

irrelevant conclusion A fallacy in which arguments that support one conclusion are used to support a different conclusion.

justification The evidence or proof that supports the proposition.

logical proof A proof that shows consistency in reasoning and conforms to the principles of validity.

observations Descriptions based on phenomena that can be sensed—seen, heard, tasted, smelled, or felt.

personal proof A proof based on the speaker's credibility and includes such speaker attributes as competence, trustworthiness, dynamism, and co-orientation.

proposition A statement of belief.

syllogism A form in logic that consists of a generalization called a major premise, a specific instance called a minor premise, and a link between the generalization and the specific instance called a conclusion.

validity The extent to which a conclusion may be logically derived from its propositions; correct form of an argument.

Answers to the exercise on "Identifying Fallacies:"

1. 7,   **2.** 10,   **3.** 5,   **4.** 2,   **5.** 3,   **6.** 1,   **7.** 7,   **8.** 5,   **9.** 3,   **10.** 10,
11. 6,   **12.** 8,   **13.** 2,   **14.** 4,   **15.** 2,   **16.** 5

chapter 6

Nonverbal Codes:

Sharing with Others

This chapter focuses on the role of nonverbal codes in communication. We will begin by considering the problems that occur in interpreting nonverbal cues. Next, we identify and define some of the major nonverbal codes including kinesics, proxemics, tactile communication, paralinguistics, and objectics. Are these terms foreign to you? They will be familiar by the time you finish this chapter. The chapter concludes with a discussion of some solutions to the problems we encounter in interpreting nonverbal codes. Let us begin our examination of nonverbal codes by considering some of the problems we face.

What you will learn?

After you have read and thought about this chapter, you should be able to answer the following questions:

1. What are three problems people have in interpreting nonverbal cues?

2. Can you identify and define the five nonverbal codes described in this chapter?

3. What are five different types of bodily movements in nonverbal communication?

4. What determines changes in the amount of personal space you use?

5. What are two factors that influence the meaning and use of touch?

6. How are objects used in nonverbal communication?

7. Can you state the three suggestions for solving problems in interpreting nonverbal codes?

A smile is the shortest distance between two people.

Victor Borge

You cannot shake hands with a clenched fist.

Indira Gandhi

When one is pretending the entire body revolts.

Anais Nin

115

I In the past five chapters, we have considered the process of understanding. In this chapter and in chapter 7, we shift our attention to sharing messages with others. One way we share messages with other people is through the nonverbal codes we use. As you shall determine in this chapter, communication often occurs without words.

Communication experts agree nonverbal communication is essential to understanding and sharing meaning.[1] *How* we say something is as important as *what* we say. Furthermore, the nonverbal aspects of our messages add depth or additional meaning to the verbal aspects of our messages.

Problems in the Interpretation of Nonverbal Cues

Nonverbal communication provides the basis for much of the misunderstanding that occurs in communication. Just as we have difficulty interpreting verbal symbols, so do we have difficulty interpreting nonverbal cues. There are at least three reasons for this difficulty: we use the same cue to communicate a variety of different meanings, we use a variety of cues to communicate the same meaning, and the intentionality of cues makes a difference.

One Cue Communicates a Variety of Different Meanings

Examples of situations in which one cue communicates a variety of different meanings will clarify this problem. Raising your right hand may mean you are taking an oath, you are demonstrating for a cause, you are indicating to an instructor you would like to answer a question, a physician is examining your right side, or you want a taxi to stop for you. We may stand close to someone because of a feeling of affection, because the room is crowded, or because we have difficulty hearing. We may speak softly because we were taught it was the "correct" way for us to speak, because we are suffering from a sore throat, or because we are sharing a secret. We may wear blue jeans because they are an acceptable mode of dress, because they symbolize our rebellion against higher-priced clothing, or because they are the only clean clothes we have that day.

A Variety of Cues Communicate the Same Meaning

An example of a variety of nonverbal cues communicating the same meaning would be the many nonverbal ways adults have to express love or affection. We may choose to sit or stand more closely to someone we love. We might speak more softly, use a different vocal intonation, or alter how quickly we

PEANUTS

speak when we communicate with someone for whom we have affection. Also, we often dress differently if we are going to be in the company of a person we love.

The "Peanuts" cartoon shows an inappropriate way of communicating affection. Yet, those of us who are parents or who have younger siblings are familiar with the tendency of young children to express their attraction to another person through physical aggression. As children grow, they begin to experiment with more appropriate nonverbal indications of affection.

Motive Determines Intentionality of a Cue

There are four possibilities in interpreting **intentionality,** or the purposefulness of nonverbal cues.[2] One possibility is *intentional nonverbal communication interpreted as intentional,* such as when you hug a friend. The hug is nonverbal, purposeful, and perceived as an intended message: I am so glad to see you.

Another possibility is *an intentional cue misperceived as having another intention,* such as when a man is reading the message printed on a woman's T-shirt and she covers her chest and quickly turns away. The reading of the shirt, a nonverbal cue, is perceived as intentional lust. A third possibility is *an unintentional cue perceived as intentional,* such as when I forget my turn signal is on, and the driver behind me thinks I intend to turn. A fourth possibility is *a cue sent and received unintentionally,* such as when a woman's blouse has a button open in the back, a man has accidently left a pricetag on a new tie, or a person has mismatched socks. The cue is noticed but is perceived as unintentional and discounted as meaningless.

In the study of nonverbal communication, the focus is on intentional nonverbal cues, including all the previously cited examples except the last example of an unintentional cue.

Definition and Identification of Nonverbal Codes

Nonverbal codes were defined in chapter 1 as codes of communication consisting of symbols that are not words. Bodily movements, facial expression, use of space, touching, vocalics, and clothing and artifacts are all nonverbal codes. Let us consider these systematic arrangements of symbols that have been given arbitrary meaning and are used in communication.

Bodily Movement and Facial Expression

The study of posture, movement, gestures, and facial expression is called **kinesics,** a word derived from the Greek word *kinesis* meaning movement. Some popular books purport to teach you how "to read" nonverbal communication, so you will know who is sexually aroused, who is just kidding, and who you should stay away from. Nonverbal communication, however, is more complicated than that. Interpreting the meaning of nonverbal communication is partly a matter of assessing the other person's unique behavior and considering the context. You don't just "read" another person's body language; instead, you observe, analyze, and interpret before you decide the probable meaning.

Assessing the other person's unique behavior means that you need to know how they usually act. A taciturn person might be unflappable even in an emergency situation. A person who never smiles may not be unhappy, and someone who acts happy might not actually be happy. You need to know how the person expresses him- or herself before you can interpret what the nonverbal communication means.

Considering the context means that the situation might alter how you interpret the nonverbal communication. Many people get talkative, candid, and sometimes stupid when they take such mind-altering drugs as alcohol. Finding someone excessively friendly at a long party might be more attributable to the proof of the drinks than anything else. People tend to be formally polite at ceremonies, emotionally unguarded in their homes, and excessively prudent when applying for a job.

To look more deeply into interpreting nonverbal communication, let us consider the work of some experts on the subject: Albert Mehrabian on the body, and Paul Ekman and Wallace Friesen on nonverbal movement and facial expression.

Mehrabian studied nonverbal communication by examining liking, status, and responsiveness.[3]

1. *Liking* was often expressed by leaning forward, a direct body orientation (e.g., standing face to face), close proximity, increased touching, relaxed posture, open arms and body, positive facial expression, and more eye contact (i.e., looking directly at the other person). For examples, watch how a group of males act when drinking beer and watching a game on television or watch newly matched couples in the Spring.
2. *Status,* especially high status, is communicated nonverbally by bigger gestures, relaxed posture, and less eye contact. Male bosses will talk to subordinates while leaning back in their desk chair with their hands behind their head and their elbows out (very relaxed), but you practically never see a subordinate acting the same way.
3. *Responsiveness* in nonverbal communication is exhibited by moving toward the other person, by spontaneous gestures, by shifting posture and position, and by facial expressiveness. In other words, the face and body provides positive feedback to the other person.

Ekman and Friesen developed categories of movement based on the functions, origins, and meanings of the nonverbal behavior. Their five categories include emblems, illustrators, affect displays, regulators, and adaptors.[4]

1. *Emblems* substitute for words and phrases. Examples of emblems are a beckoning first finger to mean "come here," an open hand held up to mean "stop," or a forefinger and thumb together to mean "O.K." Be wary of emblems, however, because they may mean something else in another culture.
2. *Illustrators* accompany or reinforce verbal messages. Examples of illustrators are nodding your head when you say "Yes," shaking your head when you say "No," stroking your stomach when you say you are hungry, and shaking your fist in the air when you say "Get out of here." These nonverbal cues tend to be more universal.

3. *Affect displays* are movements of the face and body used to show emotion. Watch people's behavior when their favorite team wins a game, see and hear the door slam when an angry person leaves the scene, and watch men make threatening moves when they are very upset with each other but don't dare openly fight.
4. *Regulators* are nonverbal moves that control communication. Examples of regulators are starting to move away when you want the conversation to stop, looking at the floor or looking away when you are disinterested, or yawning and looking at your watch when you are bored.
5. *Adaptors* are movements that you might fully perform in private, but only do partially in public. For example, we might scratch our nose in public, but we don't scratch everywhere it itches.

Finally, Ekman and Friesen determined that our facial expressions provide information to others about how we feel, while our body orientation suggests how intensely we feel.[5] Put facial expression and body orientation together, and your interpretation of nonverbal message will become more accurate.

To illustrate the importance of nonverbal communication, consider the finding that audiences who can see the speaker understand more of the message than audiences who cannot see the speaker.[6] Apparently, bodily movement and facial expression increase the ability to interpret meaning.

Space

Anthropologist Edward T. Hall introduced the concept of **proxemics,** the human use of space, in 1966 in his book *The Hidden Dimension*. Robert Sommer analyzed the topic further in 1969 in *Personal Space: The Behavioral Basis of Design*. These researchers and others have demonstrated the role space plays in human communication.[7] Two concepts considered essential to the study of the use of space are territoriality and personal space.

1. *Territoriality* refers to *our need to establish and maintain certain spaces as our own*. In a shared dormitory room, the items on the common desk area mark the territory. On a cafeteria table, the placement of the plate, glass, napkin, and eating utensils mark the territory. In a neighborhood, it might be fences, hedges, trees, or rocks that mark the territory. All are nonverbal indicators that signal ownership.
2. *Personal space* is *the personal bubble of space that moves around with you*. It is the distance you maintain between yourself and others, the amount of room you claim as your own. Large people usually claim more space because of their size, and men often take more space than women. Observe, for example, who claims the armrests in the lecture hall to see who takes them as part of their personal bubble.

Hall was the first to define the four distances people regularly use. His categories have been useful in understanding the communicative behavior that might occur when two communicators are a particular distance from each other. Beginning with the closest contact and the least personal space and moving to the greatest distance, Hall's four categories are intimate distance, personal distance, social distance, and public distance.[8]

1. *Intimate distance* extends from you outward to eighteen inches and is used by people who are relationally close to us. Used more often in private than in public, this intimate distance is employed to show affection, to give comfort, and to protect. It usually shows positive response because we tend to stand and sit close to people to whom we are attracted.[9]
2. *Personal distance* ranges from eighteen inches to four feet, and it is the distance used by most Americans for conversation and other nonintimate exchanges.
3. *Social distance* ranges from four to twelve feet and is used most often to carry out business in the workplace, especially in formal, less personal situations. The higher the status of the other person, the greater the distance.
4. *Public distance* exceeds twelve feet and is used most often in public speaking such situations as lecture halls; churches, mosques, and synagogues; courtrooms; and convention halls. Professors often stand at this distance while lecturing.

Distance, then, is a nonverbal means of communicating everything from the size of your personal bubble to your relationship with the person to whom you are speaking or listening. In fact, sex, size, and similarity seem to be among the important determiners of your personal space.

Men tend to take more space because they are often bigger. Women take less space, and children take and are given the least space.[10] Women exhibit less discomfort with small space and tend to interact at closer range.[11] Perhaps because women are so often given little space, they come to expect it. Also, women and children in our society seem to desire more relational closeness than do men.

Your relationship to other people is related to use of space. You stand closer to friends and farther from enemies.[12] You stand farther from strangers, authority figures, high-status people, physically challenged people, and people from racial groups different from your own. You also stand closer to people you perceive as similar or unthreatening because closeness communicates trust.

The physical setting also can alter our personal space. People tend to stand closer together in large rooms and farther apart in small rooms.[13] In addition, physical obstacles and furniture arrangements can affect personal space.

Conversational Space

Visualize your living room at home. Are the chairs and couches arranged to encourage or discourage conversations? How many conversational groupings are encouraged by the arrangement of the furniture? Do tables, lamps, and other objects interfere with conversations? How closely are chairs placed to each other? Does the lighting in the room, the colors of the walls, or the textures of the fabrics on the upholstered furniture add to, or detract from, the possibility that people will enjoy conversations in the room?

Contrast your living room with a lounge in the student center on your campus. What similarities and differences exist? What general conclusions can you draw about the two rooms for communicative purposes?

The cultural background of the people communicating also must be considered in the evaluation of personal space. Hall was among the first to recognize the importance of cultural background when, in 1963, he was training American service personnel for service overseas. Hall wrote:

> Americans overseas were confronted with a variety of difficulties because of cultural differences in the handling of space. People stood "too close" during conversations, and when the Americans backed away to a comfortable conversational distance, this was taken to mean that Americans were cold, aloof, withdrawn, and disinterested in the people of the country. USA housewives muttered about "waste-space" in houses in the Middle East. In England, Americans who were used to neighborliness were hurt when they discovered that their neighbors were no more accessible or friendly than other people, and in Latin America, exsuburbanites, accustomed to unfenced yards, found that the high walls there made them feel "shut out." Even in Germany, where so many of my countrymen felt at home, radically different patterns in the use of space led to unexpected tensions.[14]

Cultural background can result in great differences in the human use of space and the interpretation, by others, of that use of space. As our world continues to shrink, more of us than ever will be working in multinational corporations, regularly traveling to different countries, and interacting with people from a variety of backgrounds. Sensitivity to space differences in different cultures and quick and appropriate responses to those variations may become imperative to survival.

Touch is a form of communication that is essential to our growth and development.

Touching

Tactile communication is the use of touch in communication. Because touch always involves invasion of another's personal space, it is not a kind of communication that can be ignored. It can be welcome as when a crying child is held by a parent or unwelcome as in sexual harassment, but our need for and appreciation of tactile communication starts early in life. Schutz observes,

> The unconscious parental feelings communicated through touch or lack of touch can lead to feelings of confusion and conflict in a child. Sometimes a "modern" parent will say all the right things but not want to touch the child very much. The child's confusion comes from the inconsistency of levels: if they really approve of me so much like they say they do, why don't they touch me?[15]

Insufficient touching can lead to health disorders, such as allergies and eczema, speech problems, and even death.[16] Researchers have found that untouched babies and small children grow increasingly ill and die.

For adults touch is a powerful means of communication. Usually, touch is perceived as positive, pleasureful, and reinforcing. The association of touch with the warmth and caring that began in infancy carries over into adulthood. People who are comfortable with touch are more likely to be satisfied with their past and their current lives. They are self-confident, assertive, socially acceptable, and active in confronting problems.[17]

Touch is part of many important rituals. In baptism, the practice in many churches is as little as a touch on the head during the ceremony to as much as a total immersion. Prayers in some churches are said with the pastor's hand touching the person being prayed for. In fundamentalist Christian churches, the healer might accompany the touch with a mighty shove right into the hands of two catchers. In medicine, physician Bernie Siegel writes the following in a new book on mindbody communication:

> I'd like to see some teaching time devoted to the healing power of touch—a subject that only 12 of 169 medical schools in the English-speaking world deal with at all . . . despite the fact that touch is one of the most basic forms of communication between people. . . . We need to teach medical students how to touch people.[18]

Religion and medicine are just two professions in which touch is important for ceremonial and curative purposes.

Touch varies with each co-culture. The findings relating touch with gender indicate that

- Women value touch more than men do.[19]
- Women are touched more than men from the sixth month on.
- Women touch female children more often than they touch male children.[20]
- Males and their sons touch each other the least.[21]
- Female students are touched more and in more places than are male students.[22]
- Males touch others more than women touch others.
- Men have more access to women's bodies than they do to men's bodies.
- Males may use touch to indicate power or dominance.[23]

On this last point, it is interesting to observe who can touch whom among people in the workplace. Although sexual harassment rules have inadvertently stopped nearly all touch except for handshaking, the general nonverbal principle is that the higher status individual gets to initiate touch, but it is not reciprocal. The president might pat you on the back for a job well done, but in our society you don't pat back.

Further, it is not only co-culture but culture that determines the frequency and kind of nonverbal communication. People from different countries handle nonverbal communication differently—even something as simple as touch. Sidney Jourard determined the rates of touch per hour among adults from various cultures. In a coffee shop, adults in San Juan, Puerto Rico, touched 180 times per hour, while those in Paris, France, touched about 110 times per hour, followed by those in Gainesville, Florida, who touched about two times per hour, and those in London, England, who touched only once per hour.[24] A more recent study indicates that North Americans are more frequent touchers than are the Japanese.[25]

We value touch from birth until death, but touch sends such a powerful message that it has to be handled with responsibility. When the right to touch is abused, it can result in a breach of trust, anxiety, and hostility. When touch is used to communicate concern, caring, and affection, touch is welcome, desired, and appreciated.

Vocal Cues

Nonverbal communication does include some sounds as long as they are not words. We call them **paralinguistic features.** The prefix *para* means along side or parallel to, so paralinguistic means "along side the words or language," namely sound features that accompany language in oral communication.

The paralinguistic feature we are examining here are **vocal cues,** which include the following:

- Pitch. The highness or lowness of your voice
- Rate. How rapidly or slowly you speak
- Inflection. The variety or changes in your pitch
- Volume. The loudness or softness of your voice
- Quality. The unique resonance of your voice, such as huskiness, nasality, raspiness, and whininess
- Sounds and silence. Such nonword sounds as *mmh, huh,* and *ahh* and pauses or absence of sound used for effect in speaking. Pronunciation, articulation, and enunciation refer not to what accompanies the word but how the word itself is correctly or incorrectly handled.
- Pronunciation is whether or not you say the word correctly.
- Articulation is whether or not your mouth, tongue, and teeth coordinate to make the word understandable to others. A lisp is an example of an articulation problem.
- Enunciation is whether or not you combine pronunciation and articulation to produce a word with clarity and distinction, so it can be understood. A person who mumbles has an enunciation problem.

These vocal cues are important because they are linked in our minds with a speaker's physical characteristics, emotional states, personality characteristics, sex differences, and even credibility.

Vocal cues frequently convey information about the speaker's physical characteristics, such as age, height, appearance, and body type.[26] For example, we associate a high-pitched voice with someone who is female rather than male, someone who is younger rather than older, and someone who is smaller rather than larger. We visualize someone who uses a loud voice as being taller rather than shorter, and larger rather than smaller. People who speak quickly may be thought to be nervous rather than calm. People who tend to speak slowly and deliberately may be given credit as high-status individuals or people who have high credibility.

A number of studies have related emotional states to specific vocal cues. Joy and hate appear to be the most accurately communicated emotions, while shame and love are among the most difficult to communicate accurately.[27] Joy and hate appear to be conveyed by fewer vocal cues, which makes their interpretation less difficult than the complex sets of vocal cues that identify emotions like shame and love. "Active" feelings like joy and hate are associated with a loud voice, a high pitch, a blaring timbre, and a rapid rate. Conversely, our "passive" feelings, which include affection and sadness, are communicated with a soft voice, a low pitch, a resonant timbre, and a relatively slow rate.[28]

Personality characteristics, too, have been related to vocal cues. Dominance, social adjustment, and sociability have been clearly correlated with specific vocal cues.[29]

While the personality characteristics attributed to individuals displaying particular vocal cues have not been shown to accurately portray the person, as determined by standardized personality tests, our impressions affect our interactions. In other words, while we may perceive loud-voiced, high-pitched, fast-speaking individuals as dominant, they might not be measured as dominant by a personality inventory. Nonetheless, in our interactions with such people, we may become increasingly submissive because of our perception that they are dominant. In addition, these people may begin to become more dominant as they are treated as though they have this personality characteristic.

Sex differences are also related to vocal cues. Men and women demonstrate different intonational patterns. For instance, women tend to state declarative sentences with an upward inflection to suggest a question rather than a declaration.[30]

Vocal cues can help a public speaker establish credibility with an audience and can clarify the message. Pitch and inflection can be used to make the speech sound aesthetically pleasing, to accomplish subtle changes in meaning, and to tell an audience whether you are asking a question or making a statement, being sincere or sarcastic, or being doubtful or assertive. A rapid speaking rate may indicate you are confident about speaking in public or you are nervously attempting to conclude your speech. Variations in volume can be used for emphasis or to create suspense. Enunciation is especially important in public speaking because of the increased size of the audience and the fewer opportunities for direct feedback. Pauses can be used in the public speech for dramatic effect and to arouse audience interest. Vocalized pauses—the *ahs, uh-huhs, ums,* etc.—are not desirable in public speaking and may distract the audience. Far better than vocalized pauses is silence. One observer noted,

> Sometimes silence is best. Words are curious things, at best approximations. And every human being is a separate language. . . . [sometimes] silence is best.[31]

Clothing and Other Artifacts

Objectics, or *object language,* refers to our display of material things and includes clothing and other artifacts. **Artifacts** are ornaments or adornments and include jewelry, hairstyles, cosmetics, automobiles, canes, watches, shoes, portfolios, hats, glasses, and even the choice of fillings in our teeth! Our clothing and other adornments communicate our age, gender, status, role, socioeconomic class, group memberships, personality, and our relation to the opposite sex. Dresses are seldom worn by men, low-cut gowns are not the choice of shy women, bright colors are avoided by reticent people, and the most recent Paris fashion is seldom seen in the small towns of mid-America.

These cues also indicate the time in history, the time of day, and the climate. Clothing and artifacts provide physical and psychological protection and are used for sexual attraction and to indicate self-concept. Our clothing and artifacts clarify for each of us the sort of person we believe we are.[32] They permit us personal expression,[33] and they satisfy our need for creative self-expression.[34] An interest in clothing predicts a high level of self-actualization.[35]

Clothing and other artifacts play an important role in nonverbal communication.

Many studies have established relationships between an individual's clothing and artifacts and his or her characteristics. An early study showed that people who dressed in a decorative style tended to be sociable and nonintellectual. People who dressed with comfort in mind tended to be higher in self-control and extroversion. People who were conformists in their clothing styles were restrained, submissive, and conforming in social situations, as well.[36] A more recent study confirms these results; conforming to current styles is correlated with an individual's desire to be accepted and liked.[37] In addition, individuals feel that clothing is important in forming first impressions.[38]

Perhaps of more importance are the studies that consider the relationship between clothing and an observer's perception of that person. In an early study, clothing was shown to affect others' impressions of status and personality traits.[39] We also seem to base our acceptance of people on their clothing and artifacts. Women who were asked to describe the most popular women they knew used clothing as the most important characteristic.[40] Finally, brightly colored clothing is associated with sophistication, immorality, and physical attractiveness.[41]

The importance of clothing and other artifacts on our perception of others cannot be overrated. A few years ago, the students in a male instructor's class told him clothing was a form of communication only among older people—like himself. They argued that young people made no judgments about other people's clothing and seldom even noticed other people's clothes. The instructor's arguments to the contrary fell on deaf ears. The next semester, while again lecturing on object language, the instructor told his new students about that previous discussion—but while he talked, he slipped off his jeans and sweater to reveal a T-shirt and running shorts. At the end of the hour, he gave a quiz on the material covered during the period. Not surprisingly, the students successfully answered the items on the material covered before he disrobed but did a poor job with the questions on material he covered afterward. These students agreed—they were distracted by his unusual and provocative attire and had difficulty concentrating on the lecture. The importance of clothing as a means of nonverbal communication to young as well as older people was established, at least in that second class.

Suggestions for Improving Your Nonverbal Communication

You can improve your use of nonverbal communication by being sensitive to context, audience, and feedback.

The *context* includes the physical setting, the occasion, and the situation. In conversation, your vocal cues are rarely a problem unless you stutter, stammer, lisp, or suffer from some speech pathology. Paralinguistic features loom larger in importance in small group communication where you have to adapt the distance and a variety of receivers. These features are, perhaps, most important in public speaking because you have to adjust volume and rate, you have to enunciate more clearly, and you have to introduce more vocal variety or inflection to keep the audience's attention. The strategic use of pauses and silence is also more apparent in public speaking than it is in an interpersonal context in conversations or small group discussion.

The *audience* makes a difference in your nonverbal communication because you have to adapt. When speaking to children, the complexity and vocabulary have to be adjusted to simplicity along with careful enunciation, articulation, and pronunciation. With an older audience or with younger audiences whose hearing has been impaired by too much loud music, you must adapt your volume. Generally, it helps to speak more slowly to children and to older people both in interpersonal and public speaking situations. The audience may determine your choice of clothing, hair style, and jewelry. A shaved head, earring in one ear, and a shirt open to the navel does not go over well in a job interview—unless you are trying for a job as an entertainer.

Your attention to *feedback* can be very important in helping others interpret nonverbal cues that might otherwise distract your listener. Some pregnant women avoid questions and distraction by wearing a shirt that says, "I'm not fat. I'm pregnant;" otherwise, listeners might wonder instead of listening.

Similarly, your listener's own nonverbal cues—quizzical looks, staring, nodding off—can provide you with information that might signal you to talk louder, introduce variety, restate, or clarify.

Summary

In this chapter, we considered the role of intentional nonverbal codes in communication. We have difficulty in interpreting nonverbal codes because we use the same code to communicate a variety of different meanings and because we use a variety of codes to communicate the same meaning.

Nonverbal codes consist of nonword symbols. Bodily movements and facial expression, personal space, sounds other than words, and clothing and artifacts are nonverbal codes. Kinesics is the study of people's bodily movements, including posture, gestures, and facial expression. Five categories of bodily movements are emblems, illustrators, affect displays, regulators, and adaptors. Proxemics is the human use of space. Territoriality—our need to establish and maintain certain spaces of our own—and personal space—the amount of physical distance we maintain between ourselves and other people—are important concepts of proxemics. Tactile communication is the use of touch in communication and is essential to our growth and development. Vocal cues are all of the oral aspects of sound except the words themselves and include pitch, rate, inflection, volume, quality, enunciation, specific sounds, such as *huh, ah,* and *mmh,* and silences. Objectics, or object language, is our display of material things, including hairstyles, clothing, jewelry, and cosmetics. Our object language communicates our age, gender, status, role, socioeconomic class, group memberships, personality, and our relation to the opposite sex.

We can solve some of the communication difficulties in interpreting nonverbal codes if we consider all of the variables in the particular communication situation, if we consider all of the available verbal and nonverbal codes, and if we use descriptive feedback to minimize misunderstandings.

Key Terms

artifacts Ornaments or adornments we display that hold communicative potential; examples include jewelry, hairstyles, cosmetics, glasses, and automobiles.

intentionality When nonverbal communication is used on purpose and is perceived as purposeful.

kinesics The study of bodily movements, including posture, gestures, and facial expressions.

nonverbal codes A code consisting of any symbols that are not words, including nonword vocalizations.

objectics The study of the human use of clothing and other artifacts as nonverbal codes; object language.

paralinguistic features nonword sounds and nonword characteristics of language, such as pitch, volume, rate, and quality.

proxemics The study of the human use of space and distance.

tactile communication Communicating by touch.

vocal cues All the oral aspects of sound except words themselves; part of paralanguage.

chapter 7

Verbal Codes:

Sharing with Others

I n this chapter, we explore the use of words in communication by discussing what verbal codes are, how verbal codes interfere with communication, and how we can prevent verbal codes from interfering with our understanding of ourselves and others and with our ability to share ourselves with others. We also examine how the verbal language that we choose provides others with information about how we conceive of ourselves, others, and the relationships between ourselves and others. This chapter is about language and how it functions in communication. Most importantly, you can use this chapter as a guide to improve your own language skills.

What will you learn?

After you have read and thought about this chapter, you should be able to answer the following questions:

1. Can you illustrate the relationship among encoding, codes, and decoding in a drawing with two people?

2. Can you distinguish the differences among semantics, general semantics, and syntactics?

3. How does a language provide a particular perception of reality?

4. In what sense does every person in the world have his or her own language?

5. What are some unconventional ways that we use language?

6. Do you know three ways we can improve our verbal skills?

7. How do co-cultural groups influence language?

8. How do operational definitions, descriptiveness, paraphrasing, concreteness, dating, and indexing increase the chances for shared meaning?

Calvin Coolidge don't say much—but when he does—he don't say much.

Will Rogers

If you don't say anything, you won't be called on to repeat it.

Calvin Coolidge

To say nothing, especially when speaking, is half the art of diplomacy.

Will and Ariel Durant

L anguage is central to communication. We use it to get what we think into the minds of others. We learn it as children, and think we are doing pretty well to use it as adults. Language is such a part of us that we might not realize how it both expands and limits the way we think and perceive. In this chapter we will find out how imperfectly language works or how to make it work better.

Verbal Codes: Sets of Words

Language is a **code, symbols,** letters, or words with arbitrary meanings arranged according to the rules of syntax and used to communicate. **Syntactics** is the study of word arrangement. A simple example is that in English we usually place the subject before the verb and the object after the verb. Other languages have other rules of syntax, including reading from right to left. We **encode** by translating our thoughts into words. When we listen to verbal communication in words we translate, assign meaning or **decode,** the words into thoughts of our own. Because language is an imperfect means of transmission, the thoughts of one person never really become the thoughts of another person entirely as we learned in chapter 2.

Words as Verbal Symbols

To understand language, you need to understand what words mean, the nature of words.

First, it will help you to know that *words are arbitrary*. They have no inherent meanings, and they have only the meanings we give them. When lots of people use a word to indicate some object or idea, the word is placed in the dictionary. Placing a word in the dictionary, however, does not keep it from changing, so the dictionary is simply a record of how a word may be used now and a history of how it was used in the past. Language is dynamic, ever changing, and always interesting to study.

Second, *words are abstractions, simplifications of what they stand for*. People who study semantics, the study of meaning, say "the map is not the territory." This expression means that a map is a simplification and abstraction of the area it depicts—the actual roads, hills, and towns. Your community may be a dot on a large map. That dot greatly oversimplifies what is really there. Similarly, the word *videogame* is a broad term for thousands of individual games. The statement "The word is not the thing" sums up the idea.

Third, *words organize and classify reality*. Because you cannot account for all of the individual things in the world when you speak, you lump them into groups; so all four-legged items with seats and backs are called *chairs,* all two-legged living things with arms and faces are called *people,* and all multiple-dwelling buildings are called *apartments.* The following is an example of how you might classify when you try to identify someone in a crowd:

"See that guy over there?"

"Which one?"

"The tall one."

"The one with short brown hair?"

"No, the thick one with glasses."

Language is used to classify—in this case—by gender, height, hair color, weight, and adornment.

Another way of saying that words are arbitrary, that they are abstractions or simplifications, and that they organize and classify reality is to say that *words are symbols.* Words represent something without being that something: the word is not the thing.

The people who study the science of meaning in language call their discipline **semantics.** They examine the way humans use language to evoke meaning in others, and they are interested in how language and meaning change over time. For example, during the last thirty years, Africans in America have called themselves Negroes, Afro-Americans, blacks, and African Americans; "girl" became an undesirable term for mature females who preferred to be called "women;" and "gay" switched from meaning happy to meaning homosexual.

An entire field called **general semantics** was started by Count Alfred Korzybski with the noble notion of changing the world through careful use of language. The general semanticists encouraged some practices that made language more certain to engender shared meanings. Two such concepts to be introduced later in this chapter are dating and indexing. Their contribution included the use of precise, concrete, specific language to encourage the transmission and reception of symbols as accurately as possible.

Language Is Personal

To support the argument that there are more than three billion different languages in the world is easy. Each of us talks, listens, and thinks in a unique language (and sometimes we have several) that contains slight variations of agreed-upon meanings and that may change each minute.

Language usage is personal and is learned over time. You already know that if you had grown up in Poland rather than the United States your language usage would be quite different. Have you ever stopped to recognize how other factors affect your language usage? Our **personal language** is shaped by our culture, country, neighborhood, job, personality, education, family, friends, recreation, gender, experiences, and age.

Figure 7.1   How would you describe this picture?

An experiment illustrates the differences in our personal language usage. The photograph in figure 7.1 was shown to three people—a sophomore enrolled in a speech communication course, a Ph.D. in speech communication, and a veterinarian. Each person was asked to define or describe the picture. Their descriptions follow:

> It is a deerlike animal with a white belly and horns. The ears appear relatively large, and the rump is higher than the shoulders.
>
> Student

> A four-legged mammal of indeterminate size with hooves, variegated horns, large ears, elongated neck, and a two-toned torso. The rear legs are larger than the front legs, as if the animal were designed for running. Its relatively large eyes are on the sides of the animal's face, so it is probably among the grazing, hunted animals, rather than the carnivorous hunters.
>
> Speech communication professor

> *Gazella dorcas.*
>
> Veterinarian

The student used relatively simple and straightforward language, the professor used a larger vocabulary and (perhaps because of her academic training or interest) a greater number of words, and the veterinarian used the fewest, but most precise and technical words. If you had only been given the three descriptions of figure 7.1 and been told the three individuals involved in this experiment were a student, a speech communication professor, and a veterinarian, you probably would have been able to match the correct description with the correct individual. All of us draw conclusions about others on the basis of the language that others use.

The personal nature of language may be a means of coming closer to others and to ourselves. The uniqueness of each individual's language provides valuable information in our attempts to achieve some common meaning with others. Nonetheless, the personal nature of language also provides some difficulties in our communication with others. As we have already observed, each of us has a unique language shaped by a variety of factors. The possibility that even a few people will share most of these characteristics at the same time in the same way is really quite remote. The personal nature of language, then, obstructs, as well as enhances, communication.

Let us examine the influence of cultures, co-cultures, the individual, and the situation and context on personal language usage, and some of the misunderstandings that can occur when people do not recognize the influence of such variables.

Cultural Influence on Language Usage

Language usage varies among different cultures for the obvious reason that different cultures have different languages. A family we know spent a summer in Europe several years ago. As they traveled from country to country—sometimes crossing two or three borders in a single day—the wife noticed a striking similarity in the behavior of the Europeans they met. Although her husband is fluent in a number of European languages, the children and she are not. After successfully communicating with the husband, the European would turn to the wife and attempt to make small talk or social conversation. She would shrug her shoulders to indicate she did not understand. The European would repeat the remark, but a bit more loudly. She would again try to say she could not understand the language. The other person would stand closer to her, use more gestures, and repeat the message very loudly. Generally, the husband intervened at this point and explained she really did not understand the language. This happened everywhere the family went. People in the Netherlands, France, Germany, Spain, Italy, and other countries all shared the assumption that speaking more loudly and more enthusiastically would result in understanding.

This European experience is similar to experiences all of us have had in this country. People often assume their words have an inherent, intrinsic meaning that is universally understood. Unfortunately, this is not correct.

Groups establish specialized language among themselves to establish a co-cultural identity.

Co-cultural Influence on Language Usage

The heading for this section is a lesson in language. For five editions of this text it said "Subcultural Influence on Language Usage" until some intelligent student pointed out that *sub*culture can mean "less than" as in the word *subordinate*. Co-culture seems to be a better label since it implies coexistence and does not have the negative connotation.

Co-cultures are groups within our dominant American culture that have a separate identity by race, organization, or interest. Co-cultures can include African Americans, Latinos, and Asians; survivalists, environmentalists, and corporations; or musicians, motorcyclists, and gangs. We are interested in how these groups' use language to communicate, to include and exclude, and to establish identity within the group.

Women can be classified as a co-culture, a marginalized group in our society with lower pay, lower status jobs, and more working for white collar managers. Women speak English but their use of language differs from that used by men. One example would be words used to name colors. Women know and use words like chartreuse, mauve, ginger, and jade. Men rarely use these words for color or, perhaps, even know what they mean. Interestingly, co-cultures seem to enrich our language more than does the dominant culture. The language of singers, rap and rock artists, musicians, gangs, and athletes is creative and dynamic. Arsenio Hall and his guests manage to introduce new words and actions to a national audience at an impressive rate.

In fact, the language of co-cultures changes so rapidly that any words used as examples could be outdated by the time this book is published. Your class and your teacher, however, can create a list used by college students and other co-cultures, words that are so new that no dictionary has recorded them. You can prove that co-cultures influence our language by enriching our vocabulary.

Individuals' Influence on Language Usage

We can demonstrate again that words do not have inherent meaning by considering the differences in personal language usage among individuals within the same co-culture. You may, for example, discover a conflict about the use of the word *gay* to define a homosexual person. Some people, homosexual and heterosexual alike, might agree that it is a nonbiased term used to refer to a specific group of people. Others of both groups might find it extremely offensive and prefer that only the term *homosexual* be used. All of these statements illustrate the different meanings a word can have and the idea that words vary in meaning from person to person.

A distinction is frequently made between the denotative and connotative meanings of words. **Denotative meaning** refers to an agreed-upon meaning or a dictionary meaning for a term. **Connotative meaning** refers to an individualized or personalized meaning that may be emotionally laden. Denotative meanings are understood and shared by a large number of people. They are meanings people hold because of a common social experience with a word. For example, the word *chair* is generally understood similarly by others through their essentially common experience with the objects we call *chairs*. Connotative meanings are limited to a single person or to a very small number of people. They are meanings others have come to hold because of a personal or individual experience with a word. For example, the word *love* holds vastly different meanings for people because of their unique experiences with the concept.

People sometimes deliberately use the connotative meaning of a word for a particular purpose. You will recall that in chapter 5 we discussed glittering generalities and loaded words, which are words intended to stir the emotions of the listener. Politicians may use the word *murder* when discussing abortion; advertisers may use the word *sexy* when referring to a car; and a faculty member may drop in the word *examination* when students are not attentively listening. In each case, the individual is purposefully using the connotative meaning of the word to gain a desired response.

Red-flag words provide an example of connotative meaning and refer to words that tend to stir up negative responses. These words are often upsetting enough to interrupt or stop communication between people. They include racial epithets; comments about one's mother; using man-linked words to refer to women (e.g., the postmaster is a woman); scornful terms for people in careers, such as the army, the police force, or internal revenue; and words that label you as mentally or physically deficient ("you retard" or "you whimp"). Sometimes ordinary words can become red-flag words when they temporarily have increased significance. "Terminate an unwanted pregnancy" becomes the more negatively charged "murder a preborn child."

In the 1950s, you could ruin a person by calling him or her a Communist (as Richard Nixon did). In the 1960s, you could start a fight by suggesting that a member of the counter-culture favored war. In the 1970s, college professors and students opposed to the war were called "nattering nabobs of negativism," and media reporters were derided as "effete snobs" by the then Vice President Agnew. In the 1980s, being considered greedy was a compliment; but by the 1990s, Vice President Quayle was attacking "cultural elites," who sneer at traditional moral values.[1] The 1990s began with a "political correctness" movement to drive out racist, sexist, and ageist language. All of these are examples of how words can be used as red-flags to anger some groups or limit their use of language.

On the other hand, new words or **neologisms** continue to find their way into the language every day from talk shows, films, videos, co-cultural groups, and everyday people.

The Influence of the Situation and Setting on Language Usage

Not only do the meanings of words vary in different cultures and co-cultures and among different individuals, they also vary with the same person, depending on the situation and the setting. We can see how this happens by looking at the number of denotative meanings for a word provided in a dictionary. For example, the *Oxford English Dictionary* provides twenty-one separate definitions and

PEANUTS

many more subtypes for the word *close;* the word *clear* has twenty-seven definitions and many subtypes; the word *head* has sixty-six definitions with two to four subtypes of each definition; and the word *come* has sixty-nine definitions, but nearly two hundred definitions when all the subdefinitions are counted.

We gain a clue about the particular denotative meaning a person has in mind for a particular word from the setting in which the word is used. For example, we would be referring to a *sale* if we were in a shopping mall, but more likely a *sail* if we were on a boat.

An additional problem with spoken English (not as great in written English) is the number of words that sound the same but have different spellings and/or meanings. The "Peanuts" cartoon calls to mind *tail* and *tale.* Unless we are sensitive to the setting and the situation, we can easily receive the unintended definition.

Words as an Obstacle to Communication

In this section, we consider how language can actually be a major obstacle to communication. We will see that people sometimes use language in unconventional ways or to distort or alter meaning.

Unconventional Language Usage

People sometimes use language in unusual ways, and clear communication is almost impossible when individuals do not follow language conventions. For example, people sometimes break the semantic and syntactical rules that others agree on, and sometimes they replace cultural language rules with those from a particular co-culture. At other times, more personal decisions dictate the choice of words and the structuring of them. For instance, we use language in an unconventional way when we make errors in grammar, word choice, or the structure of our sentences; or when we use colloquialisms, clichés, euphemisms, slang, jargon, regionalisms, or street language.

Some errors in language usage have become fairly commonplace; nonetheless, they still cause confusion. For instance, if someone exclaims, "There's a woman with a baby all over the place!" the meaning is unclear. Is the baby actually "all over the place" or are there several women carrying babies walking around town? A more clear statement would have been "Look at all the women on the street who are carrying babies!"

Similarly, incorrect syntax creates problems. If someone told you, "I like to write on my book," you might not be sure if he liked to write and scribble on the cover of his book or if he liked writing and was authoring a book. The statement he made suggests the former conclusion. If he had been trying to express the latter, he should have said, "I like writing my book."

Colloquialisms include words and phrases used informally. Sometimes, colloquial words and phrases are unclear particularly to strangers to your region. International people may be particularly confused by colloquialisms. Similarly, people from other co-cultures may not understand your intended meaning. Some typical examples of colloquialisms are, "Have a happy day," "Good to see you," "Take care now," and "See you."

Metatalk refers to talk in which the meaning is beyond the words. For instance, everyday phrases like "Call me," "How are you," "Let's have lunch," and "We must get together" do not derive their meaning from the words. "Call me" generally means you are too busy to talk right now and the other person should call if he or she really needs to talk. "Call me" translates as "I can't talk now." "How are you?" is a greeting that acknowledges the other person's presence. The speaker is not inquiring about his or her physical or psychological health. "Let's have lunch" is a mildly positive comment suggesting that the two people might get together, but only if they are both without other plans. "We must get together" is similarly positive, but the likelihood that the speaker will actively attempt to arrange a social occasion is very low. Metatalk is confusing to anyone who is not familiar with American customs.

Clichés are words or phrases that have lost their effectiveness because of overuse. Examples include "Don't cry over spilled milk," "As old as the hills," and "A dime a dozen." In addition to being overused, clichés may be unclear to individuals who are unfamiliar with the underlying ideas of a particular cliché.

Euphemisms, sometimes called *double talk,* are inoffensive words substituted for words considered offensive. These, too, confuse others. For instance, we may say "tinkle" for "urinate"; "inequitable distribution of wealth" to account for the poor; and "unsheltered" for homeless. Euphemisms are frequently substituted for short, abrupt words, the names of physical functions, or the terms for some unpleasant social situations. Although euphemisms are frequently considered more polite than the words for which they are substituted, they also distort reality. For example, we find it easier to discuss "substandard living" than the horrors of starvation, and we can soften the reality of child and spouse abuse by calling it "intrafamily conflict." Communication based on delusion allows us to ignore real human problems and to avoid unpleasant situations.

Unconventional Language

Each of us uses a variety of unconventional language forms. Try to list at least two clichés, two euphemisms, two slang expressions, and two examples of jargon you use. If you have difficulty identifying such forms in your own language, use someone else's expressions. It is sometimes easier to identify unconventional language in other people's communication.

Clichés: 1. _____

                  2. _____

Euphemisms: 1. _____

                  2. _____

Slang: 1. _____

                  2. _____

Jargon: 1. _____

                  2. _____

Slang refers to a specialized language of a group of people who share a common interest or belong to a similar co-culture. While slang is understood by many people, it is generally not used in formal oral or written communication. Slang is often associated with teenagers, African-Americans, and women. It is temporary in nature. In the 1950s, the terms used by young women and men were *scuzz* and *zilch*. In the 1960s, young people used the words *pig, groovy,* and *uptight*. In the 1970s, young people used the terms *turkey, gross,* and *queer*. In the 1980s, they used such words as *really, I mean, rad,* and *wick*.

Today, students use a final *not* to deny the sentence they just said as in "She's really a nice person—not;" *Yeah right; kickin'* as in "That's a kickin do" (that's an attractive hairdo); or *dissed* as in "You really dissed him" (you really disrespected him). However, the half-life of slang is so brief that even these expressions will be out-of-date in nine months.

Jargon is the technical language developed by a professional group, such as physicians, educators, electricians, economists, and computer operators. Some examples of jargon include *CPR, InCo, brief,* and *storyboard.* Jargon can be an efficient and effective aid in communicating with those who share an understanding of the terms. However, like slang, it can lead to confusion when individuals who understand such terms attempt communication with others who do not.

Regionalisms are words or phrases specific to a particular region or part of the country. The word *coke* in Texas has the same meaning as the word *soda* in New York and the word *pop* in Indiana. When people from different parts of the country try to talk with each other, clarity may break down.

Street language consists of words or phrases specific to one locality. "Boys in the hood" is street language for the gang in the neighborhood. Students refer to "the quad," "the green," "the statue," and "the square" for parts of the campus. This language unifies the groups with terms that are unique to the group and difficult for outsiders to interpret.

These names for different kinds of language are not mutually exclusive, that is, a particular expression could fit in more than one category. Can you see how this brief sentence could be a colloquialism, a cliché, metatalk, and perhaps even a regionalism—"How's it going?" Nonetheless, the idea is to introduce a vocabulary you can use to describe the language you hear every day.

Distorted Language or Language that Alters Meaning

All of us confuse ourselves and others with language. For example, a friend asks, "How do I look?" and we respond with a compliment rather than with an honest response. People sometimes press us to state a point of view before we have had time to think it through. If pressed too hard, we may make a vague response to gain more time to consider the issue. We also sometimes answer vaguely when someone asks for information we do not have. Through ambiguity, we attempt to convey the idea that we really know more than we do.

Politicians provide abundant examples of language intentionally used to obstruct communication. People running for political office often use abstract terms and vague phrases to say nothing or everything. They recognize that specific and concrete terms will offend one group or another, so they seek the safety of empty and meaningless language.

Advertisers, too, often intentionally use language to confuse the consumer. Under current law, "lite" beer can have more calories than regular beer, a "serving" can vary from a teaspoon to a cup, and "natural" foods can have the same ingredients as foods full of refined flour, sugar, and chemical colors. Similarly, a "sale" item can cost the same as it did when it was not on sale, and

Metaphoric Language

As you have seen in this chapter, language is fluid and continually changing. In this exercise, you will have an opportunity to experience this idea. Metaphors are figures of speech in which a word is transferred from the object it ordinarily represents to an object it designates only by implicit comparison. For example, we may talk about the "autumn of one's years," the fog that comes in on "tiny cat feet," or "the song of the sea." Metaphors are generally fresh and lively comparisons; they are not to be confused with clichés, which are overworked or overused terms. For each of the concepts listed below, try to determine one to three metaphors. Compare your phrases or words with those of your classmates.

1. Springtime _____
   _____

2. Love _____
   _____

3. Friendship _____
   _____

4. Twilight _____
   _____

5. Anger _____
   _____

6. Success _____
   _____

7. Human babies _____
   _____

8. Surprise _____
   _____

a "going out of business sale" can go on forever. Like the sign in "The Wizard of Id" cartoon that advertises a "100-foot pool," such words and phrases do not convey a clear message.

Improving Verbal Skills

We have observed that words are symbolic and highly personal. In addition, we have noted that sometimes we use language in unconventional ways, and we intentionally attempt to confuse others with our language. Words need not be obstacles to communication, however. We can make specific changes in our verbal usage that will help us to become more effective communicators. Before we discuss those specific changes, we should observe two warnings.

First, we are limited in our language changes by factors we do not always understand or control. Before you read this chapter, you may have been unaware of all of the different influences—such as your culture, co-culture, religion, gender, and neighborhood—on your language. Even now, you may be influenced by factors we have not fully discussed or of which you are unaware.

For example, the intimate relationship between language and perception creates difficulties for us in changing our language and, simultaneously, in changing our perceptions. Edward Sapir, a linguist, and Benjamin Lee Whorf, a fire-insurance expert, first discussed the relationship between language and perception. The **Sapir-Whorf hypothesis,** as it has become known, states that our perception of reality is determined by our thought processes, and our thought processes are limited by our language. Our perception of reality is dependent on our language.[2] To understand how the Sapir-Whorf hypothesis works, we might tell a doctor we feel "discomfort" or "tension." The doctor however, can recognize "digestive distress" or "angina."

Another example may help to clarify the Sapir-Whorf hypothesis. In your lifetime, you have engaged in countless conversations. However, before you read the material on nonverbal communication in chapter 6, you may not have "seen" those interactions in the same way. Now you may notice the bodily movement of others, their use of space, the amount of touching in which they engage, their paralanguage, and the influence of their clothing on the many "messages" they send. Your familiarity with the language of nonverbal communication may create greater sensitivity in your perception of interactions.

The second warning we must consider when experimenting with new language behavior concerns the purpose of the former behavior and the purpose of the new verbal patterns. Sometimes ambiguous, colloquial, or distorted language serves an important purpose for an individual. We may use such practices to protect ourselves—to establish a healthy self-concept or to maintain a distorted self-concept, to deny self-awareness or to gain time to develop self-awareness. We also use such forms to protect others—to help them maintain a selective view of reality, to help them distort their world, or to help them acknowledge successes or deny difficulties. A "gifted child" may feel pressure to succeed. The term *sanitation specialist* changes our perception of a "garbage man." The clichés "No pain no gain" and "Whoever has the most when he dies wins," are substituted for overstrenuous exercise and greed, respectively.

Our choice of language provides information to others about how we see ourselves, how we see others, and what relationships we believe are established between ourselves and others. You may relax around friends and use language deemed "inappropriate" by your parents or coworkers. If you are being interviewed for a job, you may use language that is particular to your profession and be careful to use correct grammar. You may use words with special meaning with an intimate or lover.

Changes in your verbal behavior must occur within the context of the situation in which you find yourself. You must consider what you wish to share with others through your language and how clearly you wish to be known. Your prior relationships with others and your current goals in the interactions are important considerations. Understanding and sharing are the ultimate benefits of verbal clarity; you must decide the extent to which such goals are possible and important. With these considerations in mind, let us consider how we can improve our verbal skills.

Avoid Intentional Confusion

Some of the verbal patterns we fall into have become so habitual that we no longer feel we are intentionally confusing; rather, we believe "everyone" speaks the way we do. We take comfort in our clichés. Edwin Newman, television news personality, talks about his own use of clichés in his books, *Strictly Speaking* and *A Civil Tongue:*

> One thing that happened to me, as a reporter on the air, was that I realized I was pushing along ideas that had no substance. I was taking phrases and using them as if they had substance, and they didn't.[3]

We should strive to become increasingly sensitive to our own use of empty language, ambiguities, clichés, and euphemisms. It is often helpful to have someone else monitor our statements and point out the problem areas. After someone else has sensitized us to our confusing phraseology, we can "take the reins in our own hands" (Er, that is, do the job ourselves!) Our goal, at all times, is to keep it simple.

Use Descriptiveness

Descriptiveness is the practice of describing observable behavior or phenomena instead of offering personal reactions or judgments. This skill was discussed in chapter 4 in the section on feedback and the section on behaviors associated with effective listening.

We can be descriptive in different ways. One of the most important ways involves making simple checks on our perception. To communicate effectively with another person, it is important to have a common understanding of an event that has occurred or of the definition of a particular phenomenon. We can check with other persons to determine if their perceptions are the same as our own. We ask another person, "Isn't it hot in here?" "It's been a long week, hasn't it?" "That was a hard test, wasn't it?" Many disagreements occur because people do not stop to make these simple checks on their perception.

For example, each of us confuses **inferences**—the drawing of a conclusion from or about things we have observed—with observations. One of the most obvious examples of this occurs when we walk through a dark room at night. We cannot see the furniture or other obstacles, but we conclude they are still where they were, and we walk around them without turning on the light. We have no problem with this kind of simple exchange of an inference for an observation—unless someone has moved the furniture or placed a new object in the room, or unless our memory is not accurate. Even simple inferences can be wrong. Many shins have been bruised because someone relied on inference rather than observation.

Another way to improve your verbal skills is to be descriptive instead of evaluative. In chapter 4, you learned about listening and the importance of describing instead of evaluating. Similarly, in chapter 5 you learned the difference between observation and inference. Part of learning how to use language with greater precision is to be aware when you are describing, evaluating, observing, and inferring. We will add two more kinds of descriptiveness that can help improve your use of language.

Paraphrasing is restating what you think you heard in your own words. You do not simply repeat exactly what you heard in the same words. This act allows the source to make corrections in case you misinterpreted what was said. In actively listening to a paraphrase, you consciously try to determine if your listener understood both the *intent* and the *content* of what you said.

Another kind of descriptiveness is using ***operational definitions,*** which define by saying specifically what behaviors are involved. For example, a professor says in her syllabus that students can have an excused absence for illness. A student spends a sleepless night studying for an exam in another course, misses class, and claims an excused absence because of illness. The student explains that he was too tired to come to class, and the teacher explains that illness is surgery, injury, regurgitation, diarrhea, or a very bad headache. This operational definition will not please the student, but it will clarify the meaning of the term by saying what behavior the professor defines as illness.

Even abstractions become understandable when they are operationalized. To say that someone is "romantic" does not reveal much compared to saying that someone dresses up, picks you up at the door, pays for a fine meal, and likes the same kind of music that you do. At present, Beuford, South Carolina, is trying to operationally define their noise ordinance to quiet down the street preachers, and some cities are trying to define giant squirt guns as outlawed weapons. To handle these problems, Beuford and other cities will have to operationally define offensive noise and offensive weapons without violating the right of free speech or the right to bear arms.

Suppose a student says, "I don't understand descriptiveness." The teacher can respond by repeating, "I heard you say you don't understand descriptiveness," or "Do you mean my explanation of that skill wasn't clear?" or "Do you mean you would like me to explain the skill further to you?" In the first reply, the teacher is merely repeating the message and has only shown that the words were heard. The second reply shows the *content* of the student's message has been understood. The third reply shows the *intent* of the message has been understood. The first response is mere repetition; the second and third are two levels of paraphrasing.

Confusion may also arise when we use unusual terms or if we use a word in a special way. If we suspect someone might not understand the terminology we are using, it is essential to define the term. We need to be careful not to offend the other person on the one hand, and to offer a definition that is clearer than the term itself on the other hand. Similarly, we need to ask others for definitions when they use words in unusual or new ways.

Be Concrete

Earlier in this chapter, we observed that general semanticists recommend individuals improve their verbal behavior by using words more critically. Concreteness is one of their specific recommendations. **Concreteness** is specificity of expression. A person whose language is concrete uses statements that are specific, rather than abstract or vague. "You have interrupted me three times when I have begun to talk—I feel as though you do not consider my point of view as important as yours," is specific; "You should consider my viewpoint, too," is not specific.

In the following conversation, notice that the student becomes increasingly concrete as she describes her reactions to a textbook:

Student:	*I don't like the book.*
Instructor:	*What book is that?*
Student:	*The book for this class.*
Instructor:	*We have three required books—to which book are you referring?*
Student:	*The big one.*
Instructor:	*Do you mean* Professional Speaking?
Student:	*Yeah, that's the one.*
Instructor:	*Why don't you like it?*
Student:	*Well, it doesn't say anything to me.*
Instructor:	*Do you mean it's not relevant to your needs?*
Student:	*Yeah, I guess so, but it's more than that.*
Instructor:	*Could you explain why you don't like it?*
Student:	*Well, the chapters are so long and boring.*
Instructor:	*Do you find the examples helpful?*
Student:	*No.*
Instructor:	*Are there specific chapters that you find to be too long?*
Student:	*I've only started to read the first one, but it's pretty long.*
Instructor:	*Why do you find it boring?*
Student:	*There aren't any cartoons, pictures, or anything but words!*

Instructor: *In other words, you find chapter 1 of* Professional Speaking *to be long and boring because it has so few, or no, illustrations?*

Student: *Right. I don't like the book because the first chapter is over forty pages long and has only one diagram, which is of a model of communication that doesn't make any sense to me. I like books that have short chapters and lots of illustrations that I can understand.*

Concreteness is any form of more specific expression. Two of the more useful subtypes of concreteness are dating and indexing. **Dating** is a skill based on the idea that everything is subject to change. Often, we view objects, people, or situations as remaining the same. We form a judgment or point of view about a person, an idea, or a phenomenon, and we maintain that view, even though the person, idea, or phenomenon has changed. Dating is the opposite of *frozen evaluation,* a term that means you did not allow your assessment to change over time. Instead of saying something is always or universally a certain way, we state *when* we made our judgment and clarify that our perception was based on that experience.

For example, if you had a course with a particular instructor four or five years ago, it is essential that your judgment about the course and instructor be qualified as to time. You may tell someone, "English 100 with Professor Jones is a snap course," but it may no longer be true. Suppose you went out with a man two years ago, and now your best friend is looking forward to her first evening with him. You might say he is quiet and withdrawn, but it may no longer be accurate: the time that has passed, the person he is with, and the situation have all changed. Such statements as "English 100 with Professor Jones was a snap course for me in 1987," and "Joe seemed quiet and withdrawn when I dated him two or three years ago" will create fewer communication problems.

Indexing is a skill based on the idea that all members of a group do not share all of the characteristics of the other members of that group. Stereotyping—making conventional, oversimplified generalizations about a group, event, or issue—is the opposite of indexing. Earlier in the chapter, we discussed the importance of being able to generalize and classify. Nonetheless, problems can arise when we generalize and classify people. We sometimes assume the characteristics of one member of a class apply to all of the members of the class. For example, you assume that because you have a good communication instructor, all instructors in the department are exceptional. You assume because your little sister is frivolous that all females are frivolous. Your last boyfriend was a jerk, so all men are jerks.

You could say, "I have a great communication instructor. How is yours?" "My little sister is so frivolous. Are all you females like that?" "John was a real jerk. How does your boyfriend treat you?"

Paraphrasing

For each of the following dialogues, identify the response as repetition, paraphrasing of content, or paraphrasing of intent. Place an *R* in the blank if the dialogue is a repetition, a *C* if it paraphrases content, and an *I* if it paraphrases intent.

1. Question or statement: If you had to do it over again, would you do the same thing?

   Response: Do you mean would I state my disagreement to my employer?

   _____

2. Question or statement: Will your wife move to the new location with you if you secure this promotion?

   Response: Are you asking if my wife will move with me to the new location if I get the job?

   _____

3. Question or statement: I'm always afraid I'm going to make a mistake!

   Response: What do you mean, you feel like you're going to make a mistake?

   _____

4. Question or statement: I've lived here for three months, but I still don't know my way around the city.

   Response: Would you like me to show you some of the principal landmarks and the main streets?

   _____

5. Question or statement: I really appreciate the time you have spent talking to me.

   Response: I would like to encourage you to come in and see me whenever you have a problem—I understand how important it is to be able to talk to your supervisor.

   _____

Answers: 1. C, 2. C, 3. R, 4. I, 5. I.

Indexing assists us in avoiding these pitfalls. Indexing is simply recognizing differences among the various members of a group. Instead of grouping all automobiles together and assuming a characteristic one car has is shared by all of the others, we recognize that the car we own could be unique. Instead of assuming all firstborn children are alike, we exhibit openness and an inquiring attitude about firstborn children, other than the ones we know.

Practicing Concreteness

To gain some practice in being concrete, rewrite each of the following statements to make the statement more specific, to date the statement, or to index
the statement. For instance, if you were given the statement, "I don't like algebra," you would date it by stating, "I don't like the algebra course I have this
quarter." If you were asked to index the statement, you might write, "I don't
like the algebra course taught by Professor Smith." If you were asked to make
the statement more specific, you might write either of the previous alternatives,
or you might write something similar to, "I don't like the algebra course
required at this university."

        1. I love "Good Morning America"

Dated alteration: _____

        2. My mom is my friend.

Indexed alteration: _____

        3. My roommate never listens to me.

More specific alteration: _____

        4. My boyfriend is hard to get along with.

Dated alteration: _____

        5. Where's my book?

More specific alteration: _____

We are indexing when we make statements like, "I have a Hyundai that
uses very little gas. How does your Hyundai do on gas mileage?" or "My older
brother is far more responsible than I. Is the same true of your older brother?"
We lack an ability to index when we state, "Hyundais get good gas mileage—I
know, I own one," or "Firstborn children are more responsible than their
younger brothers and sisters."

Summary

In this chapter, we have explored the use of words in communication. Words
are symbolic; that is, they stand for something else. Verbal codes consist of
sets of words. Semantics is the study or science of meaning in language forms.
General semanticists emphasize improving human behavior through more critical, concrete use of words and symbols. Words are organized into larger units
known as languages. Syntactics is the study of how we put words together to
form phrases and sentences.

Language is personal. Each of us possesses a unique language, although we share some meanings with others. Denotative meaning refers to an agreed-upon or a dictionary meaning, while connotative meaning refers to an individualized or personalized meaning of a term. The culture, the co-culture, the individual, and the situation and setting all influence our language usage.

Words can be an obstacle to communication because we sometimes use language in an unconventional way, such as when we make structural and grammatical errors, or when we use colloquialisms, metatalk, clichés, euphemisms, slang, jargon, regionalisms, or street language. Words can also be an obstacle to communication when we use language to distort or alter meaning.

We sometimes have limited success in improving our verbal skills because we are unaware of the factors that affect our language or we cannot control those factors. In addition, we sometimes purposely distort what we state to protect ourselves or to protect others. Nonetheless, we can change and improve our use of language.

We can use language to communicate more effectively by first defining the terminology we use and by avoiding unconventional usage. Second, we can check our perception of something by becoming increasingly descriptive. Paraphrasing the intent and content of others' messages—one form of descriptive feedback—can be highly useful in our attempts at verbal clarity. Third, we can improve our verbal skills by making an effort to be more concrete; that is, we should try to use statements that are specific, rather than abstract or vague. Both dating and indexing are useful methods of being increasingly concrete.

Key Terms

clichés   Words or phrases that have lost their effectiveness because of overuse; examples include "Don't lose any sleep over it," "Give them an inch and they'll take a mile," "Watch him like a hawk," and "You can't take it with you."

co-cultures   Groups within our dominant American culture that have a separate identity by race, organization, or interest.

code   Any systematic arrangement or comprehensive collection of symbols, letters, or words given arbitrary meanings and used for communication.

colloquialisms   Words and phrases used informally, such as "Have a happy day," "Good to see you," "Take care now," "How you doin'?" and "See you."

concreteness   Specificity of expression; using words that are not ambiguous or abstract.

connotative meaning   Individualized or personalized meaning for a term; the emotional content of words.

dating   A subtype of concreteness; identifying and stating when we make an inference or observation.

decode   To assign meaning to verbal codes we receive.

denotative meaning   An agreed-upon meaning of a word or phrase; a formal meaning determined by agreement within a society or culture.

descriptiveness The describing of observed behavior or phenomena instead of offering personal reactions or judgments.

encode To put an idea or thought into a code.

euphemisms Inoffensive words or phrases substituted for words considered vulgar or that have unacceptable connotations; for example, "washroom" as a substitute for "toilet."

general semantics A field of study proposed by Alfred Korzybski that emphasizes improving human behavior through a more critical use of words and symbols.

indexing A subtype of concreteness; identifying the uniqueness of objects, events, and people and stating our observations and inferences are specific rather than generalizable.

inferences Conclusions drawn from observation.

jargon The technical language reserved by a special group or profession, such as physicians, educators, economists, or computer operators; examples of jargon include *angina, duodenal, dyadic interaction, bytes,* and *CPU.*

metatalk Talk in which the meaning is beyond the words, such as "How are you," or "Call me."

neologisms New words that come into usage as other terms become outdated.

operational definitions A definition that consists of stating the process that results in the thing being defined; hence, a cake can be operationally defined by a recipe, a particular house by its blueprints, and a job by its description.

paraphrasing Restating the other person's message by rephrasing the content or intent of the message.

personal language The language of the individual, which varies slightly from the agreed-upon meanings because of past experiences and present conditions.

red-flag words Words that tend to stir up negative responses in people.

regionalisms Words or phrases specific to a particular region or part of the country; for example, the word *coke* in Texas is similar to the word *soda* in New York and is the same as the word *pop* in Indiana.

Sapir-Whorf hypothesis The theory that our perception of reality is determined by our thought processes, and our thought processes are limited by our language; therefore, language shapes our perception of reality.

semantics The study or science of meaning in language forms, especially with regard to historical change; the examination of the relationship between words and meaning.

slang A specialized language of a group of people who share a common interest or belong to a similar co-culture, such as teenagers, African-Americans, women, and members of the drug culture.

street language Words or phrases specific to one section of one city used by a group to demonstrate their unity.

symbol Something that stands for, or represents, something else by association, resemblance, or convention.

syntactics The study of how we put words together to form phrases and sentences.

part 2

Interpersonal Communication

Interpersonal communication is the process of understanding and sharing meaning in pairs and in small groups. Chapters 8 through 10 explore why we have interpersonal relationships and how they function in small decision-making or problem-solving groups.

Chapter 8, "Interpersonal Relationships: Close Encounters," covers the nature of relationships, how they are defined, and why they are important. You will discover the stages of relationship development, maintenance, and disintegration. You will also learn the role of self-disclosure and its importance in human relationships.

Chapter 9, "Intercultural and Co-cultural Communication," addresses the importance of communicating between and among groups of people bonded by interest, identity, and language. This chapter examines problems faced in such communication situations and solutions to those problems.

Chapter 10, "Small Group Communication: Leadership and Conflict Resolution," reveals when groups should be used and when they should not. This chapter covers important concepts in group communication, such as norms, roles, productivity, cohesiveness, commitment, consensus, and member satisfaction. The process of small-group discussion includes topic selection, wording the discussion question, and organizing the discussion. The section on leadership reviews leadership styles and how the leader functions in a group. Finally, the portion on solving conflict analyzes the various modes of resolving conflict and reveals which modes are most advantageous in a small group.

chapter 8

Interpersonal Relationships:

Close Encounters

W hat will you learn in this chapter? First, you will discover that interpersonal relationships are complicated, but important to each of us. They help us understand ourselves, others, and our world, fulfill our needs, and increase and enrich positive experiences. A number of stages in relational development, maintenance, and deterioration have been identified. You will see what each of these stages are and how to recognize them from both verbal and nonverbal behaviors. Self-disclosure, the revealing of personal information, is part of the developing relationship and is considered in detail. Conflict occurs in virtually all interpersonal relationships. How is it effectively resolved? You will learn about specific methods of conflict resolution. Finally, we will consider how we can improve our communicative abilities within interpersonal relationships. Although relationships are complex, our communication can lead to more satisfaction within them.

What will you learn?

When you have read and thought about this chapter, you will be able to answer the following questions:

1. Can you define interpersonal relationships?

2. Can you list five reasons why we engage in interpersonal relationships?

3. Can you provide an example of each of Knapp's relational stages?

4. Can you define self-disclosure and name two dimensions of the concept?

5. Why is self-disclosure important?

6. Can you contrast supportive and defensive behaviors and provide examples of them?

7. How are behavioral flexibility and androgynous behavior related?

8. What are some ways you can become a more effective interpersonal communicator?

Life is truly a boomerang. What you give, you get.

Dale Carnegie

Seeing ourselves as others see us would probably confirm our worst suspicions about them.

Franklin P. Jones

It is those who have not really lived—who have left issues unsettled, dreams unfilled, hopes shattered and who have let the real things in life . . . pass them by—who are most reluctant to die. It is never too late to start living and growing.

Elisabeth Kübler-Ross

I n this chapter we will consider the importance of communication in interpersonal relationships. The skills and concepts discussed thus far are particularly relevant to successful interpersonal communication. For example, how we see ourselves is largely dependent on the relationships we have with others, and the interpersonal relationships we have with others help us to define who we are. Also, perceptual differences are often apparent as we engage in interpersonal relationships and may lead to the deterioration of a relationship. Our ability to listen is another skill critical to the development of an interpersonal relationship. Finally, we rely on verbal and nonverbal codes to express our understanding of others and to share ourselves with them.

The Nature of Interpersonal Relationships

Definition of Interpersonal Relationships

On the simplest level, relationships are associations or connections. Interpersonal relationships, however, are far more complex. **Interpersonal relationships** may be defined as associations between two or more people who are interdependent, who use some consistent patterns of interaction, and who have interacted for some period of time. Let us consider the different elements of this definition in more detail.

First, *interpersonal relationships include two or more people.* One person does not comprise a relationship. Often, interpersonal relationships consist of just two people—a dating couple, a single parent and a child, a married couple, two close friends, or two coworkers. Interpersonal relationships can also involve more than two people—a family unit, a group of friends, or a social group.

Second, *interpersonal relationships involve people who are interdependent.* Interdependence refers to people being mutually dependent on each other and having an impact on each other. Friendship easily illustrates this concept. Your best friend, for example, may be dependent on you for acceptance and guidance. You, on the other hand, might require support and admiration. When individuals are independent of each other, or when dependence only occurs in one direction, the resulting association is not defined as an interpersonal relationship.

Third, *individuals in interpersonal relationships use some consistent patterns of interaction.* These patterns may include behaviors generally understood across a variety of situations and also behaviors unique to the particular relationship. For example, a husband may always greet his wife with a kiss. This kiss is generally understood as a sign of warmth and affection. On the other hand, the husband may have unique nicknames for his wife not understood beyond the confines of the relationship.

Communication is central to the development of interpersonal relationships.

Fourth, *individuals in interpersonal relationships generally have interacted for some time.* When you nod and smile to someone as you leave the classroom, when you meet a girlfriend's siblings for the first time, or when you place an order at a fast-food counter, you do not have an interpersonal relationship. Although participants use interpersonal communication to accomplish these events, onetime interactions do not constitute interpersonal relationships. We should note, however, that interpersonal relationships may last for varying lengths of time—some are relatively short and others extend for a lifetime.

Importance of Interpersonal Relationships

Interpersonal relationships are essential for all of us. Five reasons we engage in interpersonal relationships are (1) to understand ourselves, (2) to understand others, (3) to understand our world, (4) to fulfill our needs, and (5) to increase and enrich positive experiences.

To Understand Ourselves

We learn about ourselves through our interpersonal relationships. Sometimes we find our perceptions of ourselves are not the same as are others' perceptions of us. At other times, our self-concepts are strengthened by the confirmation we receive from others' reactions. We do not share the same perspective as others, and we learn more about ourselves as we listen to the alternative perceptions others hold of us.

The Johari Window, introduced in chapter 3, is useful in illustrating how we come to understand ourselves better through interpersonal relationships. To review, the *open self* consists of information about yourself known to you and other people; the *blind self* consists of information about yourself known to others but not to you; the *hidden self* includes information you are aware of about yourself but you have not shared with others; and the *unknown self* includes information about yourself unknown both to you and others.

Through our interpersonal relationships, we can increase the size of the open self and decrease the size of the other three quadrants. For instance, if you discuss a difficult relationship in your life, you may suddenly realize a hidden source of the tension. If you talk about some happy experiences in your life with your friends, you might learn that others see you as an especially optimistic, positive person. Since your friends hold this perception of you, and you were unaware of it, you reduce the blind self on the Johari Window and increase the open self.

We should observe the self is different in each relationship in which we are involved. We share more of ourselves with some people than we do with others. Consequently, the open self is different in size for each relationship. A different Johari Window would be necessary to depict each of our relationships. Nonetheless, the Johari Window illustrates that our interpersonal relationships result in greater understanding of ourselves.

To Understand Others

Similarly, interpersonal relationships assist us in learning about others. Many times, we may feel we "know" someone before we have a relationship with them. We make judgments, draw inferences, and reach conclusions about others without really knowing very much about them. Professors Charles R. Berger and Richard J. Calabrese label this phenomenon the **uncertainty principle**.[1] This principle simply suggests when we initially meet others, we know little about them, and we rid ourselves of this uncertainty by drawing inferences from the physical data with which we are presented. This tendency is similar to the process of closure discussed in chapter 2. Additionally, the urge to lessen uncertainty motivates further interpersonal communication.

Sometimes we want so much for someone we like to fit our own preconceived ideas that we see what we want to see in them. When we actually involve ourselves in a relationship with that person, however, we may find our initial reactions were inaccurate. For example, the quiet woman you work with, who seems aloof, may actually be a warm person who is introverted and shy. The large man you see on the street who has a stern expression on his face isn't necessarily mean; he may have just learned that he lost his job. Your friend's mother, who reacted coldly when you first met her, may actually just be intimidated by strangers.

We develop interpersonal relationships in order to understand other people.

People can be quickly stereotyped, categorized, and forgotten; however, we cannot learn about others through snap judgments and initial interactions. Interpersonal relationships allow us to continue to grow in our knowledge of other persons. In the same way others help us to increase our open self in the Johari Window, we can, through our interpersonal relationships, expand the open self of others.

To Understand Our World

In addition to learning more about ourselves and about others through interpersonal relationships, we also learn more about our world—our environment. Our environment is made up of other people, physical objects, events, and circumstances. Our knowledge of the environment comes largely through the interactions we have in our relationships. For example, who most greatly influences your future plans? How did you come to form your life philosophy? Your responses to these questions probably indicate you learned about these people, ideas, and issues through your interpersonal relationships with acquaintances, friends, and family.

In addition to developing interpersonal relationships to learn more about our environment, we often develop interpersonal relationships to *cope* with our environment. For instance, when we encounter everyday stresses, such as tough exams, pressuring parents, and confusing relationships with the opposite sex, we need to feel there is someone who is able to empathize. It is reassuring to discuss these difficulties with friends and to discover creative ways of handling them. These relationships truly help us in coping with our complex world.

Another more specific example involves those who are substance abusers, such as alcoholics. They encounter pressure from, among other things, a society that sometimes promotes drinking as a way to relax or have a good time. These people may find that when they form friendships or relationships with members of a support group, their environment is no longer difficult to understand. These interpersonal relationships enable them to put their problems in perspective and to see how others like themselves interact in our world.

To Fulfill Our Needs

Individuals have many needs. In chapter 3, we discussed Maslow's hierarchy of needs, which included physical, safety and security, social, esteem, and self-actualization needs. According to William Schutz, we also have three basic interpersonal needs that are satisfied through interaction with others. These are (1) the need for **inclusion,** or becoming involved with others; (2) the need for **affection,** or being cared for by others; and (3) the need for **control,** or the ability to influence others, our environment, and ourselves.[2] Although we may be able to fulfill some of our physical, safety, and security needs through interactions with relative strangers, we can only fulfill the other needs through our interpersonal relationships.

The interdependent nature of interpersonal relationships suggests people mutually satisfy their needs in this type of association. Interdependence suggests one person is dependent on another to have some need fulfilled, and the other person or persons are dependent on the first to have the same or other needs fulfilled. For example, a child who is dependent on a parent may fill that parent's need for control. The parent, on the other hand, may supply the affection needed by the child when hugging, kissing, or listening to the child.

Complementary relationships—those in which each person supplies something the other lacks—provide good examples of the manner in which we have our needs fulfilled in interpersonal relationships. The popular male involved with the intelligent female is an example of a complementary relationship, since the woman may find herself involved in the social events she desires, and the man may find himself increasingly successful in his classes. Another example of a complementary relationship is a friendship between an introverted and an extroverted individual. The introvert may teach her friend to be more self-reflective or to listen to others more carefully. The extrovert might, in exchange, encourage her to be more outspoken or assertive.

Interpersonal communication involves bargaining with the other person.

Our needs also may be fulfilled in **symmetrical relationships**—those in which the participants mirror each other or are highly similar. A relationship between two intelligent persons may reflect their need for intellectual stimulation. Two people of similar ancestry might marry, in part to preserve their heritage.

Whether the other person or persons are similar to us or highly different, our needs are generally fulfilled through the relationships we have with others.

To Increase and Enrich Positive Experiences

We also enter into interpersonal relationships to increase and enrich positive experiences and/or to decrease negative experiences. One theory, the **cost-benefit theory,** suggests individuals will only maintain relationships as long as the benefits of the relationship outweigh the costs.[3] Some of the benefits of a relationship include personal growth, improved self-concept, increased self-knowledge, assistance with particular tasks, greater resources, and an improved capacity for coping. The costs include the amount of time spent on the relationship, the amount of energy that goes into the relationship, psychological stress created by the relationship, perhaps physiological stress, and social limitations. According to the cost-benefit theory, if the costs begin to outweigh the benefits, we may decide to terminate the relationship. If the benefits appear to outweigh the costs, we may escalate relationship development.

Interpersonal relationships are not so simply translated into a cost-benefit model, however. More often, we engage in bargaining in our interpersonal relationships. **Bargaining** occurs when two or more parties attempt to reach an agreement on what each should give and receive in a transaction between them. Bargains may be explicit and formal, such as the kinds of agreements we reach with others to share tasks, to attend a particular event, or to behave in a specified way. Bargains may also be implicit and informal. For example, you might agree not to tell embarrassing stories about your boyfriend in public in exchange for receiving a compliment from him every day. You may not even be aware of some of the implicit, tacit agreements you have with others with whom you communicate.

In a study on interpersonal bargaining, three essential features of a bargaining situation were identified:

1. All parties perceive the possibility of reaching an agreement in which each party would be better off, or no worse off, than if no agreement is reached.
2. All parties perceive more than one such agreement that could be reached.
3. All parties perceive the other or others to have conflicting preferences or opposed interests with regard to the different agreements that might be reached.[4]

What are some examples of bargaining situations? You may want to go out with friends when your date would prefer a quiet evening at home. A wife might prefer to go hiking, while her husband is more eager to take a cruise. One person could use the term "forever" to mean a few days or weeks, while another assumes it refers to a much longer period of time. In each of these instances, the disagreement can be resolved through bargaining.

Two researchers underlined the importance of bargaining in interpersonal communication:

> The point should be made . . . that whatever the gratifications achieved in dyads, however lofty or fine the motives satisfied may be, the relationship may be viewed as a trading or bargaining one. The basic assumption running throughout our analysis is that every individual voluntarily enters and stays in any relationship only as long as it is adequately satisfactory in terms of rewards and costs.[5]

This statement emphasizes the central role of bargaining in interpersonal relationships, and it also underlines the notion of cost-benefit analysis.

Stages in Interpersonal Relationships

Communication and relationship development are symbiotic; that is, communication affects relational development and relational development affects communicative behavior.[6] The association between communication and relational development have encouraged communication researchers to study **relational development**, **relational maintenance**, and **relational deterioration**.

Current theories rest on the original work of researchers Altman and Taylor. These authors developed the **social penetration theory,** which explains the development and deterioration of interpersonal relationships. In essence, the theory states interpersonal exchanges move from superficial, non-intimate information transfers to exchanging more intimate information through the process of revealing personal information. The amount of interaction increases as the relationship develops. Further, cost-reward considerations determine how quickly or slowly relationships develop. Finally, dissolution or depenetration is the reverse process of development or penetration.[7]

Professor Mark L. Knapp of the University of Texas expanded on Altman and Taylor's levels of relationship development by identifying ten interaction stages of interpersonal relationships. These stages are depicted in table 8.1. Professor Leslie A. Baxter and others have experimentally attempted to validate these stages. While they have found the termination stages are not reverse images of the developmental stages, the model that Knapp presents generally appears valid.[8] Furthermore, this developmental model helps to organize and explain relational changes.

The first five stages cover the development of a relationship:

1. **Initiating** is stage one and involves the first impressions, the sizing up of the other person, and the attempts to share commonality. An example is "scouting" at a party where you might break off the initiating stage when you don't find what you are seeking in the person you have just met. If this first stage goes well, you might move to stage two in a first meeting.
2. **Experimenting** occurs when the two people have clearly decided to find out more about each other, to quit scouting, and to start getting serious about each other. This stage includes self-disclosures at a safe level: what music, people, classes, professors, food you like or dislike. In a situation where you are "captive" in an airplane seat, waiting for a concert to begin, or seated next to someone for three or four months, this stage could start early and last for weeks.
3. **Intensifying** involves active participation, mutual concern, and an awareness that the relationship is developing because neither party has broken it off, and both people are encouraging its development. The information exchanges get more personal, more intimate, and more self-disclosive. Both act comfortable with each other, use private jokes and language, and provide expressions of commitment.
4. **Integrating** means the two start mirroring each other's behavior in manner, dress, and language. They merge their social circles, designate common property, and share interests and values. They know more about each other than anyone except long-term best friends, and others see them as a pair.

Table 8.1

An Overview of Interaction Stages

Process	Stage	Representative Dialogue
Coming Together	1. Initiating	"Hi, how ya doin'?" "Fine. You?"
	2. Experimenting	"Oh, so you like to ski . . . so do I." "You do?! Great. Where do you go?"
	3. Intensifying	"I . . . I think I love you." "I love you too."
	4. Integrating	"I feel so much a part of you." "Yeah, we are like one person. What happens to you happens to me."
	5. Bonding	"I want to be with you always." "Let's get married."
Coming Apart	6. Differentiating	"I just don't like big social gatherings." "Sometimes I don't understand you. This is one area where I'm certainly not like you at all."
	7. Circumscribing	"Did you have a good time on your trip?" "What time will dinner be ready?"
	8. Stagnating	"What's there to talk about?" "Right. I know what you're going to say and you know what I'm going to say."
	9. Avoiding	"I'm so busy, I just don't know when I'll be able to see you." "If I'm not around when you try, you'll understand."
	10. Terminating	"I'm leaving you . . . and don't bother trying to contact me." "Don't worry."

From Mark L. Knapp and Anita L. Vangelish, Interpersonal Communication and Human Relationships, *2d ed. Copyright © 1992 by Allyn and Bacon. Reprinted with permission.*

5. **Bonding** is the final stage in relational development. They may exchange personal items as a symbol of commitment; they may participate in a public ritual that bonds them, as in the case of marriage; or they may vow to be friends for life and demonstrate that commitment by always being present at important points in the other's life. Living together, marrying, having children, buying a home, or moving together to another place would be examples of this stage of relational development.

The second five stages—numbered six through ten—occur as a relationship disintegrates:

6. **Differentiation** occurs when the two partners start emphasizing their individual differences instead of their similarities. Instead of going to movies together, he plays basketball with his friends, and she goes out with her friends. Some separate activities are healthy in a relationship; but in differentiation, the pulling apart is to get away from each other.
7. **Circumscribing** is characterized by decreased interaction, shorter times together, and less depth to sharing. The two people might go to public events together but do little together in private. The individuals figuratively draw a circle around themselves, a circle that does not include the other person. The exchange of feelings, the demonstrations of commitment, and the obvious pairing are disappearing.
8. **Stagnating** suggests a lack of activity, especially activity together. Interactions are minimal, functional, and only for convenience. The two people now find conversation and sharing awkward instead of stimulating. During this stage, the individual may be finding an outlet elsewhere for developmental stages.
9. **Avoiding** brings a reluctance to interact, an active avoidance, and even hostility. The two former partners are now getting in each other's way, seeing the other person as an obstacle or limitation. The amount of their talk may actually increase, but the content and intent are negative. Arguing, fighting, disagreeing, and flight mark their interactions.
10. **Terminating** occurs when the two people are no longer seen by others or themselves as a pair. They increasingly dissociate, share nothing, claim common goods as individual property, and give back or get rid of the symbols of togetherness. Divorce, annulment, and dissolution are manifestations of this stage, as are people no longer living together, former friends who have nothing to do with each other, and roommates who take separate and distant quarters.[9]

Knapp acknowledged that individuals do not move in a linear way through these escalating or de-escalating stages. He suggests people might move within stages in order to maintain their equilibrium or stability. In other words, people might behave in a way that is more characteristic of one stage even though they are generally maintaining the interaction patterns of another stage.

Similarly, we do not move through these stages with everyone we meet. We base decisions to develop relationships on such factors as physical attractiveness, personal charisma, and communication behaviors. In general, we are more likely to attempt to develop a relationship with individuals who are attractive, emotionally expressive, extroverted, and spontaneous.[10]

Although Altman and Taylor as well as Knapp briefly consider relational maintenance, neither cover it in very much detail. Professor William Wilmot of the University of Montana felt Knapp's notion of movement within relationship stages were "minor adjustments" and that features characteristic of stable relationships need to be identified. He suggests relationships stabilize when the partners reach at least some level of agreement about what they want from the relationship. In addition, he states relationships can stabilize at any level of intimacy. Finally, he observes even "stabilized" relationships may have internal movement.[11]

Although we initially develop a relationship on the basis of such factors as attractiveness and personal charisma, relationships are maintained for different reasons. In our maintained relationships, we desire certain levels of predictability or certainty.[12] Indeed, we attempt to create strategies that will provide us with additional personal information about our relational partners.[13] We are also less concerned with partners' expressive traits—being extroverted and spontaneous—and more concerned with their ability to focus on us—to be empathic, caring, and concerned.[14] Indeed, as relationships are maintained, partners not only are empathic, they mirror the behaviors of the other.[15] In this manner, partners develop their own systems of interacting that may appear unusual to outside observers, but solidify the couple and the relationship.[16]

Deterioration of relationships is a communicative process often characterized by increased talk as former friends or mates confront each other with complaints, prepare each other for the exit, and tell other friends and relatives about the demise of the relationship. In the final phases of a failing relationship people go through a "grave dressing phase" in which they create their story of the relationship and its demise to tell others.[17] All of this activity toward the end of a relationship involves intense talk between the two people who are splitting and the circle of people who care about them.

Some writers have criticized those theorists who have equated relational development with the communication of personal information. Professor Malcolm Parks, of the University of Washington, for instance, believes such an ideology devalues less intimate, but more prevalent relationships.[18] Similarly, others have suggested that the view of relationship development should be refocused.[19] Nonetheless, relationship development, maintenance, and deterioration have guided a great deal of contemporary theorizing. Furthermore, they are a useful way to demonstrate the relevance of communication to relationship development.

Self-Disclosure

Definition of Self-Disclosure

The relationship development stages change as the intentional revealing of personal information changes. The term **self-disclosure** includes statements a person makes about himself or herself that another person would be unlikely to know or discover. Self-disclosure can be as unthreatening as talking about your last vacation or revealing how well you think you did on an exam. It can be as difficult as discussing your sexuality or confiding that you were abused as a child.

Self-disclosure can be analyzed in a number of ways. Two important dimensions are valence (positive or negative information) and amount. Although we cannot supply prescriptive answers to the desirable amount of self-disclosure, self-disclosure should be reciprocal. In other words, you should use the other person's disclosure as a guide to the amount of information you should disclose. We usually provide positive information to others about ourselves before we provide negative information. An extremely high level of negative information early in relational development may doom further development.

To whom do teenagers confide? The telephone pie charts in figures 8.1 and 8.2 suggest that both males and females are more likely to disclose to same-sex friends. Their second choice is their mother. Fathers are not mentioned by female teens and are in last place for male teens. To whom do you disclose?

Importance of Self-Disclosure

Self-disclosure is important for two reasons. First, it allows us to establish more meaningful relationships with others. Second, self-disclosure allows us to establish more positive attitudes toward ourselves and others. Let us examine these two reasons for self-disclosure in more detail.

To Establish More Meaningful Relationships with Others

Consider your communication with the person to whom you feel closest. Have you engaged in a great deal of self-disclosure? Now consider what you say or write to someone with whom you have only an acquaintanceship. How does your self-disclosure differ? Self-disclosure is offered most frequently and regularly to close friends. Self-disclosure allows relationships to grow in depth and meaning. If we use self-disclosure appropriately, our relationships move from being fairly superficial to being deeper and more meaningful. We find when we self-disclose more to others, they, reciprocally, disclose more to us.

An inability to self-disclose, on the other hand, can result in the death of a relationship. One common explanation for divorce given by women is their need to self-disclose. Divorced women are increasingly identifying their own lack of opportunity to express who they are as the cause of the breakup of their marriages. Without opportunities for self-disclosure, relationships appear to be doomed to shallowness, superficiality, or death.

To Establish More Positive Attitudes toward Ourselves and Others

In an article entitled "Shy Murderers," psychologists Lee, Zimbardo, and Bertholf discuss people who are overcontrolled and shy, and who, because of their frustration, attack others. They suggest these people need to learn how to express feelings directly to others. They continue:

> The social skills we've outlined should be learned by every child as a normal part of socialization. Children should be encouraged to express their feelings and to like themselves. They should come to see other people as sources of positive regard and interest, not as critical, negative evaluators who might reject them. They, and we, must be seen *and* heard.[20]

Figure 8.1 To whom do female teenagers confide? Copyright 1989, *USA Today.* Reprinted with permission.

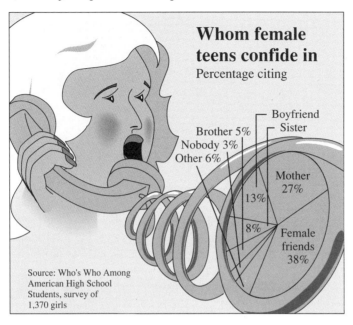

Figure 8.2 To whom do male teenagers confide? Copyright 1989, *USA Today.* Reprinted with permission.

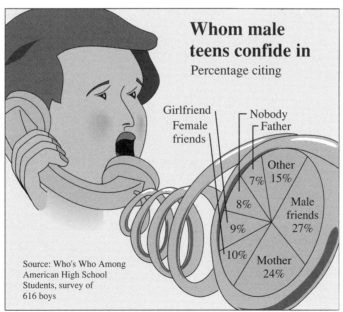

Both positive and negative self-disclosure can result in more positive attitudes about ourselves and others. If we disclose positive information about ourselves, we share the joy we feel about ourselves. When we tell others about our hopes and dreams, when we share happy moments, and when we recall exciting experiences, we feel encouraged. Others reinforce our feelings by offering their support, enthusiasm, and encouragement.

Although it may seem paradoxical, negative self-disclosure can also result in more positive attitudes about ourselves and others. When we are able to expose our negative qualities, our mistakes, our failings, and our shortcomings to others, and when others are able to do the same with us, we recognize we are all fallible. No one is perfect. We become more understanding and forgiving, and we develop more positive attitudes about all humankind.

Interference with Self-Disclosure

If self-disclosure is an aspect of interpersonal communication important to the way we view ourselves and others, we should consider why we are often unwilling to self-disclose to others. In general, we can say people are reluctant to self-disclose because of their negative feelings about themselves or their negative feelings about others. In other words, they do not respect themselves, they do not trust others, or both.

Many writers have discussed the risk involved in self-disclosure. For example, in *The Shoes of the Fisherman,* Morris L. West wrote:

> It costs so much to be a full human being that there are very few who have the enlightenment or the courage to pay the price. . . . One has to abandon altogether the search for security and reach out to the risk of living with both arms. One has to embrace the world like a lover. One has to accept pain as a condition of existence. One has to court doubt and darkness as the cost of knowing. One needs a will stubborn in conflict, but apt always to total acceptance of every consequence of living and dying.[21] (Reprinted by permission of William Morrow & Company, Inc. from *The Shoes of the Fisherman* by Morris L. West. Copyright © 1963 by Morris L. West.)

In *Why Am I Afraid to Tell You Who I Am?* John Powell writes he asked a number of people the question, "Why are you afraid to tell me who you are?" The response of one of his friends was to the point. He answered, "Because if I tell you who I am, you may not like who I am, and that's all that I have."[22] In essence, his friend was stating he did not respect himself enough to trust others with the information. Frequently, our lack of positive feelings about ourselves or about others contributes to our inability to self-disclose.

We are probably taught very early in our lives to avoid self-disclosure. The same kinds of responses that interfere with our self-awareness (see chapter 3) contribute to our difficulty in self-disclosing. Our parents taught us positive

Self-disclosure may be avoided because of people's negative feelings about themselves or about others.

self-disclosure was bragging. Significant others responded negatively when we made negative self-disclosures. The message we seemed to hear was self-disclosure should be avoided.

Men and women might avoid disclosure for different reasons. One study suggested men avoid self-disclosure in order to maintain control over their relationships, while women avoid self-disclosure in order to avoid personal hurt.[23] Another investigation showed men were shown to disclose more to strangers and casual acquaintances, while women were more willing to disclose to intimates. The authors state stereotypically successful men are expected to compete and win, and competitiveness is not conducive to intimacy. They conclude one form of winning is exploiting another person's weakness, so men may cut themselves off from others in order not to expose their vulnerability.[24]

Two communication behaviors are related to our unwillingness to self-disclose. If we feel insecure about ourselves, we may be overly defensive. If we are unsure of our own responses and believe others are superior to us, we may be **nonassertive.**

Defensiveness, the tendency to protect oneself against danger or injury, was mentioned in connection with feedback and listening in chapter 4. We observed in chapter 4 that defensiveness may occur when individuals receive negative feedback, and they may not listen effectively to others because of their defensive posture. Defensiveness is also relevant to self-disclosure.

Table 8.2

Defensive versus Supportive Communication Behaviors

Defensive Behaviors	Supportive Behaviors
1. Evaluation	1. Descriptive statements
2. Control	2. Problem orientation
3. Strategy	3. Spontaneity
4. Neutrality	4. Empathy
5. Superiority	5. Equality
6. Certainty	6. Provisionalism

Defensiveness may occur because we believe the kind of person we are is not consistent with the kind of person we are supposed to be. In other words, our "real" self is discrepant from our "idealized" self. The difference between these two selves causes us to feel uneasy because we are concerned we will show others our "real" self and be discounted.

Six behaviors have been identified as contributing to defensiveness in individuals. These behaviors and their counterparts, which lead to a supportive communication climate, are listed in table 8.2. Let us consider each of these categories in more depth.

1. *Evaluation* refers to judgmental, evaluative statements as contrasted with *descriptive statements*. "You are doing failing work" is a highly evaluative statement that invites a defensive response. "Your paper was graded lower because of one run-on, two fused, and one incomplete sentence" is a more descriptive statement. You will hurt fewer feelings and get in a lot fewer difficulties with others if you communicate with description and observation instead of evaluation and inferences.

2. *Control* refers to commands, statements that say others must do as you do or as you say. "If you would study as I do, you would get better grades" is an example of a control statement. The parallel supportive behavior is *problem orientation*. Problem orientation suggests that a number of alternatives are possible and you can find a good solution together. "What do you think you could do to improve your grades?" or "What could I do to help you gain higher grades?" are examples of this method.

3. *Strategy* implies an element of manipulation in assuming a defensive posture toward others. The term *strategy* also suggests that an idea was generated for protection as a reason for one's behavior. Late for a lunch appointment, the defensive person might decide on a strategy that will cover the *faux pas* by saying, "I had a long distance call that held me up for ten minutes." The alternative supportive behavior, called *spontaneity*, suggests a more honest expression, such as, "I'm sorry I am late. I don't have some great excuse; I just lost track of the time. I apologize."

4. *Neutrality* reflects a lack of interest or concern for another person. Unresponsiveness or statements, such as "I could care less" or "That's your problem" are examples. On the other end of this continuum is *empathy* in which you try to adopt the other person's perspective. "I know how you must feel" or "I have an idea what you could try" are examples of empathy.

5. *Superiority* implies that what you have to say is somehow better, more important, or more effective than what someone else has to say. "You will see that I am right" and "Glad to see that you are catching up" are examples of superiority. *Equality* is the supportive mode in which the other person is treated as a respected human being. "None of us has all the answers" and "by working together we can both do better" suggest equality.

6. *Certainty* implies that you have all the answers and that others are simply at fault for not recognizing it. Your words sound like commandments, perfect and chipped in stone. "I can't help it that those fools didn't vote for the best person—me" is an example of certainty. *Provisionalism,* at the other end of the continuum, suggests that you are not infallible, that you do not know who is at fault, and that there may be a number of "right answers."[25] "There were three strong candidates, and maybe I need to try harder next time" would be an example of provisionalism. Some words that suggest provisionalism are *perhaps, maybe, might,* and *possibly*—to name a few.

Defensiveness may be a regular response pattern resulting from strong negative feelings about self, or it may be a function of current statements from others. Occasionally feeling defensive as a result of people making evaluative, controlling, strategic, neutral, superior, or certainty statements is a natural response. However, recognizing that you respond defensively may assist you in altering your behavior in these occasional circumstances.

We may dismiss occasional defensiveness on the basis that it occurs on rare occasions, it occurs in response to another person's comments, or it is not overly destructive to effective communication. Regular defensiveness, however, can be a problem. Never being open and honest in communication can lead to shallow interpersonal relationships and a distrust of others. Further, regular defensiveness can lead to a communication climate in which people learn to expect such behaviors as evaluation, control, strategy, neutrality, superiority, and certainty. If you feel you use defensiveness as a regular response to others, you may want to consider ways to overcome your negative feelings about yourself to be free of the potential negative effects of defensiveness in your communication behavior.

While defensiveness should be avoided and supportiveness encouraged, **assertiveness,** the ability to communicate feelings and ideas directly and honestly, is desirable. People with strong self-concepts, high self-esteem, and good verbal skills do not invite others to speak for them, allow others to say what their feelings should be, or disregard their feelings and ideas. Marginalized people, powerless people, and timid people are the common victims of unassertiveness; they find the world always in other's control—including how they are supposed to feel.

Assertive people own their feelings, that is, they are willing to say what they think and how they feel. Unassertive people avoid saying what they think. They might say, "Well, I've heard other people say they don't like him," or "Republicans believe in the pro-life position" instead of owning up to feelings and thoughts by saying "I don't like him" or "I believe in the pro-life position." Assertive people tell others, even those with power over them, what their expectations, problems, and feelings are. Otherwise, the other person assumes that everything is satisfactory, and nothing is done about problems that need solutions and feelings that remain hurt.

People in service roles and helping professions—mothers, nurses, sales personnel, and human services workers—often spend all of their time serving others without having their needs met. Service to others and even sacrifice are noble activities, but they may be unhealthy if they inspire undermining, resentment, and anger. Everyone has rights and assertive people act to support their rights. However, you also have to avoid being overly assertive or aggressive.

Aggressiveness is assertiveness carried to an extreme, standing up for your rights at the expense of others, caring about your needs but no one else's. Aggressiveness might help you get your way a few times, but ultimately, others will avoid you and let their resentment show. Both aggressive and unassertive people may suffer from a negative self-concept. Both have trouble with self-disclosure. They may feel that they have to overpower others to get their way. Unfortunately, their intense competitiveness often denies them the acceptance they seek.

Interpersonal Communication with Friends

With millions of people in this world, how do we decide which few should be our friends? How are we attracted to them? Why do we cultivate a relationship with them? How does communication figure into the equation?

First, let us examine how we select our friends. **Proximity** or location is obvious but important. You are not going to have a friend from all those places you have never been. You are most likely to find your friends where you spend most of your time. For this reason, a roommate can easily become a friend. People who go to the same religious services, belong to the same social clubs, or are members of the same gang are most likely to become friends. People in the same major, dormitory, cafeteria, car pool, and part of the seating chart are also likely candidates. To underline the potency of proximity, consider the observation that changes in location (high school to college and college to job) often changes our pattern of friendships.

Second, we select from all the people we see the ones we find high in **social attractiveness,** a feature that takes three forms: task, social, and physical.[26] In other words, a person who is desirable to work with, seems to have "social value" in that others also show interest in him or her, and physically looks good to us is socially attractive.[27] Because of perceptual differences, you will not be looking for the same person as everyone else. In fact, someone who is "too good looking" may be perceived as unattainable, as inviting too many competitors, or as too difficult to sustain a relationship with as a friend.

Responsiveness is another feature of attraction. Not everyone responds positively to us, but someone who does is likely to get our attention. Few characteristics are more attractive than someone who actively listens to us, thinks our jokes are funny, finds our vulnerabilities wonderful, and our faults amusing. In short, we practically never select our friends from among those who dislike us, and we almost always find our friends. People who like us respond positively.

Similarity is another feature of attractiveness. Our friends might look like us, act like us, or think like us. Whatever we consider most important is the similarity we seek, so some friends are bound by their interests, others by their ideology, and still others by their mutual likes and dislikes. A hard core environmentalist is unlikely to be close personal friends with a developer, and the developer is likely to select friends from people in the same business, country club, and suburb. Thousands of people find their friends in the same circle where they work: clerical workers with clerical workers, managers with managers, and bosses with bosses. Similarity is a powerful attracter.

Complementarity is still another feature of attractiveness. Where similarity matches interests, likes and dislikes, and roles, complementarity seems more matched with personality. Because you a slightly shy, your friend may be assertive, and she is assertive for you. The math-loving engineer finds friendship with the people-loving communication major who takes care of the engineer's social life, while the engineer helps his friend with math courses. Having friends who are too much alike can result in competitiveness that destroys the friendship.

"We distinguish between friendships and acquaintanceships," according to a current text on interpersonal communication, "on the basis of choice and of positive regard. We choose our friends; we do not accidently have friendships."[28] Another truism, relevant here, is the old statement: "You can't make friends; you have to be a friend, and then others will make you a friend."

Friendship is characterized by a host of qualities. Friends are available, they share in your activities, they care about you and the relationship, they disclose personal information, they are loyal, and they demonstrate understanding.[29] Notice that all these characteristics operate through verbal and nonverbal communication. You can show availability and loyalty only by physically being there for a friend. You can self-disclose and show understanding only by talking and listening. Communication between people is what friendship is all about.

To summarize the findings on friendship, we will turn to a study that revealed some basic rules of behavior:

> The most consistently held rules indicate that friends are expected to (1) share news of success with each other, (2) show emotional support for each other, (3) volunteer to help in times of need, (4) strive to make each other happy while in each other's company, (5) demonstrate trust in each other, and (6) stand up for each other in their absence. It seems that friendships do involve a certain degree of commitment and trust in each other's unconditional support.[30]

Improving Communication in Interpersonal Relationships

We all want to have successful interpersonal relationships. We want to be able to trust others and to self-disclose to them. We want to be able to handle conflict and to use conflict resolution techniques that are mutually satisfying. Nonetheless, countless people find themselves in dissatisfying and unhappy relationships.

The Possibilities for Improvement

Can we improve our communication in interpersonal relationships? Until relatively recently, many people felt we could not learn to relate more effectively to others. Today, most individuals feel such a possibility does exist. Are such changes easy? Generally, they are not. We should not expect to take an introductory course in communication and solve all of our relational problems. Self-help books that promise instant success will probably result only in permanent disillusionment. Courses on assertiveness training, relaxation techniques, and marital satisfaction provide only part of the answer.

If we wish to improve our communication within our interpersonal relationships, we must have a commitment to learning a variety of communication skills. We must understand the importance of perceptual differences among people, the role of self-concept in communication, the nature of verbal language, and the role of nonverbal communication. We must be willing to share ourselves with others as we self-disclose, and we must be willing to attempt to understand another person through careful and conscientious listening. In addition, we must recognize that, even when we thoroughly understand these concepts and are able to implement them in our behavior, our interactions with others may not be successful. Communication is dependent on the interaction between two communicators, and one person cannot guarantee its success. Others may have conflicting goals, different perspectives, or less ability to communicate competently.

Interpersonal conflict is inevitable in relationships and may be destructive or constructive.

Learning individual communication concepts and specific communication skills is essential to effective interaction. We also need to understand the impact of these skills. For example, we know we do not communicate at home the way we do in the classroom. Self-disclosure, which is especially appropriate and important within the family context, may be out of place in the classroom. Preparation and planning are important in an interview, but they may be seen as manipulative in a conversation between a husband and wife.

Behavioral Flexibility

In addition to communication concepts, skills, and settings, our interactions may be greatly enhanced by an underlying approach to communication behavior called behavioral flexibility. **Behavioral flexibility** is defined as "the ability to alter behavior in order to adapt to new situations and to relate in new ways when necessary."[31] Behavioral flexibility allows you to relax and let your guard down when you are with friends and allows you to be your formal self while interviewing for a job. The key to behavioral flexibility may be self-monitoring, always being conscious of the effect of your words on this audience in this context.

Flexibility is important in a variety of fields. For example, biologists and botanists have demonstrated that extinction of certain living things often occurs because of an organism's inability to adapt to changes in the environment. Psychologists have suggested women and men who are **androgynous**—who hold both male and female traits—are more successful in their interactions than are people who are unyieldingly masculine or absolutely feminine. Flexibility in our psychological gender roles is more useful than a static notion of what it means to be a man or a woman in our culture. For instance, if you are a single parent, you may be called upon to behave in a loving and nurturing way to your child, regardless of your biological gender. If your goal is to be a successful manager in a large corporation, you may have to exhibit competitiveness, assertiveness, and a task orientation, regardless of your biological gender. As you move from interactions with co-workers to interactions with your family and friends, you may need to change from traditionally "masculine" behaviors to those that have been considered "feminine."

Behavioral flexibility is especially important in interpersonal communication today because relationships between people are in constant flux. For example, the family structure has gone through sharp changes in recent years. In addition, the United States today has a growing older population. Changes in the labor force also require new skills and different ways of interacting with others. People travel more often and move more frequently. As a result of these types of changes, people may interact differently today than in the past.

What kinds of changes might you expect in your own life that will affect your relationships with others? You may change your job ten or more times. You may move your place of residence even more frequently. You probably will be married at least once, and possibly two or three times. You probably will have one child or more. You will experience loss of family members through death and dissolution of relationships. You may have a spouse whose needs conflict with your needs. Other family members may view the world differently than you and challenge your perceptions. When your life appears to be most stable and calm, unexpected changes will occur.

How could behavioral flexibility assist you through these changes? A flexible person has a large repertoire or set of behaviors from which to draw. This individual is confident about sharing messages with others and about understanding the messages that others provide. The flexible person is able to self-disclose when appropriate but does not use this ability in inappropriate contexts. The flexible person can demonstrate listening skills but is not always the one who is listening. The flexible person can show concern for a child who needs assistance, can be assertive on the job, can be yielding when another person needs to exercise control, and can be independent when called on to stand alone. The flexible person does not predetermine one set of communication behaviors he or she will always enact. The flexible person is not dogmatic or narrow-minded in interactions with others.

Behavioral Flexibility

For each of the three situations given, suggest how a behaviorally flexible person and a person who is not behaviorally flexible might respond.

1. You are a man who believes women and men are different and men should be the final arbiter of decisions. Your wife believes the two of you should reach decisions together by talking about the situation until a solution is determined. How might you respond to your wife if you were behaviorally flexible? How would you respond if you were behaviorally inflexible?

2. You are a woman who cares a great deal about children. As a consequence, you take a job in a day-care center. You find you form many attachments to the children who come each day and you suffer a certain amount of anguish and sadness each time one of the children is moved to a different school. You try to resolve the problem by becoming even closer to the new children who enroll. However, you know this is no solution since these children too will at some time leave the day-care center. What would you do if you were behaviorally flexible? What would you do if you were behaviorally inflexible?

3. You are a person who likes to date only one individual at a time. You have had several fairly long-term relationships, but each relationship has ended with the other person gradually fading out of the picture. You do not know why others leave you, but you feel a certain amount of distress that you cannot maintain a relationship. What would you do if you were behaviorally flexible? What would you do if you were behaviorally inflexible?

It is also important to remember that changes are not always negative. In fact, a great deal of change is positive. For instance, when we graduate from college, the changes that occur are generally perceived as positive. When we enter into new relationships, we generally encounter positive change.

Change is stressful, however, even when it is positive. Nonetheless, we cannot remain the same; we must change. As Gail Sheehy, author of *Passages: Predictable Crises of Adult Life,* writes:

> We must be willing to change chairs if we want to grow. There is no permanent compatibility between a chair and a person. And there is no one right chair. What is right at one stage may be restricting at another or too soft.[32]

Summary

In this chapter, we examined interpersonal relationships, one context in which people communicate with each other. Interpersonal relationships are associations between two or more people who are interdependent, who use some consistent patterns of interaction, and who have interacted for some period of time. We establish interpersonal relationships for a variety of reasons, including to understand more about ourselves, to understand more about others, to understand our world, to fulfill our needs, and to increase and enrich our positive experiences. Relationships go through definable stages of development, maintenance, and deterioration, which affect self-disclosure.

Self-disclosure consists of verbal and nonverbal intentional statements about ourselves that other people are unlikely to know. Self-disclosure is important in interpersonal relationships because when we tell others about ourselves, we become closer to them and are able to establish more meaningful relationships. Self-disclosure also allows us to establish more positive attitudes about ourselves and others. Women and men exhibit different self-disclosure patterns. Some people choose not to self-disclose because they have negative feelings about themselves, do not trust others, or both. Two communication behaviors related to an unwillingness to self-disclose are defensivness and nonassertiveness.

Communication can be improved in interpersonal relationships but it is not a simple matter. In addition to understanding communication concepts, skills, and settings, we need to develop behavioral flexibility. Behavioral flexibility refers to our ability to alter our behavior in order to adapt to new situations and to relate in new ways when necessary. Interpersonal relationships are constantly changing, and individuals who wish to be successful in them must demonstrate flexibility.

Key Terms

affection   The need to be cared for by others; one of the three basic interpersonal needs satisfied through interaction with others.

aggressiveness   Standing up for one's rights at the expense of others.

androgynous   The term used to describe an individual who possesses stereotypically female and male characteristics.

assertiveness   The ability to communicate our feelings, attitudes, and beliefs honestly and directly; a communication skill associated with a positive self-concept.

avoiding   The ninth stage of Knapp's relationship development model that is characterized by a reluctance to interact.

bargaining   An interaction that occurs when two parties attempt to reach an agreement on what each should give and receive in a transaction between them; may be explicit and formal, or implicit and informal.

behavioral flexibility   The ability to alter behavior in order to adapt to new situations and to relate in new ways when necessary.

bonding   The fifth stage of Knapp's relationship development model where partners commit to each other.

circumscribing   The seventh stage of Knapp's relationship development model marked by a decrease in interaction duration and depth.

complementarity   The idea that we sometimes select as friends people whose strengths are our weaknesses.

complementary relationships Relationships in which each person supplies something the other person or persons lack; relationships based on differences rather than on similarities.

control   The ability to influence others, our environment, and ourselves; one of the three basic interpersonal needs satisfied through interaction with others.

cost-benefit theory   A theory of interpersonal relationships that suggests we alter our relationships with others on the basis of a consideration of the costs and benefits involved.

defensiveness   Protecting and supporting our ideas and attitudes against attack by others; induced by the feeling that the self and validity of self-expression are threatened.

differentiation   The sixth stage of Knapp's relationship development model where partners emphasize their individual differences rather than their similarities.

experimenting   The second stage of Knapp's relationship development model where partners attempt to discover information about the other.

inclusion   The need to become involved with others; one of the three basic interpersonal needs satisfied through interaction with others.

initiating   The short beginning period of an interaction. This is the first stage of Knapp's model of relationship development.

integrating   The fourth stage of Knapp's relationship development model where partners become more aware of each other and actively participate in the relationship.

intensifying   The third stage of Knapp's relationship development model where partners become more aware of each other and actively participate in the relationship.

interpersonal relationships   The association of two or more people who are interdependent, who use some consistent patterns of interaction, and who have interacted for some period of time.

nonassertiveness   Associated with a negative self-concept and indicates an inability to stand up for one's own rights, or, to stand up for oneself in a dysfunctional way.

proximity   A person or object's physical location.

relational deterioration   The process by which relationships de-escalate.

relational development   The process by which relationships grow.

relational maintenance The process by which people attempt to keep their relationship at an acceptable level of intimacy.

responsiveness The idea that we tend to select our friends from people who demonstrate positive interest in us.

self-disclosure Verbal and nonverbal statements we make about ourselves that are intentional and that the other person or persons are unlikely to know.

similarity The idea that our friends are usually people who like or dislike the same things we do; our friends tend to look, act, and think as we do.

social attractiveness A concept that includes physical attractiveness, how desirable a person is to work with, and how interested others are in a person.

social penetration theory A theory that explains how relationships develop and deteriorate through the exchange of intimate information.

stagnating The eighth stage of Knapp's relationship development model that is marked by a lack of activity. Interaction during this stage is awkward and difficult.

symmetrical relationships Relationships between people who mirror each other or who are highly similar.

terminating The tenth and final stage of Knapp's relationship development model. At this stage the couple demonstrates both distance and disassociation.

uncertainty principle The principle that suggests that, when we initially meet others, we know little about them, and we rid ourselves of this uncertainty by drawing inferences from the physical data with which we are presented.

c h a p t e r 9

Intercultural and Co-cultural Communication

C ultural and co-cultural communication is the topic of this chapter. You will learn how assimilation and accommodation perspectives have helped us envision our development as a country. You will discover how our frequent interactions with other cultures and co-cultures are affecting our society; how co-languages develop within a group; the role of argot, jargon, and slang; the meaning of coenetics; potential problems that occur in intercultural communication—ethnocentrism, stereotyping, assumed similarity and denial of differences, to name a few; and some strategies for improving intercultural communication. When you have completed the chapter and applied what you have learned, you should feel more comfortable understanding and sharing through intercultural communication.

What will you learn?

When you have read and thought about this chapter, you will be able to answer the following questions:

1. Why has the world become a "global village"?

2. What is the difference between the assimilation and the accommodation perspectives on diversity?

3. Do you think this country is in an assimilation mode, an accommodation mode, or some other mode?

4. What is culture and how does it affect communication?

5. What is a co-culture, and what are some examples of co-cultures in your locale?

6. What are co-languages, and what are some examples that you know about?

7. Can you explain the term *coenetics* and relate it to the discussion of nonverbal communication?

8. What are some problems that often occur in intercultural communication?

9. What are some strategies you can use to avoid, overcome, or solve problems that can occur in intercultural communication?

10. What can you do in your daily life to improve relationships with people from other cultures and co-cultures?

In the 21st century—and that's not far off—racial and ethnic groups in the U.S. will outnumber whites for the first time. The "browning of America" will alter everything in society, from politics and education to industry, values and culture.

William A. Henry III

Rap is scaring people now. But if you remember back to the '60s and '70s, when everybody became hippies and had their own dress and music, people got scared. It was just that kids wanted their own identity. They wanted to be noticed, they wanted to be understood. All of this [now] is just people crying out for help.[1]

Deonna McWilliams, 15, a student at Manhattan's Cathedral High

I think whites really need to listen [to rap]. They're the ones who don't know the message.[2]

Scott Smith, 18, a new graduate from the Collegiate School in Manhattan

T o be an effective communicator means understanding and sharing with people from various racial, ethnic, and cultural backgrounds. This chapter stresses the importance of communicating in an ever changing world, the influence of culture on communication, and the types and functions of co-languages. In addition, this chapter will identify potential problems and will suggest strategies for improving your communication effectiveness.

Intercultural Communication

Intercultural communication refers to the process of understanding and sharing meaning with individuals from various cultures. Although some scholars make fine distinctions among interracial, interethnic, crosscultural, contracultural, and transcultural acts,[3] we will use the term *intercultural communication* to mean any communication between persons of different cultures. The following are some examples:

- The Director of a local advertising agency negotiates student internships with an administrator from the University de Paris.
- The Vice-President of General Motors discusses a project with a staff member from a Japanese investment company.
- Two new students at a state university—one from Mexico and the other from Canada—are assigned as roommates.
- A new elementary school teacher—born, reared, and educated in a small town in Idaho populated by European-American Mormons—accepts a position with the Cleveland public school system.
- An African-American woman brings her significant other—a man from Uganda—home to meet her family in Oakland.
- A newly-hired Italian American is assigned to supervise a staff consisting of Korean-American, African-American, Filipino-American, and Puerto Rican administrators.

Not long ago, intercultural communication involved only missionaries, jet-setting business executives, foreign correspondents, and some national political figures. These individuals were few in number. Most people in the United States interacted with other people like themselves. Now, however, developments in technology and shifts in demographics have created a society where intercultural communication is nearly inevitable.

Today, communication satellites, digital switches, and fax machines instantly connect all parts of the world. Traveling to other countries once took days, and it is now possible to make the same trip in a matter of hours. New developments in technology and population shifts have created one world community. A wide variety of careers—oil workers, business people, professors, politicians, developers, and marketers—require intercultural communication skills. We have truly become the **global village,** described years ago by

Our increasingly diverse society invites us to learn how to communicate with co-cultures.

Marshall McLuhan, where people cannot avoid one another. No nation, group, or culture is isolated. Contact with people who are different from us is something for which each person must be prepared.

The United States, Diversity, and Changing Demographics

Large changes are occurring in the demographic composition of this country. The **melting pot theory** portrayed the United States as a country where individuals lost their original heritage and identified themselves instead as Americans. The Latin slogan *E pluribus unum,* or "one formed from many," promoted the **assimilation** perspective that was prevalent in our country. Assimilation refers to the absorbing of cultural groups into a dominant culture. New immigrants from Ireland were expected to relinquish their Irish culture and blend into American society. A contrasting view has many ethnic groups entering the country with an **accommodation** perspective. Accommodation refers to a willingness by the dominant culture to accept cultural difference in others. According to this perspective, a degree of autonomy in each group is important to the survival of the whole culture. Under accommodation, the Irish keep their Irish heritage as they are incorporated into the dominant American culture.

The melting pot perspective represented a process where all groups would blend together to form a new group—Americans. The U.S. was viewed as a huge melting pot.

The melting pot metaphor or assimilation perspective depicts an American society that blends different ethnic groups to make Americans of them all. With assimilation, ethnic groups are like butter, cream, sugar, and cocoa that when blended become a completely different thing—fudge.

On the other hand, the accommodation perspective depicts an American society in which different ethnic groups blend without losing their particular flavor. In other words they become a stew in which the carrots, potatoes, celery, and meat become a stew (i.e., Americans) but not by giving up their uniqueness.

The metaphor of the melting pot is a valuable one, but if all the people are the same flavor our society becomes pretty boring. "Variety is the spice of life" is the contrasting view. Appreciation of variety would seem a good assimilation perspective for America, a country with many cultures that contribute to what it means to be American. Each culture is incorporated into a larger entity and allowed to maintain its distinct "flavor." In short, we need to maintain a balance between the assimilation and accommodation perspectives.

The United States population is experiencing drastic changes in its composition. By the middle of the twenty-first century, people of color may compose the majority of U.S. citizens. A recent cover story in *Time* magazine estimates that one out of four Americans presently defines himself or herself as "Hispanic or nonwhite."[4] These projections assume current immigration trends and population growth. By the end of the twentieth century, the Hispanic/Latino population is expected to grow by 22 percent, the Asian population by 21 percent, the Africans in America by almost 12 percent, and European American population by a little more than 2 percent. Figures 9.1 and 9.2 reflect these projections.

Demographic changes in this country will affect politics, education, government, and business. *U.S. News and World Report* states that in 1980 white males comprised 52 percent of the work force. In 1986, that percentage was reduced to 43 percent, and it continues to shrink.[5] The same article projects that by 1995 over 75 percent of workers entering the job market will be minorities—women and people of color. With the changes in demographics, technology, and global communication, instances of intercultural communication will become commonplace.

Figure 9.1 Assuming that immigration trends continue, the number of non-Hispanic whites will decrease as a percentage of the total population (Projection based on United States Census figures).

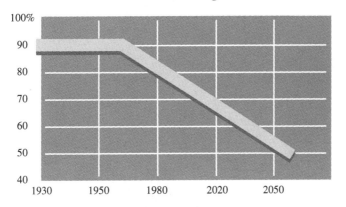

Figure 9.2 Because of immigration and/or birth rates, the Asian, Hispanics, and African Americans are growing faster, as indicated on the bar graph below (Projections based on United States Census figures).

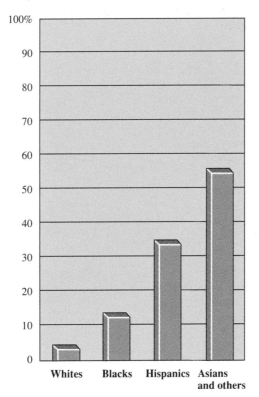

Members of a co-culture bond through language, dress, and proximity.

Cultures and Co-cultures

Culture can be defined as a system of shared beliefs, values, customs, behaviors, and artifacts that the members of a society use to cope with one another and with their world. Transmitted from generation to generation through social learning, culture can also be seen as the mechanism that allows human beings to make sense of the world around them. Cultures include a wide variety of races, ethnic groups, and nationalities, not just international cultures from outside the United States. However, the definition offered above can also relate to a number of other groups of people that may be considered a distinct "culture."

In the United States, a number of co-cultures exist based on race, religion, economics, age, gender, and sexual orientation. **Co-cultures** involve groups of persons united by a common element who live in a culture operating within a dominant culture. We use the term *co-culture* rather than the more common term *subculture* because the latter implies that these groups are somehow less than or inferior to the dominant culture. In the United States, the Anglo-Saxon, male, middle-upper class is the dominant culture. Examples of co-cultures are Cuban Americans, Korean Americans, Appalachians, Baptists, and adolescents. Some experts would add the hearing and visually impaired, gay males, and lesbian women to name a few.[6] The premise of Deborah Tannen's book, *You Just Don't Understand: Women and Men in Conversation,* is that women function in a distinct co-culture.[7]

While these people live in the dominant American culture, they experience a life which differs from that of the Anglo-Saxon, male, middle-class culture. Their life experiences seem worlds away from typical interactions that occur in the larger society. An individual can belong to a number of co-cultures. For example the same person can be identified as an American (culture), an African American (co-culture), a Baptist (co-culture), and an avid soccer fan (co-culture).

The distinctions between cultures and co-cultures are clear to individuals who live in a co-culture. However, for members of the dominant society, the description of a co-culture can appear unimportant. Some co-cultures may seem clear—Puerto Rican Americans, Californians or Roman Catholics—while others may appear not so clear or even insignificant—academic departments, musicians, soccer players, and bridge clubs. However, if an individual is unaware of the unique cultural experiences of each co-culture, serious communication problems may arise. We turn next to a discussion of co-languages and coenetics, the verbal and nonverbal communication of a co-culture.

Co-languages

Obvious problems can occur when individuals are speaking different languages. Not as obvious are problems that occur when people use different co-languages. These exist within a co-culture and enable group members to communicate effectively with each other. **Co-languages** refer to specialized languages used by co-cultures. Within the larger society that employs a dominant language (in this country's case standard English), a co-culture creates a specific language adapted to its experiences. As with the dominant language, co-languages vary and change over time, but they always perform some function for the group.

Functions of Co-languages

Co-languages serve two primary functions for members of a co-culture. They facilitate effective communication and provide a sense of belonging and identity with the group. Specific examples will help clarify the functions of co-languages.

First, co-languages allow effective communication among members. The co-culture creates convenient terms to identify, classify, and describe their unique experiences and relationships. Words often are substituted for longer phrases. For example, communication scholars speak of "high comm apps" for "high communication apprehensives," SCA for the Speech Communication Association, and CSMC for *Critical Studies in Mass Communication.* The co-language allows efficient communication.

Second, a co-language creates a sense of belonging or identity with the group. Many new words, especially in the medical and scientific fields are created to describe new ideas and common experiences. To a physician a bruise is "a subcutaneous hematoma." A gang will have an entire vocabulary to talk about weapons, drugs, and the legal system. Within the co-culture, the language is effective and efficient. To outsiders it is supposed to be confusing and difficult to translate. Once the terms are adopted by the dominant culture, they are quickly changed by the co-culture, so it can maintain its uniqueness. By the time a Wall Street banker starts using the word *fresh*, the co-culture has dropped the language.

Specialized languages are used for mutual identification, alienation of non-members, and privacy. One example of co-language is the specialized language used by young people. OP-language was a special language used by the children in some neighborhoods. The key to OP-language was to add the suffix "op" to each letter as the word was spelled out. Syllables were included as normal. "Call me later" became "cop-a-lop-lop mop-e lop-a-top-e-rop." OP-language revealed who was cool and who was not. Parents, teachers, and "noncool" kids were out of the loop. OP-language demonstrated identification, alienation of nonmembers, and communication privacy. Three examples of co-languages—argot, jargon, and slang—are explained here to illustrate the different purposes served.

Argot

Argot refers to a specialized vocabulary used by a particular group of nonprofessional people (figure 9.3). Argot is also known as **cant.** Specialized language used by drug dealers, prostitutes, truck drivers, and CB operators are examples of co-language. The drug culture changes its vocabulary too fast for ordinary mortals to keep up, but cocaine has been called "coke," "blow," and "snow" in the past. Marijuana is "grass," "reefers," "joints," "Mary Jane," "herb," and "weed." Street people call police "the man," "getting pinched" means getting arrested, and "stretch" refers to the length of a prison sentence.

Argot in its purest form is not understood by people outside the co-culture. However, media portrayals of co-cultures have increased public awareness of argot. Again, co-cultures change their specialized co-language when it is adopted by the dominant culture.

Jargon

Jargon refers to the technical language used by a particular trade, profession, or group. Jargon differs from argot or cant because it is more technical and professional in nature. College professors, computer scientists, physicians, investors, and lawyers are noted for their jargon. Even professional athletes have their jargon. A water skier might say, "I made 3 at my 34 pass at 15 off,"

Figure 9.3   People are so interested in the specialized language of co-cultural groups that *Newsweek* publishes a list of them. In this case, it is the argot spoken by baseball umpires. *Newsweek*, June 15, 1992. Reprinted by permission.

BUZZWORDS

Nobody ever interviews them after the game, but umpires have plenty to say on the field. Here are some colorful terms you might hear between calls:

Rats: The players.

He loves to dance: A manager prone to arguing.

Working the stick: Home-plate duty, closest to the batwielding rats.

Working the rocking chair: Third-base duty, which is usually pretty dull.

The balloon: A chest protector.

Dusting the jewel: Cleaning off home plate.

Z-baller: A minor leaguer called up to the big league.

Breaking in the puppy: Ejecting a Z-baller.

which translates into "I made three out of fifteen attempts at 34 miles per hour." Tricks performed inside the wake are "surface tricks," barefoot starts are "deep water starts," and the tow rope is "the line."

The group's jargon facilitates communication. The vocabulary depicts their experiences and remains mysterious to others. The jargon involves vocabulary that more precisely describes specific items the co-culture frequently uses. Professionals, like other groups who use co-languages, stress the functions that this specialized language fulfills.

Slang

Slang refers to terms derived from argot that are widely known to the dominant culture but are not acceptable for use in formal settings. Slang is creative, playful, vivid, and often metaphorical language. It includes such terms as *pissed off, hammered, NOT, skeeze, slammin',* and *dis.* Commonly used on the street, these terms are regarded as too colloquial for formal written and oral communication.

An example of coenetics is this traditional Japanese greeting.

Slang is derived from argot. It is temporarily popular, then it is used less and less, and finally, it is abandoned—often before it gets into the dictionary. A few slang terms become socially acceptable expressions in the dominant culture: couch potato, booze, and psycho are examples. You should be aware that some people regard all slang terms—even the most commonly used—as inappropriate in formal settings.

Coenetics

Edward Hall, in his book *The Silent Language,* discusses the importance of recognizing both verbal and nonverbal behaviors in intercultural communication. To communicate effectively with someone from a different culture or co-culture, you must learn both the verbal and the nonverbal systems of those cultures.[8]

Coenetics is the study of culturally significant nonverbal communication. The fundamental premise of coenetics is that a nonverbal behavior in one culture may have quite a different meaning in another culture. In 1991, President Bush traveled to Australia and was photographed giving the peace sign to Australian citizens waving to his passing car. Imagine his surprise when he learned that his nonverbal sign in that culture meant the same as "flipping the bird" in America. Similarly, when President Nixon toured several Latin American countries, he gave the "A-O.K." sign nonverbally, a gesture that in many Latin American countries means "screw you." Effective intercultural communication can be greatly hampered by ignoring nonverbal behavior.

O. L. Taylor has found a number of differences in the nonverbal communication patterns of co-cultures in the United States.[9] According to Taylor, African Americans, Hispanic/Latino Americans, Native Americans, and Asian Americans have drastically different perspectives on nonverbal communication. Among the differences are the use of eye contact, enunciation, vocal volume, body movements, gestures, time, and space. The following incidents illustrate how nonverbal communication across cultures can be misinterpreted with negative consequences.

> Dr. Smith, a professor of English, noticed that one of his Japanese students, Satoshi, did not participate overtly in his writing class. Attempting encouragement, Dr. Smith casually patted Satoshi on the back. The next day, Satoshi asked Dr. Smith to sign a drop-add slip so he could switch sections. Dr. Smith was unaware that in Japanese culture, class participation is not perceived in the same way Americans see it. Furthermore, the Japanese view a slap on the back as highly insulting.

> Chris, an Italian-American student at a large Midwestern university was driving by the student center with a couple of friends when he noticed a group of African-American students standing outside and loudly greeting one another with a familiar hand gesture—a closed fist with the thumb and small finger extended. Chris, recognizing this popular gesture to mean "hang five" or "coolin'," immediately jumped up and yelled while waving the friendly gesture. Before he knew what was happening, several African-American students began yelling insults and rushed toward the car. Only later did Chris discover that the gesture was the sacred hand sign for members of the Alpha Phi Alpha Fraternity, the oldest predominantly African-American fraternity in the United States. By using this gesture without being a member of the group, he had insulted that group.

> Two European-American police officers were called to investigate a possible illegal drug deal. As soon as the officers arrived on the scene, people began to scatter in all directions. Officer, Dale McClary, began to chase a young Latino boy who turned out to be Ignacio Osio, a boy around six or seven years old. After McClary caught him, he began to ask Ignacio questions about what he was doing in that area. The officer wanted to know because

drug dealers used young boys as "runners" who often became heavily involved in the drug trafficking. Ignacio did not answer any questions; instead, he remained silent, looking at the ground. Charged with adrenalin from the chase and angry that all he had collared was a suspect who wouldn't talk, McClary's questioning grew louder, more insistent, and decidedly threatening. Tears welled in Ignacio's eyes, and he reached in his pocket for a tissue. McClary, wound tight and worried that Ignacio was armed, quickly drew his service revolver and shot him. Before Ignacio's funeral, a Latino officer explained to McClary that young Latino children are taught not to have eye contact with adults—especially when being disciplined—and not to talk back because these acts signify disrespect in their culture. Tragically, what was regarded as respect in one culture—answering questions directly when asked without looking guilty—was disrespect in another culture.

Potential Problems for Effective Intercultural Communication

Intercultural communication is subject to all of the problems that can hamper effective interpersonal communication. However, several additional problems may occur during intercultural interactions. We identify these issues to avoid problems or to reduce their effects. Keep in mind that the barriers identified here can be problematic but do not occur in every exchange.

Ethnocentrism

The largest problem that occurs during intercultural communication is the ethnocentric perspective that each person brings to the interaction (figure 9.4). **Ethnocentrism** is the belief that your own group or culture is superior to all other groups or cultures. To some extent, each of us operates from such a perspective, but problems arise when we interpret and evaluate other cultures by the norms and standards of our own culture. Generally, a lack of interaction with another culture fosters higher levels of ethnocentrism and encourages the notion that one culture is somehow superior to another. Ethnocentrism can be dangerous because it invites defensiveness on the part of the person who is being treated as in some way deficient or inferior.

Stereotyping

A **stereotype** is a belief that all members of a group are more or less alike and think and act in similar fashion. You might remember the idea better if you know that the word *stereotype* came from the printing industry where it meant a metal printing plate that could turn out multiple copies of the same

Figure 9.4 Advertising is different in other cultures as this article about Japanese advertising indicates.
© 1992 USA Today. Reprinted by permission.

INSIDERS

BEHIND THE SCENES IN THE WORLD OF BUSINESS

Japanese ads: Abstract sells

Here's a typical Japanese beer commercial. Camera focuses on staircase in house. Guy rushes down staircase, runs into kitchen, grabs two Kirin beers from the fridge, rushes back upstairs. Seconds later, he zooms down the stairs again, grabs the cat, runs back up. Cut to the final scene: guy watching fireworks from the roof, drinking beer, cat on lap. The tag line: "By the way, Kirin beer tastes really good."

No beach volleyball, no buddies, no babeacious waitresses — in fact, at the end of the spot, even the cat jumps down and walks off.

"Japanese stuff, it's fairly incomprehensible," says John Padfield, an art director for McCann-Erickson in Italy.

Consider this ad for Parco department store: a man in a business suit swimming in Tokyo Bay. The only narration: "How many hours were you alive yesterday?"

"Sometimes the ideas are very European," says Jaap Back, of the Dutch government information office, who watched a showing of 100 Japanese ads here Wednesday. "Sometimes . . . I didn't get it."

REPORTER'S NOTEBOOK

FROM THE INTERNATIONAL ADVERTISING FILM FESTIVAL IN CANNES, FRANCE

By MARTHA T. MOORE

He's not alone. Unlike Japanese products, Japanese advertising doesn't come highly recommended here.

Akira Kagami, a creative director at Dentsu, Japan's largest ad agency, summed up the attitude: "They're just too much. (Westerners) don't understand them at all. They drive them crazy."

During the screening, Kagami pointed out to a largely Western audience that in ad-saturated Japan, consumers look to ads for entertainment more than information. Music from popular ads can become hits; actors in a hot spot can become stars.

"We want people to really enjoy the commercial. The commercial is the product. The commercial is the face of the client," Kagami says.

199

words and graphics. A stereotype, as we use the word now, means multiple copies of the same kind of people who seem relatively indistinguishable from each other by people outside the group.

In one way stereotyping is unavoidable. When you think of lawyers, physicians, gardeners, and bag people a generalized image comes to mind. Stereotyping becomes troublesome in communication when people make assumptions about the individual based on their simplified notion of the group to which he or she belongs. Assuming that a physician will know what is wrong with you, that a mechanic can fix your car, or that a lawyer will win your case are some examples of positive assumptions based on stereotypes. Assuming that athletes are dimwits, blondes are empty-headed, and gay men prey on children are negative stereotypes that are injurious to individuals and groups alike.

Assumed Similarity and Denial of Differences

Stereotypes invite us to see others as if they were all alike. The other side of this coin is the **ethnocentric perspective** in which we assume not only that others think and act as we do, but they ought to do so. The ethnocentric person sees his or her own worldview as superior to others and assumes that others should see and act as he or she does. The intercultural communicator is cautious about assuming similarity and recognizes differences.

In most human exchanges, the individuals seek common ground, and to that extent, seeking similarity is a positive practice. Where it becomes troublesome is when you assume that the other person thinks as you do, believes the same things you do, and even acts as you would act. Denial of differences also causes problems. Sometimes people strive so hard to be politically correct that they psychologically deny that they are talking to someone in a wheelchair, someone with white skin, or someone who has a decidedly Spanish accent. While it is wrong to assume that a Korean American loves Korean food and knows about every Korean restaurant, it is not wrong to recognize that they are of Korean descent. It is fine to find out what you have in common with that person, but do not assume that he or she feels the same way you do about politics, racial strife, or mathematics. Denying that any differences exist may lead to misunderstandings which are easy to avoid by accepting the idea that there will be differences.

Misinterpretation of Codes

As you learned in the chapter on language, words have arbitrary meanings, multiple meanings, and continually changing meanings. **Misinterpretation of codes** refers to ambiguities or different uses of words that confuse the interpreter of the code. The inaccurate translations can occur verbally, nonverbally, or both.

Language and Race

In the aftermath of April 29, 1992, when Los Angeles burned over the legal resolution of the Rodney King incident, there was much introspection about African-American anger, brown involvement, and Anglo ignorance. Discuss in class the following quotes about co-cultural language as it occurs in music and in social policy.

> While pols cling to nice talk about a harmonious society that's just a social program away, musicians and fans, black and white, are declaring the massive schism between the races—consuming the rift as entertainment, a worldview and a beat you can dance to.[10]
>
> After nearly three decades of reflecting the promises of integration, pop music—from country to hard-core rap—has become our most pointed metaphor for volatile racial polarization. Whether the candidates get it or not, we've moved past the warm and fuzzy age of "We Are the World."[11]
>
> Our history and our present have taught us that the language we use to talk about race can vary widely from our behavior. The word *diversity*, which is in vogue these days, ought to indicate wide variety but is often used by companies, schools and universities to mean two African Americans in a group of 50 whites. These were all the code words, used principally by politicians to whip fear and ignorance into votes. . . . It's the language of stereotype, the American shorthand that keeps the discussion, and the people, circumscribed. . . ."[12]

New Englanders, for example, who attend college in the Midwest sometimes have difficulty with word usage. The New Englander uses such words as *soda, grinder, sneakers,* or *bubbler,* which the Midwesterner cannot easily interpret. The New Englander orders a soda and receives an ice cream float. The New Englander seeks a bubbler, but the Midwesterner doesn't even know he or she wants water.

Frustration and Early Termination

Effective intercultural communication can often take considerable energy, time, and commitment. Seemingly insurmountable problems, especially during early interactions, can become frustrating. Instead of investing more time in understanding the differences that cause problems, it may seem easier to ignore

Figure 9.5   A Misinterpretation of Codes?
(Reprinted with permission from *The Athens (Ohio) Messenger.*)

Activists call for board member to quit

CINCINNATI (AP)   A white school board member said he overreacted when he wrote that black families' outbursts at a high school graduation explain why black students are disciplined more often than whites.

"I very much regret that this incident diminishes in any way our pride in the achievement of our graduating seniors," Vice President William Seitz said at a school board meeting Monday night.

During the meeting, several black and white community leaders and residents demanded that Seitz resign because of a June 3 letter he wrote to a lawyer working on the school district's desegregation agreement. He copied the letter to nine district officials.

Seitz wrote in the letter that 74 percent of black families disrupted a recent graduation ceremony with screams and shouts, compared with 29 percent of white families.

He drew a parallel between those incidents and district statistics showing that black students are expelled or suspended twice as often as whites.

problems or simply to stop talking. Remember that intercultural communication invites participants to learn from each other. To stop trying to communicate is to quit learning.

A more productive strategy is to solve problems that may occur during initial interactions and use those incidents as learning experiences for the future.

Figure 9.5 appeared in a local newspaper during the summer of 1992. Read the article and keep in mind the things you have learned in this chapter on intercultural communication. How would you explain the situation in terms of coenetics and co-cultures? Some scholars, like Thomas Kochman,[13] suggest that African Americans function within a co-cultural system which is vastly different than that which European Americans use. The African-American culture is a great deal more vocal, interactive, and expressive especially in times of celebration, so the Vice President's initial response was based on a misinterpretation of the nonverbal codes used by the African-American families.

Strategies to Improve Intercultural Communication

Some individuals would like a "Ten Easy Steps" approach to ensure effective intercultural communication, but there is no foolproof plan to guarantee effective communication. The strategies presented here are offered as possible ways to avoid potential problems.

Practice supportive communication behaviors. The same skills you learned in earlier chapters have application here. Supportive behaviors, such as problem orientation, spontaneity, empathy, and provisionalism can encourage success in intercultural interactions. Defensive behaviors will hamper effectiveness.

Practice personal self-assessment. One of the first steps in improving your intercultural skills is an honest assessment of your own communication style, prejudices, ethnocentrism, and stereotyping. Understanding the other person must begin with a self-analysis of who you are. Often ignored, this strategy of self-assessment is crucial to understanding others. Because your identity is something you take for granted, asking you to define specific characteristics of yourself can be difficult. However, challenging your socialization into a particular cultural system is excellent preparation for participating in intercultural communication.

Avoid the trap of stereotyping and drawing hasty generalizations. As discussed earlier, stereotyping can be viewed as a form of "lazy communication." It is easier to rely on existing stereotypes than to discover another person's uniqueness. Sometimes a person's belonging to some category is of secondary importance even to him. Because stereotypes pervade every aspect of your life, you must consciously remember to challenge them—especially in intercultural communication.

Develop sensitivity toward diversity. A healthy communication perspective is that you can learn something from all people, and diverse populations provide ample opportunity for learning. Diversity in investments, gene pools, ideologies, and modes of thought also provide strength that is unavailable to populations that are highly homogenous. Being sensitive to differences includes interacting with them without evaluation, criticism, or ridicule. It also involves challenging ethnocentric beliefs that view others as inferior, abnormal, or unworthy of your consideration and respect.

Some communication concepts that enhance sensitivity to others include empathy, role playing, and understanding of verbal and nonverbal codes. It includes **code sensitivity,** or using verbal and nonverbal behaviors appropriate to the culture or co-culture with which you are interacting. Learning as much as you can about a culture is a good way to prepare for future interactions with members of that culture.

You should seek shared codes. The arbitrary nature of words can result in many words meaning the same thing or one word having several interpretations. Our discussion of co-languages and coenetics illustrated how verbal and nonverbal codes are influenced by culture. An effective intercultural communicator will develop a **tolerance of ambiguity,** a cognitive style that emphasizes open-mindedness about differences. It involves developing a sense of communicative flexibility. Individuals adapt communication behavior to fit different situations with which they are confronted. A key ingredient in establishing shared codes is tolerating ambiguity while you analyze which communication style to adopt during intercultural communication.

Use and encourage descriptive feedback. Feedback encourages adaptation. In intercultural communication, effective feedback is crucial. It allows us to correct, adjust, and sharpen our communication during future interactions.

During intercultural interactions, participants must encourage descriptive feedback. Both individuals must be willing to accept feedback and exhibit supportive behaviors. The feedback should be immediate, honest, specific, and clear. Using and encouraging feedback is a strategy available to both individuals in an intercultural encounter.

Open communication channels. Intercultural communication can be frustrating. One important strategy to follow during these interactions is to keep the lines of communication open. No matter how bad a situation is, it is important to remain available for future exchanges. Sometimes an interaction starts out more poorly than expected, but by following the strategies suggested in this chapter, you can overcome seemingly impossible barriers.

Summary

In this chapter, you examined intercultural communication and the effects that culture has on communication. Because of recent advances in technology and changes in demographics, instances of intercultural communication are becoming more commonplace and important.

Initially, our country's assimilation perspective, the melting pot, invited different ethnic groups to become Americans. The accommodation perspective, on the other hand, invited the dominant culture to accept differences in minority cultures that kept more of their ethnic identity. This book took the position that balance should be maintained between these contrasting perspectives: diverse groups can maintain their heritage and still become Americans.

Culture influences communication. The experiences of co-cultures are vastly different from that of the dominant culture. Their specialized languages facilitate effective communication and distinguish between members and nonmembers. Argot, jargon, and slang are examples of co-languages. Coenetics refers to the study of culturally significant nonverbal patterns.

You examined potential problems spawned by ethnocentrism, stereotyping, assumed similarity, denial of differences, misinterpretation of codes, frustration, and early termination of the interaction. An awareness of potential problems reduces the cultural barriers before they become problems.

Several strategies can improve intercultural communication. Practicing supportive behaviors, avoiding defensive behaviors, completing a self-assessment, avoiding stereotypes and hasty generalizations, developing a sensitivity toward diversity, seeking shared codes, using and encouraging feedback, and keeping lines of communication open are some strategies for improving intercultural communication. In our ever changing world, an effective communicator must possess the skills to communicate with diverse cultures and co-cultures. You should now have a more complete understanding of the relationship between culture and communication.

Key Terms

accommodation   A perspective on diversity that includes a willingness on behalf of the majority culture to accept cultural differences.

argot   A specialized language system used by nonprofessional groups.

assimilation   One perspective on diversity in which individual cultural groups are expected to transcend ancestral heritage to form a new identity with the dominant culture.

cant   A synonym for *argot.*

code sensitivity   Using verbal and nonverbal language appropriate to the cultural or co-cultural norms of the individual with whom you are communicating.

coenetics   The study of culturally significant nonverbal communication patterns.

co-cultures   Groups of people who are united by a common element and who have a culture of their own within the dominant culture.

co-languages   Specialized languages used by co-cultures to facilitate effective communication and to distinguish members from nonmembers of the group.

culture   A population characterized by socially transmitted behavior, beliefs, language, values, arts, and customs.

E pluribus unum   A Latin phrase appearing on American coins which means "one formed from many," symbolic of the assimilation perspective.

ethnocentric perspective   The assumption that not only do others think and act as we do, but they ought to do so.

ethnocentrism   The belief that your own group or culture is superior to other groups and cultures; the tendency to judge other cultures by the values of your own.

global village   The small world phenomenon engendered by improved travel and high technology communications.

intercultural communication The process of understanding and sharing meaning among individuals from different cultures.

jargon The technical language used by a particular trade, profession, or group.

melting pot theory A metaphor that views American society from the perspective of assimilation.

misinterpretation of codes Ambiguities or different uses of words that confuse the interpreter of the code.

slang A specialized language derived from argot; known to the dominant culture but not regarded as acceptable in formal discourse.

stereotype A belief about other groups or individuals based on previously formed opinions and attitudes.

tolerance of ambiguity A cognitive style that emphasizes open-mindedness about differences.

chapter 10

Small Group Communication, Leadership, and Conflict Resolution

S mall group communication is everywhere these days. Government, business, and education use it almost excessively, but everyone who is going to be anyone needs to know about it. What is small group communication? How does it work? How can you use it to make decisions and solve problems? What should we expect to happen in a small group discussion? Finally, you will learn about leadership in small group communication, styles of leadership, and some functions of leadership. When you have completed this chapter, you should be ready to practice making decisions and solving problems through groups.

W hat will you learn?

When you have read and thought about this chapter, you should be able to answer the following questions:

1. What is small group communication and when should it be used?

2. Can you define and explain norms, roles, productivity, cohesiveness, commitment, consensus, member satisfaction, and group organization?

3. What differences do male and female communication differences make in small group communication?

4. Can you distinguish among the panel, the symposium, and the forum?

5. Can you explain how small group discussion works in decision making and problem solving?

6. What are some qualities that would help you become more effective as a small group discussant?

7. Who is perceived as the leader in small group communication?

8. What are some approaches to leadership?

9. Can you explain how conflict can be constructive in small group communication?

10. Can you name and explain some types of conflict resolution?

T he average executive spends about 60 percent of his [her] time in meetings and conferences. This recent survey finding points up the fact that ability to work in and through small groups is one of the most useful skills a manager can have.[1]

Louis Cassels

W ithout leadership, there is no focus about which a number of individuals may cluster to form a group.[2]

Cecil Gibb

T he successful organization has one major attribute that sets it apart from unsuccessful organizations: dynamic and effective leadership.[3]

Paul Hersey and Kenneth Blanchard

Many of you aspire to be managers in business, industry, volunteer organizations, education or government. As a manager, you will spend much of your time in committee meetings, strategy sessions, sales conferences, information-sharing meetings, and planning sessions. Even college professors spend an average of eleven hours per week in committee meetings;[4] the managers—department chairs, directors, deans, and vice presidents—spend even more time at meetings. Generally speaking, those high on the organizational ladder spend considerably more time at meetings than do those who are lower in the hierarchy. Since many of you plan to be high on the organizational ladder, you would be wise to learn what small group communication is all about.

These meetings are what we call **small group communication,** small assemblies invited together to solve problems and make decisions. Small groups are another context of interpersonal communication which so far in this text has been concerned with dyadic or two-person groups. Because small groups are omnipresent in our democratic culture and because this may be the most important form of interpersonal communication used by college students,[5] you can be much more effective in our society if you know how they work, how they can be used for social and business reasons, who is selected to lead small group discussions, and who earns the leadership role.

Let us begin our exploration of small groups by determining what a small group is and when the small group is most appropriately used.

The Nature of Small Group Communication

Definition of Small Group Communication

Many definitions of small group communication have been proposed. Professor Jack Brilhart, now retired from the University of Nebraska at Omaha, combined elements from various definitions to present five minimal characteristics all small group communication must meet. He asserted that small group communication involves the following:

1. A sufficiently small number of people (from two to rarely more than twenty), so that each group member is aware of and has some reaction to each other group member.
2. A mutually interdependent purpose, and the success of each person is contingent upon the success of the small group in achieving this goal.
3. For each person, a sense of belonging or membership.

4. Oral interaction (not all of the interaction is oral, but a significant characteristic of a discussion group is reciprocal influence exercised by talking).
5. Behavior based on norms, values, and procedures accepted by all members.[6]

To summarize, small group communication consists of a relatively small number of persons who have a mutually interdependent purpose and a sense of belonging, demonstrate behavior based on norms and values, use procedures accepted by the group, and interact orally. We discount small numbers of people who do not have shared interests, do not communicate regularly with each other, and do not all contribute to the functioning of the group.

All small groups have two primary concerns: (1) accomplishing the task and (2) maintaining healthy relationships among the group members. Groups have distinctive tasks they accomplish: to solve a problem, to share information, to determine a policy, to clarify values, or to introduce social opportunities. Regardless of the task, all groups also have a relational function as they attempt to encourage individuals to establish and maintain positive associations with the others in the group. Group decision making is dependent on its ability to satisfy essential decision functions.[7]

Appropriate Use of Small Group Communication

Although small group communication is an essential part of our lives, we need to observe that it is most appropriate under certain conditions. Some of these conditions follow:

1. *When a variety of different ideas is preferable over a smaller number of less diverse ideas.* Individuals working together in a group setting are likely to encourage each other to think of a larger number of different ideas than will individuals attempting to generate ideas by themselves.
2. *When differing amounts and levels of information, expertise, or experience are necessary to solve the problem.* The group setting is ideal for combining people with different information, ideas, and backgrounds.
3. *When time constraints are not present.* Groups often take longer than individuals to reach a decision.
4. *When individuals desire an opportunity to be involved in the information sharing or decision making.* If people wish to be part of the decision-making process or the information-sharing opportunity, it is wise to include, rather than exclude, them from the possibility.
5. *When members' commitments are needed to implement decisions.* If decisions cannot be put into place unless most group members agree and feel some sense of commitment, a group rather than one individual or a small subgroup should be used. If a manager determines a new production schedule without consulting his or her subordinates, he or she may be surprised by the resistance that is present.

6. *When a group decision is a requirement.* If a group—rather than an individual—decision must be made, the group setting is a superior place in which to have that decision made. Asking individuals privately about their opinions will result in a different and less useful outcome than will occur if the entire group is allowed to interact. Examples of required group decisions include a jury selecting a "foreman," an ongoing group selecting a chairperson, or an intact group determining how it shall be governed.

A group is more than the sum of its members, just as a whole is more than the sum of its parts. Groups consist of people who individually have energy, information, abilities, and ideas. When these people are placed together in a group, the psychological combination leads to a level of productivity the members could not achieve if they were working alone. Small groups are useful and important. Let us consider the basic components of the small group discussion.

Concepts Important in Small Group Communication

Although the small group shares characteristics with other forms of interpersonal communication, it also has some unique features. The terms *norms, roles, productivity, cohesiveness, commitment, consensus, member satisfaction,* and *communication networks* are applied in a special way to the small group setting. Let us consider each of these concepts as it relates to the small group.

Norms

Norms refer to whatever develops as standard practice in a group. Some examples would be that the chair always starts the meeting with approval of the agenda, the meeting always lasts for one hour, or the group members always sit in certain seats. The norms include the kind of language used in the group, the way individuals relate to each other, and the way decisions are made.

Norms can be explicit or implicit. An example of an explicit norm is when a group adopts the rules of parliamentary procedure for giving reports, making motions, and passing motions. Some examples of implicit norms are that the group always meets in the student center, practically never meets for more than one hour, and group members always eat their bag lunch during the meeting.

Norms make groups more predictable for members. The people in a group feel more comfortable when members follow the explicit and implicit norms. The member who always comes prepared as the others do, always does the work expected, and always respects the opinions of others is simply following the norms of the group. The member who attends sporadically, comes unprepared, and causes conflict frequently may be violating group norms. People who violate the norms of social and work groups are often subjected to pressure by other members of the group. Observe what happens to the person who "depledges" a fraternity or sorority, a person who wears clothing that differs from what others wear to the office, or a person who rarely does what others expect in a small group situation.

New members of a group are wise to hang back a bit at first to learn the group norms. Every group has its own way of deciding issues. You should not stay out of the discussion so long that your silence becomes normative, but you should observe a group long enough that you do not violate important norms that might render you less important to the group. On the other hand, there are some norms that invite breaking. One such is the norm that happens in so many business, government, and education groups where the males assume the functions of leadership, and the female and minority voices are conveniently left out of the decisions. Changes are taking place in small group norms.

Roles

Everyone in a small group plays a **role,** a pattern of behavior perceived, expected, and enacted by a member of a small group. Why should you know about roles? Role expectations in small group communication can be so strong that an individual is not allowed to be anything other than what the remainder of the group permits. In many organizations where Asian Americans, African Americans, Hispanics, or women are few, the group unfairly expects them to be spokespersons for their co-culture, often to the exclusion of any other function within the group. If you are aware that people tend to get frozen into roles, you can help by bringing out other aspects of that individual's knowledge and skills. After all, the sole African American on a committee might know little about "how black people feel" on some issue, but he or she might know considerable information about the issue generally. A role, in other words, can become a kind of mini-stereotype where only certain behavior is invited and expected of an individual.

What are some roles? You can generate your own names for roles in small group communication. Researchers have made up hundreds of them: leader, initiator, analyst, recorder, tension releaser, conciliator, clarifier, researcher, detail person, motion-maker, summarizer. To help keep all the possible roles straight, you can remember that two things occur continuously in small group discussion: accomplishing the task and maintaining the relationships. Task-oriented roles push the agenda, concentrate on the decision-making process, keep the discussion on track; relationship maintenance roles keep the tension tolerable, increase conciliation, and encourage participation.

You will probably find that you are better at some roles than at others. Charismatic leaders, for example, are sometimes great at cheerleading, bringing up the issues, and maybe even solving them, but they may not be best at finding the available information, keeping the group on task, and recording

Our interactions as a group establish our role.

the results of the meeting. There is nothing wrong with having a role at which you excel, but highly effective individuals tend to exhibit role flexibility. They are able to assume a number of roles competently in the group.

Productivity

Productivity refers to the relative success the group has in completing a specific task. If the objective of your small group is to choose a topic for a class project, and you have not accomplished this within a week, your group will likely be judged as having low productivity. On the other hand, if your task is to develop a topic, do research, conduct three interviews, write a fifty-page paper, and present your work, you will probably not be judged as harshly when this is not accomplished at the end of the week.

Productivity is a measure of the dimension of the task and ranges from low to high. The group's productivity is affected by both its procedures and the members' ability to communicate.[8]

Cohesiveness

Cohesiveness refers to the "stick-to-itiveness" of the small group. Small group members must feel a sense of belonging. This sense of unity with the group depends on each member's attraction to the group. Small groups sometimes are very cohesive because group members feel they have a great deal in common with the other members. They perceive their needs and interests as matching the needs and interests of the others. The group also may reinforce individuals for belonging to the group, which increases a feeling of cohesiveness.

Commitment

Commitment is closely related to cohesiveness. Group members feel commitment to a group when the group is cohesive. Commitment to a group may arise because of interpersonal attraction among group members; because of commonality in beliefs, attitudes, and values; because of fulfillment of needs; or because of the reinforcement the group offers. Groups that meet to solve a problem or to share information should also feel a commitment to their task. A lack of commitment to an assigned task can be very disruptive to the functioning of a small group.

Consensus

Consensus refers to an agreement among group members, due to active participation in the process, to implement and support group decisions. Consensus is more than no one objecting to a particular decision. Occasionally, a group will make a decision that appears to be unanimous because no one voices a dissenting opinion. Later, members resign from the group or show their disapproval by not assisting the group in carrying out the decision. They may privately report they felt obligated to "go along" with the decision because of the vociferous arguments made by the proponents or that they felt unable to articulate their own position. Such decisions cannot be considered to be achieved by consensus. Consensus requires genuine agreement and commitment by group members. Groups high in cohesiveness, commitment, and productivity often achieve consensus; similarly, when groups are able to reach decisions by consensus, they typically find increases in cohesiveness, commitment, and productivity.

Member Satisfaction

Member satisfaction refers to the positive or negative evaluation of the group by the members. A political campaign, for instance, may form for the purpose of raising money for and supporting a townsperson who is running for mayor. If they mishandle their money, however, or lack a leader with the required organizational skills, member satisfaction is apt to be low. If they generate a lot of publicity for the candidate, on the other hand, or bring important issues to the attention of the town, a high level of member satisfaction is a likely result.

Member satisfaction is dependent on the extent to which a group fulfills the expectations of its members, uses appropriate procedures, and has members with competent communication skills.[9] Member satisfaction can result in increased cohesiveness, and cohesiveness may be a contributing factor to member satisfaction. Similarly, member satisfaction may be positively related to productivity in the group as both a cause and an effect.

Group Organization

The appointment or assignment of a group leader and the group's access to each other influence both task accomplishment and group satisfaction. **Group organization** refers to hierarchy and the group's access to each other.

When the group has an **appointed leader** or the members of the group have hierarchial titles—president, vice president, secretary, treasurer—the group membership's participation may be influenced adversely by the status of the individuals. Low-status individuals may contribute less, or the group may value their contributes less. On the other hand, a group may be leaderless or a leader may simply emerge from the group membership. An **emergent leader** is a person who acquires the functions of a leader but does not discourage individual contributions because there are fewer status differences.

Groups characterized by hierarchy are superior in simple problem solving, but the more democratic leaderless or emergent leader-headed groups where all members feel a sense of equity are better at solving complex problems. The latter groups are also higher in group satisfaction.[10] A group leader who cares about the contributions of all—even an appointed leader or someone with a high title—can enhance group satisfaction by helping everyone in the group feel that their contributions are of value and that they are not taking risks in speaking their minds.

Gender Differences in Small Group Communication

Some teachers and students have difficulty with this section on gender in small group communication. Especially, some people believe that the results are replete with sexist findings. Consider whether you think it is sexist to say that in the one hundred meter dash, men's best times are better than women's best times. It is a fact, but is it sexist to say so? The research findings in this section are similar in that sometimes they reflect negatively on women and sometimes on men. Also, sometimes women and men behave in small groups in a stereotypical fashion—not necessarily as we would like them to behave.

This section reviews some of the conclusions researchers in small group communication have offered.[11] Many of the findings are general differences that may not apply to you or to all men and women. You should also know that we are not recommending that individuals in small groups behave in stereotypical ways.

Some research has shown men talk more in the small group setting than do women, and they demonstrate more task-related behavior than do women. Women offer more positive responses than do men, and they are also more opinionated than men. Men, on the other hand, are more informative, objective, and goal-oriented.[12] If the interaction is not pleasant, women are more likely to withdraw, while men are inclined to talk even more.[13]

A common task of the small group is to solve problems. Some early research suggested women were superior at tasks that were personally interesting, but men were superior at abstract multiple-choice problems.[14] Although men may be superior to women in solving problems, this difference is reduced when mixed-sex groups are examined, and when women are highly motivated to solve problems.[15] Motivated women may be just as effective at problem-solving as motivated men. Further, mixed-sex groups may produce superior outcomes to all-male or all-female groups.

Nonetheless, women are sometimes perceived to be less competent than men in problem solving or decision making in the small group.[16] What can women do when they are placed in such situations? Professor Patricia Bradley of Indiana University suggested women can overcome negative perceptions by increasing their demonstrated competence. She showed that women who demonstrated high task-related competence were treated with friendliness, reason, and relatively few displays of dominance from their male counterparts. However, she also found these women held low interpersonal attraction for the men in the group.[17] The competent woman is perceived as effective as a small group member, but she is not seen as an attractive social partner.

Risk taking occurs with more frequency in the small group than in individual behavior. Studies on individual risk taking by women and men suggest men take more risks than women when they are behaving individually.[18] Mixed-sexed groups are most likely to take risks, followed by all-male groups, than all-female groups.[19] Consistent with individual behavior, women tend to take fewer risks in a small group. The higher incidence of risk taking in the mixed-sex groups allows for interesting speculation, however.

Cooperation and competition are important in the small group setting. Most studies suggest women tend to be more cooperative than men, and they are more willing to share their resources with their opponents than are men.[20] Women appear to be more interested in fair outcomes than in winning.[21]

Men and women engage in and resolve conflict differently, as well. Men are more likely to engage in aggression than are women.[22] They are also more likely to gain their own way through deception and deceit than are women.[23] Men are more likely to use antisocial modes of behavior, including revenge, verbal aggression, and physical violence.[24] Women, on the other hand, are more likely to engage in socially acceptable behavior, including reasoning and understanding, to resolve conflict than are men.[25]

Coalitions, or subgroups, sometimes form in the small group. Both women and men tend to join the majority coalition, but they do so in different situations. Women are more likely to do so when they are weak, while men are more likely to do so when they are strong.[26] When three men are placed together in a group, the men tend to engage in a dominance struggle in which the two strongest males form a coalition and the weakest male is excluded.[27]

When three-person groups include two men and a woman, the men compete for the woman's attention.[28] When women are in the majority, they tend to include any person who may be left out, regardless of his or her biological gender.[29]

Do men and women prefer to work in same-sex or mixed-sex groups? Women prefer to work with all women if the group is small; they prefer the inclusion of men only when the group is large. Men, conversely, prefer to have women present regardless of the size of the group. In addition, cohesiveness within a small all-male group takes a longer time to materialize than in mixed-sex or all-female groups.[30]

As our culture changes, women and men may behave differently in the small group than they have in the past. Some recent studies suggest such changes are already occurring.[31] One's **psychological gender**—an individual's internalization of characteristics associated with men or women in a particular culture—may be more relevant to understanding gender in the small group than one's biological gender. Masculine individuals compete for control in predictable patterns of relational interaction, while feminine individuals use equality and submissiveness in predictable patterns. Androgynous individuals—persons who are both masculine and feminine—are more moderate and use patterns of idea initiation.[32]

The Process of Small Group Discussion

A variety of types of public presentation formats are possible for the small group discussion. Among the primary formats are the panel, the symposium, and the forum. The **panel** is the most familiar type of public discussion. It involves a discussion among people who attempt to solve a problem or make a policy decision. A panel generally includes one person whose job is to moderate the discussion by asking questions, encouraging everyone to participate, and keeping the discussion orderly.

The **symposium** is more formal than the panel and is closer to being public communication than it is to being interpersonal communication. The symposium is actually not a discussion if we define a discussion as an opportunity for equal give-and-take among members. The symposium generally includes a number of speeches oriented around a topic. Each symposium speaker typically addresses one part of the topic.

The **forum** occurs when audience members participate in a public discussion. A forum may follow a speech, a symposium, or a panel discussion. A forum may also occur without a prior discussion. For example, a forum could follow a play when the director is willing to converse with the members of the audience after the play is shown. The director would serve as the moderator even though anyone who wished would be permitted to speak.

In your class, you may be asked to participate in a panel discussion, a symposium, a panel-forum (a discussion followed by questions and answers from the audience), or a symposium-forum (a symposium followed by participation from the audience). Within these presentation formats, you may be involved in either information sharing or problem solving. Since the problem-solving discussion is more complex than the information-sharing discussion and since the preparation for, and presentation of, a problem-solving discussion requires more steps than that of an information-sharing discussion, we discuss the problem-solving discussion here in detail. If you are able to understand and carry out the suggestions for the problem-solving discussion, you should have no difficulty adapting the suggestions to an information-sharing discussion.

Preparation for the Discussion

The steps in preparing for the problem-solving discussion include: (1) selecting a topic, (2) wording the question to be discussed, (3) researching the topic, (4) evaluating the research, and (5) organizing the discussion. Let us discuss each of these steps in detail.

Selecting a Topic

The first step in preparing for a group discussion is to select a topic. The method most often recommended is brainstorming. **Brainstorming** is a technique in which you list or name as many ideas as you can within a stated period of time. Alex Osborn, who introduced the technique almost forty years ago, listed four rules governing brainstorming: (1) don't criticize any ideas, (2) no idea is too wild, (3) quantity is important, and (4) seize opportunities to improve on, or add to, ideas suggested by others.[33]

Wording the Question to Be Discussed

After you have selected a topic, the next task is to word the question to be discussed. The wording of the question is very important—it can lead to a fruitful or a wasted group discussion. The question clarifies the purpose of the discussion, suggests the avenues of research, and largely determines the agenda.

Categories of Discussion Questions.   In general, questions to be discussed can be placed into one of three categories. **Questions of fact** deal with truth and falsity. They are concerned with the occurrence, the existence, or the particular properties of something. **Questions of value** require judgments of good and bad. Such questions are grounded in the participant's motives, beliefs, and cultural standards. Desirability and satisfaction are often central to

questions of value. **Questions of policy** concern future action. The purpose of a policy question is to determine a course of action to be taken or supported in a specific situation. The word *should* often appears in a question of policy.

Characteristics of Good Discussion Questions. All discussion questions should meet a minimum set of standards. Characteristics of good discussion questions—whether they are questions of fact, value, or policy—are that they should be simple, neutral, open, and controversial. By *simple,* we mean the question should be written with the fewest number of words possible and should be easily understood by all who read or hear it. In addition, the question should be appropriate for the time available, the research available, and the individuals who will be discussants. A discussion question, such as "How will ethnographic studies contribute to our understanding of the impact of androgyny on the economic structure?" does not meet the criterion of simplicity.

A discussion question should be written *neutrally.* It should not imply "correct" answers. People reading the question should be able to suggest alternative answers. For example, the question "Is Presidential candidate John Brown, a weak man who will bring economic ruin and unemployment, capable of running a great nation like ours?" does not meet the criterion of neutrality. The framing of this leading question implies that "no" is the only reasonable answer.

A discussion question should be *open* rather than closed. Open questions allow a number of alternative answers. Closed questions allow only a "yes" or "no" response. Open discussion questions can be answered in a variety of different ways.

Finally, the discussion question should be controversial. It should not be a question with a predetermined answer. Nor should it concern a matter that has an already agreed-upon solution. The question should be timely—of current international, national, or local concern; interesting to the group members; and worthwhile to those involved. The following questions are not suitable: Out of date—"should women be allowed to vote?"; irrelevant to a particular group—"Should all daycare operators be licensed by the state?"; and not worthwhile—"Should four years of school be required to get a degree?"

Organizing the Discussion

Each category of discussion questions requires a different kind of discussion organization. A question of fact requires you (1) define key terms in the question, (2) gather relevant information, and (3) compare your information to the terms and classifications you have made. A question of value requires you (1) define key terms in the question, (2) establish criteria of "goodness" or value for the question, (3) gather relevant information, and (4) compare your information to the criteria you have established.

Questions of Fact, Value, and Policy

Fact

How has the divorce rate changed in the last fifteen years?
How many Hispanic students graduate from high school each year?
What percentage of college students graduate in four years?
How often on average does a person speak each day?
What occupations earn the highest annual income?

Value

Why should people seek higher education?
How should Americans treat international students?
Does our legal system provide "justice for all?"
How should young people be educated about AIDS?
What is the value of standardized tests for college admission?

Policy

What courses should students be required to take?
Should the state's drunken driving laws be changed?
What are the arguments for and against mandatory retirement?
Should the U.S. intervene in foreign disputes for humanitarian reasons?
What advantages should government provide for businesses willing to develop in high risk areas of a city?

For many years, it was believed a discussion involving a question of policy could only be organized according to **Dewey's method of reflective thinking,** which required discussants to do the following:

1. *Recognize the problem.* The group must acknowledge a problem exists and group members are concerned about that specific problem. For example, the group might recognize that handling waste—paper, glass, metals, and garbage—is a big problem in our communities.
2. *Define the problem.* The group must identify the nature of the problem and define the critical terms. For instance, the term *waste* needs to be defined, and the problem must be limited, perhaps by eliminating industrial, chemical, and hazardous waste from consideration.
3. *Analyze the problem.* The group must suggest the problem's cause, extensiveness, limits, implications or effects, and who the problem affects. The group might decide the problem is caused by our "throw away" society with disposable packaging, daily newspapers, cans, and bottles. They

might find out how big the problem is locally and limit their consideration to the local area. They might consider the costs both aesthetically and in money, and they might decide that the problem affects everyone in the community.

4. *Establish criteria for evaluating solutions.* The group must decide what standards will be used to evaluate their solution and which standards are most important to them. Examples of criteria for solving the waste problem might be that the cost needs to be low enough for the citizens to afford; the solution must be convenient enough for complete participation by individuals; and the solution must not depend on the cooperation of others as in the case of shipping the waste out-of-state.

5. *Suggest solutions to the problem.* By brainstorming or other techniques, the group lists possible solutions to the problem. The group might consider such solutions as recycling, constructing a solid waste disposal plant, incineration, or higher taxes to pay for the problem.

6. *Select the best solution.* After many solutions have been offered, group members apply their predetermined criteria to the specific solutions to arrive at the one that best meets the standards. The group might, for example, decide that recycling will be mandatory in the community.

7. *Test the solution.* The final step in Dewey's method of reflective thinking is testing the solution, finding out what the consequences of adopting the best solution would be. The group could discover on reflection that some cities have found recycling problematic because the costs recovered by sale of metal, glass, and paper are greater than the earnings. If the solution does not test well, the group has to return to its proposed solutions to find a better one.

More recently, authors have suggested that a strict adherence to this organizational pattern results in planned performances rather than decision-making processes. These authors have demonstrated that many questions are not susceptible to solution by Dewey's method of reflective thinking, and a number of alternative organizational patterns have been created for the use of small groups. Basically, however, all problem-solving discussions must include two questions: (1) What is the nature of the problem? and (2) How can we solve it? Subsidiary questions can be added to this most simple organizational pattern to meet the group's needs.

For example, a group may find the problem it is considering requires a very loosely structured pattern. Group members also may find they require a very prescriptive pattern of organization. The appropriate organizational pattern will depend on the nature and composition of the group as well as on the nature of the problem. Regardless of what specific organizational pattern seems appropriate, it is essential the discussion be organized.

As mayor this official has opportunities to demonstrate leadership abilities.

Leadership in Small Groups

Leadership is defined as the verbal and nonverbal communication behavior that influences the group to move toward its goals. The leader may be emergent or appointed. An ideal situation might be one in which the leadership functions are a shared responsibility, where a number of people are leaders of the group.

An appointed leader may or may not have good leadership skills, but often an appointed leader does view the appointment as a reason to take responsibility for the group.[34] The emergent leader, on the other hand, achieves leadership because he or she exhibits leadership skills. Nonetheless, appointed leaders gain some authority by being appointed as is evidenced by the fact that group members agree more with statements by appointed leaders than statements by emergent leaders.[35]

Styles-of-Leadership Approach

The **styles-of-leadership approach** suggests that if we examine an individual's influential communication, patterns of behavior emerge that typify a particular leadership style. Styles of leadership have been placed on a continuum

Figure 10.1 Styles of leadership.

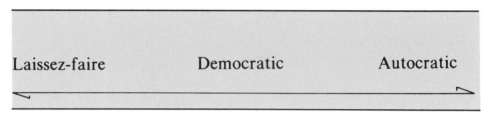

from *laissez-faire* to autocratic (figure 10.1). Halfway between these extremes is democratic leadership. Since these three positions exist on a continuum, many other leadership styles fall between them, but we will only deal with these three basic styles.

In general, the *laissez-faire,* democratic, and autocratic leadership styles are defined in terms of the amount of control exercised by the leader. **Laissez-faire leadership** is the most permissive, and group members are offered almost no direction. **Autocratic leadership** contrasts sharply with *laissez-faire* leadership in that the leader has complete control and group members have very little freedom. **Democratic leadership** allows the leader some control, but group members also have some freedom.

Style of leadership may be a function of many variables. The personality of the leader may affect style of leadership. For example, firstborn children are more likely to develop task-oriented, directive leadership styles, while later-born children are more interpersonal, relationship-oriented leaders.[36] In other words, firstborn children are more likely to fall on the end of the continuum between democratic and autocratic leadership, while later-born children are more likely to fall on the end of the continuum between *laissez-faire* and democratic leadership.

What style of leadership is superior? *Laissez-faire* leadership results in the least amount of work and the poorest quality of work. Autocratic leadership generally produces more work than does *laissez-faire* leadership, but member satisfaction is diminished since hostility and aggression often result. In many situations, democratic leadership seems to be the most successful because work motivation is higher, more originality in ideas is demonstrated, and group members indicate a preference for this kind of leadership.

Past research suggested democratic leadership frequently promoted more friendliness, permissiveness, and member satisfaction than did other styles of leadership, even though democratic decision making and problem solving took more time than the other styles of leadership.[37] However, a number of limitations of these studies should be noted. First, our cultural bias in favor of democratic leadership may skew the results of the older research. Particularly in the 1940s and 1950s, people may not have wanted to believe ruling in an autocratic manner was preferable to the democratic style. Second, the democratic leader has been defined in terms of culturally preferred characteristics. Third, the democratic leader has been positioned halfway between the two extreme positions. This style of leadership may merely represent a "happy medium" between two extremes. Fourth, the ambiguity of leadership styles that fall between the democratic style and the extreme ends of the continuum calls into question the meaningfulness of the research findings. Finally, it appears intuitively incorrect that one style of leadership would always be superior in all situations and with all people, and current research supports this. For instance, a small group that must act quickly and has a highly informed person as a leader might find the autocratic style of leadership is more effective. The democratic style of leadership is no longer considered superior for all situations.

The preferred style of leadership is dependent on the type of task, the context of the small group, and the individuals involved.[38] For example, effective leadership styles vary for women and men. A directive, autocratic leadership style has been rated even more unfavorably when displayed by a female than a male, and male workers have stated that a woman who employs such a style would be less effective. The rated effectiveness of a leader and the satisfaction of subordinates may decrease to the extent that the leader adopts a style inconsistent with the expected stereotype.[39] Women who are directive and men who are *laissez-faire* may find that others rate them as ineffective.

Because of these kinds of problems, the styles-of-leadership approach no longer enjoys a central role in our understanding of leadership that it once did.

Participation in Leadership in the Discussion Group

You may be asked to share leadership functions in a small group discussion or to exhibit your leadership abilities in a problem-solving or information-sharing group discussion in your communication class. Your role in the group discussion may be that of an appointed leader or someone who shares leadership functions with others.

What leadership functions are important in the group discussion? Jack Brilhart suggests the functions of leaders can be categorized into "initiating, organizing, spreading participation, stimulating both creative and critical thinking, facilitating understanding, promoting cooperative interpersonal relationships, and developing the group members."[40] While this list may sound overwhelming, these classes of behaviors are comprehensive and may be shared among members.

Initiating may include icebreaking activities or other action by which the members of the group learn the names of the other members and are introduced to each other. During this stage, procedures, purposes, and other plans

Communication skills are basic to leadership. Ministers, lawyers, actors and broadcasters have language and presentational skills that help in leadership positions.

should be outlined. Opening remarks may be made, and necessary arrangements, such as securing and running a tape recorder, appointing a secretary, or arranging the room, should be handled. The group members should be made to feel comfortable during this initial phase.

Organizing refers to orderliness. The group leader should help keep the group moving toward its goal by summarizing, making transitions, and bringing the group to a conclusion. When the group digresses from the topic, the leader should direct the group back to the topic. When the group repeats itself, the leader should be sensitive to the need to move on. When the group spends a great deal of time on one aspect of the problem, the leader should remind the group of time constraints and help the group budget its time appropriately.

Spreading participation means the group leader should help equalize or divide participation among group members. Individuals in the group should not feel obliged or forced to speak if they have nothing to contribute, but talkative members should not be allowed to prevent the contributions of other members. The leaders should carefully observe members to determine if they

ANIMAL CRACKERS

wish to speak and should listen actively to determine what points need extension or clarification. The leader should ask questions to encourage participation and should use follow-up questions or probes to gain additional information. Acceptance should be shown toward the contributions of all group members—no matter how trivial the remark. Highly evaluative verbal or non-verbal responses may discourage individuals from future participation.

Stimulating both creative and critical thinking refers to simultaneously encouraging novel and unique ideas and careful analysis of ideas. While it is difficult to encourage at the same time; both kinds of thinking are essential to the successful small group discussion. Criteria by which solutions or answers will be measured should be uniformly understood; ideas should not be dismissed until they have been carefully and thoughtfully measured against existing criteria; and new approaches should be encouraged.

Facilitating understanding means the leader models active and empathic listening, and he or she encourages others to engage in this kind of listening as well. Pointing out areas of agreement, stressing commonalities, suggesting visualizations, and offering analogies all contribute to understanding among members.

Promoting cooperative interpersonal relationships is another function of the leader. Tension within the group should be reduced so group members can work together effectively. Not allowing conflict over personalities or personal issues is useful. The leader can encourage humor as a tension-reliever in groups that are particularly serious or have an especially difficult task. When conflict does arise, using such conflict-reduction methods as compromise, negotiation, consensus, or arbitration, may be helpful.

Developing the group and its members suggests the leader helps the group and group members to grow and change. Sometimes, these goals are at cross-purposes, but usually, helping individuals develop their repertoire of roles within a group or learn more about a certain topic also helps the group develop and grow. Similarly, helping the group develop by establishing consensus and member satisfaction frequently results in individual growth in the members. Growth of the group at the cost of the individuals has short-term benefits. Also, helping individuals grow and develop without regard to the group's goal has limited benefit.

Effective leadership is essential to successful problem solving in the small group. As we stated earlier, the leadership of a small group discussion is generally shared, but the designated leader has the responsibility of ensuring that all of the leadership functions are performed. If you are selected as the leader of a small group or if you emerge as the leader, you should review the functions that must be provided by leadership and ensure that you or someone else is fulfilling them.

Solving Conflict in Small Groups

We are accustomed to thinking of **conflict** or the clash of wills or ideas as being a negative occurrence. However, in small group communication, in decision-making and problem-solving groups, conflict is inevitable. Conflict can also be productive, and it can force the group to consider the better of two or more alternatives. In this section, we will focus on some methods of conflict resolution to provide ideas on how you can better handle conflict when it occurs in your meetings.

Before moving to the methods of resolution, however, you should know that conflict invariably leads to increased tension in the group, whether the tension is focused on an individual or on a part of the group who challenges what the group is saying. Tension, like conflict, is inherent in the small group. We should say that groups without tension are often boring and unproductive. Tension can get out of control, but as long as it stays in the realm of verbal combat and as long as no one bears lasting psychological or physical scars, tension can be healthy, especially when it provokes thought, movement, and progress.

Five methods of conflict resolution are considered here: (1) denial, (2) suppression, (3) power, (4) compromise, and (5) collaboration. Some are desirable methods and some are not.

Denial

Leaders or groups who use **denial,** an undesirable means of resolving conflict, simply believe their group does not have problems. They either refuse to define what is happening in the group as conflict, or they ignore the conflict and act as if it never occurred. Unfortunately, denial is a common occurrence, and it does not resolve the problems.

The following is an example of denial in a small group. Yolanda Saunders arrives late for nearly every meeting and sometimes leaves early. She is not contributing to the group effort and is leaving the work of the group to the others. The members of the group all define the tardiness and the early leaving as "not a problem," so nothing is done about the delinquent member. Meanwhile, Yolanda may think that nothing is wrong because nobody says anything about it.

Suppression

Another method for resolving conflict that we do not recommend is **suppression.** While denial means that no one acknowledges a problem, suppression means that the group is aware of the problem but chooses to minimize its importance. Fiorella Gomez is a very likable group member, but she dominates every meeting with talk about her social life. The group has trouble trying to accomplish the group task. People in the group don't want to hurt Fiorella's feelings, so they continue to meet time and time again accomplishing little or nothing.

Power

A third undesirable method of conflict resolution is the use of **power** to decide or block, including the power of vested authority, position, majority, or insistent minority.

Bill Blanchard, the boss's son, is chair of the company's personnel committee. When he wants someone hired over the objections of the others, he asks them if they want to keep their jobs. Bill resolves conflict by using the power of vested authority and position and by threatening the other members of the group.

Elizabeth Weber has lots of friends on the community improvement board. She usually gets her way on issues by calling all of her friends before the meeting, lining up the votes, and swaying the votes at the meeting—no matter what the few remaining individuals might think. Elizabeth uses the power of a majority to determine board decisions.

Mahmoud Hammoud has only two friends on the City Council, but he manages to block many decisions on issues by crying loudly to the press that the entire council is prejudiced against people from the Middle East. He and his friends have the entire board in gridlock because every issue is determined by the three of them to be racist. Mahmoud uses the power of a minority to stop decision making on the council.

Compromise

This method of resolving conflict is one of the recommended methods. **Compromise** means that the conflicting parties give up part of their plan to arrive at a third alternative that encompasses some of what each group wants. Compromise implies sacrifice. Each part of the group has to give up something to gain something, but both parts get some of what they want as well.

Teacher Jacqueline Mulhern has given student Seok Kim a grade. He appeals to the departmental appeals committee, consisting of two students and three faculty members. The senior faculty member is the appointed chair. The two students think that Seok Kim has earned a B in the course, but two of the faculty think the D that Dr. Mulhern gave him was appropriate. Deadlocked, the chair resolves the conflict in the second meeting by suggesting that Dr. Mulhern be asked to change the grade to a C. Neither the two students nor the two faculty members got their way, but both got part of what they wanted in this compromise.

Collaboration

Collaboration is a recommended method of conflict resolution in which the group considers the problem and negotiates a solution satisfactory to all. Everyone respects the abilities and expertise of everyone else. The focus is on the problem, and the assumption is that a group decision is superior to that of any individual decision. This method uses a problem orientation and a supportive climate without any majority, minority, or autocratic leader trying to control the group's decision making.

Bryan Hall and Pickering Hall are supposed to build a float for the homecoming parade. Six members of each hall have been elected to plan the float. At first, the members from Bryan Hall thought that a theme float with skinny males playing the role of the opposing Tigers would be good, but Pickering Hall had envisioned a float on which the Tigers were being whopped by the college band. At their first meeting, however, the two groups decided to avoid an impasse by constructing a float with a large dunking barrel into which a hapless Tiger would be sent flying by a combined Bryan and Pickering Hall team representing the local football team.

The moral of the story is that in small group communication it is unwise to be too wedded to your own point of view or to that of a majority or minority. Instead, you should allow the small group decision-making process to take advantage of everyone's ideas and come up with the best idea that nearly everyone in the group can embrace. People who only pretend to be group members but who are really there to advance their own agenda are not truly members of a decision-making group. Embracing what the group decides, whether it is your own idea or not, is one of the responsibilities of group membership.

Summary

Small group communication was defined as small assemblies gathered together to solve problems and make decisions. The primary concern in small groups is to accomplish the task and to maintain healthy relationships among group members. You discovered that small, decision-making groups are appropriate only under certain conditions. You also learned some concepts important in small group communication: norms, roles, productivity, cohesiveness, commitment, consensus, satisfaction, and group organization. You also learned that there are appointed and emergent leaders.

Males and females behave differently in small group communication. You discovered among other things that men tend to talk more in small groups, mixed-sex groups tend to produce superior outcomes, women high in task-related competence are seen as low in attraction by men, mixed-sex groups take the most risks, and men are more likely to be aggressive in a group.

You learned the types of small discussion groups: the panel, the symposium, and the forum; and you learned the three kinds of questions for discussion groups: questions of fact, value, and policy. You discovered how to organize a discussion according to Dewey's method of reflective thinking.

Leadership in small groups was defined as the verbal and nonverbal communication behavior that influences the group to move toward its goals. You learned three styles of leadership: *laissez-faire,* democratic, and autocratic. Finally, you learned leadership functions important to small group communication.

Under the aegis of conflict resolution, you learned three poor ways to handle conflict—denial, suppression, and power—and two recommended ways to resolve conflicts in a small group—compromise and collaboration.

Key Terms

appointed leader   A person formally selected to lead.

autocratic leadership   Leadership that exerts complete control over a group.

brainstorming   Listing or naming as many ideas as a group or an individual can within a limited period of time.

cohesiveness   The sense of belonging within a group.

collaboration   The group considers the problem and negotiates a solution satisfactory to all; a recommended method of conflict resolution.

commitment   Individual dedication to a group because of interpersonal attraction, commonality, fulfillment, or reinforcement.

compromise   Combining part of two conflicting plans to create a third plan that partially satisfies each conflicting party of a group; a recommended method of conflict resolution.

conflict   The clash of wills or ideas.

consensus   Complete agreement among group members and their support of group decisions.

democratic leadership Leadership that exerts a balance of control and freedom over a group.

denial An undesirable mode of conflict resolution in which no one acknowledges any problems of conflict in the group.

Dewey's method of reflective thinking A sequence of steps for organizing, defining, researching, and solving problems in groups.

emergent leader An individual not selected to be leader, but a person who emerges as the group continues to meet and work.

forum The forum occurs when audience members participate in a public discussion; a forum may follow a speech, a symposium, or a panel discussion.

group organization The group hierarchy and the group's access to each other.

laissez-faire **leadership** Leadership that exerts only minimal control on a group.

leadership Verbal and nonverbal communication behavior that helps to clarify or achieve a group's goals; influence.

member satisfaction The positive or negative evaluation of a group by its members.

norms Unwritten rules of acceptable and unacceptable behavior in a group.

panel A discussion among people who attempt to solve a problem or make a policy decision; a panel generally includes one person whose job is to monitor the discussion.

power Vested authority or position to decide issues; an undesirable method of conflict resolution.

productivity The relative success the group has in completing a specific task.

psychological gender An individual's internalization of characteristics associated with men or women in a particular culture.

questions of fact Discussion questions that deal with truth and falsity; concern the occurrence, existence, or particular properties of something.

questions of policy Discussion questions that concern future action or policy.

questions of value Discussion questions that require a judgment of good or bad.

role Behavior expected by others because of the social category in which a person is placed.

small group communication Small assemblies invited together to solve problems and make decisions; consists of a few people (usually more than two but fewer than twenty) with a mutually interdependent purpose and a sense of belonging.

styles-of-leadership approach An approach to leadership that suggests if we examine the influential communication of an individual, patterns of behavior emerge that typify a particular leadership style, such as *laissez-faire,* democratic, or autocratic.

suppression The group is aware of a problem but chooses to minimize its importance; an undesirable method of conflict resolution.

symposium A form of small group communication that does not allow equal give-and-take among its members but does include a number of speeches oriented around a topic.

part 3

Public Communication

Public communication is the process of understanding and sharing that occurs in the speaker-to-audience situation. Public communication, like interpersonal communication, is a transaction in which people simultaneously give and receive meaning from each other.

Our exploration of public communication begins with chapter 11, "Topic Selection and Audience Analysis," which provides methods of discovering good speech topics and explains how to interpret information about the audience. Chapter 12, "Communication Apprehension and Speaker Credibility," begins by discussing the fear of public speaking and then examines the dimensions of credibility and means of improving credibility as a public speaker. In chapter 13, "Finding Information," we explain where to find information in written sources and from people. Ways to develop sentence and key-word outlines and a number of patterns of speech organization are presented in chapter 14, "Organizing Your Speech." Chapter 15, "Delivery and Visual Aids," discusses vocal and bodily aspects of public speaking—including voice, eye contact, gestures, and movement. This chapter also has an expanded section on why and how to use visual aids in your speech. In chapter 16, "The Informative Speech," we provide detailed directions on how to compose a speech whose primary purpose is to increase the audience's knowledge. Preparing a speech designed to change an audience or to invite the audience to action is the subject of chapter 17, "The Persuasive Speech."

chapter 11

Topic Selection and Audience Analysis

T his chapter focuses on two topics: topic selection and audience analysis. How do you select and limit a topic for a public speech? Individual brainstorming and personal inventories help you begin the process. Other considerations are your involvement in, and knowledge of, the topic. Analyzing the audience must occur on four levels. Is the audience captive or voluntary? What demographic qualities do audience members hold? How interested in, and knowledgeable about, the topic is the audience? What are the audience's attitudes, beliefs, and values? How can you analyze your audience in all of these ways? The chapter explains how to use observation, inference, and the questionnaire. Adapting to an audience means adapting yourself, adapting your verbal and nonverbal codes, adapting your topic, adapting your purposes, and adapting your supporting materials. When you have completed this chapter, you will be able to select an appropriate topic for a public speech and you will be more adaptive to an audience.

W hat will you learn?

When you have read and thought about this chapter, you should be able to answer the following questions:

1. How do brainstorming and personal inventories help you discover topics for speeches?

2. Can you think of five topics that meet your criterion for topic involvement?

3. Can you take a general topic for a public speech and show how to make it narrow enough for a five-minute speech?

4. Can you analyze an audience using all four levels of audience analysis?

5. Can you give an example of one belief, one attitude, and one value that you hold and indicate how easy or difficult each would be to change in you?

6. What do you think is the relative effectiveness of the three methods of audience analysis for a topic of your own choosing?

7. What are some methods of audience adaptation performed by the competent public speaker?

8. What is audience sensitivity?

T here are no uninteresting things; there are only uninterested people.

G. K. Chesterton

O ne of the finest accomplishments is making a long story short.

Kim Hubbard

N one are so deaf as those who will not hear.

Matthew Henry

C hoosing a topic for a speech can be a problem. You may have already discovered that, when you are assigned to write a paper or to deliver a speech, the first step of finding something to write or speak about is difficult. You may not be able to think of a topic as soon as you hear the assignment. Instead, you may find yourself mulling over the assignment for days, sharpening your pencil, drinking water or coffee as you think, and only selecting a topic after most of your time for completing the assignment has slipped away. This chapter is designed to save you time by finding an appropriate topic quickly and to increase your effectiveness through audience analysis.

Selecting and Limiting the Topic

Let us begin by examining some methods of finding a topic. The two methods discussed here are individual brainstorming and conducting a personal inventory.

Individual Brainstorming

Group brainstorming is a useful technique for selecting a topic for group discussion. Individual brainstorming can be equally effective for finding a topic for your public speech. **Brainstorming** is thinking of as many topics as you can in a limited time so you can select one topic that will be appropriate for you and your audience.

What is individual brainstorming, and how can you use it to help you find a topic? First, give yourself a very limited time, say five minutes. Without trying to think of fancy titles or even complete thoughts, write down as many topics as you can. When your time is up, you should have a rough list of the ideas or topics easiest to arouse in your mind. This step can be repeated if you want to have an even larger list from which to choose. The second step is to select three items from your list that have the most appeal as topics for you. Third, choose one of these three topics you feel would be appealing not only to you, but also to your audience.

This technique of individual brainstorming can generate many speech topics from which you can choose. Many students find this method more productive than trying to think of one topic for their speech.

Personal Inventories

Another way to find a topic for your speech is to conduct **personal inventories** of your reading and viewing habits. Choosing one topic from thousands of possible topics requires some self-analysis.

You make choices every time you read or watch something. You can discover your own interests by examining carefully what you choose to read or watch. What kind of books do you read? The person who reads science fiction

The selection of a topic for a public speech may emerge from your own interests or experiences.

exhibits quite a different interest than the person who reads biographies, auto-biographies, or mysteries. Do you watch films? The person who watches inter-national films is reflecting quite a different interest than the person who watch-es horror films, musicals, or X-rated movies.

Public speaking starts with the self, with what you know, have experi-enced, or are willing to learn. The two inventories that follow demonstrate how self-analysis can help you assess those areas in which you are qualified to speak. You could do the same kind of inventory with music, books, films, plays, and art.

Your personal inventories of television and newspaper reading habits are just two rough indications of your own interests. Other inventories you could conduct might include:

Hobbies	Jobs
Leisure activities	Elective courses
Organizations	Talents
Magazines	Academic major courses

Personal inventories should help you identify your own interests and pref-erences—including some you may not have been fully aware you have. How the topic relates to self is an early step in topic selection; how the topic relates to the listeners comes later. Now you are ready to assess your personal involvement in and knowledge of the topic.

Involvement in the Topic

After you have selected a possible topic area, you should evaluate the topic to see if you have the appropriate involvement in and knowledge of the subject. **Involvement** is simply a measure of how much a topic means to you.

Your brainstorming and personal inventories might have shown that you have an interest in many items. However, you may not be involved in these items. For example, you could be interested in sports because they allow you a kind of escape from everyday concerns, but you might not be highly involved in sports. How can you tell the difference between mere interest and involvement? What difference does it make whether a speaker is involved in a topic?

One measure of involvement is how much time you put into a topic area. What if you find, through brainstorming and conducting personal inventories, that one of your interests is computers? You could probably consider yourself involved in computers if you spend time around them, learn how they work, read books about them, and spend time around computer shops to see what new hardware and software is available. The amount of time you spend with your topic is, then, one measure of your involvement.

A second measure of involvement is how much effort you expend with a particular interest. The person who is really involved in politics is much more than a passive observer. He or she knows the candidates and politicians, works on campaigns, helps bring out the voters, reads about politics, talks with other interested persons and joins groups with a similar interest. Involvement, then, is measured by the time and effort you commit to your subject.

To tell whether or not a speaker is involved in a speech topic is easy. An involved speaker speaks with more conviction, passion, and authority. The involved speaker gives many verbal and nonverbal indications that he or she cares about the topic. The person who is only trying to fulfill an assignment cannot convey the sense of involvement so important in public speaking. Usually, you will find the speaker who really cares about the topic being discussed is often successful at getting you involved in the topic as well.

Knowledge of the Topic

After you have selected a topic area and determined your own involvement in the subject, you need to assess your personal knowledge of the subject. What do you know about the subject that can, and should, be communicated to your audience? Your knowledge about the topic comes primarily from three sources: yourself, other people, and such resources as books, films, magazines, television, and newspapers.

First, determine what you know about your subject from *your own experience.* Do you have experience that has not been shared by many other people? Have you raised children, worked at interesting jobs, served in the armed forces, traveled to unusual places, or done things that few can claim?

The importance of speaking from personal experience was demonstrated at a large university where over seven hundred students were invited to select the best speeches made in their individual speech classes. The winners delivered their speeches in a runoff contest, and the three best speakers gave their speeches to everyone taking the course. Those three speakers, selected by their classmates, were two African-American males and a handicapped white female—but, of the seven hundred competitors, very few were black and even fewer were handicapped. All three spoke about topics in which they were highly involved and to which they were committed. The two African-American men spoke about being black students in a predominantly white university, and the woman told what it was like to be a student confined to a wheelchair. The African-American men told about being stared at in class, having classmates constantly asking them about being black, and being misunderstood. The handicapped woman told of having practically nobody speak to her no matter where she was, of people moving to the other side of the sidewalk when she approached, and of being considered an oddity. All three students had special knowledge of, and experience with, the topics on which they based their speeches.

After determining what you know about a topic from your personal experience, you should *turn to other people* who might know more about the topic than you do. You can make your speech stronger by talking to people in your community or in your college or university who are knowledgeable about your topic. A telephone call or personal interview can often provide you with some ideas and quotations for your speech that will show you cared enough about the subject to bring your audience current expert information.

You can also bolster your knowledge of a topic by *turning to resources* like magazines, books, films, newspapers, or television. These resources can help you to fill in information about your topic that you do not already know, and they will increase your credibility as a speaker. Finding such information is discussed in more detail in chapter 13.

It is important to remember that, when you get information from another person or from some resource, you must credit that person or resource. In other words, you must tell your audience that you got the information from someplace other than your personal experience.

Robert M. Smith, of Alma College in Michigan, suggests there are four benchmarks in selecting a topic. First is the speaker and whether he or she can handle the topic. Second is whether the topic is appropriate, given the audience's chronological, educational, political, or religious characteristics. Third is the occasion. Can the speaker fit the selected topic into the class and the time limits? A speech from a class at 8:00 P.M. may not work in class at 8:00 A.M.

Finally, a speaker must consider if he or she can find the available information within the deadline. Can the information be gathered within the week or month?

Narrowing the Topic

Brainstorming techniques and personal inventories can yield topic areas appropriate for you. However, these topics are probably too large or abstract for a brief speech. A personal inventory may show that a speech on the topic of small business administration is a good one for you because you are involved in the topic, and you read and know about it. Unfortunately, a speech on small business administration could take days or weeks to deliver because so much information is available on the subject. You might try *narrowing the topic* so much that, at first glance, it might appear you would never be able to find enough information on the topic. The advantage in starting with a very narrow topic is that it renders much information on the subject irrelevant. Only a small amount of the available information will be related to your narrowed topic; thus, your research on the topic will be highly focused, and you will not end up spending a lot of time obtaining information you cannot use.

The most common way to narrow a topic is to make it more specific and concrete. The small business administration topic, for instance, can be narrowed down to health care administration in your part of the country. You may even find it necessary to narrow the topic further, such as administration in hospitals, or leadership in facilities for those with eating disorders. After carefully considering the audience's interests in the various kinds of small business administrations, you might end up delivering a speech on the administrative hierarchy in southeastern Ohio's psychiatric wards.

One method of narrowing a topic is suggested by the small business administration example just described. An abstract category discovered through brainstorming or personal inventories can be narrowed by listing smaller categories directly related to that topic. The abstract topic *college,* for example, might yield the following smaller categories directly related to it:

- Application process for state colleges
- Application process for out-of-state schools
- Where to apply for financial aid
- On-campus residence
- Programs of study

A slightly different approach to narrowing a topic involves taking a broad category, such as music, and listing as many smaller topics as you can that are at least loosely related to that topic:

- The development of country western music
- The influence of rock music on our youth
- Rap artists
- Music therapy
- Why any good song sounds bad in an elevator
- Music education at the elementary school level
- The history of the mandolin
- Country singers who serve as role models

The list of more specific and concrete topics can be extended until you have a large number from which to choose.

How will you know if your topic is narrow enough? There is no easy answer? Several things to consider are (1) the amount of information available on the narrowed topic, (2) the amount of information that can be conveyed within the time limits for the speech, and (3) whether or not the narrowed topic can be discussed with enough depth to keep the audience interested and increase their knowledge.

The advice in this section on how to find and narrow a topic should help you choose a topic for your speech. If all of these suggestions fail, you may wish to examine the potential speech topics on p. 242 and those in chapters 16 and 17 on informative and persuasive speaking. These topics came from successful student speeches. Another idea worth considering is to generate a similar list of current topics with your classmates.

Now we will turn from selecting a speech topic to adapting your topic to an audience.

Analyzing Your Audience

Why should you analyze your audience? Especially, why should you analyze your audience if it consists of your own classmates? Before we start talking about *how* to analyze an audience, we need to explain *why* we anlayze an audience.

One professor who used this text commented he never used the chapter on audience analysis because his students spoke only to their own classmates and, therefore, did not need to analyze the audience. Naturally, we were startled because we assumed a public speaker always needs to know about an audience before knowing how to state a message. Would you give the same speech in the same way no matter who constituted the audience?

Potential Speech Topics

AIDS protection
Birth control
Hazards of smoking
Cancer
Women and career goals
Pro-life/Pro-choice
Symptoms and treatments of chronic
  fatigue syndrome
How to organize your day to your
  advantage
Child abuse
Spouse abuse
Superstitions
How to deal with stress
How to be environmentally conscious
The use of drug testing in the
  American work force
The plight of the American homeless
Diabetes
Why you need your rest
Earning your way through school
Why African Americans are angry
How to decide which personal
  computer is best for your needs
Get in shape and lose weight
Fathers and child support
Why be a democrat?
Should corporal punishment be used
  on high school students?
Cruelty to animals in lab experiments
Legalization of marijuana
Add humor to your life
Women's rights
Donate organs
Why you should not drink and drive
Donate your body to science
Adopt a child
Problems with the Supreme Court
How to study more effectively
Capital punishment

History of pizza
How Greek life has changed
Should the drinking age be lowered to
  twenty?
What jobs are most profitable?
The components of physical fitness
Safe sex
Destruction of rain forests
Greenhouse effect
Rape and date rape
Are divorce rates increasing?
Mental benefits of exercise
How students can get financial aid
Third world culture
Cholesterol levels
Contraception
Suicide—the signs to watch for
Limiting terms of office
The problem with "living together"
Give blood
Take vitamins
Dental health
Become a big brother or big sister
Pizza is healthy
College-aged alcoholics
Need to vote
Recycling
Buying software
Volunteerism
Gay rights
Animal rights
Toxic waste
Skin cancer from tanning
Against marriage
Control the pet population
Government intervention in other
  nations
Gun control
Why integrate?

Classroom speakers generally face a captive audience.

Let us say you are going to give an informative speech on interest rates. Would you give that speech in the same way to a beginning communication class that consisted mainly of business majors as you would if the class consisted mainly of arts and sciences majors? Let us say you are going to give a persuasive speech on abortion. Would it matter to you that the audience consisted of many persons whose religious beliefs prohibited abortion? In short, how would you know the majors, religious beliefs, and interests of your audience unless you analyzed the audience in some way?

Audience analysis is similar to target marketing, which business majors and business people use. It can be as simple as "eyeballing" a group to estimate age, gender, and race, or it can be as complicated as polling people to discover their predispositions on your topic. The information that follows is designed to make you more insightful about how you approach an audience and to invite you to think carefully about the people to whom you speak so you can be as effective as possible.

To begin, we survey four levels of **audience analysis.** The categories are called *levels* because the first is relatively easy and the last is the most difficult to understand and to use. In that sense, the levels are like grade levels in school; the ideas and concepts increase in difficulty. The four levels begin with the distinction between captive and voluntary audiences.

Level 1: Captive and Voluntary Audiences

A **captive audience,** as the name suggests, is an audience that did not choose to hear a particular speaker or speech. The teacher of a required class addresses a captive audience. A disc jockey who broadcasts commercial announcements between the songs you want to hear addresses a captive audience. Similarly, a student who addresses fellow students in a required speech class is addressing a captive audience.

Why should a public speaker distinguish a captive from a voluntary audience? One reason is a captive audience did not choose to hear from you or about your subject—you may have to motivate them to listen. Another is that captive audiences are **heterogeneous,** characterized by the wide variety of differences among individuals. The speaker must adapt the topic and the content of the speech to a wider range of information and to more diverse attitudes toward the subject. One of the advantages of a captive audience is that it gives the speaker an opportunity to present ideas to people who, under ordinary circumstances, might never have heard the information or the point of view embodied in the speech.

The **voluntary audience** chooses to hear the particular speaker or speech. The most important characteristic of the voluntary audience is that the participants have some need or desire to hear the speech. The people who go to listen to a politician are usually sympathetic to the speaker's ideas. The students who stop to hear a traveling evangelist speak on the campus lawn are usually curious about, or perhaps even committed to, the speaker's religious beliefs. The advantage of a voluntary audience is the speaker addresses an audience that is more **homogeneous,** that is, audience members are more like one another. Addressing a captive audience is like attempting to attract new customers to a product; addressing a voluntary audience is like attempting to please customers who have purchased the product before. Both salesperson and speaker are helped by knowing whether the audience is voluntary or captive because the nature of the audience affects the topic, rationale, approach, and goal of the speaker.

The task of determining the character of an audience is far from simple. A specific example can demonstrate its complexity. At first, you might guess a congregation is a voluntary audience—people choose to attend a particular church to hear a particular minister. What about the children in the congregation? Did they choose to hear the sermon, or did their parents make them go to church? What about some of the husbands and wives? How many people are there because their spouses wanted them to come along? To what extent did social pressures persuade some of these people to attend church? Did the audience members really know what the minister was going to say, or are they captives of the message that is being delivered? Even this first level of audience analysis is more challenging than it appears. The minister of a congregation addresses an audience that is in some ways voluntary and in some ways captive, and must adapt the message to those differences.

How can you, in your class, make the distinction between the voluntary and the captive audience? You may find your audience is more captive than voluntary—the members of the audience did not enroll in the class to hear you or your speech. On the other hand, they are there to learn how to give and to listen to speeches. You may have to adapt to your student audience by ensuring they know why *you* are speaking to *them* about *this* particular subject. You will actually find yourself more dependent than most speakers on the other kinds of audience analysis covered in this chapter. Most public speakers work with voluntary audiences. They know, from experience and investigation, what their audience wants to hear and what they can do. You will probably have to learn about your audience through the methods suggested in this chapter.

Level 2: Demographic Analysis

Demographics literally means "the characteristics of the people." **Demographic analysis** is based on the kind of characteristics you write on forms: name, age, sex, home-town, year in school, race, major subject, religion, and organizational affiliations. Such information can be important to public speakers because it can reveal the extent to which they will have to adapt themselves and their topics to that audience.

A closer look at one item might demonstrate the importance of demographic information about the audience. Let us see what the effect might be of your audience's majors. Suppose you plan to speak about the cost of littering in your state. Your audience consists of twenty-two students: seven have not chosen a major subject, three are mathematics majors, four are biology majors, six are majoring in business administration, and one is an English major. This information gives you no reason to assume that any of them knows much about littering, but you can assume from nine to thirteen audience members have a basic understanding of numbers. The six business majors may have a better understanding of costs than the others, and the students majoring in math and science may find the cost-benefit approach attractive as well.

If you add more demographic information to that small bit of information, then you can find even more to guide you. Does your college attract students who are likely to be concerned about the expense of littering? Is your audience likely to be knowledgeable about rural or urban littering? Do any students in your audience belong to organizations concerned about conservation? Whatever your topic, the demographic characteristics of your audience can imply the audience's receptiveness to your topic.

Public speakers usually rely heavily on demographic information. Politicians send personnel ahead to find out how many blue-collar workers, faithful party members, elderly people, union members, and hecklers they are likely to encounter. They want to know how many and what cultural and co-cultural groups are likely to be present. They consult opinion polls, population

Demographic characteristics reveal important information about an audience.

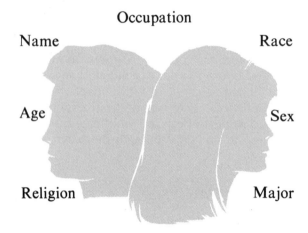

studies, and reliable persons in the area to discover the nature of a prospective audience. Conducting a demographic analysis of your class can serve a similar purpose—it will help you design a speech better adapted to your audience.

Level 3: Audience Interest in and Knowledge of the Topic

As you move up the levels of audience analysis, the information you are asked to discover becomes more difficult to find. On level 3, your task is to determine the degree of **audience interest** in your topic and **audience knowledge** of the topic. The following are another way to ask the same questions about interest and knowledge in a topic: How familiar is your audience with the topic? This question is important because if your audience is disinterested in, or unfamiliar with, your topic, you will have to generate that interest in your speech.

One means of finding an audience's interest in, and knowledge of, a topic is to consider the age of the topic. Age and familiarity are closely related because the longer a topic has been around and the more recently it has gained importance, the more likely the audience is to know about it. Your classmates may know much about a topic that has been a burning issue in the student newspaper, but they may not know a great deal about nuclear fusion, power satellites, or the latest fashions. A topic that is old to a forty-five year old person can be new to a nineteen-year-old student. If you were addressing classmates of mixed ages, you would have to adapt to those persons who are familiar with the topic and to those who are not. Fortunately, old topics have new variations. Topics, like people, live, change, and die—some have long and varied lives, while others pass quickly.

How can you gauge the audience's interest in, and knowledge of, your topic? One way to find out is to ask questions. You can ask demographic questions to help assess audience interest in your topic. The audience members' ages, majors, year in school, and organizational memberships can suggest their familiarity with, knowledge of, and interest in your topic. Ask your fellow students before and after classes, in the hallways and the cafeteria. Ask them in writing through a questionnaire, if your instructor encourages that kind of analysis. You can even ask for some indication of interest during your speech, by asking your classmates to raise their hands in response to such questions as: How many of you watch television news? How many of you have been to Washington, D.C.? How many of you have read an unassigned book in the last three months?

Level 4: The Audience's Attitudes, Beliefs, and Values

An **attitude** is a tendency to respond favorably or unfavorably to some person, object, idea, or event. The attitudes of audience members can be assessed through questionnaires, by careful observation, or even by asking the right questions. If your audience comes from a place where many attitudes, beliefs, and values are shared, your audience analysis may be easy. A speech about safe sex would be heard in some colleges with as much excitement as a speech on snails; but at other colleges, the same speech could be grounds for dismissal. Attitudes towards politics, sex, religion, war, and even work, vary in different geographical areas and co-cultures. Regardless of the purpose of your speech, the attitudes of audience members will make a difference in the appropriateness of your topic. Some examples of different attitudes follow:

Pro-war	Pro-business
Anti-Communist	Anti-materialism
Pro-government	Pro-choice
Anti-gun control	Anti-intellectual
Pro-conformity	Pro-life
Anti-pollution	Anti-exercise
Anti-immigration	Pro-conservation
Pro-animal rights	Anti-recycling

A **belief** is a conviction. Beliefs, or convictions, are usually considered more solid than attitudes, but our attitudes often spring from our beliefs. Your belief in good eating habits may lead to a negative attitude toward overeating and obesity and to a positive attitude toward balanced meals and nutrition. Your audience's beliefs make a difference in how they respond to your speech. They may believe in upward mobility through higher education, in higher pay through hard work, in the superiority of the family farm, in a lower tax base, or in social welfare. They may not believe in any of these ideas.

Choose from thousands of possible topics the ones that are most appropriate for you and your audience.

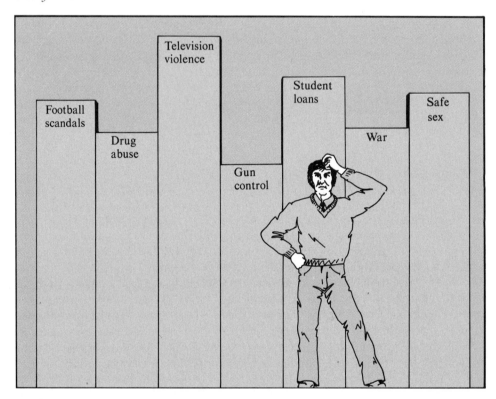

Beliefs are like anchors to which our attitudes are attached. To discover the beliefs of our audience, we need to ask questions and to observe carefully. Some examples of beliefs follow:

Hard work pays off.
Minority persons cannot get a fair trial.
No one is concerned about crime victims.
Taxes are too high.
Anyone can get rich.
There is an afterlife.

The Bible is God's word.
Democrats are spenders.
Women are discriminated against.
War is natural.
The world gets better and better.
Work comes before play.

Values are the deeply rooted beliefs that govern our attitudes. Both beliefs and attitudes can be traced to some value that we hold. (Relationships between attitudes, beliefs, and values are illustrated in figure 11.1.) Learned from childhood through the family, the church, the school, and many other sources, values are often so much a foundation for the rest of what we believe and know that they are not questioned. Sometimes, we remain unaware of our

Topics

Consider the appropriateness of some of these subjects with your instructor and your classmates. The answers you receive will tell you a lot about your classmates' attitudes.

Gun control	Divorce
Birth control	Interest rates
Abortion	Swear words
Weapons	AIDS
Secret societies	Gambling
Sexual mores	Equal pay
Value of a college education	Gay rights
Marriage	Drugs and alcohol

primary values until they clash. For example, a person might have an unquestioned belief that every individual has the right to be and do whatever he or she wishes—a basic value in individuality and freedom—until it comes to homosexuality. Sexual affectional orientation as an aspect of individual freedom may clash with the person's value for individuality. The following are some examples of values:

Marriage	Salvation	Beauty
Love	Pleasure	Self-expression
Friendship	Equality	Law and order
Courage	Wisdom	Sexual freedom
Freedom	Happiness	Work
Individual rights	Independence	Privacy
Patriotism	Excitement	Family
Religion	Peace	Competition

The values held by your audience and the order in which these values are ranked by individuals can provide valuable clues about your audience's attitudes and beliefs. The speaker who addresses an audience without knowing the values of audience members is taking a risk that can be avoided by careful audience analysis.

Figure 11.1 Relationships between attitudes, beliefs, and values.

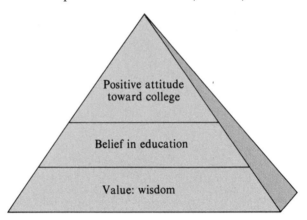

Three Methods of Audience Analysis

Method 1: Observation

Effective public speakers must engage in active **observation** of the behavior and characteristics of their audience. An effective lawyer selects an audience by questioning prospective jurors. The lawyer asks questions designed to discover prejudice, negative and positive attitudes, beliefs, and values. Later, as the witnesses testify, the lawyer observes their verbal and nonverbal behavior and decides which arguments, evidence, and witnesses are influencing the jurors. Evangelists know, from their many sermons, which Bible verses, parables, and testimonials bring sinners to the altar. People who speak on behalf of business associations, unions, political parties, colleges, and the underprivileged have usually spent years watching others and learning which approaches, arguments, and evidence are most likely to be accepted by an audience.

You can learn to do the same thing in your class. For every speech you give, you might listen to twenty or twenty-five. You have a unique opportunity to discover your classmates' responses. Do they respond well to speakers who come on strong and authoritatively or to speakers who talk to them like equals? Do they like speeches about work, leisure, getting ahead, or getting the most out of their education? Do they respond well to numbers and statistics, stories and examples, graphs and posters, or pictures and slides? As a listener in the classroom, you have a unique opportunity to observe your own and your classmates' responses to a variety of speakers.

You can also observe some demographic characteristics of your classmates: age, gender, race, and group affiliations (athletic jackets, fraternity pins). You can see how they respond to a speaker who keeps his or her eyes

The public speaker must consider differences in values among audience members.

on the audience and how they respond to one who depends heavily on notes. You can observe whether you and the audience respond favorably when the speaker is deeply involved in the speech. Every speech you hear will, in some way, indicate the speaker's attitudes, beliefs, and values, and the response of the audience.

Even though your audience may be more captive than most, you have an advantage over most public speakers. How many public speakers have an opportunity to hear every one of their listeners give a speech? Instead of sitting back like a passive observer, take advantage of the situation by listening actively, taking notes about the speaker's characteristics, and recording the audience's responses. You can analyze your audience continually during a round of speeches by careful observation.

Method 2: Inference

To draw an **inference** is to draw a tentative conclusion based on some evidence. We draw an inference when we see someone dressed in rags and tentatively conclude the person is poor. Our inferences are often accurate—we infer from his wedding band that a man is married, from the children tugging at his sleeve he is a father, and from the woman holding his arm that she is his wife. We are basing these inferences on thin data, but they are probably correct. Inferences may also be incorrect. The more evidence on which you base an inference, however, the more likely it is to be true.

Ranking Values

Rank the following values in their order of importance to you. If you can persuade some of your classmates, or the entire class, to do this as well, you will have information that will help you prepare your speech.

Wisdom	Equality	Fame
A comfortable life	Wealth	Health
A world at peace	Leisure	Love
Freedom	Security	Beauty
Maturity	Fulfillment	Relational satisfaction

How does your ranking compare to your classmates'? What other values might help you with your speech?

From Robert L. Heath, "Variability in Value System Priorities as Decision-Making Adaptation to Situational Differences" in Communication Monographs 43:325–33. © 1976 Speech Communication Association. *Reprinted by permission.*

You can base inferences on observed characteristics in your audience, on demographic information, and on questionnaires. You can also draw inferences either indirectly or directly. An indirect way to draw inferences is by observation. You might, for example, find that 85 percent of students at a particular university hold part-time jobs (an observation). You might infer that it is an expensive school, that financial aid is limited, or that the cost of area housing is high. You might also infer, from your limited information, that most of the students in this school value their education, are exceptionally well-motivated, or believe in saving money for future plans.

A more direct way to gather data on which to base inferences is to ask questions. You could, for example, ask either orally or in writing, to determine how many students in the class have part- or full-time jobs; how many are married, have families, have grown children; how many plan to become wealthy; whether they were raised in an urban or rural setting; and how many have strong religious ties. The answers to these questions would provide valuable information about your audience.

To illustrate how this method works, let us examine one question, one answer, and some inferences that could be drawn from the information. The question is: How many students in your class are married? The answer may be four out of twenty-five. From this data, several inferences can be drawn. First, the students are probably older than the average person enrolled in college. Second, they may be part-time students who are also raising a family or holding a job. Finally, they are motivated and mature enough to prepare for a class and handle a marriage and home. These inferences can assist you in preparing the content of your speech. For example, if your strongest inference is that these individuals are also raising a family, certain topics will hold greater interest for them than others. Such topics as setting priorities or saving money for the future may engage this audience. Conversely, speeches about dorm policy, intermural athletics, or study abroad may be met with disinterest.

Method 3: The Questionnaire

A more formal way to collect data on which you can base inferences is to ask your audience to fill out a **questionnaire** you or others have developed to determine demographic and attitudinal information. Demographic information can be easily gathered and summarized from questions similar to those that follow:

____ 1.   I am   *(a)* a first-year student.

  (b) a sophomore.

  (c) a junior.

  (d) a senior.

____ 2.   I am   *(a)* under 18.

  (b) 18–21 years old.

  (c) 22–27 years old.

  (d) over 27.

____ 3.   I am   *(a)* single.

  (b) married.

  (c) divorced or separated.

  (d) widowed.

____ 4.   I have   *(a)* no children.

  (b) one child.

  (c) two children.

  (d) more than two children.

The audience members do not have to identify themselves by name to provide this information. Keeping the questionnaires anonymous (no names) encourages honest answers and does not reduce the value of the information.

Attitudinal information can be collected in at least three ways. *One way is to ask questions that place audience members in identifiable groups,* as these questions do:

___ 5. I (*a*) am active in campus organizations.

        (*b*) am not active in campus organizations.

___ 6. I see myself as (*a*) conservative.

        (*b*) liberal.

        (*c*) independent.

___ 7. I see myself as (*a*) strongly religious.

        (*b*) moderately religious.

        (*c*) unreligious.

A second method of gaining attitudinal information is to ask people to rank values, such as hard work, higher education, high pay, and security. People's ranking of their values can suggest additional information about their attitudes and beliefs.

The third method of collecting data about people's attitudes involves listing word-concepts that reveal attitudes and then asking your respondents to assess their attitudes toward these specific issues. One way to do this involves using an attitudinal scale like the one on page 255. The reactions to these and similar words or phrases can provide information that will help you approach your audience successfully. For example, if most persons in your audience are neutral to mildly favorable toward abortion, then your speech advocating abortion could be designed to raise their attitudes from mildly to favorable to strongly favorable. If the responses are negative, then you may have to work just to move your audience closer to a mildly disfavorable attitude or toward neutrality.

Adapting to the Audience

Analysis of an audience yields information about your listeners that enables you to adapt yourself and your verbal and nonverbal codes to that audience. A speech is not a message imposed on a collection of listeners; a speech is negotiated between a speaker and an audience designed to inform, entertain, inspire, teach, or persuade that audience. This negotiation is based on your analysis of your audience.

An important question to consider in adapting to an audience is: How do I adapt to an audience without letting the audience dictate my position? The answer is you do not analyze the audience to discover your own position but to discover theirs—how much do they know about the topic? What approach is most likely to persuade persons with their attitudes, beliefs, and values? To find, for example, an audience is likely to be utterly opposed to your position is not an indication that you should alter your position on the issue. It is an indication that you may have to adopt a more gradual approach to changing them than you would have liked to use. Similarly, to discover the audience is even more ignorant of the topic than you thought only indicates you will have to provide more background or more elementary information than you had originally planned. In short, you have to adapt yourself, your verbal and non-verbal codes, your topic, your purpose, and your supporting materials to the particular group of people you will face in your speech.

Adapting Yourself

In previous chapters, you learned about self-concept and about how people in interpersonal contexts and small group settings adjust to each other. *In public speaking, the speaker also has to adjust to information about the audience.* Just as the college senior preparing for a job interview adapts to the interviewer in dress, manner, and language, the public speaker prepares for an audience by adapting to its expectations. How you look, how you behave, and what you say should be carefully adjusted to an audience you have learned about through observation, experience, and analysis. As you will discover in chapter 12 on speaker credibility, there are ways you can help an audience perceive you as a credible person.

The public speaker must adapt to the audience through both verbal and nonverbal codes.

Adapting Your Verbal and Nonverbal Codes

The language you employ in your speech, as well as your gestures, movements, and even facial expressions, should be adapted to your audience. Does your experience, observation, and analysis of the audience's attitudes indicate your language should be conversational, formal, cynical, or technical? Does your analysis indicate your listeners like numbers and statistics? Do your observations indicate you should pace the stage or stand still behind the lectern? Does your analysis indicate you should not use taboo words in your speech lest you alienate your group, or does the audience like a little lively language?

Adapting Your Topic

Public speakers should be permitted to speak about any topic that fits the assignment. In the classroom, at least, you should select a topic that relates to you. Remember, you will be giving your speech to an audience of classmates; therefore, the topic you select must be adapted to them. Audience analysis is a means of discovering the audience's position on the topic. From information based on observation, description, and inference, you have to decide how you are going to adapt your topic to this audience.

DOONESBURY

Audience analysis can tell you what challenges you face. If you want to speak in favor of nuclear energy and your audience analysis indicates the majority of your listeners are opposed to that position, you need not conclude the topic is inappropriate. You may, however, adapt to the members of your audience by starting with a position closer to theirs. Your initial step might be to make audience members feel less comfortable about their present position so they are prepared to hear your position.

Your analysis might indicate your audience already has considerable information about your topic. You then may have to adapt by locating information they do not have. For example, you may want to deliver an informative speech about the latest world crisis, but your analysis may indicate the audience is not only already interested, but it also has sufficient information of the sort you planned to offer. You can adapt your topic by shifting to the area of the subject about which the audience is not so well informed: What is the background of the situation? What are the backgrounds of the personalities and the issues? What do the experts think will happen? What are the possible consequences?

Adapting Your Purpose

You should also adapt the purpose of your speech to your audience. Teachers often ask a student to state the purpose of a speech—what do you want your audience to know, understand, or do? It may help you to think of your speech as one part of a series of informative talks your audience will hear about your topic. They have probably heard something about the topic before and are likely to hear about the topic again. Your particular presentation is just one of the audience's exposures to the topic.

Still, your immediate purpose is linked to some larger goal. The goal is the end you have in mind. In the "Doonesbury" cartoon, Ms. Slade's immediate purpose is to announce her candidacy for the United States Congress; her larger

Writing Immediate Purposes

To gain practice in writing immediate purposes for speeches, write five purposes for an informative speech and five purposes for a persuasive speech. Use the general topics suggested on pages 387–88. for informative speeches and on pages 413–15 for persuasive speeches. Make sure the immediate purposes are specific, use the phrase "should be able to," use an action verb, and are written from the audience's perspective.

goal is to be elected to office. Some examples of immediate purposes and long-range goals will illustrate the difference. The following are examples of immediate purposes and long-range goals of an informative speech:

Immediate Purpose	**Long-Range Goal**
After listening to this speech, the audience should be able to identify three properties of flying saucers.	To increase the number of people who will read articles and books about flying saucers.
After listening to my talk, the audience should be able to name six expressions that are part of the street language used by urban African Americans.	To help the listeners understand and appreciate the language employed by some African-American students.

The following are some examples of the immediate purposes and the long-range goals of a persuasive speech:

Immediate Purpose	**Long-Range Goal**
After my presentation, the audience should be able to state three positive characteristics of the candidate for mayor.	To have some of the audience members vote for the candidate at election time.
After my speech, the audience should be able to explain the low nutritional value of two popular junk foods.	To dissuade the listeners from eating junk food.

You should note that the immediate purpose has four essential features. First, it is highly specific, it is not ambiguous or vague. Second, it includes the phrase "should be able to." Third, it uses an action verb such as state, identify, report, name, list, describe, explain, show, and reveal. Fourth, it is stated from the viewpoint of the audience. You are writing the purpose as an audience objective.

The more specific your immediate purpose, the better you will be able to determine whether you accomplished it. You should also employ audience analysis to help you discover whether your purpose is appropriate. Suppose half the people in your class are going into fields where a knowledge of food and nutrition is important. They already know more than the average person about nutritional values. Consequently, it is probably not appropriate to deliver a speech about junk food. It may also not be wise to speak to a group of athletes about the importance of exercise. You should adapt your purpose to the audience by considering the level of their information, the novelty of the issue, and the other factors discussed in this chapter.

Adapting Your Supporting Materials

Your personal knowledge, your interviewing, and your library research should provide more material for your speech than you can use. Again, audience analysis helps you select materials for this particular audience. Your analysis might reveal, for example, your classmates do not have much respect for authority figures. In that case, you might be wasting your time informing them of the surgeon general's opinion on smoking; your personal experience or the experience of some of your classmates might be more important to them than an expert's opinion. On the other hand, if your audience analysis reveals that parents, teachers, pastors, and other authority figures are held in high regard, you may want to quote physicians, research scientists, counselors, and health-service personnel.

As a public speaker, you should always keep in mind the choices you make in selecting a topic, choosing an immediate purpose, determining a long-range goal, organizing your speech, selecting supporting materials, and even creating visual aids are all **strategic choices.** All of these choices are made for the purpose of adapting the speaker and the subject to a particular audience. The larger your supply of supporting arguments, the better your chances of having effective arguments. The larger your supply of supporting materials, the better your chances of providing effective evidence, illustrations, and visual aids. Your choices are strategic in that they are purposeful. The purpose is to choose, from among the available alternatives, the ones that will best achieve your purpose with the particular audience.

Summary

This chapter has two purposes: to help you select a speech topic appropriate for you and for your audience and to help you analyze and adapt to your audience.

Brainstorming and personal inventories are two methods of topic selection. Involvement in, and knowledge of, a topic are two means of evaluating the topic's appropriateness for you. Once you have chosen a topic, it is important to narrow the topic to fit the subject, audience, and time allowed.

To discover if a topic is appropriate for your audience, you have to analyze your audience at four levels. Level 1 distinguishes between voluntary and captive audiences. Level 2 is demographic analysis in which the characteristics of the audience members are evaluated. Level 3 analyzes the audience's interest in, and knowledge of, a topic. Level 4 determines the audience's attitudes, beliefs, and values.

Three methods of analyzing an audience are observation, inference, and the questionnaire. Observation involves actively watching your audience and learning from its behavior. Inference uses incomplete data to draw tentative conclusions about an audience; conclusions that may make the audience's response more predictable. The questionnaire can be used to garner demographic and attitudinal information about the audience.

Adapting to an audience after audience analysis requires you to carefully adapt yourself, your verbal and nonverbal codes, your topic, your purpose, and your supporting materials to that particular group of people.

Key Terms

attitudes A predisposition to respond favorably or unfavorably to some person, object, idea, or event.

audience analysis The collection and interpretation of data on the demographics, attitudes, values, and beliefs of the audience obtained by observation, inferences, questionnaires, or interviews.

audience interest The relevance and importance of the topic to an audience; sometimes related to the uniqueness of the topic.

audience knowledge The amount of information the audience already has about the topic.

belief A conviction; often thought to be more enduring than an attitude and less enduring than a value.

brainstorming Listening or naming as many ideas as a group or an individual can within a limited period of time.

captive audience An audience that did not choose to hear a particular speaker or speech.

demographic analysis The collection and interpretation of data about the characteristics of people, excluding their attitudes, values, and beliefs.

heterogeneous The amount and variety of differences that exist between individual audience members.

homogeneous The similarity between individual audience members.

inference Conclusions drawn from observation.

involvement The importance of the topic to the speaker; determined by the strength of the feelings the speaker has about the topic and the time and energy the speaker devotes to that subject area or topic.

observation Seeing and sensing the behavior and characteristics of an audience.

personal inventories A speaker's surveys of his or her reading and viewing habits and behavior to discover what topics and subjects are of personal interest.

questionnaire A method of obtaining information about an audience by asking written questions about audience members' demographic characteristics or attitudes.

strategic choices What you choose to do in your speech from the words to the arguments; evidence should be used to help you adapt your speech to the audience.

value A deeply rooted belief that governs our attitude about something.

voluntary audience A collection of people who choose to listen to a particular speaker or speech.

chapter 12

Communication Apprehension and
Speaker Credibility

I n this chapter, we cover two areas of great concern to students of public speaking. The first area is fear. Many people are afraid of public speaking. In fact, at least one source reports it as the most common phobia in this country.[1] The person who does not feel some fear as a beginning public speaker is rare, so if you look forward to public speaking with some apprehension, you are normal. On the other hand, some students exhibit a more serious problem as they face the prospect of giving public speeches. Their problem is called speech anxiety or communication apprehension. This chapter explores the normal and more serious fears people have about public speaking and also looks at some of the ways of coping with this fear.

The second area of concern to students of public speaking is speaker credibility. Why will people listen to a particular speaker when he or she speaks? What do audiences perceive as the signs a speaker is believable? Can a speaker do anything to help an audience recognize he or she has earned the right to speak on a topic? These and other dimensions of credibility focus our attention on sharing ourselves with an audience.

What will you learn?

When you have read and thought about this chapter, you should be able to answer the following questions:

1. What is high communication apprehension?

2. What are five symptoms of normal apprehension?

3. Can you explain six strategies for overcoming normal fear of public speaking?

4. Can you distinguish among the four aspects of source credibility by defining and explaining them?

5. What are two important ways you could improve your credibility as a public speaker?

6. What does research tell us about source credibility and its effects?

7. What information would you provide about yourself for someone who has to introduce you to improve your credibility?

8. What would you say about yourself in the beginning of a public speech to establish your credibility on the topic?

No one can make you feel inferior without your consent.

Eleanor Roosevelt

You can't build a reputation on what you are going to do.

Henry Ford

In the future everyone will be world-famous for 15 minutes.

Andy Warhol

Fear of Public Speaking

The fear of speaking in public goes by many different names. Once called "stage fright" because it was a fear most often seen in beginning actors, it is now called **communication apprehension.** The term covers many kinds of communication fears in diverse situations: fear of talking on the telephone, fear of face-to-face conversations, fear of talking to authority figures or high-status individuals, fear of speaking to another individual, fear of speaking in a small group, and fear of speaking to an audience.

Why should you know about communication apprehension? Even the question is controversial. Some teachers of public speaking feel that discussing communication apprehension—even in a textbook—is questionable because students who read about the fear of public speaking may see themselves as more apprehensive than those who do not know about it. However, as more teachers learn about communication apprehension, they want the subject discussed in texts.

There are at least two reasons why you should know about communication apprehension. The first is you need to be able to see the difference between the normal fear most people experience before they give a speech and high communication apprehension, which is a more serious problem. The second reason is people who are highly apprehensive about communication should receive special treatment for their problem, or they will spend a lifetime handicapped by their fear.

Let us look first at the scope, symptoms, and effects of high communication apprehension. Then we will examine some solutions to this problem.[2]

High Communication Apprehension

About one out of every five persons is communication apprehensive, that is, 20 percent of all college students. Fortunately, that statistic means that four out of every five students, or 80 percent, are not apprehensive. Communication apprehensive people may not appear apprehensive unless they are engaging in a particular type of communication. High communication apprehension seems unrelated to general anxiety and intelligence. You may show no overt signs of anxiety in such activities as playing football, studying, eating, watching television, or walking to class. However, the high communication apprehensive (HCA) person has such strong negative feelings about communicating with other people that he or she typically avoids communication, or exhibits considerable fear when communicating. The scope of the communication apprehension problem may not appear large, but millions of people suffer from the fear of communicating.

One symptom of communication apprehension is the HCA tries to avoid communication situations. Two researchers conducted a study to find out what would happen if HCA students had a choice of an interpersonal communication course or a public speaking course. They found HCA students overwhelmingly chose the interpersonal communication course. The researchers suspected students perceived the public speaking course as much more threatening than the interpersonal communication course.[3] Similarly, in small group communication, HCA students tend to be nonparticipants in the class or to repeatedly register for, and drop, the class. HCA students try to avoid participating in the kind of communication that arouses their fears.

What are some other choices characteristic of HCA people? They will choose rooms away from other people at the ends of halls in dormitories or housing away from busy streets and playgrounds in a housing development. HCA people will sit away from others or in places in which leadership is not expected (along the side of the table, far from the end). When HCA persons do find themselves in a communication situation, they talk less, show less interest in the topic, take fewer risks, and say less about themselves than their classmates do. HCA people may be difficult to get to know. Even when they do find themselves in a situation where communication is unavoidable, they discourage talk with signs of disinterest and silence.

The effects of high communication apprehension can be serious. HCA persons are rarely perceived as leaders. They are seen as less extroverted, less sociable, less popular, and less competent than their peers.[4] They are not perceived as desirable partners for courtship or marriage. They are viewed as less composed, less attractive socially, and less task-attractive. Because they communicate reluctantly and seem so uneasy when they do, HCA people are perceived negatively by others. Therefore, they tend to do poorly in interviews and tend not to get the same quality of jobs as nonapprehensive people do. However, they are not less intellectual, mentally healthy, or physically attractive.[5] The consequences of being HCA seem serious enough to encourage us to look next at solutions.

One way to solve high communication apprehension is to be aware of the malady and to understand that people with anxiety actually prepare differently, and less effectively, than do people without anxiety. Professor John Daly, of the University of Texas at Austin, and three doctoral students showed that anxious people are overly concerned with self and are negative in their assessments. They choose speech topics with which they are less familiar and have less sensitivity to public speaking situations.[6] A self-fulfilling prophecy is thus created. Anxious individuals are fearful, they prepare less effectively, and perform worse, which reinforces their fear about the public speaking situation. The cycle may be broken by more effective preparation, which is discussed later in this chapter.

A second way to resolve feelings of high apprehension is through relaxation. Two techniques are possible. First, you can practice muscle relaxation, which will assist you with the physical symptoms you may have. When you deliberately tense a muscle and then relax it, you experience physical relaxation. You can become less physically tense by consciously tensing and relaxing the muscles in the various parts of your body. You may wish to systematically work from head to toe or in another reasonable progression. You may want to sit in a comfortable position or lie down as you relax your muscles.

The other side of relaxation is stopping those thoughts that make you nervous. When you begin to have anxiety-producing thoughts, you may wish to consciously calm yourself. The textbook writers Teri and Michael Gamble describe this technique.

> A variation on the "calm technique" is to precede the word *calm* with the
> word *stop*. In other words, when you begin to think upsetting thoughts, say to
> yourself, "Stop!" Then follow that command with, "Calm." For example:
> "I just can't get up in front of all those people.
> Look at their cold stares and mean smirks."
> "Stop!"
> "Calm."[7]

These two techniques can calm your physical and mental fears and allow you to be more relaxed in a communication situation.

Another remedy for high communication apprehension is professional help. The negative feelings about communication in the HCA person have often been developing since childhood. They do not disappear easily. Many schools and colleges have psychologists and counselors who have had professional training in reducing students' fears about speaking in public. Treatments that include training in the control of anxiety appear to be particularly helpful.[9] If you think you are among the small minority of people who have unusually high fear in a public speaking situation, then you may want to talk to your public speaking teacher about any services available to you.

A final possibility for fear of public speaking is called systematic desensitization. **Systematic desensitization** is the repeated exposure to small doses of whatever makes you apprehensive. A public speaking student might be asked over a number of weeks to think of what is frightening (e.g., going to the front of the room to speak) and then to immediately follow the frightening thought with thoughts that relax as in the accompanying exercise. This process repeated over time tends to diminish a person's anxiety about communicating.

So far, this section on fear of public speaking has concentrated on the individual with extreme fear. What about the vast majority of persons who have a normal fear of public speaking? What are the signs of normal fear, and what can you do about reducing this normal fear—or even getting it to work *for* you instead of *against* you?

Normal Communication Apprehension

Most human beings feel fear when they speak in public. New teachers march into their first classes armed with twelve hours worth of material—just to be sure they will have plenty to say in their one-hour class. Experienced speakers

Calming Normal Communication Anxiety

In order to practice the relaxation techniques, do the following.

1. Sit in a comfortable chair or lie down in a comfortable place. As much as possible, rid the area of distracting noises. If possible, play relaxing music or a tape with the sounds of nature.

2. Begin with your face and neck and tense the muscles. Then relax them. Repeat the tensing and hold the tensed position for 10 seconds. Relax again.

3. Tense your hands by clenching your fists. Relax. Tense again and hold for 10 seconds. Relax.

4. Tense your arms above your hands and to your shoulders. Relax. Tense again and hold for 10 seconds. Relax.

5. Tense your chest and stomach. Relax. Tense again and hold for 10 seconds. Relax.

6. Tense your feet by pulling the toes under. Relax. Tense again and hold for 10 seconds. Relax.

7. Tense your legs above the feet and up to the hips. Relax. Tense again and hold for 10 seconds. Relax.

8. Tense your entire body and hold for 10 seconds. Relax and breathe slowly.

9. Repeat the word *calm* to yourself. This will help you to relate the word to the relaxed feeling you are now experiencing. In the future, when you feel anxious the word *calm* should help you arrest the apprehension you experience.[8]

feel fear when they face audiences that are new to them. Nearly all of the students in a public speaking class feel anxiety when they think about giving their speeches and when they deliver them.

What are the classic symptoms of communication apprehension for the public speaker? The authors of this book have given hundreds of speeches but still cannot sleep well the night before an important speech—one sign of anxiety or fear. Another common symptom is worry: you can't seem to get the speech out of your mind. You keep thinking about what giving the speech is going to be like, and you keep feeling inadequate for the task. When you actually give the speech, the common symptoms of fear are shaking—usually the hands, knees, and voice; dryness of the mouth—often called cottonmouth; and sweating—usually on the palms of the hands. One wit noted public speakers suffer so often from dryness of the mouth and wetness of the palms that they should stick their hands in their mouth. For the public speaker, however, fear is no laughing matter. Let us turn from what the normal speaker *feels* to how the normal speaker *behaves* when afraid.

The speaker who is afraid—even with normal fear—tends to avoid eye contact, speak softly, utter vocalized pauses, ("Well," "You know," "Mmmmm"), speak too slowly or too quickly, not know what to do with hands or feet, stand as far away from the audience as possible, and place as many obstacles as possible between the speaker and the audience (distance, lecterns, notes). The speaker who is overcoming fear looks at the audience; speaks so all can hear easily; avoids vocalized pauses; speaks at a normal rate; moves body, arms, and feet in ways that do not appear awkward; stands at the usual distance from the audience; and uses the lectern to hold notes instead of as a hiding place.

Research on audience responses to public speakers indicates the importance of overcoming fear of public speaking for improved effectiveness. For example, one study shows that speakers who look at their audience are judged as credible and are seen as more persuasive than those who do not.[10] Another study shows apprehensive speakers who employ more vocalized pauses or hesitations are less persuasive.[11] Finally, speakers who appear unusually slow or powerless are perceived as less knowledgeable about the topic and, therefore, as less credible.[12]

Now that you understand the fear of public speaking and the way a speaker acts when afraid, you need to focus on the more positive topic of what to do about reducing normal fear.

Reducing the Fear of Public Speaking

If you expect to overcome your fear of public speaking, the first thing you need is a strong desire to overcome it. You need incentive, motivation, and determination. The Dale Carnegie organization has taught public speaking skills to millions of adults who did not believe in the merits of public speaking until they got out of school. An executive from the Dale Carnegie organization once admitted that before he took the Dale Carnegie course he was so afraid of public speaking and so outraged that his fear limited his life in so many ways, that he decided to overcome his fear by sheer determination. Ironically, the man who was so afraid of public speaking ended up devoting his life to teaching others how to become effective public speakers.

Fortunately, there are some other things besides sheer determination you can do to help overcome normal fears of public speaking:

1. *Know your topic.* Know more than most of your audience about the topic, find information and interview others about the topic, and organize your speech into the time allowed.
2. *Know your audience.* Know who is in your audience, what they are interested in, and how they are likely to respond to your topic.

Anxiety about public speaking can be reduced if you have a strong desire to overcome the fear.

3. *Know yourself.* If you feel good about yourself—your intelligence, talents, and competence—then you will be more secure and less afraid.
4. *Know your speech.* Practice your speech so you know the ideas, the order in which they appear, and the main messages you want to communicate to the audience.
5. *Focus on the message, not yourself.* If you have selected a topic important to you and your audience and you see your purpose as successfully communicating that message to the audience, then you will not be thinking about your hands, mouth, or knees—and neither will your audience.
6. **Recognize your value and uniqueness.** You are the only one who can share what you know with audience members—they cannot get it anywhere else.

Your instructor may be able to suggest some additional ideas for reducing your anxiety about public speaking, and you may be able to think of some ideas for reducing fear yourself. When some students in a beginning public speaking class were asked what they did to reduce their fears, they mentioned the following ideas:

1. Walk to the lectern calmly and confidently because acting confident and poised can make you feel confident and poised.

Reducing Your Fear during Your Speech: A Checklist

Check each of the following items to ensure you have thought about them before your speech and to improve the chances you will do them during your speech.

_____ 1. I will look at the audience members during my speech.

_____ 2. I will speak loudly enough for people in the back row to hear me with ease.

_____ 3. I will have my thoughts ready to avoid hesitations.

_____ 4. I will avoid vocalized pauses.

_____ 5. I will try to move and gesture naturally.

_____ 6. I will not avoid my audience with distance or obstacles.

_____ 7. I will speak calmly at a conversational pace.

_____ 8. I will look my best to feel my best.

_____ 9. I will sleep and eat before I speak.

_____10. I will practice my speech in the actual setting if possible.

_____11. I will imagine facing my audience until it worries me less.

_____12. Most importantly: I will reduce my fear by focusing on communicating my message to my audience.

2. Do not start talking until you feel comfortable up in front. Look at the people in your audience before you start talking to them, just as you would in a conversation.
3. Focus on the friendly faces in the audience—the people who nod affirmatively, smile, and look friendly and attentive—they will make you feel good about yourself and your speech.
4. Have your introduction, main points, and conclusion clear in your head and practiced. The examples and supporting materials come to mind easily when the important items are remembered.

Perhaps you will not find this information startling, but the best cure for normal fear of public speaking is exactly what you are doing: take a course in which you are invited to deliver a number of supervised public speeches to an audience that is sympathetic because the audience members have to speak too. In other words, the speech classroom is a laboratory in which you can work systematically to reduce your fears. Your instructor's comments and those of your classmates can help you discover your strengths and weaknesses. Repeated experiences in front of an audience tend to reduce fear and permit the learning of communication skills that have application both inside and out-side the classroom. In short, you are now in the process of reducing your normal fear of public speaking.

Fear of public speaking is a burden for the few who suffer from high communication apprehension. For most of us, however, the fear can be reduced to levels where it helps, rather than hinders. Ask anybody who has to deliver the same lecture three times a day. Often, the second lecture is the best because of the confidence borne of practice. The third lecture is usually the worst because there is so little fear left that delivering the lecture becomes a bit boring, even to the speaker.

You *can* learn to control and reduce your fear of public speaking. You can look your audience members in the eye, move and gesture with purpose, speak conversationally but with strength, and focus on the reason for your speech: to communicate your message to your audience.

Source Credibility

More than twenty-three hundred years ago, Aristotle noted a speaker's "character may almost be called the most effective means of persuasion he possesses."[13] Scholars have continued to study the importance of the source or speaker since that time because they correctly believed *who* says something determines *who* will listen.

In the public speaking classroom, you are the source of the message. You need to be concerned about how the audience will perceive you. You may feel you do not have the same credibility as a high public official, a great authority on some topic, or an expert in some narrow field. That may be so. However, you can still be a very credible source to your classmates, fellow workers, or friends. A teacher may be credible to his or her students; a father may be credible to his child; a lawyer may be credible to her or his clients. The same teacher, however, may not be credible in his or her family; the father may not be credible in the office; and the lawyer may not even be credible to her or his peers.

To understand the concept of **source credibility,** you must first recognize it is not something a speaker possesses, like a suit of clothes. Instead, the audience determines credibility. Credibility, like beauty, "is in the eye of the beholder."[14] Some people are like Woodstock in the "Peanuts" cartoon; they think a certain characteristic will give them credibility. The concept of credibility is much more complex.

A speaker's credibility depends in part on who the speaker is, the subject being discussed, the situation, and the audience. Have you served in the armed forces overseas? You may have earned the right to speak on foreign policy. Have you worked your way through college? You may have earned the

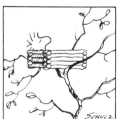

right to speak on the pros and cons of supporting yourself. Have you grown up in another country? You may have earned the right to speak on another country's culture, food, or social customs.

Similarly, you might be more credible to some audiences than you are to others—your classmates might find you credible and the local Teamsters Union might not. The personality characteristics of the audience members also affects the relative proportion of their response to your message and to you as a source of that message.[15] Some people are more inclined to respond positively to a speaker simply because he or she is attractive, while others focus on the content of the speech. For example, people who are high in **self-monitoring,** the ability to be sensitive to the communication situation and flexible in response, are more concerned with good arguments than with good looks.[16]

How do we gain credibility with an audience? The answer is public speakers *earn* the right to speak. They earn the right through their lives, experiences, and accomplishments. As one person observed, "Before you express yourself, you need a self-worth expressing." You may have earned the right to speak on a number of subjects. Have you worked in a fast-food restaurant? You may have earned the right to comment on the quality of fast food and service. Have you raised children? You may have earned the right to speak on the problems and pleasures of family life. Think about it. What have you experienced, learned, or lived through that has earned you the right to speak?

Four Aspects of Credibility

What do audience members perceive that gives them the idea a speaker is credible? If credibility is based on judgments by individuals in the audience, then what is the basis for those judgments? On what will your classmates be rating you when they judge your credibility? According to recent studies, *four of the most important aspects of credibility are competence, trustworthiness, dynamism, and co-orientation.*[17]

Competence

The first aspect of credibility is **competence.** A speaker who is perceived as competent is perceived as qualified, trained, experienced, authoritative, expert, reliable, informed, or knowledgeable. A speaker does not have to live up to all of these adjectives; any one, or a few, might make the speaker credible. The machinist who displays his metalwork in a speech about junk sculpture as art is as credible as the biblical scholar who is demonstrating her ability to interpret scripture. They have different bases for their competence, but both can demonstrate competence or expertise in their own areas of specialization.

Your own competence as a speaker is conveyed by your words, visual aids, and air of authority. What can you build into your speech that will help the audience see and understand the basis for your authority? What experience have you had that is related to the subject? What special training or knowledge do you have? How can you suggest to your audience that you have earned the right to speak about this subject? The most obvious way is to tell the audience the basis of your authority or expertise, but a creative speaker can think of dozens of ways to hint and suggest, competence without being explicit, without seeming condescending, and without lying.

A speaker also signals competence by knowing the substance of the speech so well that the speech is delivered without reading from notecards, without unplanned or vocalized pauses, and without mispronounced words. The speaker who knows the technical language in a specialized field and who can define the terms for the audience is signaling competence. The speaker who can translate complex ideas into language the audience can understand, who can find ways to illustrate ideas in ways the audience can comprehend, and who is familiar with people who know about the subject and with books and articles about the subject is signaling competence to the audience.

Trustworthiness

The second aspect of credibility is **trustworthiness.** How honest, fair, sincere, friendly, honorable, and kind does the audience find the speaker? These descriptors are also earned. We judge a person's honesty both by past behavior and present estimates. Your classmates will judge your trustworthiness when you speak in front of them. How do you decide whether or not other speakers in your class are responsible, sincere, dependable, or just? What can you do to help your audience perceive you are trustworthy?

You may have to reveal to your audience why you are trustworthy. Have you held jobs that demanded honesty and responsibility? Have you been a cashier, a bank teller, or a supervisor? Have you given up anything to demonstrate you are sincere? The person who pays her own way through college ordinarily has to be very sincere about education, and the person who chooses a lower-paying job because he or she feels a sense of public service is displaying sincerity about the job. Being respectful of others' points of view can

The speaker who uses facial expression, gestures, movements, and voice to make a point exhibits dynamism.

be a sign of your fairness, and being considerate of other people can be a sign of your kindness and friendliness. What can you say about yourself that will show your trustworthiness?

Dynamism

The third aspect of credibility is **dynamism**—the extent to which an audience perceives the speaker as bold, energetic, and assertive. Audiences value behavior described by these adjectives. Perhaps when we consider their opposites—timid, tired, and meek—we can see why dynamism is attractive. People who exude energy and show the spirit of their convictions impress others. Watch the television evangelists and ministers and note how dynamic they look and sound. You can learn to do the same. Evidence indicates that the audience's perception of your dynamic qualities will enhance your credibility.

Dynamism is exhibited mainly by voice, movement, facial expression, and gesture. The person who speaks forcefully, rapidly, and with considerable vocal variety; the speaker who moves toward the audience, back behind the

Jane Fonda's bold, energetic, and assertive delivery demonstrates dynamism.

lectern, and over to the visual aid; and the speaker who employs facial expression and gestures to make a point are all exhibiting dynamism. What can you do with your voice, movement, facial expressions, and gestures to show the audience you are a dynamic speaker?

Co-orientation

Co-orientation refers to the sharing of values, beliefs, attitudes, and interests.[18] It is not a mask of agreement worn to fool the audience. Co-orientation may involve having the welfare of others in mind. Co-orientation is telling the audience explicitly how you agree with them. This kind of information sharing is not just demographic—sharing similarities about hometowns, family sizes, and so on—but is also ideological. That is, the speaker tells the audience which ideas he or she has in common with the audience. An informative speech may require less co-orientation. A persuasive speech requires the speaker go beyond areas of complete agreement into areas where the speaker is trying to make a case for acceptance of his or her point of view on the issue.

Examples of student speeches the authors have heard in which the speaker employed co-orientation include speeches about student housing, dormitory food, and honors societies. The student who spoke about student housing was complaining about the use of three-person rooms in the dormitories. He knew the majority of the students in the class had suffered through a year or two of these same living conditions, and he established co-orientation by simply recounting some of his experiences in trying to study, entertain, and sleep in a three-person room. The student who spoke about the low quality of dormitory food knew most of the audience members had tasted it. She brought in a tray of dormitory food to remind them and to establish co-orientation. The student who spoke about honors societies was in an honors section full of students who had received invitations to join various honors societies. Unfortunately, most of the societies met only once and cost a high fee to join. The speaker established co-orientation by recounting a common experience of receiving such letters and of being uncertain whether to join. What can you do to establish co-orientation with your audience?

Reading the long list of adjectives describing the four aspects of credibility, you might feel establishing credibility is beyond your capability. However, you do not have to fit all of the adjectives or score well on all the aspects. Many highly credible speakers are not dynamic; in fact, all they may possess is their specialized knowledge. Some speakers may be considered credible simply because they exude sincerity, even though they lack knowledge, expertise, and dynamism.

You do not have to excel in all four aspects of source credibility to be an effective speaker. Competence, trustworthiness, dynamism, and co-orientation are the grounds on which your audience is likely to evaluate your credibility, so consider ways to ensure you come across as a credible source.

To continue our examination of source credibility, we next turn to some research about increasing credibility.

Research Findings about Increasing Credibility

Credibility can be achieved before, during, or after a public speech. A speaker can have a reputation before arriving at a hall; that judgment can be altered during the presentation; and the evaluation can change again, long after the speech has ended. You might think that some speakers are great before you hear them. Their dull presentation reduces their credibility. In the weeks after the speech, your evaluation of such speakers might rise again because you discover their message has given you new hope. In other words, credibility is not static—it is always in flux, always changing, always alterable.

Nor is credibility, we should remind you, something a speaker always possesses. It depends on topics, audiences, and situations. That makes the concept of source credibility a challenging one to public speakers. We intend these comments about the changing nature of credibility as a caution in interpreting the research findings that follow.

Reminding Your Audience of Your Credibility

Most of the studies that try to measure the effect of a speaker's message on an audience indicate highly credible speakers change opinions more than speakers whose credibility is poor.[19] At least when the speech is delivered, a person perceived as credible can seek and achieve more changes of opinion.[20]

However, as time passes, an interesting phenomenon called the **sleeper effect** occurs.[21] Apparently, the source of the speech and the message become separated in the listener's mind—"I don't remember who said this, but. . . ." The result of this separation of source and message is that the message loses impact as audience members later forget they heard it from a highly credible speaker. The speaker with little credibility benefits from the opposite effect. As time passes, the audience forgets the source of the information, and the message gains impact. In one study, three or four weeks after a speech, a highly credible speaker and a speaker with little credibility had pulled about even with respect to their ability to change opinions.

The lesson for the public speaker is that the effect of credibility may be short-lived. In most speech classes, several weeks or more may elapse between your presentations. In between, your classmates are exposed to other speakers and speeches. They need reminders of your credibility. We like to think audiences remember us and our speeches, but it is sometimes difficult for students to remember a speech they heard the day before yesterday, much less weeks earlier. Effective speakers remind the audience of their credibility. Remind your audience about your major subject, your special interest in the topic, your special knowledge, or your special experience. Credibility decays over time and must be renewed if you want to have the maximum effect on your audience.

Establishing Common Ground with the Audience

To establish **common ground** with an audience is to emphasize what you share with the audience—in the present situation, in your experience, in your ideas, or in your behavior. You can establish common ground by sharing the situation you and your classmates have in common—you all have speeches to give and exams to take. You can share ideological common ground—values, beliefs, or ideas. One way to earn an audience's trust is to point out some of the important ways you are like the audience. Revealing shared attitudes, beliefs, and values establishes co-orientation. You can address members of your audience as fellow students (common ground) or as people who believe grades are destructive to learning or that bookstore prices are too high (co-orientation). The use of the pronoun *we* tends to help audience members see their commonality with the speaker.

Some studies indicate areas of agreement should be established early in a speech for maximum effect; others say *when* commonality is established is not important, as long as it is established sometime during the speech. All of the studies agree speakers can enhance their relationship with the audience by talking about something they have in common with the audience. Some degree of commonality with voluntary audiences may be assumed, but it is necessary to be explicit to captive audiences.

Other Research-Based Findings about Credibility

The following generalizations and conclusions are based on a summary of nearly thirty years of credibility studies.[22]

The introduction of a speaker by another person can increase the speaker's credibility. The credibility of the person making the introduction is as important to the speaker's credibility as what is said in that introduction. Your credibility may also be enhanced if the audience believes your introducer is highly credible. A close friend introducing you can reveal information that could enhance or harm your status. To be safe, the speaker should always provide the introducer with information that could potentially increase credibility by showing the speaker's competence, trustworthiness, dynamism, or co-orientation. Your introducer can make evaluative statements about you that might sound self-serving were you to say them.

The way you are identified by the person introducing you also can affect your credibility. Students who are identified as graduate students are thought to be more competent than undergraduates. Graduate students are also seen as more fair-minded, likeable, and sincere.[23] It is possible, therefore, that your identification as a sophomore, junior, or senior might contribute to your credibility with a student audience.

The perceived status of a speaker can make a difference in credibility. Speakers of high status are consistently rated as more credible than speakers of low status. Even more striking is the finding that listeners judged credibility and status during the first ten or fifteen seconds of the speech.[24] The probable explanation of this finding is the audience receives a barrage of cues about the speaker at the very beginning of the speech. They see how the speaker is dressed and make judgments about the speaker's appearance. They hear the speaker's voice, and they get an initial impression of the speaker's confidence, competence, trustworthiness, and dynamism. This finding is true in interpersonal situations, too. We decide if we are attracted to someone within the first seconds of an encounter.

Strategies for Improving Your Credibility: A Checklist

A checklist you can use to make sure you have considered the possible ways to improve your credibility follows. Place a check in the blank on the right to indicate you have considered the implications of the statement.

1. Have you selected a topic in which you are involved, so you can be perceived as sincere, responsible, reputable, and trustworthy? _____

2. Have you considered the relationship between your apparent competence and your credibility by building cues into your speech that indicate your experience, training, skill, and expertise in the subject? _____

3. Have you considered the relationship between your apparent trustworthiness and your credibility by building trust through concern for your audience's welfare, objective consideration of your audience's needs, friendly rapport, and responsible and honest handling of the speech content? _____

4. Have you selected a means of delivery and content that will help the audience see you as dynamic—energetic, strong, empathic, and assertive? _____

5. Are you indicating in your speech one or more ideas, beliefs, attitudes, or characteristics you hold in common with most of the people in your audience? _____

6. Can you ask your instructor or someone else who introduces you to say something praiseworthy about you or your qualifications? _____

7. Have you reminded your audience, descriptively, of your qualifications to speak on the subject? _____

8. Are you dressed appropriately for this audience? _____

9. Given the classroom situation, your class audience, and the topic you have selected, will you be perceived as competent, trustworthy, dynamic, and interested in this audience's well-being? _____

10. Have you carefully pointed out how your topic is related to the audience, selected appropriate supporting materials, organized the content, and found a way to deliver your speech that will help your audience learn and retain what you say? _____

The organization of your speech can affect your credibility. Students who listen to a disorganized speech think less of a speaker after the speech than they did before the speech.[25] This judgment by the audience may be based on its expectations. In the public speaking classroom, students expect good organization; and when they perceive a speech as poorly organized, they lower their evaluation of the speaker. The lesson from this study is clear. The classroom speaker should strive for sound organization, lest he or she lose credibility even while speaking.

Other interesting findings about credibility are related to delivery, fluency, and repetition. *A speaker whose delivery is considered effective, whose use of voice, movement, and gesture is effective, can become more credible during a speech.*[26] A payoff exists for the student who practices a speech and who learns to be comfortable enough in front of an audience to appear natural, confident, and competent. Nonfluencies—breaks in the smooth and fluid delivery of the speech—are judged negatively. Vocalized pauses, such as *mmb* and *abb* are nonfluencies. Another kind of nonfluency is the repetitive use of certain words and phrases, such as *well, like,* and *you know* at every transition. These nonfluencies decrease the audience's ratings of competence and dynamism but do not affect the speaker's trustworthiness.[27]

Competent speakers are constantly aware of their personal impact on the speech and the audience. We have examined four aspects of credibility; competence, trustworthiness, dynamism, and co-orientation. We have reviewed the results of studies indicating that a highly credible speaker has an advantage at the time of the speech; establishing common ground can help your speech; the introduction of a speaker can help or harm credibility; the speaker's status, sincerity, and organization can influence credibility; and effective delivery can enhance credibility. The credibility of your sources, or the value of the material you find to support what you say in a speech, also affects the success of your speeches. We explore this area in detail in chapter 13.

Ethical Considerations

Credibility is a perceptual variable; that is, credibility is in the "eye of the beholder." It is not based on external measures of competence, trustworthiness, dynamism, and co-orientation. However, you retain an ethical obligation to be the sort of person you project yourself as being. The well-known cliché, "You can fool all of the people some of the time," may be accurate; but the ethical communicator attempts to avoid "fooling" anyone.

In order to determine if you are behaving ethically, ask yourself the following questions:

1. Are your immediate purpose and your long-range goal sound? Are you providing information or recommending change that would be determined worthy by current standards? Attempting to sell a substandard

product or to encourage people to injure others would clearly not be sound; persuading people to accept new, more useful ideas and to be kinder to each other would be sound.

2. Does your end justify your means? This time-honored notion suggests that communicators can have ethical ends, but they may use unethical means of bringing the audience to that conclusion. What are some of the ethical considerations you should make in presenting your message? Professor Stephen E. Lucas, from the University of Wisconsin in Madison, offers four suggestions:

   a. Be well informed about your subject.
   b. Be honest in what you say.
   c. Use sound evidence.
   d. Employ valid reasoning.[28]

In chapter 5, you learned a great deal about critical thinking, that will help you use sound evidence and employ valid reasoning. Being well informed and honest are equally important to the ethical communicator.

Credibility does lie in the audience's perception of you, but you also have an ethical obligation to be the sort of person you project yourself to be. In addition, you must consider the influence of your message on the audience. Persuasive speeches, particularly, may make far-reaching changes in others' behaviors. Are the changes you are recommending sound and consistent with standard ethical and moral guidelines? Have you thoroughly studied your topic so you are convinced of the accuracy of the information you are presenting? Are you presenting the entire picture? Are you employing valid and true arguments? In short, are you treating the listeners in the way you wish to be treated when someone else is speaking and you are the listener? The Golden Rule has application to the communication situation.

Summary

This chapter opened with a consideration of communication apprehension, the fear of communicating with others. The 10 to 20 percent of the population who suffer from high communication apprehension show their fear by avoiding communication with others. They tend to live away from other people, sit away from other people, and speak and disclose less than others. They also tend to be judged negatively by others. In the public speaking situation, people suffering from high communication apprehension exhibit the signs of fear that make them seem ineffective as speakers: they look at the floor, hesitate, pause unexpectedly, and appear powerless and slow. Remedies for high communication apprehension include professional help and systematic desensitization.

Fortunately, most people have only normal anxiety about public speaking and can overcome their fear through self-determination and by knowing their topic, audience, speech, and themselves; focusing on communication, not themselves; and recognizing their value and uniqueness.

This chapter also explored the concept of source credibility by examining what qualities people seek in a speaker and how they judge a speaker's worthiness. The four dimensions of source credibility are competence, trustworthiness, dynamism, and co-orientation. High credibility speakers have an initial advantage in changing audience opinion. To be a competent speaker, you should establish common ground with the audience. As a speaker, your credibility can be influenced by who introduces you and how you are introduced. A speaker's status, organization, and delivery also can influence credibility.

Key Terms

communication apprehension   The generalized fear of communication, regardless of context.

common ground   Experiences, ideas, or behaviors that are shared by both the speaker and the audience.

competence   The degree to which the speaker is perceived as skilled, experienced, qualified, authoritative, and informed; an aspect of credibility.

co-orientation   The degree to which the speaker's values, beliefs, attitudes, and interests are shared with the audience; an aspect of credibility.

dynamism   The degree to which the speaker is perceived as bold, active, energetic, strong, empathic, and assertive; an aspect of credibility.

self-monitoring   The ability to be sensitive to the communication situation and flexible in response.

sleeper effect   An increase in changes of opinion created by a speaker with little credibility; caused by the separation of the message content from its source over a period of time.

source credibility   The audience's perception of a speaker's competence, dynamism, trustworthiness, and co-orientation.

systematic desensitization   A theory for reducing high communication apprehension by repeated exposure to small doses of whatever makes one apprehensive in a situation designed to reduce or eradicate the fear.

trustworthiness   The degree to which the speaker is perceived as honest, fair, sincere, honorable, friendly, and kind; an aspect of credibility.

chapter 13

Finding Information

This chapter is about how to answer your questions. How do you find information? Where do you look for it? To whom can you speak about your topic? Once found, how do you use information in your speech? In this chapter, we take you from your initial question to the places where the answers wait for your discovery. The task of finding information is exciting if you select something exciting to explore.

What will you learn?

After you have read and thought about this chapter, you will be able to answer the following questions:

1. What are three main sources of information for a speech?

2. What are two reasons for citing sources and using oral footnotes?

3. Can you cite sources in writing with footnotes and in your speech with oral footnotes?

4. Can you define these supporting materials: surveys, testimonies, statistics, raw numbers, analogies, explanations, and definitions?

5. Can you find appropriate supporting materials to support your position on an issue?

6. What is the difference between proof and clarification when discussing supporting materials?

Some books are to be tasted, others to be swallowed, and some few to be chewed and digested . . .

Francis Bacon

Nothing you cannot spell will ever work.

Will Rogers

Knowledge is the only instrument of production that is not subject to diminishing returns.

J. M. Clark

285

A college sophomore had agreed to teach medieval history to a summer class of high school ninth and tenth graders. The college student was smart enough to know these teenagers would be bored by his lectures on the subject. Instead of telling them about people in the Middle Ages, he gave them a task. They had to answer questions: What would one find in the home of a serf? Could a third daughter of a titled father marry the son of a wealthy but untitled merchant? What was it like in a monastery? If you owned a castle, how many people would it take to operate it? The student who taught the class told his students a few things about medieval times, but mainly he supplied them with books that provided answers to their questions. The students learned more about history by answering their questions than they would have learned in a series of lectures. Why? Because they had interesting questions and a way to find answers to those questions.

In your public speaking class, you are in a similar situation. The students mentioned in the previous paragraph wanted to learn history in an interesting way. You want to learn public speaking, but you want to learn it in an interesting way. The important ingredients missing for you—but provided to the students described in the previous paragraph—are the interesting questions. You have to find some interesting questions to pursue. You have to find a topic that invites questions, the answers to which will be interesting to you and to your classmates.

A speech on dogs becomes, "Which breed is best for an apartment-dwelling college student on a limited income?" A speech on the economy becomes, "What is the difference between recession and depression?" A speech on cars becomes, "What do you need to know about buying a used car?" In each case, the topic becomes an interesting question you can pursue by exploring your own experience; reading papers, magazines, and books; watching films, television, or videotapes; or talking to other people. The teacher made medieval history interesting to his students; you can make your own speech interesting to yourself and to your audience by picking a topic about which you can ask interesting questions. First, you need to know where you can find information for your speech.

Information Sources

Information sources for your speech include your personal experiences, written and visual resources, and other people. Let us look at each of these areas.

Personal Experiences

The first place you should look for materials for the content of your speech is within yourself. Your **personal experience** is something you can talk about with some authority. One student had been a "headhunter," a person who tries to find employees for employers who are willing to pay a premium for specific kinds of employees. This student gave a speech from his personal experience concerning what employers particularly value in employees. Another student had a brother who was retarded and who died at age nine. She gave a speech about retarded individuals and the way they are treated in our society. Your special causes, jobs, and family can provide you with firsthand information you can use in your speech.

You should not, however, use your personal experience uncritically. Important questions should be asked about personal experience before you employ it in your speech. Is your experience typical? If you are among the very few who had an unfortunate experience with a local bar, you should think carefully before you generalize and assume that many people have been treated similarly. You can ask some questions about your personal experience that will help you evaluate it as evidence—data on which proof may be based—of what you plan to say in your speech:

1. Was your experience typical?
2. Was your experience so typical it will be boring?
3. Was your experience so atypical it was a chance occurrence?
4. Was your experience so personal and revealing that the audience may feel uncomfortable?
5. Was your experience one this audience will appreciate, or from which this audience can learn a lesson?
6. Does your experience really constitute proof or evidence of anything?

Not all personal experiences can be shared with an audience. Only a limited number of them really can be used as evidence or proof.

Another question about your experience is whether it was firsthand or the experience of someone else. If the information is not firsthand, it is usually questionable. It may have been distorted in transmission. You might find yourself passing along a falsehood to your audience unless the experience is your own.

Written and Visual Resources

A second place you can look for substance for your speech is in **written and visual resources.** Perhaps the quickest and most efficient way to find information in written sources is to go to the ***Reader's Guide to Periodical Literature.*** This multivolume work lists articles that have appeared in magazines. You can look up a topic, such as *cocaine,* and find a listing of all the articles that recently have appeared in popular magazines on the subject. If you want to explore the topic further, you can look up key words in the *Reader's Guide* that will lead you to still other sources. For example, you could explore the subject of cocaine further by looking up such key words as *drugs, law enforcement, international regulation, medicine,* and *crime.* It would be difficult to think of a topic not covered in the popular literature. As a

Written and visual resources aid in preparing a speech.

student of public speaking, you should learn how to use the *Reader's Guide,* the *Index to the Humanities,* and the *Index to Social Sciences* to help you learn more about your topic. Better yet, your library may have computer information systems like CD-ROM indices and other retrieval systems to aid your search.

The following are some additional sources frequently used by public speaking students for finding information:

1. Frequently used yearbooks include the *World Almanac,* the *Book of Facts, Facts on File,* and the *Statistical Abstract of the United States.* These sources contain facts and figures about a wide variety of subjects, from population to yearly coal production. The encyclopedias contain short bibliographies and background material about many topics. Among the popular encyclopedias are the *Encyclopedia Americana* and the *Encyclopedia Britannica.*

2. Sourcebooks for examples, literary allusions, and quotations include Bartlett's *Familiar Quotations,* George Seldes' *The Great Quotations,* Arthur Richmond's *Modern Quotations for Ready Reference,* and *Respectfully Quoted,* a dictionary of quotations requested from the congressional research service.

3. Biographies of famous persons can be found in *Who's Who in America, Current Biography,* and the *Dictionary of American Biography* (deceased Americans).

4. Newspaper files are helpful, especially if your college has the *New York Times,* one of the few newspapers that has an index. Newspapers tend to be most useful for recent information.

5. Professional journals, which are also indexed, are collected by many libraries. You can find articles about communication, psychology, sociology, economics, chemistry, mathematics, and many other subjects.

6. Many modern libraries own volumes of material on microfilm. Media resource centers on campuses have lists of slides, films, and other visual materials.

7. The reference librarian is an expert at helping locate other materials.

You can also use information from television news and documentaries, films, and tapes. An effective public speaker becomes like a skilled debater—he or she learns rapidly where to find good supporting materials.

Still another resource important to the public speaker is the **card catalog.** The card catalog lists every book in the library by author, title, and subject. The books are usually cross-indexed, so you can find them by simply looking at the cards collected under a particular subject heading. If you pick a subject in which you are involved and to which you are committed, you should not have to read a large number of books on the subject. On the other hand, if the subject is truly of interest to you, you may *want* to read some of the books. Usually, it is sufficient to check out several of the best books on the topic and to read them selectively for information most usable to you in your speech. The kinds of information selected are usually quotations and evidence or proof that support your position on the issue. As in interviewing, it is important to take good notes, to record the information accurately and precisely, and to credit the author of the book in your speech when you deliver it. An entry like the one in figure 13.1 on an index card or a separate sheet of paper usually helps. Be sure to include author, title, publisher, place of publication, date of publication, and page reference, as well as the information.

You may find that your college or university library has access to its holdings through a computerized system. An increasing number of such systems allow students to gather information about the library's holdings if they have a computer equipped with a modem. You may be able to sit in a computer lab, your dormitory, or your own home and gather materials for your speech. At

Figure 13.1 Index card: a speaker's notes from a book.

```
                    Working Mothers in America

Arlie Hochschild, The Second Shift (New York: Avon Books, 1989).
p. 2.


  * Before 1950 so few women worked outside the home that the
    Bureau of Labor Statistics did not record figures.


  * By 1950, 28% of married women with children between the ages
    of six and seventeen worked outside the home.


  * By 1986, 54% of women with children between the ages six and
    seventeen worked outside the home.


  * Two-thirds of all mothers are now in the labor force, more
    mothers have paying jobs than do nonmothers, and two-job
    families now make up 58% of married couples with children.
```

the very least, you can determine if the library has sources useful to you and if those sources are currently on the shelves or checked out to another person. The convenience of such systems is clear.

In your search for information you can use in your speech, you might also want to examine the written resources listed in figure 13.2. The indices will lead you to other sources, the dictionaries and encyclopedias will provide definitions and explanations, and the yearbooks will provide facts and statistics.

The Importance of Citing Sources

When you write an outline, compose a manuscript speech, or deliver a speech, *you are expected to indicate where you found your information.* Two reasons exist for this expectation: a rule of scholarship dictates any ideas that are not your own must be credited to the person whose ideas they are; and writers and speakers must be able to verify what they say. What if a speaker claims that homosexuality is entirely hereditary? Your first response might be, "Who says?" The speaker might reveal a source. You might come up with ten other sources who disagree. The notion of citing sources, of crediting others with ideas that originated with them, and of challenging sources and the credibility of authors is an important aspect of speech composition, delivery, and criticism.

Figure 13.2 Written resources for the public speaker.

General Indexes to Periodicals

Book Review Digest. 1905–. (Author, title, subject)

New York Times Index. 1913–. (Author, subject)

Reader's Guide to Periodical Literature. 1900–. (Author, title, subject)

Social Sciences and Humanities Index. 1965–. (Author, subject)

Special Indexes to Periodicals

Art Index. 1929–. (Author, subject)

Bibliographic Index. 1937–. (Subject)

Biography Index. 1946–. (Subject)

Biological and Agricultural Index. 1964–. (Subject)

Book Review Index. 1965–.

Business Periodicals Index. 1958–. (Subject)

Catholic Periodical Index. 1930–. (Subject)

Communication Abstracts. 1978–. (Subject)

Education Index. 1929–. (Author, subject)

Engineering Index. 1884–. (Subject)

Index to Book Reviews in the Humanities. 1960–.

Index to Legal Periodicals. 1908–. (Author, subject)

Music Index. 1949–. (Author, subject)

Psychological Abstracts. 1927–. (Author, subject)

Public Affairs Information Service. 1915–. (Subject)

Quarterly Cumulative Index Medicus. 1927–. (Author, subject)

Sociological Abstracts. 1952–. (Subject)

Specialized Dictionaries

Partridge, Eric. *A Dictionary of Catch Phrases.* 1979.

Partridge, Eric. *A Dictionary of Cliches* 5th ed., 1978.

Roget, Peter M. *Roget's University Thesaurus.* 1981.

Webster's New World Bible Dictionary. 1986.

Webster's New World Dictionary of Business Terms. 1985.

Webster's New World Dictionary of Synonyms. 1984.

Specialized Encyclopedias

Adams, J. T. *Dictionary of American History.* 6 vols. 1942.

Encyclopedia of the Social Sciences. 15 vols. 1930–35.

Encyclopedia of World Art. 1959–.

Grove's Dictionary of Music and Musicians. 9 vols. 1954. (Supplement, 1961.)

Harris, Chester W. *Encyclopedia of Educational Research.* 1960.

Hastings, James. *Interpreter's Dictionary of the Bible.* 4 vols. 1962.

McGraw-Hill. *Encyclopedia of Science and Technology.* 15 vols. 1966.

Munn, Glenn G. *Encyclopedia of Banking and Finance.* 7th ed., 1973.

Van Nostrand's *Scientific Encyclopedia.* 4th ed., 1968.

Worldmark Encyclopedia of the Nations. 5 vols. 1963.

Yearbooks

Americana Annual. 1923–.

The Annual Register of World Events. 1958–.

Economic Almanac. 1940–.

Facts on File. 1940–.

Information Please Almanac. 1947–.

New International Year Book. 1907–.

Statesman's Year-Book. 1864–.

Statistical Abstract of the United States. 1878–.

World Almanac and Book of Facts. 1868–.

Lest we appear to understate the importance of citing sources in written and spoken discourse, we should point out that *neglecting to cite sources is an offense* called **plagiarism,** a crime punishable in many colleges and universities by measures as serious as expulsion. Outside the classroom, plagiarism can result in disgrace, fines, and even jail. Do not forget to reveal where you got your information: there is a moral and a legal obligation to do so.

Formats for Citing Sources

A number of different forms are used in citing sources, including the *Publication Manual of the American Psychological Association* and the *MLA Handbook for Writers of Research Papers.* Some, including MLA, use the footnote form in manuscripts and outlines when you want to reveal where you found the information. The footnote typically follows the information cited and is signaled by an elevated number in the manuscript.

> Bettinghaus argues "the study of *proof* is vital to the student of communication."[1]

In this case, the footnote follows a direct quotation, a statement set apart with quotation marks that states the exact words used in the source. A *paraphrased* statement, a statement based on another's idea but recast in your own words, is also footnoted:

> Bettinghaus argues students of communication should study the nature of proof.[2]

If a direct quote is longer than three sentences, it should be indented on both the right and the left margins, stated exactly as the source states it, typed single-spaced, and followed by a footnote.

> As Bettinghaus says in his book *The Nature of Proof:*

> Modes of proof have changed greatly over the centuries, but the concept of proof is recognizable over a span of two thousand years. Ancient Greeks recognized confessions obtained from the torture of witnesses as valid evidence—and perfectly good proof—in their courts. During the Roman era, a defendant was allowed to parade his weeping wife and children before the judges as proof of his innocence. During the Middle Ages, the "water test" could establish the proof of a man's guilt. The accused was thrown into a lake or pond. If he swam, he was judged guilty; if he drowned, he was believed to have been innocent.[3]

Similarly, you indicated you are paraphrasing a number of sentences based on somebody else's idea or information, following it with an elevated number but without indenting and separating it from the body of the text.

Knowing Your Library

You are more likely to use reference works if you know where they are in the library and if you know what kind of information is in them. The exercise that follows will help to better acquaint you with the library and its reference works.

1. From the card catalog or the computerized system at your library, find the author and title of one book that deals with your topic.

Author _____

Title _____

2. From the *Reader's Guide to Periodical Literature,* find the title and author of one article on your topic.

Author _____

Title _____

3. Using a specialized index to periodicals, give the author, title, and name of the publication for an article on the topic you have selected.

Author _____

Title _____

Publication _____

4. Using an encyclopedia or a yearbook, find specific information about your topic. In one sentence, explain what kind of information you found.

_____

_____

Source _____

As you might suspect, you have to do more than simply place an elevated number after a direct quotation or a paraphrased statement. The elevated number indicates the source is cited or listed either at the bottom of the page (thus the name "foot" note) or at the end of the paper in endnotes. The footnotes or endnotes should be in a consistent form.

If the footnote cites an article from a magazine or journal, you should indicate the author, the title of the article (in quotation marks), the name of the magazine or journal (underlined), the volume number, the date (in parentheses), and the page on which you found the information. For a single-authored magazine article, the footnote would look like this:

[1]George F. Will, "Battle of the Bantamweights." <u>Newsweek</u> 15 June 1992, p. 72.

The first line is indented three spaces; the second line (if one exists) moves out to the left margin. Notice also when you include a volume number, you do not write "p." or "pp." before the page reference.

If the footnote cites a newspaper, you use the same basic format:

[1]Richard Heck, "Effective Crime Watch Never Stops," The Athens Messenger, 12 June 1992, p. 1

A footnote for a book looks like this:

[1]Shad Helmstetter, Choices (New York: Pocket Books, 1989), pp. 46–47.

In a footnote for a book, the publication information is placed in parentheses, and the pages are indicated either with a "p." for a reference from a single page or with a "pp." for material from more than one page. The name of the book, like the names of magazines, journals, and newspapers, is underlined when you type, or set in italics when it appears in print.

A quotation or paraphrased material from an interview, lecture, or television program follows the same basic format except that the footnote contains slightly different information, including the person's qualifications when the reader is unlikely to know them.

[1]Interview with H. Wells Singleton, Dean of the College of Education, Ohio University, 13 June 1992.

[2]Boris Yeltsin, first democratically elected leader of Russia, in a speech to the U.S. Congress, 16 June 1992.

With pamphlets, the amount and type of information you can provide may be quite different:

[1]U.S. Department of Agriculture. *"Controlling Garden Pests."* Pamphlet, available through State University's agricultural extension office, p. 3.

Remember that the purpose of citing sources and writing footnotes is to provide sufficient information to lead the reader to the source for verification or for further reading. The basic footnote format suggested here is just one of a number of acceptable forms that you can find in stylebooks.

Footnotes might be fine in written manuscripts or outlines, but what are you to do about indicating your sources in a speech? The answer is oral footnotes. An **oral footnote** is simply an abbreviated manuscript or outline footnote that tells the audience where you found your information. In a speech, the footnotes would sound like this:

"A recent *Newsweek* article by conservative columnist George Will pointed out that . . . ."
"*The Athens Messenger* reported that an angry burglary victim is organizing . . . ."
"Dean Singleton from Education agrees that the future for entry level teachers will be . . . ."

In other words, in a speech, the speaker indicates the information or idea came from a magazine, newspaper, book, or interview by providing some signal to the audience that the material came from some other source.

Citing sources provides verification and invites further reading.

We have already discussed the moral and legal obligation to reveal your sources of information, and now you know how to indicate where you got your information, both in written compositions like outlines and manuscripts, and in oral performances. Another reason for citing sources of information should not be overlooked: sometimes, quotations from a credible source can improve your own credibility. Audience members who may not be impressed with your statements on a topic might be more favorably influenced if you demonstrate that people important to them support your ideas.

People Sources

One student wanted to do his speech on a topic in which he was involved, but almost every source he located through the library's reference works had been vandalized. Most of the written sources in newspapers, magazines, and journals had been cut out by someone who had researched the topic earlier. The student was so angry he stormed into his professor's office, ready to quit the course. "What is the point in trying to write well-prepared speeches if the information isn't even available in the library?" he asked.

The student was asked to do one thing before dropping the course: see the director of libraries about his complaint. The director of libraries not only made an appointment with the student, she also showed considerable interest in the student's complaint. The director was chairing a task force for sixteen colleges and universities who were delving into the problem of mutilation, the destruction of library holdings by students who thought it was all right to destroy sources for everyone who came after them. The director spoke to the student for an hour. She gave him facts, figures, arguments, and ideas about the mutilation of library holdings. The student ended up delivering an excellent speech—not on the topic he had originally planned—on the problem of library mutilation and what to do about it.

The point of this actual account is that speakers often overlook the most obvious sources of information—the people around them. You can get information for your speech from personal experience, written and visual resources, *and* from other people. The easiest way to secure information from other people is to ask them through an information interview.

Finding People to Interview

As a person who needs information about a particular topic, your first step is to find the person or persons who can help you discover more about your topic. Your instructor might have some suggestions about whom to approach. Among the easier and better sources of information are professors and administrators who are available on campus. They can be contacted during office hours or by appointment. Government officials, too, have a certain obligation to be responsive to your questions. Even big business and industrial concerns have public relations offices that can answer your questions. Your object is to find someone, or a few people, who can provide you with the best information in the limited time you have to prepare your speech.

Conducting the Interview

An interview can be an important and impressive source of information for your speech—if you conduct the interview properly. After you have carefully selected the person or persons you wish to interview, you need to consider these proprieties:

1. *On first contact with your interviewee or the interviewee's secretary, be honest about your purpose.* For example, you might say, "I want to interview Dr. Schwartz for ten minutes about the plans for student aid for next year so I can share that information with the twenty students in my public speaking class." In other words, it is good to reveal why you want to talk to the person. It is also good to reveal how much of the interviewee's time you need to take, and it is smart to keep time short. If your interviewee wants to give you more time than you requested, that should be the interviewee's choice. Finally, it is unwise to be deceptive about why you want to talk to the person, or not to reveal why you want to talk, because you want the interviewee to trust you.

2. *Prepare specific questions for the interview.* Think ahead of time of exactly what kinds of information you need to satisfy yourself and your audience. Keep your list of questions short enough to fit the time limit you have suggested to the interviewee.

3. *Be respectful toward the person you interview.* Remember the person is doing you a favor. You do not need to act like Mike Wallace on "60 Minutes." Instead, dress appropriately for the person's status, ask your questions with politeness and concern, and thank your interviewee for granting you an interview.

4. *Tell the interviewee you are going to take notes on his or her answers so you can use the information in your speech.* If you are going to record the interview on a tape recorder, you need to ask the interviewee's permission, and you should be prepared to take written notes in case the interviewee does not wish to be recorded.

5. *When you quote the interviewee or paraphrase the person's ideas in your speech, use oral footnotes to indicate where you got the information:* "According to Dr. Fred Schwartz, the Director of Financial Aids, the amount of student financial aid for next year will be slightly less than it was this year."

Sometimes, the person you interview will be a good resource for still other information. For example, if the interviewee is an expert on your topic, he or she may be able to lead you to other people or additional written resources for your speech. Remember, too, how you behave before, during, and after the interview is a reflection on you, the class you are taking, and even your college or university.

Finding Appropriate Supporting Materials

You already know that indices, card catalogs, and interviews will lead you to new ideas and information about your topic, but what should you seek when you find the magazine articles, journals, and books, or interview the expert on the topic? You might find additional materials that help clarify information or arguments you can use to persuade. The most useful materials you can find are the abundant **supporting materials,** those materials you can employ to support your ideas, to substantiate your arguments, and to clarify your position. The supporting materials we examine most closely are examples, surveys, testimonial evidence, statistics, analogies, explanations, and definitions. Some of these supporting materials are used as evidence or proof; others are used mainly for clarification or amplification, but all are found in researching your topic.

Examples

Examples, the use of a specific instance or two to illustrate your point, are among the most common supporting materials found in speeches. Sometimes, a single example helps to convince an audience; at other times, a relatively large number of examples may be necessary to achieve your purpose. For instance, an argument that a university gives admission priority to out-of-state students could be supported by showing the difference between the number of in-state and out-of-state students that are accepted, in relation to the number of students that applied in each group. Likewise, in a persuasive speech designed to motivate everyone to vote, you could present cases where several more votes would have meant a major change in an administration.

You should also be careful when using examples or specific instances. Sometimes, an example may be so unusual that an audience will not accept it as evidence or proof of anything. The student who refers to crime in his hometown as an example of the increasing crime problem is unconvincing if his hometown has considerably less crime than the audience is accustomed to. A good example must be plausible, typical, and related to the main point before it will be effective in a speech.

Two types of examples are factual and hypothetical. If the example is laconic, it is called brief. If it is a detailed or long example, it is called extended. The following is an example of a brief factual example and an extended hypothetical example.

> A Brief Factual Example
> According to the *Consumer Reports: 1992 Buying Guide Issue,* the Sears Craftsman model 38023 is a "best buy" with no serious disadvantages, and the Atlas model 20-2231 has serious flaws.
> An Extended Hypothetical Example
> An example of a good excuse for a student missing class would be that the student has a serious auto accident on the way to class, ends up in the hospital, and has a signed medical excuse from a physician to prove hospitalization for a week. A poor excuse for a student missing class is that the student knows when the final examination is scheduled before taking the class but schedules a flight home the day before the exam and wants an "excused absence."

The factual example is verifiable; it can be supported by a source that the audience can also find. The hypothetical example is one that is a composite of actual excuses, but it is combined as an example that a professor might have experienced. The hypothetical example cannot be verified in the same way as the factual example. The length of the example determines whether it is brief or extended.

Surveys

Surveys are a source of supporting materials commonly used in speeches. **Surveys** are found most often in magazines or journals and are usually seen as more credible than one person's experience or an example or two because they synthesize the experience of hundreds or thousands of people. Public opinion polls fall into this category. One person's experience with alcohol can have an impact on an audience, but a survey indicating one third of Americans are abstainers, one third are occasional drinkers, and one third are regular drinkers provides better support for an argument.

As with personal experience, there are some important questions you should ask about the evidence found in surveys:

1. *How reliable is the source you used?* A report in a professional journal of sociology, psychology, or communication is likely to be more thorough and more valid than one found in a local newspaper.
2. *How broad was the sample used in the survey?* Was it a survey of the entire nation, the region, the state, the city, the campus, or the class?
3. *Who was included in the survey?* Did everyone in the sample have an equally good chance of being selected or were volunteers asked to respond to the questions?
4. *How representative was the survey sample? Playboy's* readers may not be typical of the population in your state.
5. *Who performed the survey?* Was it a nationally recognized survey firm like Lou Harris or Gallup, or was it the local newspaper editor? Was it performed by professionals like professors, researchers, or management consultants?
6. *Why was the survey done?* Was it performed for any self-serving purpose—for example, to attract more readers—or did the government conduct it to help establish policy or legislation?

Testimonial evidence can be very convincing.

Testimonial Evidence

Testimonial evidence, a third kind of supporting material, is using the words of others to substantiate or clarify your points. The three kinds of testimonial evidence you can use in your speeches are lay, expert, and celebrity.

One assumption behind testimonial evidence is that you are not alone in your beliefs, ideas, and arguments; other people also support them. Another assumption behind testimonial evidence is that the statements of others should help the audience accept your point of view.

An example of **lay testimony** is when an ordinary person substantiates, supports or backs what you say. In advertising this kind of testimony shows ordinary people using products, buying goods, and stating their fine qualities. In a speech, lay testimony might be to pass on the words of your relatives, your neighbors, or colleagues concerning some issue. Such testimony shows the audience that you and other ordinary people support the idea. Other examples of lay testimony are when alcoholics at an Alcoholics Anonymous meeting, fundamentalist Christians at a church gathering, or alumni at a recruiting session confess their addiction, witness their faith, or state the wonderful qualities of their college.

An example of **expert testimony** is when someone who has special knowledge or expertise is quoted about an issue or idea. In your speech, you might quote a mechanic about problems with an automobile, an interior decorator about the aesthetic qualities of fabrics, or a political pundit about the elections. The idea is to demonstrate that people with specialized experience or education support the positions you advocate in your speech.

Celebrity testimony is when you use the words of some public figure who is known to the audience. In advertising, a famous basketball player may endorse a particular brand of athletic shoes. In your speech, you might point out that a famous politician, a syndicated columnist, or a well-known entertainer endorses the position you advocate.

Although testimonial evidence may encourage your audience to adopt your ideas, you need to use such evidence with caution. An idea may have little credence even though many lay people believe in it; an expert may be quoted on topics well outside his or her area of expertise; and a celebrity is often paid by a vendor for endorsing a product. To protect yourself and your audience, you should ask yourself the following questions before using testimonial evidence in your speeches:

1. Is the person you quote an expert whose opinions or conclusions are worthier than most other people's opinions?
2. Is the quotation about a subject in the person's area of expertise?
3. Is the person's statement based on extensive personal experience, professional study or research, or another form of firsthand proof?
4. Will your classmates find the statement more believable because you got it from this outside source?

Numbers and Statistics

A fourth kind of evidence useful for clarification or substantiation is numbers and statistics. Because numbers are easier to understand and digest when they appear in print, the public speaker has to simplify, explain, and translate their meaning in a public speech.

For instance, what if a speaker says that there were 323,462 high school graduates in your state this year? That **raw number,** a specific figure or count, is very difficult to process when you hear it. How can you make it easier for the audience to understand? You can simplify it by rounding it off by just saying "over three hundred thousand (300,000)." You can explain it by placing it in a context by saying "that number is a lot smaller than the number who graduated from high school last year." You can translate it by stating it a different way by saying "that is a 20 percent reduction in the number of high school graduates in a single year."

Some suggestions for using raw numbers in a speech include rounding, writing the number on the board or a poster, placing the number in a context, and translating by using another form of explanation or familiar comparisons. An example of the latter would be to say that 300,000 high school graduates are equivalent to the entire population of Lancaster (or some city the audience will recognize). The number dropped from the year before was equivalent to the population of Circleville (or some town known to the audience). Each of these techniques will simplify and clarify the meaning of the number.

Similarly, you need to be wary of statistics in a public speech because they are at least as difficult for an audience to interpret as raw numbers. A **percentage,** for example, is just another name for the ratio or fraction of one hundred. If you say in your speech that Honda sales increased 47 percent, your audience is unlikely to know what that figure means. Again, you can round off the figure to "nearly 50 percent;" you can reveal the raw number of sales this year and last year—100 sold last year and 150 sold this year;" and you can help the audience interpret the significance with a comparison—"that is a bigger increase in sales than experienced by any domestic or imported car dealer in our city this year."

Statistics is a kind of numerical shorthand that summarizes data for easier consumption, but in oral communication, it can mystify more than it clarifies unless you take precautions. For instance, an **average** or statistical **mean**—the total of a list of numbers divided by the number of items—can be very misleading. Take the statement: the average per capita income in our community is $15,480. In some communities, practically no one would earn the average income because the population consists of a relatively small number of very wealthy people and a relatively large number of very poor people. Also, *per capita* means that the entire population is counted, not just the people who earn money.

You might clarify the statistic by revealing the **range,** the lowest and the highest incomes; the **mode,** the most commonly recurring income; or even the **median,** the midpoint among the incomes. For example, you might say "the lowest paid person earns only $1,500 per year, while the highest earns $50,000;" "the amount that the largest number of people earn is $16,000;" and "the median amount is $15,000." You probably can see the problem already; spoken statistics are hard to interpret. Your statistics will be easier to understand if you round them, provide them in writing, provide comparisons, and translate them into family income instead of per capita income.

Imagine that you are giving a speech on the changing nature of minorities in the United States. You have found the enclosed article. What statistics would you report? Why? What would you omit? Why? How would you determine how many of the numbers reported that you would include in your speech? Do you believe the author distorted the situation with his use of numbers? If so, how did he do so?

The Fracturing of America
by Peter Brimelow
Forbes

"Within ten years there will not be a word of English spoken [in Miami] . . . one day residents will have to learn Spanish or leave."

With a few months left to run, this 1982 prediction of Miami's then mayor, Maurice Ferré, may not have come true . . . quite. But Linda Chavez finds that Florida sales clerks now invariably respond to her sparkling dark eyes and glossy black hair with Spanish salutations—or point silently, and perhaps sullenly, at the appropriate price.

Chavez, 44, a former aide in the Reagan and Carter White Houses and a former teachers union official to boot, is now a senior fellow with New York's Manhattan Institute think tank. Her recent book *Out of the Barrio: Toward a New Politics of Hispanic Assimilation* (Basic Books) announces good news: The bad news about her fellow Hispanics is wrong. They are assimilating, economically and even linguistically, ex-mayor Ferré notwithstanding.

The bad news: No one wants to know the good news—especially Hispanic leaders, but also some allegedly conservative politicians, and even corporations.

The Hispanic presence in the U.S. has surged since the 1965 Immigration Act, which reoriented U.S. immigration intake away from its traditional European sources. About 40% of the 13.5 million legal immigrants in the last three decades have been Hispanics. Officially, a total of some 20 million Hispanics now live in the U.S., about 9% of the population, up from less than 3% in 1950. Additionally, an estimated 3.5 million live here illegally. Some demographers project that Hispanics will be a third of the U.S. population within 100 years (*see chart*).

Will this big chunk of immigrants follow the traditional path and become Americanized? "We cannot assimilate—and we won't!" This slogan, Chavez reports, came from the Arnold Torres, former executive director of the League of United Latin American Citizens, in a debate with her at Stanford. She says it represents a wide consensus among officials in Hispanic organizations.

Statistics appear to provide support for the view that Hispanics are different. Thus, median income of Mexican-Americans in the Southwest—the largest element in the Hispanic community—was 57% of non-Hispanic median income in 1959, and exactly the same percentage in 1989. Education, earnings, poverty rates and other indicators are also static.

So why is Chavez optimistic about integration? There is, she points out, a major factor distorting these statistics: the wave of unskilled, uneducated immigrants that has swamped the established Mexican-American community in particular. (Indeed, the most recent "Mexican" arrivals are ethnic Indians who cannot properly be called Hispanic because they do not even speak Spanish.)

Analyzing unpublished government data, Chavez found that weekly earnings for U.S.-born Mexican-Americans were 83% of non-Hispanics'—and that adjusted for other factors, like education, region of residence and experience, the difference virtually disappeared. Similarly, U.S.-born Hispanics seem to be converging with non-Hispanics in education levels. Some researchers claim the pace of educational convergence slows with the third generation—but Chavez says this is exactly the pattern that previous immigrant groups followed.

About a quarter of all Hispanics do live in poverty, twice the proportion of the general population. But again, poverty levels among U.S.-born Hispanics are significantly lower. In fact, according to the Bureau of the Census, a striking 42% of all Hispanics owned or were buying their own homes in 1989.

A second factor distorting Hispanic statistics: There are, actually, no "Hispanics." It's a catchall category invented by the Census Bureau under political pressure from "Hispanic" politicians ambitious to increase their leverage on Washington. It covers some very disparate groups.

For example, the economic success of Cubans is widely acknowledged: Cuban males overall earn about 90% of what non-Hispanics do and females actually earn more than non-Hispanics—although, as Chavez notes, the Cuban influx has not been as uniformly high-skilled as popularly supposed. Less appreciated is the relative success of Dominicans. They make up 40% of New York's Hispanics, but own 70% of the Hispanic small businesses and enjoy average incomes 30% higher than Puerto Ricans'.

The status of Puerto Ricans is somewhat surprising. They are the only Hispanic group that shows signs of developing into a permanent underclass—a paradox, since as U.S. citizens they are the only Hispanic group that automatically qualifies for benefits. In New York, where more than half of U.S. Puerto Ricans live, they have higher welfare participation rates than any

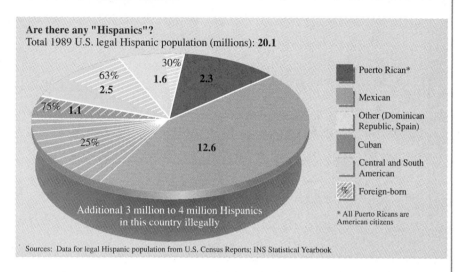

Are there any "Hispanics"?
Total 1989 U.S. legal Hispanic population (millions): **20.1**

30%
63%
75%
25%
1.6
2.3
2.5
1.1
12.6

Puerto Rican*
Mexican
Other (Dominican Republic, Spain)
Cuban
Central and South American
% Foreign-born

Additional 3 million to 4 million Hispanics in this country illegally

* All Puerto Ricans are American citizens

Sources: Data for legal Hispanic population from U.S. Census Reports; INS Statistical Yearbook

other group. "They have been smothered by entitlements," writes Chavez, "which should serve as a warning to other Hispanics." Outside of New York, where social programs are not as developed, Puerto Ricans do significantly better.

The ultimate indicator of Hispanic assimilation: In California more than half of all Mexican-Americans marry non-Hispanics. By the third generation, Chavez says, most Hispanic Americans speak only English, as she does herself. (Which is why Spanish-language advertising strategies are being questioned; see FORBES, *Dec. 23, 1991.*)

Chavez is optimistic about the capacity of the U.S. to assimilate Hispanics—and all of the current influx of immigrants. But, she says, "It's not something that can't be wrecked with the wrong policies."

Foremost among these wrong policies: bilingual education, or the idea that linguistic minorities can be introduced to English and education only in their own tongue rather than being plunged into the mainstream.

Although contrary to historic American practice and a mounting body of research findings, bilingual education has been institutionalized since the 1960s through a combination of judicial rulings, federal bureaucratic pressure and lobbying from the burgeoning bilingualism establishment. Increasingly, it is justified, not as a transitional measure, but as "cultural maintenance." Often it is imposed on Hispanic children even if they can speak English. The

Washington, D.C. public school system placed Chavez's son in bilingual classes, apparently on the basis of his name, even though he can speak no Spanish at all.

Opinion polls show Hispanics generally more conservative and willing to learn English than their leaders—who, Chavez points out, are financed largely by non-Hispanic sources like the Ford Foundation. Certainly some of the leaders' reactions to her book have been hysterical. She has been prevented from speaking on college campuses and even assaulted.

Nevertheless, the Bush Administration listened to those leaders, even though their standing was questioned within the communities they claimed to represent. The Administration allowed the drift to bilingualism to resume—for example, by appointing Rita Esquivel director of the Office of Bilingual Education.

But big corporations are equally misguided, Chavez says. She reports that, while she gets calls from corporations about their Hispanic hiring, "They give me the cold shoulder when they realize where I'm coming from. The personnel departments are full of affirmative action types."

She doesn't care. "I don't want to be a professional Hispanic," she says.

Shortly, Chavez is to become director of the Manhattan Institute's Center for the New American Community, which will study the common heritage threatened by what she calls multiculturalism's "fracturing of America."

Observe how much easier you could say:

People in our community earn an average family income of $25,000 per year, a figure that is very close to the state and national average. Of course, we have people in our community who earn a lot less than half that amount and a few wealthy families who earn three times that amount. What makes our community different is that we have considerably more elderly people on fixed incomes from social security and pensions, people who are unlikely to vote for increases in taxes for schools.

You can greatly increase your effectiveness as a speaker if you translate your numbers by using visual aids, such as pie charts, line graphs, and bar graphs. You can help your audience by both saying and showing your figures. You also can help your audience to visualize your statistics by comparisons and even visual imagery. An example of the latter is to say "that amount of money is greater than all of the money in all of our local banks," "that number of people could stand hand to hand from coast to coast," or "that many discarded tires would cover our city six feet deep in a single year." You can use numbers and statistics for support and substantiation if you can think of creative ways to help your audience simplify them, place them in a context, and interpret and translate them into their language. Your responsibility as a speaker is to help the audience understand your figures. Your responsibility as a listener is to seek clarification if you do not understand the meaning or significance of figures used in a speech.

Analogies

Another kind of supporting material used in public speeches is the analogy. An **analogy** is a comparison of things in some respects, especially in position or function that are otherwise dissimilar. For instance, human beings and bees are different, but one could draw a comparison of these two different groups by pointing out that, in many ways, human beings are like bees—we have people who are like the queen bees, who are pampered and cared for by others; we have the drones, who do nothing and yet are cared for; and we have the workers, who seem to do all of the labor without any pampering care. Similarly, analogies can be used to show that Roman society is analogous to American society, that a law applied in one state will work the same way in another, and that if animals get cancer from drinking too much diet soda, so will human beings.

An analogy often provides clarification, but it is not proof because the comparison inevitably breaks down. Therefore, the speaker who argues that the American society will fail just as Roman society did can carry the comparison only so far because the two societies exist in a different time frame, because the form of government and the institutions in the two societies are quite different, and so on. Likewise, you can question the bee/human being analogy by pointing out the vast differences between the two things being compared. Nonetheless, the analogy can be quite successful as a way to illustrate or clarify.

Explanations

Explanations are another important means of clarification and persuasion you can find in written and visual sources and in interviews. An **explanation** clarifies what something is or how it works to the audience. How does Freud account for our motivations? What is *catharsis* and how is it related to aggression? What do *id, ego,* and *superego* mean? A discussion of psychology would offer explanations and answers, as well as their relation to the field.

A good explanation usually simplifies a concept or idea for an audience by explaining it from their point of view. William Safire, once a presidential speech writer and now a syndicated columnist, provided an explanation in one of his columns about how the spelling of a word gets changed. In his explanation, he pointed out that experts who write dictionaries observe how writers and editors use the language. "When enough citations come in from cultivated writers, passed by trained copy editors," he quotes a lexicographer as saying, "the 'mistake' becomes the spelling."[4] You may find, too, much of your informative speaking is explanation, explaining what an idea means or how something works.

Definitions

Some of the most contentious arguments in our society center around **definitions** or explanations of what a word or concept means. Experts and ordinary citizens have argued for years about definitions. When does art become pornography? Is abortion murder or just birth control? Is withdrawal of life-support systems euthanasia or humanitarian concern? How you define the concept can make a considerable difference.

Definitions in a public speech are supposed to enlighten the audience by revealing what a term means. You can accomplish that goal with explanations, comparisons, examples, analysis, and simplification. Most importantly, you need to state definitions in terms the audience will understand. Sometimes you can use definitions that appear in standard reference works, such as dictionaries and encyclopedias, but more often you can simply try to explain the word in language the audience will understand. For example, what is meant by the term *subcutaneous hematoma?* This term is jargon that a physician uses when he or she spots a dark blotch on your skin. How could you explain that jargon to an audience of ordinary people? You could say, "The word *subcutaneous* means 'under the skin' and the word *hematoma* means 'swelled with blood,' so the words mean 'blood swelling under the skin' or what we lay people call a bruise."

Using Evidence as Proof

Supporting material in your speech can be nearly anything that provides backing for your argument. It can be as simple as, "I know this works because I did it myself," or as complex as a fifty-page report by a government body about a topic. *Evidence* is both a stronger and a narrower term than the term *supporting material.* **Evidence** refers to data or information from which you can draw a conclusion, make a judgment, or establish the probability of something occurring. In the legal system, strict rules govern what may or may not be used as evidence. In public speaking, the rules are considerably looser, but common sense still applies. For instance, a single example is supporting material and it is probably even evidence, but a single example is usually insufficient evidence on which to base a claim. Evidence is often described as being strong or weak. The statement, "This works for me," is weak evidence compared to, "This has worked for millions of people."

If supporting material can be considered an umbrella term for nearly anything that supports a contention, and if evidence is a stronger term on which a conclusion or judgment can be based, then the term *proof* is the strongest. **Proof** is sufficient evidence to convince your audience that what you say is true. Sufficient evidence could be a single example or hundreds of experiments. Evidence becomes proof depending on its acceptability to the audience.

How can you handle evidence in a speech so it will be regarded as proof? The central concern is in knowing what kind and how much evidence will convince an audience your assertions are true. Some audiences—students grounded in math, business, and economics come to mind—are partial to statistics and numerical treatments of a topic. Other audiences are actually repelled by numbers and respond more favorably to long, dramatic stories or examples. How much evidence to use is also an important consideration. Sometimes, one example proves the point for most of the people in your audience. At other times, all the examples in the world would be insufficient to prove a point to an audience.

Actually, no rules govern how much or what kind of evidence should be used in your speech. Instead, you have to apply your intelligence to the problem. Given your skills and the nature of this audience, what can you say about your topic that will convince the audience of the truth of your statements?

One last bit of advice concerning evidence: standard ways of presenting evidence in a speech exist. *First, you need to be highly selective about which of the many possible claims you intend to make in your speech.* Literally hundreds of claims can be made about any given issue. You need to choose the ones most important to you and your audience.

Second, you need to be highly selective about which evidence you use in your speech to support your claims. Literally hundreds of pieces of evidence can be used to support a claim. You need to choose the evidence most important to you and to your audience.

Finally, you need to arrange your argument with a statement either before, after, or both before and after the evidence that reveals what you are trying to prove. Many names for this kind of statement exist—argument, assertion, proposition, claim, and main point. Whatever the name, the content of the statement is a claim that invites evidence, that needs to be proved. It might be a statement of policy: "The United States should approve a single six-year term for our president." It might be a statement of value: "Ohio University has the strongest College of Communication in the country." It might be a statement of fact: "The School of Telecommunications is the largest school of radio-television east of the Mississippi." Statements of fact are evaluated for truth and accuracy because there is a "right answer" to a question of fact.

Statements of value and policy are endlessly debatable because the answer ultimately comes down to what the audience is willing to believe and what the audience will consider as proof.

For example, you may decide that, given your audience and the particular occasion on which you intend to speak, your best approach might be to state first the position you want to prove and then provide what you think is sufficient evidence to prove it:

Claim: *Central States University (CSU) has the best general education requirements in the region.*

Evidence: *CSU requires every student to master English composition by passing a first- and third-year course.*

Evidence: *CSU requires every student to pass at least one quantitative course in mathematics, statistics, computer science, or logic.*

Evidence: *CSU requires every student to take thirty credits in three of five broad areas, such as science, the arts, third-world cultures, literature, and applied engineering.*

Evidence: *CSU requires every student to take a capstone course in the senior year that synthesizes a body of knowledge.*

In another situation with a different audience, you may decide to begin with the evidence and end with the claim.

The important point to remember about proof is that it is perceived differently by different people. The speaker is responsible for demonstrating the truth or probability of a claim. Intelligent analysis of the audience helps the speaker to discover which claims and which evidence will be perceived as proof.

Summary

This chapter focused on how to find information for the content of your speech and how to use that information once you have found it. Sources to consider when gathering information for a speech include your personal experiences, written and visual resources, and other people. Personal experiences are something you can discuss with authority, but care must be taken to evaluate personal experiences as evidence.

Written and visual resources can lead you to important information on a wide variety of topics, but it is important to know and understand how to use a variety of sources, such as the ***Reader's Guide to Periodical Literature,*** yearbooks, encyclopedias, sourcebooks, newspaper files, journals, and the card catalog, to find your information. Explaining where you found your information through written and oral footnotes helps you avoid charges of plagiarism and enhances your credibility.

Interviewing other people is another way to obtain information for your speech. The interviewee can provide expert information, quotations, and examples, and sometimes he or she can lead you to other experts or additional written resources.

Supporting material is information you can employ to support your ideas, to substantiate your arguments, and to clarify your position. The supporting materials discussed in this chapter are examples, surveys, testimonial evidence, statistics, analogies, explanations, and definitions.

Evidence refers to data or information from which you can draw a conclusion, make a judgment, or establish the probability of something occurring. Proof is sufficient evidence to convince your audience that what you say is true. Knowing what kind and how much evidence will be regarded as proof is an important consideration for a speaker. Knowing how to select and organize a claim and its evidence so the audience will accept it as proof is also important.

Key Terms

analogy A kind of supporting material in which the speaker compares or points out similarities between two things that are basically unalike, such as comparing the British and the American medical systems.

card catalog A source of information about books in the library.

celebrity testimony Statements of a public figure that support a point of view.

definitions Revealing what something is through description, comparison, explanation, or illustration.

evidence Anything that constitutes proof of a proposition.

examples Evidence consisting of illustrations drawn from specific instances.

expert testimony Statements of someone who has special knowledge or expertise that support a point of view.

explanation Means of clarification by simplifying, amplifying, or restating.

lay testimony Statements of ordinary people that substantiate, support, or back a point of view.

mean or average The arithmetic sum of a series of numbers divided by the total number of items in the series.

median The midpoint in a series of numbers, the middle score.

mode The most frequently recurring number in a series of numbers.

oral footnote An abbreviated manuscript footnote that tells the audience where you found your information.

percentage The ratio or fraction of one hundred represented by a specific number; obtained by dividing the number by one hundred.

personal experience The use of your own life as a source of information for your speech.

plagiarism The use of someone else's ideas or words without giving them credit.

proof Evidence offered in support of a proposition.

range The highest and lowest numbers in a distribution.

raw numbers Exact numbers cited in measures of population, production, and other measures of quantity.

statistics Numbers that summarize numerical information or compare quantities.

supporting material Any information used to support an argument or idea.

surveys Studies in which a limited number of questions are answered by a sample of the population to discover opinions on issues.

testimonial evidence Written or oral statements of the experience of people other than the speaker used by the speaker to substantiate or clarify his or her points.

written and visual resources The use of books, newspapers, magazines, broadcasts, and documentaries for information, arguments, and evidence for your speech.

chapter 14

Organizing Your Speech

I n this chapter, we examine the three main parts of a speech: the introduction, the body, and the conclusion. First, we discuss the five functions of an introduction along with many ways you can fulfill those functions. Then we turn to the body of the speech, with special emphasis on the functions of the body and the many kinds of organizational patterns that can be used to organize the content of the speech. Finally, we examine the functions of a conclusion.

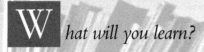

What will you learn?

After you have read and thought about this chapter, you will be able to answer the following questions:

1. What are five functions of an introduction?
2. What are some creative ways to gain and maintain attention?
3. Why is outlining a useful skill for the public speaker?
4. What are the seven principles of outlining?
5. What are four functions of the body of a speech?
6. Can you distinguish between a sentence and a word outline?
7. Can you distinguish among the six organizational patterns?
8. How do you correctly organize information in a bibliography?
9. Can you give an example of a transition and a signpost?
10. What are the four functions of a conclusion?

O rder and simplification are the first steps toward mastery of a subject.

Thomas Mann

W ithout discipline, there is no life at all.

Katharine Hepburn

D on't agonize. Organize.

Florynce R. Kennedy

315

Organizing your speech is one of the most important skills you can learn. Why? First, it requires that you learn how to select from a large amount of information essential to you and your audience. It requires selectivity. You have to determine what your arguments, main points, and evidence will be. Second, outlining demands that you establish priorities with all that important information. You need to decide which of your arguments are strongest and where they should be placed. You need to decide which evidence will be most potent with this audience and where it should be placed. Third, outlining teaches you how to limit and define your topic as economically as possible. Just as it is tougher to write a great paragraph than to write a whole page, it is more difficult to compose a great three-minute speech than to simply fill ten minutes with talk.

Speech organization also highlights some differences between oral and written communication. Readers can go back in your written composition to see what you said. As a speaker, you must build in redundancy, repetition, previews, summaries, transitions, and signposts which are essential because the listener cannot return to the script as a reader can. If you confuse a listener, he or she will remain confused until you clarify your message. A well organized speech that recognizes the unique qualities of oral communication can reduce or eliminate such confusion.

Not only will you get your message across more clearly and effectively with a well organized speech, the audience will also think more highly of you as a speaker. Yes, listeners judge harshly those speakers whose speeches are perceived as disorganized, confusing, or overly complex. A tightly organized speech enhances audience understanding and speaker credibility.

As you begin your study of speech organization, you need to understand how this chapter is organized. This chapter takes you through a speech from beginning to end—from introduction to body to conclusion—with emphasis on the functions that each part fulfills in a public speech. The problem is that you cannot really compose your speech in that order. For example, one function of an introduction is to forecast the organization and development of the body. To do that you need to know what is in the body of the speech. Essentially, you need to know what is in the body in order to compose an effective introduction or an effective conclusion. Read the chapter in any order that satisfies you as long as you recognize that this chapter is organized in linear order but you are likely to compose your speech by starting with the body.

The Introduction

The **introduction** is *the first few minutes of your speech*. It is important because audiences use the introduction to "size up" a speaker. In the first few sentences and certainly in the first few minutes of a speech, audience members decide whether or not to listen to you. They also decide whether your topic is important enough to warrant their consideration. In those crucial minutes early

The introduction of a public speech gains and maintains audience attention.

in the speech, you can capture your audience's attention and keep it, or you can lose it—perhaps for the remainder of the speech. This section of the chapter is devoted to helping you compose the best possible introduction—an introduction that will grab your audience's attention and keep their minds on your topic.

The five functions of an introduction follow:

1. Gain and maintain audience attention
2. Arouse audience interest in the topic being presented
3. Reveal the purpose of your speech
4. Establish your qualifications for speaking on the topic
5. Forecast the development and organization of the speech

These five functions are not necessarily fulfilled in the order indicated. Gaining audience attention often comes at the very beginning, but it is an important function throughout the speech. Forecasting organization often comes toward the end of an introduction, but it does not have to be the last item.

Several of the functions of the introduction can be fulfilled by using the same words. For example, you could start your speech with words that both gain attention and establish your credibility to speak on a certain topic: "I have been a steelworker for twelve years. That is why I am interested in telling you today about what imported steel is doing to one of our biggest industries."

To assist you in composing an introduction for your public speech, we will move systematically through the five functions, explain each, and provide examples.

Gaining and Maintaining Audience Attention

We begin by presenting twelve ways to gain and maintain audience attention. Perhaps these suggestions will inspire you to think of even better ideas for your own speech. Remember, these suggestions are not just a bag of tricks you perform for their own sake. Instead, you gain and maintain the audience's attention by relating your topic to your audience.

1. *Bring the object or person about which you are going to speak.* Examples: A student speaking on health foods brings a small table full of health foods, which he shares with the audience after the speech; a student speaking on weight lifting brings her 250-pound friend to demonstrate the moves during the speech; or the student demonstrating the fine points of choreography employs the dancing talents of six friends.

2. *Invite your audience to participate.* Examples: Ask questions and ask audience members to raise their hands and answer; teach the audience first-aid techniques by having them do some of the techniques with you; or have audience members move their chairs closer together for your speech about overcrowded housing.

3. *Let your attire relate to your speech.* Examples: A nurse talking about the dangers of acute hepatitis wears a nurse's uniform; the construction worker dons a hard hat; or the private security person wears a uniform and badge.

4. *Exercise your audience's imagination.* Examples: Have the audience members close their eyes and imagine they are standing on a ski slope; standing before a judge on an operating-while-intoxicated charge, or entering the warm waters of Hawaii when it is freezing in Cleveland.

5. *Start with sight or sound.* Examples: One minute of classical music from a speaker encouraging others to listen to classical music stations; a large poster-size picture showing the horrors of war; or the sounds of forest birds chirping in the cool dawn. One student gave a powerful speech on motorcycle safety. He showed slides as he talked about the importance of wearing a helmet while driving or riding on a motorcycle. Only one item appeared in color on each slide: a crushed, smashed, or battered helmet that was worn by someone who lived through a motorcycle accident.

6. *Arouse audience curiosity.* Example: One student began his speech by saying, "A new sport has hit this state, yet it is a national tradition. Held in the spring of the year in some of our most beautiful timbered areas, this sport is open to men and women alike. It is for responsible adults only and requires common sense and patience. This sport of our grandparents is . . ." Naturally, by this time, the audience was very curious about the student's topic and anxious to hear more about it.

7. *Role-play.* Examples: A student invites an audience member to pretend to be a choking victim. The speaker then "saves" the victim by using the maneuver she is teaching the audience. Speakers themselves can, for

example, play the role of a mechanic fixing a small engine, a nurse showing how to take vital signs, or an architect selling a proposal. Audiences can be asked to play the role of people whose cars will not start, of paramedics learning what to do in the first few minutes with an accident victim, or of a board of directors considering a new building.

8. *Show a few slides or a very short film.* Examples: A football player speaking on violence in that sport shows a short film of a punt return while he points out which players were deliberately trying to maim their opponents with faceguards—as they has been taught to do; an international student shows a few slides of her native land; or a student speaking on city slums presents a mind-grabbing sequence of twelve-slides showing winos in doorways, rats in a child's room, and a family of ten people living in three rooms.

9. ***Present a brief quotation or have the audience read something provided by you.*** Examples: Sometimes, reading a few lines by T. S. Eliot, Wordsworth, or Malcolm X can prepare the audience for your message. One enterprising student wrote a letter to every student in his class. When class members opened their letters, they read a personalized invitation to report to their local draft board for induction into the armed services of the United States.

10. ***State striking facts or statistics.*** Examples: "Scientists have discovered the bones of a seventeen-million-year-old apelike creature, a creature that could be the common ancestor of the great apes and human beings";[1] or "Women under fifty years of age could reduce their heart attacks by 65 percent by simply quitting smoking, according to a study in the ***Journal of the American Medical Association.***"[2]

11. ***Self-disclosure.*** Tell audience members something about yourself—related to the topic—they would not otherwise know. Examples: "I took hard drugs for six years"; "I was an eagle scout"; or "I earn over fifty thousand dollars a year—legally."

12. ***Tell a story, a narration.*** Example: "I want to tell you about Tiow Tan, a friend of mine. Tan was a big success at South High: he lettered in track and football, and he was second highest for grades in our senior year. Tan was just as good in college: he had a 3.5 GPA, drove a Corvette, and was selected for a student internship with IBM. But you read about my friend Tan in last week's newspaper. Maybe you didn't know who he was, but he was the one who died in a car wreck with his girlfriend out on Route 340. They were killed by a drunken driver." If you choose to use a narration, you should indicate to your audience whether the story is hypothetical, fiction, or an actual account.

The preceding twelve suggestions for gaining and maintaining audience attention certainly are not the only possibilities. Indeed, you could begin your speech by stating a problem for which your speech proposes a solution; you could depict dramatic conflict between labor and management, teachers and students, or conservatives and liberals; or you could simply inform the audience about everyday items we only partially understand: stock market reports, barometric pressure readings, or sales tax. Your introduction should not simply imitate something you read in this book; think of ideas of your own that work best for you and your audience.

This section on gaining and maintaining audience attention concludes with a warning. The warning is *you should always make sure your attention-getting strategy is related to your topic.* Some speakers think every public speech must start with a joke. Starting with a joke is a big mistake if you are not good at telling jokes or if your audience is not interested in hearing them. Jokes can be used in the introduction of a speech if they are topically relevant, but they are just one of hundreds of ways a speaker can gain attention. Another overused device is writing some word like S-E-X on the chalkboard and then announcing your speech has nothing to do with sex but that you wanted to get the audience's attention. Again, the problem with this approach is that the attention-getting strategy had nothing to do with the topic.

Avoid being overly dramatic. One of our colleagues had a harrowing experience in class. She was still writing down some comments about the previous speech when the next student rose to deliver his speech. She heard a horrifying groan and looked up to see the student on the floor with his whole leg laid open and bleeding. The students in the class leaped up and surrounded the injured student while she ran to the office to call for emergency assistance. The student planned to give a speech on first aid. He had gotten a plastic leg wound in living color from the student health center. He had a bag of simulated blood on his stomach which he squeezed rhythmically so it would spurt like a severed artery. Unfortunately for the student, his attention-getting action introduction was too realistic. Instead of capturing the audience's attention, he managed to get so much adrenalin into their bloodstreams they were in no mood to listen to any more speeches that day.

Arousing Audience Interest

A second function of an introduction is to arouse audience interest in the subject matter. The best way to arouse audience interest is to clearly show how the topic is related to the audience. A highly skilled speaker can determine how to adapt almost any topic to a particular audience. Do you want to talk about collecting coins? Thousands of coins pass through each person's hands every year. Can you tell your audience how to spot a rare one? If you can arouse the audience's interest in currency, you will find it easier to encourage them to listen to your speech about the rare coins you have collected. Similarly, speeches about your life as a mother of four, a camp counselor, or the manager of a business can be linked to audience interests. The following is a good example of relating the topic to the audience, and it occurred in a student speech on drinking and driving.

Do you know what the leading cause of death is for people who attend this college? Some of you might think it is a disease that causes the most deaths—cancer, heart attacks, or AIDS. No, the leading cause of death among students at this college is car accidents. Not just ordinary car accidents, but accidents in which the driver has been drinking.

The speaker related her topic to the particular audience by linking a national problem to her own college. She prepared the audience to receive more information and ideas about this common problem.

Stating the Purpose

A third function of an introduction is to state the purpose of your speech. Why state the purpose? Informative speeches invite learning, and learning is more likely to occur if you reveal to the audience what you want them to know. Consider the difficulty of listening to a history professor who spends fifty minutes telling you every detail and date related to the Crusades. Observe how much easier you can listen to a history professor who begins the lecture by stating what you are supposed to learn from it: "I want you to understand why the Crusades began, who the main participants were, and when the Crusades occurred."

The following are some examples of statements of purpose:

Today I will tell you three ways to make your car last longer.

What I want you to remember from my speech are the reasons why our national debt is costing a billion dollars per day.

You will learn in this presentation several methods of protecting your credit card from crooks.

In speaking, as in teaching, the audience is more likely to learn and understand if you are clear about what is expected from them. That goal can be accomplished by stating the purpose in the introduction. One word of caution: sometimes in a persuasive speech—as you will learn in the chapter on persuasive speaking—you may wish to delay any statement of purpose until you have set the stage for audience acceptance. Under most circumstances—and especially in informative speeches—you should reveal your purpose in your introduction.

Establishing Your Qualifications

A fourth function of an introduction is to describe any special qualifications you have, to enhance your credibility as explained in chapter 12. You can talk about your experience, your research, the experts you interviewed, and your own education and training in the subject. You should be wary about self-praise, but you need not be reserved in stating why you can speak about the topic with authority. The following is one example of posing a common problem through self-disclosure:

> I am a Catholic girl and I have a Baptist boyfriend. Our different religions have challenged us both but have strengthened, rather than weakened, our relationship because we have to explain our faiths to each other. With that in mind, I'd like to share with you the similarities between two seemingly different religions.

Chapter 12 provided considerably more information about what behaviors audiences look for in a speaker, along with some suggestions concerning what information should be included about the speaker.

Forecasting Development and Organization

A fifth function of an introduction is to forecast the organization and development of the speech. The forecast provides a brief outline of your organization. It is a preview of the main points you plan to cover. Audience members feel more comfortable when they know what to expect. You can help by revealing your plan for the speech. Are you going to discuss a problem and its solution? Are you going to make three main arguments with supporting materials? Are you going to talk for five minutes or for twenty? Let your audience know what you plan to do early in your speech. Two forecasts follow. Are they adequate in forecasting the organization and development?

> Follow my advice this evening and you can earn ten dollars an hour painting houses, barns, and warehouses. First, I will show you how to locate this kind of work. Next, I will teach you how to bid on a project. And, last, I will give you some tips on how to paint well enough to get invited back.

> My purpose is to help you understand your own checking account. I will help you "read" your check by explaining the numbers and stamps that appear on the face; I will help you manage your checking account by showing you how to avoid overdraw charges; and I will demonstrate how you can prove your check cleared.

The Body

Earlier, you learned that most speakers begin composing their speech with the body rather than the introduction. The order used in composing a speech differs from the order used in delivering a speech because the speaker needs to know the content of the speech to write an effective introduction.

The **body** of a speech is the largest portion of the speech in which you place your arguments and ideas, your substantiation and examples, and your proofs and illustrations. Since you usually do not have time to state in a speech everything you know about a subject, you need to decide what information to include and what information to exclude. Since the remaining material may not all be of equal importance, you need to decide where in the body to place it—first, last, or in the middle. Selecting, prioritizing, and organizing are three skills that you will employ in developing the body of your speech.

Just as the introduction of a speech has certain functions to fulfill, so does the body. The main functions of the body follow:

1. Increase what an audience knows about a topic (informative speech)
2. Change an audience's actions about a topic (persuasive speech)
3. Present a limited number of arguments and/or ideas
4. Provide backing, support, or substantiation for your arguments and/or ideas
5. Indicate the sources of your information, arguments, support, and substantiation

All of these functions are fulfilled within a particular organizational structure.

You already know something about organization. Every sentence you utter has organization. The words are arranged according to rules of syntax for the English language. Even when you are in conversation, you employ some organization. The first statement you make is often more general than that which follows. For instance, you might say, "I don't like DeMato for Congress" after which you might say why you don't like DeMato. You probably don't start by stating some specific fact, such as DeMato's voting record, his position on abortion, or his torrid love life. Likewise, when we compose a speech, we tend to limit what we say, say it in some priority order, and back it as necessary with substantiation—all organized according to principles we have either subconsciously learned (as in the case of the rules of syntax for language) or consciously studied (as in the rules of organization).

Outlining

To help you learn how to organize your speech, you will begin with the outline. An **outline** is a written plan that uses symbols, margins, and content to reveal the order, importance, and substance of your speech. The outline shows the sequence of your arguments or main points, indicates their relative importance, and states your arguments, main points, and substantiations. The outline is a simplified, abstract version of your speech.

Why learn outlining? First, outlining is a useful skill that can be used to develop written compositions, to write notes in class, and to compose speeches. Second, outlining teaches important skills, such as selecting the information and ideas most important for you and your audience, discriminating between what is more important and less important, and placing arguments, ideas, and support in some structure that will encourage learning and behavioral change. A third advantage is that an outline encourages you to speak extemporaneously and conversationally. Some of the best speakers learn how to deliver their speeches from an outline, instead of having every word written out in a manuscript. Useful, important, and readily applicable in a speech communication class, the outline is an overall organizational plan that you need to understand.

Principles of Outlining

The outline form is versatile and relatively easy to learn as long as you keep a few principles in mind. *The first principle of outlining is that all of the items of information in your outline should be directly related to your purpose.* The **immediate purpose** is what you expect to achieve by the end of your speech. You might want the audience to be able to state your three main arguments; you might want the audience to respond to your speech by reading an article, signing a petition, or by trying some synthetic food; or you might want audience members to start changing their minds about the topic by discussing it with others. The **long-range goal** is what you expect to achieve over a longer time period. Eventually, you may want the audience to vote for your candidate; to act more tolerantly toward persons of your race, gender, or religion; or to join an activist group for a cause you represent. The first principle of outlining is that the content of your outline should reflect your immediate purpose and your long-range goal.

The second principle of outlining is that the outline should be an abstract of the speech you will deliver. It should be less than every word you speak but should include all important points and supporting materials. Some instructors say an outline should be about one-third the length of the actual speech if the speech were in manuscript form. However, you should ask what your instructor expects in an outline, because some instructors like to see a very complete outline and others prefer a brief outline. Nonetheless, the outline is not a manuscript. It is an abstract of the speech you intend to deliver, a plan that includes the important arguments or information you intend to present.

The third principle of outlining is that the outline should consist of single units of information, usually in the form of complete sentences that express a single idea. The following example is incorrect because it expresses more than one idea in more than one sentence:

I. Gun control should be employed to reduce the number of deaths in the United States that result from the use of handguns. Half of the deaths from handguns are because criminals murder other people with them.

The same ideas can be outlined correctly by presenting a single idea in each sentence:

I. Government regulations of handguns should be implemented to reduce the number of murders in this country.
   A. Half of the murders in the United States are committed by criminals using handguns.

B. Half of the murders in the United States are committed by relatives, friends, or acquaintances of the victim.

The fourth principle of outlining is that the outline should indicate the importance of an item with an outlining symbol. In the example, the **main points** or most important points are indicated with Roman numerals, such as I, II, III, IV, and V. The number of main points in a five-to-ten-minute speech, or even a longer speech, should be limited to the number you can reasonably cover, explain, or prove in the time permitted. Most five-minute speeches have from one to three main points. Even hour-long speeches must have a limited number of main points because audiences seem unable to remember more than seven main points.

Subpoints, those supporting the main points or those of less importance, are indicated with capital letters, such as A, B, C, D, and E. Ordinarily, two subpoints under a main point are regarded as the minimum if any subpoints are to be presented. As with the main points, the subpoints should be limited; otherwise, the audience may lose sight of your main point. A good guideline is to present two or three of your best pieces of supporting material in support of each main point.

Sub-subpoints are even less important than the subpoints; they are introduced with Arabic numbers, such as 1, 2, 3, 4, and 5. Typically, the number of sub-subpoints is limited like the number of subpoints. Sub-subpoints usually do not exceed three in number. If you should have to present any additional ideas under a sub-subpoint, they are presented with lowercase alphabetical letters, such as a, b, c, d, and e.

The fifth principle of outlining is that the outline should provide margins that indicate the relative importance of the items. The larger the margin on the left, the less important the item is to your purpose. However, the margins are coordinated with the symbols explained previously so main points have the same left margin, the subpoints have a left margin with slightly more space on the left, the sub-subpoints have a left margin with slightly more space on the left, and so on. A correct outline with the appropriate symbols and margins looks like this:

I. The constitutional right to bear arms is being threatened by ineffective gun control.[3]
   A. Murders are being committed with handguns by psychopaths, criminals, and ordinary people.
      1. A psychopath killed John Lennon, a famous singer, with a .38-caliber handgun.[4]
      2. The same week, an ex-convict killed a famous physician, Dr. Michael Halberstam, with a .32-caliber handgun.[5]
      3. Of the twenty thousand persons killed by handguns each year, only two thousand are murdered by criminals engaged in crime.[6]

B. The number of handguns in circulation is immense.
  1. Nationally, 55 million handguns are in circulation.[7]
  2. Every year, about 2.5 million handguns add to the total.[8]
  3. Handgun Control in Washington, D.C., estimates we will have 100 million handguns in circulation by the end of the century.[9]
II. The solution may be federal gun control or harsher punishment for handgun offenders.
  A. *New York Times* columnist Tom Wicker recommends gun control.[10]
  B. Columnist James J. Kilpatrick recommends the death sentence for persons who murder with handguns.[11]

The sixth principle of outlining is that the content of an item in an outline should be less than or subordinate to the content of items with higher-order symbols or smaller left-hand margins. Notice in the outline just illustrated that the items with the highest-order symbols (I, II) and the smallest margins are larger or more important ideas than the items that appear below them with lesser-order symbols (A, B) and larger left-hand margins. Similarly, those items beneath the subpoints—the sub-subpoints—are less than or subordinate to the items that appear above them. The sub-subpoints merely amplify or provide additional evidence; hence, items in an outline are ranked in importance by symbols, margins, and content.

The seventh principle of outlining is that the items should appear in **parallel form.** *"Parallel" in this instance means similar or same, and "form" means simple sentences, phrases, or words.* The principle of parallel form means that you should consistently use either sentences, phrases, or words in an outline.

An example of incorrect parallel form follows:

I. Three measures of educational quality are college entrance tests, teacher-pupil ratios, and expenditures per pupil
  A. College entrance tests:
    1. Top SAT states—New Hampshire, Oregon, and Vermont
    2. Top ACT states—Wisconsin, Iowa, and Minnesota
  B. Teacher-pupil ratios:
    1. Connecticut and Wyoming tie for first
    2. Others in top ten: New York, Washington, D.C., New Jersey, Oregon, Delaware, Maryland, Wyoming, Rhode Island, and Massachusetts

An example of correct parallel form follows.[12]

I. Three measures of educational quality are college entrance tests, teacher-pupil ratios, and expenditures per pupil.
  A. The two most often used college entrance tests are the ACT (American College Test) and the SAT (Scholastic Aptitude Test).
    1. The top-scoring states on the ACT are Wisconsin, Iowa, and Minnesota.

   2. The top-scoring states on the SAT are New Hampshire, Oregon, and Vermont.
B. The teacher-pupil ratio is a second measure of educational quality.
   1. The top states in the nation in teacher-student ratio were Connecticut and Wyoming, who tied for first place.
   2. The other states in the top ten included New York, Washington, D.C., New Jersey, Oregon, Delaware, Maryland, Wyoming, Rhode Island, and Massachusetts.

The example of incorrect parallel form is incorrect because it mixes sentences, phrases, and words instead of consistently using one form, such as complete sentences. The example of correct parallel form uses complete sentences throughout; it is parallel because it repeats same or similar forms.

Developing a Rough Draft

Before you begin composing your outline, you can save time and energy by (1) selecting a topic appropriate for you, your audience, and the situation; (2) finding arguments, examples, illustrations, quotations, and other supporting

Once you have gathered materials consistent with your purpose, you can begin by developing a rough draft of your outline.

materials from your experience, from written and visual resources, and from other people; and (3) narrowing your immediate purpose so you have to select the best materials from a much larger supply of available items than you could include in your outline and your speech.

Once you have gathered materials consistent with your purpose, you can begin by developing a **rough draft** of your outline, a tentative plan for the ordering or arranging of your points. The most efficient way to develop a rough draft is to find the main points important for your purpose and your audience. The number of main points should be limited. In the outline about gun control in the previous section, the speaker decided the best approach to talking about gun control was to explore the problem first (item I) and then to discuss the two possible solutions (item II).

Next, you should see what materials you have from your experience, from written and visual resources, and from other people to support these main ideas. In the outline in the previous section, the speaker determined the number of murders and the number of handguns in circulation illustrated the lack of effective gun control. Similarly, you need to find out if you have any supporting materials that back up your subpoints—facts, statistics, testimony, and examples. In the same outline, the speaker found two famous people murdered by handguns within a week and a statistic that illustrated the scope of the problem. In short, you assemble your main points, your subpoints, and your sub-subpoints for your speech always with your audience and purpose in mind. What arguments, illustrations, and supporting materials will be most likely to have an impact on the audience? Sometimes, speakers get so involved in a topic they select mainly those items that interest them. In public speaking, you should select the items likely to have the maximum impact on the audience, not on you.

Composing an outline for a speech is not easy. Even professional speech writers may have to make important changes on their first draft. Some of the questions you need to consider as you revise your rough draft follow:

1. Are my main points consistent with my purpose?
2. Are my subpoints and sub-subpoints subordinate to my main points?
3. Are the items in my outline the best possible ones for this particular audience, for this topic, for me, and for the occasion?
4. Does my outline follow the principles of outlining?

Even after you have rewritten your rough draft, you would be wise to have another person—perhaps a classmate—examine your outline and provide an opinion about its content.

The Sentence Outline

One of the most useful forms of speech organization is the **sentence outline.** This kind of outline shows in sentence form your order of presentation and where and what kind of arguments, points, supporting materials, and evidence you plan to use in your speech. A look at your own outline might indicate, for example, you have insufficient information to back one of your points or, perhaps, a surplus of information for another.

In addition to the sentence outline itself, you may want to write in the functions being served by each part of your outline. For example, where are you trying to gain and maintain attention? Where are you trying to back up a major argument with supporting materials like statistics, testimony, or specific instances? The result of a sentence outline along with sidenotes indicating functions is a blueprint, a plan for your speech, that can strengthen your speech performance by aiding you in presenting evidence or supporting materials that will make sense to audience members and that will help inform or persuade them.

The outline that follows is based on a student's speech. The immediate purpose of the speech was to challenge the belief in a materialistic society based on consumption by having audience members state at the conclusion of the speech some qualities of life besides wealth for which they should strive. As you read the outline, see if you think the main points are consistent with the immediate purpose and the long-range goal, which is to convince the audience to adopt a nonmaterialistic life-style after college. Notice the outline is a sentence outline because every entry, whether it is a main point, a subpoint, or a sub-subpoint, is a complete sentence.

Functions	A Life-Style Designed for Permanence

Topic-relevant rhetorical questions to gain attention	**Introduction**
	I. I want to ask all of you three general questions.
	    A. Do you want to preserve the world's natural resources?
	    B. Do you want our country to be independent of other nations for energy supplies?
	    C. Do you want to ensure a good future for your children?

Questions to relate the topic to the audience	II. Next, I want to ask you three questions that pertain to us as college students.
	    A. Do you want to become wealthy?
	    B. Do you want to drive a big, prestigious luxury car?
	    C. Do you want to live in a big house?

Qualifications of speaker on this topic	III. I have been listening to and reading about some very serious facts concerning the scarcity of natural resources in the world.
Forecast and statement of expectations	IV. I am going to show you that, if you answered "yes" to the first three questions, then you are going to have to answer "no" to the last three.

Paraphrase an authority to demonstrate the speaker has read about the topic and to make the first main point in the speech	**Body**
	I. E. F. Schumacher's book *Small Is Beautiful* says our most fateful error is in believing that the problems of production have been solved.
	    A. We have come to believe anything can be produced by technology and good old American ingenuity.
	    B. Unfortunately, our technology depends on fossil fuels, which are being rapidly depleted.

Speaker gives the audience credit for what they have done before, asks them to do more	II. We are trying to conserve our resources by decreasing energy consumption.
	    A. Statistics indicate mass transit systems are being utilized more and more.
	    B. The automobile industry has greatly increased the production of small cars.

Paraphrases an authority, presents second main point, and demonstrates again the speaker's interest in the topic	III. Kenneth Boulding, a world-renowned economist, gave a lecture last week on campus in which he promoted the idea of a new moral order within a new life-style.
	    A. The new moral order is based on being, living, and working together.
	    B. The new life-style is one in which we learn to get along with less and accept it.

Third subpoint with three sub-subpoints to clarify the idea

C. Boulding's "mature world" has implications for our careers, for production, and for our attitudes.

1. Instead of seeking jobs to give us wealth, we should strive for occupations that enable everyone to have a decent existence.

Advances the idea of smaller places of production
Examples of one change

2. Instead of large-scale, highly complex, and highly capital-intensive production, we should try smaller units of production.
   a. Instead of one big factory, we should have many smaller plants located closer to where resources are located.

Advances the idea of area instead of national companies

   b. Instead of encouraging bigger and bigger megacorporations, we could encourage a wider assortment of smaller, locally or regionally owned companies.

Mentions an attitude that must be overcome

3. We have to overcome our "bigger is better" notion that has been encouraged during most of this century.

Conclusion

I. A life-style designed for permanence is possible!

Challenge to the audience: two alternatives

A. Do we want a world where quality means more than quantity?
B. Do we want a world that exhausts its resources on the way to self-destruction?

II. Americans need to learn how to "live small".

Based on a speech manuscript composed by Jane Wolf in *Speech 211H,* Iowa State University.

The Key-Word Outline

Speakers who use a manuscript of their entire speech sometimes become too dependent on the manuscript. It reduces their eye contact and minimizes their attention to audience responses. Nonetheless, some speakers become very proficient at reading from a manuscript on which they have highlighted the important words, phrases, and quotations. A complete sentence outline may be superior to a manuscript in that it forces the speaker to extemporize, to maintain eye contact, and to respond to audience feedback. Key words and phrases can be underlined or highlighted on a sentence outline. An alternative method is to simply use a **key-word outline,** which includes only those items you would normally highlight on a complete sentence outline.

The key-word outline consists of important words and phrases that remind the speaker of the topic or main idea being addressed. However, it may contain statistics or quotations that are too long or complicated to memorize. The key-word outline abstracts the ideas in the speech considerably more than a sentence outline. The key-word outline that follows is based on the same speech upon which the sentence outline presented in the previous section was based. A comparison of the two types of outlines illustrates how much more the key-word outline abstracts or reduces the content to the bare essentials.

A Life-Style Designed for Permanence
Introduction
  I. Three questions
      A. Preserving resources?
      B. Energy independence?
      C. Good future?
  II. Three questions
      A. Wealth?
      B. Expensive car?
      C. Big house?
  III. Facts on scarcity
  IV. Yes to three; no to three
Body
  I. Production problems not solved—Schumacher
      A. Technology and ingenuity
      B. Fossil fuels
  II. Decreasing energy consumption
      A. Mass transit
      B. Small cars
  III. New moral order—Boulding
      A. Togetherness
      B. Getting along with less
      C. Boulding's "Mature world"
         1. Occupations
         2. Smallness
            a. Small factories
            b. Small companies
         3. Bigness attitude
Conclusion
  I. Permanence
      A. Quality
      B. Resources
  II. "Live small"

The key-word outline fits easily on 3-by-5-inch or 4-by-6-inch notecards or on 8 1/2-by-11-inch paper. If you choose notecards on which you write or type a key-word outline, the following suggestions may be helpful:

1. Write instructions to yourself on your notecards. For instance, if you are supposed to write the title of your speech and your name on the chalkboard before your speech begins, then you can write that instruction on the top of your first card.
2. Write on one side of the cards only. It is better to use more cards with your key-word outline on one side only than to write front and back because the latter method is more likely to result in confusion.
3. Number your notecards on the top so they will be unlikely to get out of order and so if they are dropped, they can be quickly reassembled.
4. Write out items that might be difficult to remember. Extended quotations, difficult names, unfamiliar terms, and statistics are examples of items you may want to include on your notecards to reduce the chances for error.
5. Practice delivering your speech at least two times using your notecards. Effective delivery may be difficult to achieve if you have to fumble with unfamiliar cards.
6. Write clearly and legibly.

Organizational Patterns

The body of a speech can be outlined using a number of **organizational patterns.** Exactly which pattern of organization is most appropriate for your speech depends in part on your purpose and on the nature of your material. For instance, if your purpose is to present a solution to a problem, your purpose lends itself well to the problem-and-solution organizational pattern. If the nature of your material is something that occurred over a period of time, then your material might be most easily outlined with a chronological or time-sequence pattern of organization.

In this section, we examine five organizational patterns—*the time-sequence pattern, the spatial-sequence pattern, the causal-sequence pattern, the problem-and-solution pattern, and the topical-sequence pattern*—in detail, giving a description, an application, and an example of each. However, you should keep in mind that these five patterns of organization are prototypes from which a skilled speaker can construct many additional patterns of organization. Also, a number of organizational patterns may appear in the same speech: an overall problem-and-solution organization may have within it a time-sequence pattern that explains the history of the problem.

Time-Sequence Pattern

The **time-sequence pattern,** most commonly used in informative speeches, is also known as chronological order because it reveals how something occurs over time. You can use this pattern in speeches that consider the past, present, and future of some idea, issue, plan, or project. It is most useful on such topics as the following:

How the Salvation Army Began   The Steps in Making a Cedar Chest
The "Today" Show: A Brief History   The Formula for Foolproof Gravy
The Naming of a Stadium   The Building of the Hearst Castle
The Future for Space Exploration   The Development of Drugs for
    Treating AIDS

Any topic that requires attention to events, incidents, or steps that take place over time is appropriate for this pattern of organization. A brief outline of a speech organized in a time-sequence pattern follows.[13]

South Africa
I. The Bushmen first came to South Africa seeking better land, only to be pushed aside and enslaved by others.
  A. The San or Bushmen were nomadic hunters.
  B. The Bushmen later worked in the African gold mines.
II. Europeans (the Dutch) established an outpost at the Cape of Good Hope in 1652.
  A. The Dutch overcame the San and the Khoikhoi.
  B. The Dutch settlers and the black natives produced a repressed class of persons labeled "coloureds."
  C. The Dutch fought formidable black tribes like the Zulu and the Xhosa.
III. The nineteenth century brought armed conflict between the English settlers and the Dutch Boers.
  A. The British won a military victory in the Boer War (1899–1902).
  B. The Boers won a political victory by becoming Afrikaners with their own language, laws, and culture.
IV. In the twentieth century, South Africans established the concept of apartheid to control blacks and coloureds.
V. By the 1990s South Africans outlawed apartheid.

Notice that the emphasis in this brief outline is on the history of South Africa, on the events that took place over the centuries and resulted in the society there today. A simpler example of a time-sequence pattern of organization is a recipe that depends on the combining of ingredients in the correct order.

The organizational pattern of your speech may depend upon your purpose and the nature of your information.

Spatial-Sequence Pattern

Another organizational pattern used mainly in informative speeches is called the **spatial-sequence organization.** It is a pattern that reveals how things relate to each other in space, position, and visual orientation. Examples are a blueprint, road map, or diagram showing furniture arrangements in a room. In a speech, it is more likely to be an explanation of an audio board, of how electricity gets from the power plant to your home, or how to best set up your speakers. The following is a more detailed example describing the parts of the human heart.

The Human Heart: Form and Function

Immediate purpose: After listening to my speech, the audience will be able to recognize the form and function of the human heart.

Introduction
    I. The human heart is the part of the body that fails or falters in more than a million people per year.

    II. Learning about how your heart is structured and how it functions can help you keep it healthy.

Body
    III. As shown on the visual aid, the heart consists of four chambers, the right and left atrium and the left and right ventricle.

IV. The atria and the ventricles have different functions.
    A. The right atrium and left atrium are thin-walled receiving chambers for blood.
    B. The right and left ventricles are thick-walled pumping chambers that pump eighteen million gallons of blood in seventy years.

Conclusion

V. The heart's structure and functions are simple, but heart failure ends life.
VI. Name the parts and the functions of the heart as a first step in guarding your own health.

Causal-Sequence Pattern

With **causal-sequence pattern,** the speaker explains the cause or causes and the consequences, results, or effects. The speech may be cause-effect, effect-cause, or even effect-effect. A speech on inflation that uses the causal-sequence pattern might review causes of inflation, such as low productivity and high waves, and review effects of inflation, such as high unemployment and high interest. Causal-sequence pattern is often used in informative speeches that seek to explain an issue. It differs from the problem-and-solution pattern because the causal-sequence pattern does not necessarily reveal what to do about a problem; instead it allows for full explanation of an issue. An example of causal-sequence pattern follows.

Alcoholism or Abstinence?

Immediate purpose: To persuade the class that social drinking leads to alcoholism.

Introduction

I. Job, school, and families bring stress that many of us try to reduce with alcohol.
II. For some the social drinking will become problem drinking, which will become alcoholism.

Body

III. Why an individual becomes chemically dependent on alcohol remains a mystery, but the reasons seem rooted in nature and nurture.
    A. Children of the chemically dependent have a much greater chance of becoming chemically dependent themselves.
    B. Persons who drink at all risk becoming chemically dependent.
IV. Social drinking can become problem drinking.
    A. The person who cannot seem to stop drinking is already a problem drinker.
    B. The person who passes out, blacks out, or cannot remember what occurred has a serious drinking problem.

       C. The person whose relationships with others begins to fail with regularity has turned from people to alcohol.

   V. The problem drinker becomes an alcoholic.

       A. The person who is unable to stop drinking has become chemically dependent.

       B. The person who is alcoholic must usually be helped by others to stop.

       C. The most common way to avoid reoccurrence is to never drink again.

Conclusion   VI. The best illustration that social drinking leads to alcoholism is that a nondrinker will never become an alcoholic.

       A. Persons with a family history of chemical dependence can protect themselves by abstinence.

       B. Persons whose families see a person becoming dependent might want to encourage nondrinking before the problem becomes worse.

Problem-and-Solution Pattern

The fourth pattern of organization, used most often in persuasive speeches, is the **problem-and-solution pattern.** As the name of this pattern suggests, the pattern describes a problem and proposes a solution. A speech based on this pattern can be divided into two distinct parts, with an optional third part in which the speaker meets any anticipated objections to the proposed solution. The problem-and-solution pattern can have other patterns within it. For example, you might discuss the problem in time-sequence order, and you might discuss the solution using a topical-sequence pattern. Some examples of problem-and-solution topics follow:

- Reducing Fat in Your Diet
- A New Way to Stop Smoking
- Eliminating Nuclear Waste
- Breaking the "Glass Ceiling" for Women
- An Alternative to Welfare
- Banning Smoking Everywhere

Each example implies both a problem and a solution: "Banning Smoking Everywhere" could be a proposal for what to do about primary and secondary smoke in restaurants and offices.

The problem-and-solution pattern of organization requires close audience analysis because you have to decide how much time and effort to spend on each portion of the speech. Is the audience already familiar with the problem? If so, you might be able to discuss the problem briefly with a few reminders to the audience of the problem's seriousness or importance. On the other hand, the problem may be so complex that both the problem and the solution cannot be covered in a single speech. In that case, you may have found a topic that requires a problem speech and a solution speech or speeches. In any case, your audience analysis should be an important first step in determining the ratio of time devoted to the problem and to the solution in this pattern.

The problem-and-solution speech in outline form might look like the following:

Physical Fitness for College Students
 I. Many college students are in poor physical condition.
   A. Fewer colleges are requiring physical education courses.
   B. Increasing numbers of college students are overweight.
   C. Increasing numbers of college students suffer from physical problems caused by poor physical conditioning.
 II. Jogging is good for social, psychological, and physical reasons.
   A. People who jog together get to know each other very well.
   B. Joggers can take out some of their frustrations, anxieties, and aggressions on the track.
   C. Joggers can gain and maintain good physical conditioning through regular workouts.
 III. The main objections to jogging are the time and energy it takes.
   A. We should take the time to keep our bodies in good condition, just as we do our minds and spirits.
   B. The effort required in jogging is its main benefit—strengthening our cardiovascular system.

The problem-and-solution pattern has many applications in speeches on contemporary problems and issues. It can be used to discuss inflation, price-fixing, poverty, welfare, housing costs, the quality of goods, the quality of services, and the problems of being a student.

Topical-Sequence Pattern

The **topical-sequence pattern,** used in both informative and persuasive speeches, addresses the advantages, disadvantages, qualities, and types of persons, places, or things. The topical-sequence pattern can be used to explain to audience members why you want them to adopt a certain point of view. It is appropriate when you have three to five points to make: three reasons why people should buy used cars, four of the main benefits of studying speech, or five characteristics of a good football player. This pattern of organization is among the most versatile. In a speech informing audience members about tarantulas, a portion of the topical-sequence outline would look like the following.

I. The name *tarantula* has an interesting history.
   A. The word *tarantula* is derived from the name of a small town in Italy.
      1. Taranto was a town in Italy where the people experienced a large number of spider bites.
      2. The people of Taranto were bitten so frequently they developed a dance to sweat the spider poison out of their blood.
   B. The name *tarantula* was applied originally to the European wolf spider, the one encountered in Taranto.
   C. The name was transferred to the tropical spider, which is now known as the tarantula.
II. The tarantula is characterized by five unusual characteristics.
   A. One unusual feature of the tarantula is its size.
      1. Tropical tarantulas are as large as three inches in body length and ten inches in leg span.
      2. Species in the United States range from one to three inches in body length and up to five inches in leg span.
   B. A second unusual feature of the tarantula is that it is nocturnal; that is, it hunts at night.
   C. A third interesting feature of the tarantula is that it can see only two inches and relies on leg hairs to sense the presence of other things.
   D. A fourth characteristic of the tarantula is that the species is cannibalistic.
   E. A fifth characteristic of the tarantula is that it moults.
      1. Moulting decreases with age.
      2. Moulting can be accompanied by regeneration of lost parts, such as legs.

Based on an outline composed by Terry Hermiston, Iowa State University.

The outline could continue to develop main points on why tarantulas make interesting and economical pets and on the myths about their poison. However, the portion of the outline shown here illustrates the main advantage of the topical-sequence outline—it can be used to organize diverse ideas into a commonsense sequence that appeals to an audience.

Organizing a Bibliography

When you have completed your outline, you may be asked to provide a **bibliography,** a list of the sources you used in your speech. In chapter 13, we examined footnote form; in this chapter, we look at the correct forms for the bibliography.

The most common source students use for their speeches is magazine articles, usually obtained by using the *Reader's Guide to Periodical Literature* or a computerized information retrieval system. The following is the correct form for a bibliographic entry for a newspaper or periodical:

Newspaper

Stahl, Fran. "Homeless: From the Depths, Man Finds 'Miracles' after Life of Drugs." *Eagle,* Marco Island, Florida, 16 Sept. 1992, p. 1.

Journal

Walther, Joseph B., and Burgoon, Judee K. "Relational Communication in Computer-Mediated Interaction." *Human Communication Research* 19 (September 1992), 50–88.

Magazine

Van Gelder, Lindsy. "A Take Charge Way to Meet New People: Love among the Classifieds." *Ms.,* Aug. 1983, pp. 39–43.

Notice that in bibliography form the name of the first author appears in reverse order so the list can be alphabetized. In the first entry, if there is no author, the bibliographic entry begins with the next available information. Your instructor may or may not require volume numbers for magazine articles, but if a volume number is included, do not write "p." or "pp." in the entry.

When there is no volume number, you should include "p." for a single page or "pp." for more than one page. Notice that, unlike the footnote form, the name of the author or authors and the title of the article are followed by a period.

The following is the correct bibliographic form for a book in your list of sources:

Chellis, Marcia. *Ordinary Women, Extraordinary Lives.* New York: Viking Penguin, 1992.

The author's name is in reverse order for accurate alphabetization. The name of the author and the name of the book are followed by a period. The place of publication is followed by a colon, the name of the publisher is followed by a comma, and the date of publication is followed by a period. A bibliographic entry must include the pages of a book that were used if the entire book was not used.

If you use an interview for your source, the bibliographic entry would look like the following:

Munshaw, Joe. Professor of Communication, Southern Illinois University at Edwardsville. Personal interview. 15 October 1992.

Pamphlets, handbooks, and manuals may not have complete information about who wrote them, who published them, or when they were published. In that case, you are expected to provide as much information as possible so others can verify the source.

Correct Bibliographic Form

To test your knowledge of correct bibliographic form, see if you can rewrite these three entries in correct form. The correct form appears on p. 348 at the end of this chapter.

1. *Educational Record: The Magazine of Higher Education.* Summer 1992. "Faculty and Collegiate Athletics Reform: Seizing the Moment." John R. Gerdy. Pages 45–49.

2. Robert N. Bellah. Richard Madsen. William M. Sullivan. Ann Swidler. Steven M. Tipton. 1991, New York: Alfred A. Knopf. *The Good Society.*

3. Mark Mayfield. USA Today. Justice: A Right Denied. Page 1. September 25–27, 1992.

The main idea behind a bibliography is to inform others of what sources you used for your speech and to permit others to check those sources for themselves. If you run across sources you do not know how to footnote or to place in bibliographic form, you can ask your bookstore or a librarian for *The Publication Manual of the American Psychological Association, The MLA Style Sheet,* or *The Chicago Manual of Style.* College composition texts also include the standard forms for footnote and bibliographic entries.

Transitions and Signposts

So far, we have examined the organization of a speech in its broadest sense. To look at the speech as a problem-and-solution or causal-sequence pattern is like looking at a house's first floor and basement. It is important we also look more closely at the design of the speech by examining whatever connects the parts of a speech together.

Transitions and signposts are two items that hold the speech together. A **transition** is a bridge from one idea to another, a link between whatever came before in a speech and whatever is coming next. It also relaxes the audience momentarily. A typical transition is a brief flashback and a brief forecast that tells your audience when you are moving from one main point to another.

The most important transitions are between the introduction and the body, between the main points of the body, and between the body and the conclusion of the speech. Other transitions can appear between the main heading and main points, between main points and subpoints, between subpoints and sub-subpoints, between examples, and between visual aids and the point being illustrated. The transitions can review, preview, or even be an internal summary, but they always explain the relationship between one idea and another. Transitions are the mortar between the building blocks of the speech. Without them, cracks appear, and the structure is less solid. Figure 14.1 gives examples of transitions.

Signposts are a way a speaker signals to an audience where the speech is going. Signposts, as the name implies, are like road signs that tell a driver there is a curve, bump, or rough road ahead; they are a warning, a sign the speaker is making a move. Whereas transitions are often several to many sentences in length, signposts are usually no longer than a sentence or a few words in length. Whereas transitions review, state a relationship, and forecast, signposts just point.

Beginning speakers often are admonished by their instructors for using signposts that are too blatant: "This is my introduction," "This is my third main point," or "This is my conclusion." More experienced speakers choose more subtle but equally clear means of signposting: "Let me begin by showing you . . . ," "A third reason for avoiding the sun is . . . ," or "The best inference you can draw from what I have told you is. . . ." Figure 14.2 gives examples of signposts.

Transitions and signposts help speakers map a speech for the audience. Transitions explain the relationships in the speech by reflecting backward and forward. Signposts point more briefly to what the speaker is going to do at the moment. Both transitions and signposts help bind the speech into a unified whole.

Figure 14.1 Transitions.

Transition from One Main Point to Another
"Now that we have seen why computers are coming down in cost, let us look next at why software is so expensive."

Transition from Main Point to a Visual Aid
"I have explained that higher education is becoming more and more expensive. This bar graph will show exactly how expensive it has become over the last five years."

Transition that Includes a Review, Internal Summary, and Preview
"You have heard that suntanning ages the skin, and I have shown you the pictures of a Buddhist monk and a nighttime bartender who hardly ever exposed themselves to direct sunlight. Now I want to show you a picture of a thirty-five-year-old woman who spent most of her life working by day in direct sunlight."

Figure 14.2 Signposts.

First, I will illustrate . . .
A second idea is . . .
Another reason for . . .
Finally, we will . . .
Look at this bar graph . . .
See what you think of this evidence . . .
Furthermore, you should consider . . .

The Conclusion

Like the introduction and the body of a speech, the **conclusion,** the review and final words of your speech, has certain functions. Informative speeches usually conclude with a summary of main points from the body of the speech. Persuasive speeches frequently end with an appeal to the audience to think or behave in some manner consistent with the persuader's purpose. The means of ending speeches are numerous. The speaker can conclude a speech with a rhetorical question ("Knowing what you now know, will you feel safe riding with a driver who drinks?"), a quotation from some famous person ("As John F. Kennedy said, 'Forgive your enemies, but never forget their names.'"), a literary passage ("We conclude with the words of Ralph Waldo Emerson, who said, 'It is one light which beams out of a thousand stars; it is one soul which animates all men.'"), or perhaps with some action that demonstrates the point of the speech (the quickly assembled electric motor works for the class to see; the speaker twirls and does the splits in one graceful motion; the experiment is completed, and the mixture of soda and vinegar boils and smokes).

Introductions and conclusions—getting started and drawing to a close—are often a challenge for beginning speakers. Because of this, these two parts of the speech should be rehearsed so they can be presented as planned. The speaker who fails to plan a conclusion may approach the end of his or her speech with nothing more to say.

Audiences need to be warned by your words, tone, or actions that the speech is nearly completed. Otherwise, you might end your speech leaving the audience dangling as you head for your seat. Audiences appreciate a sense of closure, completeness, and finality in the conclusion of a speech. Speakers who ignore this expectation risk offending the very people they seek to influence.

In conversations with friends, we indicate the conversation must stop by our words, facial expressions, gestures, and movements. Similarly, in public speaking, you indicate the end of your speech is near by signaling your audience with words and actions. Notice how the following ending signals the impending conclusion of the speech: "Now that you have heard my three arguments summarized concerning why we should encourage the student newspaper to cover assaults on campus, I want to leave you with these words from the editor of the student newspaper. . . ." You can also supplement the conclusion of your speech with your movement—some speakers literally fade back and away from the audience as they draw to a conclusion because they want to show they are almost finished. Others end their speech with a challenge in which they approach the audience for their final words. Either may be appropriate depending on whether a tranquil or a challenging ending is invited by the topic. Finally, you can simply tell your audience you are finished by using the words that most often signal a conclusion: "Finally . . . ," "To summarize . . . ," "And my final words for you tonight are . . . ," or "Jesse Jackson once summed up the main message I have tried to convey to you this afternoon when he said. . . ."

The following functions are fulfilled by a conclusion:

1. Forewarn the audience you are about to stop, which is the brakelight function
2. Remind the audience of your central idea or the main points in your message
3. Specify precisely what the audience should think or do in response to your speech
4. End the speech in a manner that makes audience members want to think and do what you recommend

Let us examine each of these functions of a conclusion in greater detail.

The first, the **brakelight function,** *warns the audience you are about to stop.* Can you tell when a song is about to end? Do you know when someone in a conversation is about to complete a story? Can you tell in a television drama the narrative is drawing to a close? The answer to these questions is usually "yes" because we get verbal and nonverbal signals that songs, stories, and dramas are about to end. How do you use the brakelight function in a speech?

One student signaled the end of her speech by saying, "Five minutes is hardly time to consider all the complications of abortion. . . ." By stating her time was up, she signaled her conclusion. Another said, "Thus, men have the potential for much greater role flexibility than our society encourages. . . ." The word *thus,* like the word *therefore,* signals the conclusion of a logical argument and indicates the argument is drawing to a close.

The second function of a conclusion—reminding the audience of your central idea or the main points in your message—can be fulfilled by restating the main points, summarizing them briefly, or selecting the most important point for special treatment. A woman who was delivering a pro-choice speech on abortion ended it by reminding her audience of her main point. Her method was to use two contrasting quotations.

> We need to protect ourselves from closed-minded opinions like that of Senator Jesse Helms who proposed the following amendment::
>
> "The paramount right to life is vested in each human being from the moment of fertilization without regard to age, health, or condition of dependency."
>
> Instead, let's consider the words of Rhonda Copelon, a staff lawyer with the Center for Constitutional Rights:
>
> "To use the Bill of Rights—which also and not incidently guarantees the separation of church and state—to establish laws as a religious belief on a matter of private moral conduct would be unprecedented. It would transform into a tool of oppression a document which guarantees rights by limiting the power of the state to invade people's lives."
>
> All I ask you to do is to look at the woman's side for a moment. Consider all the implications upon her life. The unborn is not the only one with a right to life. The woman has one too.

Whether you agree with the position stated in the conclusion or not, it was an insightful way to restate the main message and reiterate the conflicting viewpoints on the issue.

The third function of a conclusion is to specify exactly what you expect audience members to do as a result of your speech. Do you want them to simply remember a few of your important points? Then tell them one last time the points you think are worth remembering. Do you want the audience members to write down the argument they found most convincing, sign a petition, talk to their friends? If so, you should specify what you would regard as an appropriate response to your speech. One student who gave her speech on unions concluded with the slogan: "Buy the union label." The ending statement specified exactly what the speaker expected of the audience.

The fourth function of a conclusion is to end the speech in a manner that makes audience members want to think and do what you recommend. Perhaps you taught the audience how to do something during the speech—how to help a choking victim, how to defend themselves, or how to find a better product. If you successfully teach audience members how to do something, they may already feel better because they know more than they did before they heard your speech. Boris Yeltsin, Russia's leader, concluded his speech to the United States Congress with a quote from Irving Berlin, a Russian-born Jew, by saying "God bless America" to which he added "and Russia too."

In concluding a speech, as in beginning one, it is possible to be overly dramatic. At one large midwestern college, the communication classes were taught on the third floor of a building. In one room, a student was delivering a speech about insanity. As the speech progressed, the class became increasingly aware the young man delivering the speech had a few problems. At first, it was difficult to understand what he was saying: words were run together, parts of sentences were incoherent, pauses were too long. Near the end of the speech, the young man's eyes were rolling, and his jaw had fallen slack. At the very end of the speech, he looked wildly at the audience, ran over to the open window, and jumped. The class was aghast. Instructor and students rushed to the window expecting to see his shattered remains. Far below, on the ground, were twenty fraternity brothers holding a large fire fighter's net with the speaker waving happily from the center.

A better idea is to conclude your speech with an inspirational statement, with words that make audience members glad they took the time and energy to listen to you. One student came up with a single line at the end of his speech on automobile accidents that summarized his speech and gave his audience a line to remember: "It is not who is right in a traffic accident that really counts," he said, "it is who is left." That conclusion was clever, provided a brief summary, and was an intelligent and safe way to end a speech.

Summary

In this chapter, we discuss the three basic parts of a speech—the introduction, the body, and the conclusion—and their functions.

The five functions of an introduction are to (1) gain and maintain audience attention, (2) arouse audience interest in the topic, (3) reveal the purpose of the speech, (4) describe the speaker's qualifications, and (5) forecast the organization and development of the speech.

The body of a speech can be organized through outlining. The seven principles of outlining are (1) relating all items in an outline to the immediate purpose and the long-range goal, (2) limiting the outline to an abstract of the speech itself, (3) expressing ideas in single units of information, (4) indicating the importance of items with rank-ordered symbols, (5) indicating the importance of items with margins that increase with decreasing importance, (6) coordinating less important content with less important symbols and larger margins, and (7) stating items in parallel form. Useful outline styles include the sentence outline and the key-word outline. Typical patterns of organization commonly used in public speaking are time-sequence, topical-sequence, the problem-and-solution, spatial-sequence, and cause-effect organization.

A completed outline should be accompanied by a bibliography that lists the sources used in your speech. Transitions are bridges from one idea to another. Signposts are a way of signaling to an audience where the speech is going. Both transitions and signposts bind the speech into a unified whole.

The functions of a speech conclusion are to (1) forewarn the audience the speech is about to end, (2) remind the audience of the central idea or the main points of your message, (3) specify the desired audience response, and (4) end the speech in a manner that encourages your audience to think and do as you recommend.

Key Terms

bibliography A list of sources used in a speech.

body The largest part of the speech that contains the arguments, evidence, and main content.

brakelight function A function of a conclusion fulfilled by forewarning the audience the end of the speech is near; can be a word, phrase, sentence, gesture, or movement.

causal-sequence pattern A method of organization in which the speaker first explains the causes of an event, problem, or issue, and then discusses its consequences.

conclusion The last part of the speech; a summary of the major ideas designed to induce some mental or behavioral change in an audience.

immediate purpose What you expect to achieve by the end of your speech.

introduction The first part of the speech; its function is to arouse the audience and to lead into the main ideas presented in the body.

key-word outline An outline consisting of important words or phrases to remind the speaker of the content of the speech.

long-range goal What you expect to achieve over a time period longer than your speech.

main points The most important points in a speech; indicated by Roman numerals.

organizational patterns Methods of arranging the contents of the speech, for example, problem-and-solution pattern.

outlining A written plan that reveals the order, importance, and substance of a speech.

parallel form The consistent use of complete sentences, clauses, phrases, or words in an outline.

problem-and-solution pattern A method of organization in which the speaker describes a problem and proposes a solution to that problem.

rough draft The preliminary organization of the outline of a speech.

sentence outline An outline consisting entirely of complete sentences.

signposts Ways in which a speaker signals to an audience where the speech is going.

spatial-sequence organization A method of organization in which the speaker explains by location in space; for example, the student who describes the instrument panel of a small airplane by moving from left to right across the instrument panel.

subpoints Those points in a speech that support the main points; indicated by capital letters.

sub-subpoints Those points in a speech that support the subpoints; indicated by Arabic numbers.

time-sequence pattern A method of organization in which the speaker explains a sequence of events in chronological order.

topical-sequence pattern A method of organization in which the speaker emphasizes the major reasons why an audience should accept a certain point of view.

transitions Linkages between sections of the speech that help the speaker move smoothly from one idea to another; principal transitions are forecasts, internal summaries, and statements of relationship.

Correct Form for Exercise (page 341)

1. Gerdy, John R. "Faculty and Collegiate Athletics Reform: Seizing the Moment." *Educational Record: The Magazine of Higher Education,* (Summer 1992) pp. 45–49.
2. Bellah, Robert N., Madsen, Richard, Sullivan, William M., Swidler, Ann, and Tipton, Steven M. *The Good Society.* New York: Alfred A. Knopf, 1991.
3. Mayfield, Mark. "Justice: A Right Denied." *USA Today,* 25–27 Sept. 1992, p. 1.

chapter 15

Delivery and Visual Aids

The delivery of a speech is an important part of public speaking. The words of a speech are only part of the message; the remainder of the message may be carried by the speaker's vocal and bodily actions. For example, the speaker can deliver a speech with a tone of voice that expresses conviction, anger, or irony. Similarly, the speaker's smile, alert posture, and forceful gestures convey a message to the audience.

In this chapter, we examine four modes of delivery, explore the vocal and bodily aspects of delivery, survey the use of visual aids, and conclude with some suggestions on how to effectively deliver your speeches. When you complete this chapter, you will be more competent in delivering speeches and using visual aids.

What will you learn?

After you have read and thought about this chapter, you will be able to answer the following questions:

1. What are the advantages and disadvantages of each mode of delivery?

2. What do you think is more important—content or delivery—and how do you support your thinking?

3. Can you name, define, and explain the seven vocal aspects of delivery?

4. What is important about each of the bodily aspects of delivery?

5. What are some suggestions for using visual aids effectively?

6. Why and when should you use visual aids?

7. What are some helpful hints for improving speech delivery?

8. Can you demonstrate effective vocal and bodily delivery in a speech of your own?

9. Can you use visual aids effectively and correctly in a speech of your own?

10. Can you evaluate the delivery of others by using the vocabulary and concepts you learned in this chapter?

I call him a master who can speak keenly and clearly to an average audience from an average point of view; but I call him eloquent who more wondrously and largely can enhance and adorn what he will, and hold in mind and memory all the sources of things that pertain to public speaking.

Cicero in *De Oratore (55 B.C.)*

Nothing great was ever achieved without enthusiasm.

Ralph Waldo Emerson

Courage is grace under pressure.

Ernest Hemingway

This chapter is designed to teach you **delivery,** the presentation of the speech by using your voice and body. After examining modes of delivery, vocal aspects and bodily aspects, you will learn how to reinforce and enlighten your audience with visual aids.

People have contradictory ideas about delivering a speech. Some people say, "It's not what you say, but how you say it that really counts." Others say, "What you say is more important than how you say it." The authors believe that what you say *and* how you say it are important, but in a contest between delivery and content, content wins.

Why do we believe content is so important? One researcher found that poor speakers are identified by their voices and by the physical aspects of their delivery, but the best speakers are identified by the content of their speeches.[1] In other words, the audience's evaluation of the speech is based more on the content with the best speakers, but poor speakers are discounted for their delivery. Actually, a well-composed speech can overcome poor delivery.[2] A review of studies on informative speaking showed the influence of delivery on audience comprehension is overrated.[3] Many of the studies cited in this chapter emphasize the importance of delivery. The researchers who challenge these findings do not say delivery is unimportant; instead, they say that in evaluating the relative importance of delivery and content, there is reason to believe content may be more important than delivery. Because we think both need to be considered by the effective public speaker, we begin our study of delivery with the four modes of delivery.

Four Modes of Speech Delivery

The four **modes of delivery** are extemporaneous, impromptu, manuscript, and memorized. Although these four modes of delivery are possible choices, students of public speaking are least likely to use the manuscript and memorized modes. They may be asked to try the impromptu mode at times, but most speech assignments require the extemporaneous mode, which we will examine first.

Extemporaneous Mode

The **extemporaneous mode** is carefully prepared and practiced, but it is delivered conversationally without heavy dependence on notes. This mode is message and audience centered with the speaker focused not on the notes but on the ideas being expressed. It is characterized by considerable eye contact, freedom of movement and gesture, the language and voice of conversation, and the use of an outline or key words to keep the speaker from reading or paying undue attention to the written script.

The word *extemporaneous* literally means "on the spur of the moment" in Latin; but as practiced in the classroom, this mode of delivery only appears to be spontaneous. The speaker may choose different words as the speech is practiced and as it is finally delivered, but the focus is on communicating the message to the audience.

The mode is seen often in the classroom, in some professors' lectures, sometimes from the pulpit, often in political and legal addresses, and usually by athletes, business people, and community leaders who are experienced speakers. It is the mode you will learn best in the classroom and the one that has the most utility outside the classroom.

Impromptu Mode

The **impromptu mode** is a speech delivered without notes, plans, or formal preparation and characterized by spontaneity and informal language. The word *impromptu* comes from Latin and French roots meaning "in readiness."

You use the impromptu mode when you answer a question in a class, when you are asked early in a course to say who and what you are, and when people ask you directions on the street. You cannot say much in these situations unless you are "in readiness," unless you know the subject matter for the class, know yourself, or know the place where someone wants to go. Ordinarily, there is no practice, no careful choice of language. The impromptu mode encourages you to "think on your feet," but it does not encourage research, preparation, or practice.

Manuscript Mode

As the name implies, the **manuscript mode** is a speech delivered with a script of the exact words to be used. The advantage of this mode is that the speaker knows exactly what was said, and the speaker is never at a loss for what to say. The disadvantages of this mode are it invites a speaker to pay more attention to the script than to the audience, discourages eye contact, and prevents response to audience feedback.

Politicians, especially those who are likely to be quoted, as well as clergy and professors sometimes use this mode of delivery, but students are not often asked to use this mode except in oral interpretation of literature.

Memorized Mode

The **memorized mode** is a speech committed to memory. This mode requires considerable practice and allows ample eye contact, movement, and gestures. However, this mode discourages the speaker from responding to feedback, from adapting to the audience during the speech, and from choosing words that might be appropriate at the moment. In other words, it lacks spontaneity, and there is always the danger of forgetting.

You have experienced this mode if you ever acted in a play where you memorized your part. Politicians, athletes, and business people who speak to the same kind of audience about the same subjects often end up memorizing their speeches. Even professors when they teach a class for the third time may find that they have practically memorized the lesson for the day.

As a student in the speech communication classroom, you need to be wary about practicing your speech so much that it becomes memorized. Most speech communication teachers respond very negatively to speeches that sound memorized. The reason teachers dislike speeches that sound memorized is that audiences respond negatively. As one of our reviewers put it: "Any presentation that 'sounds memorized'—and most memorized presentations do—never lets the audience get beyond the impression that the speaker's words are not really his or her own, even if they are."

The mode you choose should be appropriate for the message, the audience, and the occasion. The extemporaneous mode is used most often when learning public speaking because it teaches good preparation, adaptation to the audience, and focus on the message. Nonetheless, mode of delivery does not determine effectiveness. Comparing extemporaneous and memorized modes, two researchers concluded that the mode is not what makes the speaker effective. Instead, the ability of the speaker was more important. Some speakers were more effective with extemporaneous speeches than with manuscripts, but others used both modes with equal effectiveness.[4]

Vocal and Bodily Aspects of Speech Delivery

Delivery, as we have already observed, is concerned with how the voice and body affect the meaning of your speech. They are important parts of the message you communicate to your audience.

Effective speech delivery has many advantages. Research indicates effective delivery—the appropriate use of voice and body in public speaking—contributes to the credibility of the speaker.[5] Indeed, student audiences characterize the poorest speakers by their voices and the physical aspects of delivery.[6] Poor speakers are judged to be fidgety, nervous, and monotonous. They also maintain little eye contact and show little animation or facial expression.[7] Good delivery increases the audience's capacity for handling complex information.[8] Thus, public speakers' credibility—the audience's evaluation of them as good or poor speakers—and their ability to convey complex information may all be affected by the vocal and bodily aspects of delivery.

Vocal Aspects of Speech Delivery

Studying the vocal aspects of speech delivery is like studying the musical notes. Musical notes are like the words of the speech. The music results in the sounds we hear when someone says the words. Just as different musicians can make the same notes sound quite different, public speakers can say words in different ways to get the audience to respond in various ways. The seven vocal aspects of delivery are pitch, rate, pauses, volume, enunciation, fluency, and vocal variety. These terms are introduced and defined in chapter 6 on nonverbal codes. We apply them specifically to the public speaking context here.

Pitch

Pitch is the highness or lowness of the speaker's voice, its upward and downward movement, the melody produced by the voice. Pitch is what makes the difference between the "ohhh" you utter when you earn a poor grade in a class and the "ohhh" you utter when you see something or someone really attractive. The "ohhh" looks the same in print, but when the notes turn to music, the difference between the two expressions is vast. The pitch of your voice can make you sound lively, or it can make you sound listless. As a speaker, you learn to avoid the two extremes: you avoid the lack of change in pitch that results in a monotone, and you avoid repeated changes in pitch that result in a singsong delivery. The best public speakers employ the full range of their normal pitch.

Control of pitch does more than make a speech sound pleasing. Changes in pitch can actually help an audience remember information.[9] Voices perceived as "good" are characterized by a greater range of pitch, more upward inflections, more downward inflections, and more pitch shifts.[10] Certainly, one of the important features of pitch control is that it can be employed to alter the way an audience will respond to the words. Many subtle changes in meaning are accomplished by changes in pitch. The speaker's pitch tells an audience whether the words are a statement or a question, whether the words mean what they say, and whether the speaker is expressing doubt, determination, or surprise.

Pitch control, whether in baseball or speech, is learned only by regular practice. An actor who is learning to utter a line has to practice it many times and in many ways before he or she can be sure that most people in the audience will understand the words as intended. The public speaker practices a speech before friends to discover whether the words are being understood as intended. Sometimes, we sound angry when we do not intend to; sometimes we sound opposed when we intend to sound doubtful; and sometimes we sound frightened when we are only surprised. We are not always the best judge of how we sound to others, so we have to seek out and place some trust in other people's evaluations.

Do not underestimate the importance of the delivery of a message.

Rate

How fast should you speak when delivering a public speech? Teachers often caution students to "slow down," but that is because talking fast is a sign of anxiety or nervousness. Debaters speak very rapidly, but usually, their opponents understand their message. What is the best way for you to deliver your speech?

Rate is the speed of delivery, or how fast you say your words. The normal rate for Americans is between 125 and 190 words per minute, but there are a lot of individual variations. The main thing you need to remember is that your rate of delivery depends on you—how fast you normally speak, on the situation—

nobody talks fast at a funeral, on the audience—children hearing a story understand better at slower rates, and on the subject matter—complex materials might require more patient timing and more built-in repetition.

Pauses

A third vocal characteristic of speech delivery is the **pause,** an intended silence during a speech. Speeches seem to be meant for a steady stream of words, without silences, yet pauses and silence can be used for dramatic effect and to get an audience to consider content. The speaker may begin a speech with rhetorical questions: "Have you had a cigarette today? Have you had two or three? Ten or eleven? Do you know what your habit is costing you in a year? A decade? A lifetime?" After each rhetorical question, a pause allows each member of the audience to answer the question in his or her own mind.

On the other hand, **vocalized pauses** are interruptions that negatively affect an audience's perception of the speaker's competence and dynamism. The "ahhhs" and "mmhhs" of the beginning speaker are disturbing to the public speaking instructor. Unfortunately, even some experienced speakers have the habit of filling silences with vocalized pauses. At least one group teaches public speaking to laypersons by having members of the audience drop a marble into a can every time a speaker uses a vocalized pause. The resulting punishment, the clanging of the cans, is intended to break the habit. A more humane method might be to rehearse your speech before a friend who signals you every time you vocalize a pause, so you do it less often when you deliver your speech to an audience. One speech instructor hit on the idea of rigging a light to the lectern so every time the student speaker used a vocalized pause, the light went on for a moment. Perhaps we should be less afraid of silence—many audiences would prefer a little silence to vocalized pauses.

One way to learn how to use pauses effectively in public speaking is to listen to how your classmates use them. You should also listen to professional speakers. Watch a talk show host like Jay Leno or Arsenio Hall during his monologue, listen to radio personalities who do commentary and opinion, and watch and listen to people who do public lectures on campus for ideas on how to use pauses effectively.

Volume

A fourth vocal characteristic of speech delivery is **volume,** the relative loudness of your voice. We are accustomed to speaking to people at a close distance, about an arm's length in conversation. To speak effectively in front of a class, a meeting, or an auditorium full of people, we speak louder or project our voices so all may hear. Telling speech students to speak louder might sound like very elementary advice, but many beginning speakers see those people in the first few rows and speak only to them. In speech instruction, the term **projection** is volume adapted to the audience and the place. For example, the elementary teacher speaking to children gathered on the floor close by may not need to speak at more than normal conversational volume, but the college professor speaking to a room of fifty students would have to increase volume to project his or her voice to the back of the room.

Volume is more than just loudness. Variations in volume can convey emotion, importance, suspense, and changes in meaning. We whisper a secret, and we use a stage whisper in front of an audience. We may speak loudly and strongly on important points and let our voices carry our conviction. Volume can change with the situation. For example, a pep rally may be filled with loud, virtually shouted speeches teeming with enthusiasm; whereas, a eulogy may be delivered at a lower and more respectful volume. An orchestra never plays so quietly that patrons cannot hear, but the musicians vary their volume. Similarly, a public speaker who considers the voice an instrument learns how to speak softly, loudly, and everywhere between to convey meaning.

Enunciation

Enunciation, the fifth vocal aspect of speech delivery, is the pronunciation and articulation of words, two terms you learned in chapter 6 on nonverbal codes. Because our reading vocabulary is larger than our speaking vocabulary, we may use, in our speeches, words we have rarely or never heard before. It is risky to deliver unfamiliar words. One student in a speech class gave a speech about the human reproductive system. During the speech, he managed to mispronounce nearly half the words used to describe the female anatomy. The speaker sounded incompetent to his audience. Rehearsing in front of friends, roommates, or family is a safer way to try out your vocabulary and pronunciation on an audience.

Your objective should be to practice words new to you until they are easy for you to pronounce and you are comfortable with them. Also be alert to the names of people you quote, introduce, or cite in your speech. Audiences are almost overly impressed when a student speaker correctly pronounces names like Goethe, Monet, and de Chardin.

The best way to avoid **pronunciation** problems, errors in how a word is sounded out, is to find unfamiliar words in a dictionary. Every dictionary has a pronunciation key. For instance, the entry for the word *belie* in the *Random House Dictionary of the English Language* looks like this:

be-lie (bi-lī´), v. t., -lied, -ly-ing. 1. to show to be false; contradict: His trembling hands belied his calm voice . . . (From *The Random House Dictionary of the English Language.* Copyright © Random House, Inc. Reprinted by permission of Random House, Inc.)

The entry illustrates the word *belie* has two syllables. The pronunciation key states the first *e* should be pronounced like the *i* in *if,* the *u* in *busy,* or the *ee* in *been.* The *i,* according to the pronunciation key, should be pronounced like the *ye* in *lye,* the *i* in *ice,* or the *ais* in *aisle.* The accent mark (´) indicates which syllable should receive heavier emphasis. You should learn how to use the pronunciation key in a dictionary, but if you still have some misgivings about how to pronounce a word, you should ask your professor for assistance.

Another way to improve your pronunciation is to learn how to prolong syllables. For example, you might say on the street, "I'm gunna go shopin'," but for an audience, you pronounce every syllable: "I am going to go shopping." Prolonging the syllables can even make that simple statement dramatic. Prolonging vowel sounds, for instance, gives your voice a resonance attractive to audiences. Prolonging syllables can also make you easier to understand, especially if you are addressing a large audience, an audience assembled outside, or an audience in an auditorium without a microphone. The drawing out of syllables can be overdone, however. Some radio and television newspersons hang onto the final syllable so long the practice draws attention to itself.

Pronunciation and articulation are the important parts of enunciation. Poor **articulation,** poor production of sounds, is so common there are popular jokes about it. One adult remembers hearing a song about Willie the cross-eyed bear in Sunday school. The actual song title was "Willing the Cross I Bear." Some children have heard the Lord's Prayer mumbled so many times they think that one of the lines is either "hollow be thy name" or "Howard be thy name."

Articulation problems are less humorous when they occur in your own speech. They occur because we often articulate carelessly. Among the common articulation problems are the dropping of final consonants and "-ing" sounds ("goin'," "comin'," and "leavin'"), the substitution of "fer" for "for," and the substitution of "ta" for "to." An important objective in public speaking, as it should be in all communication, is to state words clearly for more accurate transmission.

Fluency

The sixth vocal characteristic of speech delivery is **fluency**—the smoothness of delivery, the flow of the words, and the absence of vocalized pauses. Fluency is difficult because it cannot be achieved by looking up words in a dictionary or by any other simple solution. Fluency is not even very noticeable. Listeners are more likely to notice errors than to notice the seemingly effortless flow of words in a well-delivered speech. Also, it is possible to be too fluent. A speaker who seems too glib is sometimes considered dishonest. The importance of fluency was emphasized in a study in which audiences tended to perceive a speaker's fluency and smoothness of presentation as a main determinant of effectiveness.[11]

To achieve fluency, public speakers must be confident of the content of their speeches. If the speakers know what they are going to say and have said it over and over in practice, then disruptive repetition and vocalized pauses are reduced. If speakers master what they are going to say and focus on the overall rhythm of the speech, their fluency improves. Speakers must pace, build, and time the various parts of the speech so they all fit together in a coherent whole.

Vocal Variety

The seventh vocal aspect of speech delivery—one that summarizes many of the others—is **vocal variety.** This term refers to voice quality, intonation patterns, inflections of pitch, and syllabic duration. Vocal variety is encouraged in public speaking because studies show it improves effectiveness. One of the founders of the national Speech Communication Association, Charles Woolbert, in a very early study of public reading, found audiences retained more information when there were large variations in rate, force, pitch, and voice quality. More recently, researcher George Glasgow studied an audience's comprehension of prose and poetry and found comprehension decreased 10 percent when the material was delivered in a monotone. A third study proved audience members understood more when listening to skilled speakers than when listening to unskilled speakers. They also recalled more information immediately after the speech and at a later date. The skilled speakers were more effective, whether or not the material was organized, disorganized, easy, or difficult. Good vocalization was also found to include fewer but longer pauses, greater ranges of pitch, and more upward and downward inflections.[12]

As you conclude this section on the vocal aspects of speech delivery, the nonverbal aspects of public speaking, you must wonder how you can improve in all of these specific areas. One thing is certainly true: reading about aspects of delivery does little or nothing to improve your performance. Delivery is not something you read about; it is something you do. Here are some specific suggestions for improving the vocal aspects of your speech.

1. *Choose some aspect of vocal delivery, and work on it until you are confident enough to move to another.* Do not think that you have to improve in all areas at once. Most likely you are already competent in some aspects of vocal delivery and only need improvement in a few areas. Select some aspect that you believe needs improvement and work on it. If you think—and others have told you—that you speak in a monotone, perhaps you ought to start working in that area. You decide what you need to improve, and then move to the following step.
2. *Try practicing the skill in your everyday life.* Most of the vocal aspects of delivery are employed in conversation: rate, volume, variety, etc. Often the person who speaks without vocal variety in a public speech talks that way to friends as well. To improve your skill in that area, you can consciously practice making your voice more expressive than it has been in the past. Do not think you can only work on improving your skills when you are performing in the classroom. You can improve every time you talk to anybody. Unlike your chemistry, biology, or physics class where

much of what you practice must be done in the laboratory, your communication class has your world as its lab, and you can do your experiments any time you want.

3. *Be doggedly determined about improvement.* You took a lot of years getting to be who you are today, and you will not change your behavior overnight. If you have always been a rapid-fire speaker, a soft-spoken whisperer, or a person who has never used a -g ending, then you are going to have to be determined to actually achieve any change in your behavior. On the other hand, you should be confident in the knowledge that thousands of people like yourself learn how to improve their vocal delivery through persistent effort. You are not being asked to do the impossible, but neither should you be deceived into thinking that changing your own vocal aspects is simple and easy to achieve.

Next, you will move from the vocal aspects of delivery to another nonverbal area—the bodily aspects of delivery.

Bodily Aspects of Speech Delivery

The four bodily aspects of speech delivery are gestures, facial expression, eye contact, and movement. These nonverbal indicators of meaning show how speakers relate to audiences, just as they show how individuals relate to each other. When we observe two persons busily engaged in conversation, we can judge their interest in the conversation without hearing their words. Similarly, in public speaking, the nonverbal bodily aspects of delivery reinforce what the speaker is saying. Audience members who can see the speaker comprehend more of the speech than audience members who cannot see the speaker.[13] Apparently, the speaker's body movements convey enough meaning to improve the audience's understanding of what is being said.

Gestures

Gestures are movements of the head, arms, and hands we use to describe what we are talking about, to emphasize certain points, and to signal a change to another part of the speech. We rarely worry about gestures in a conversation, but when we give a speech in front of an audience, arms and hands seem to be bothersome. Perhaps we feel unnatural because public speaking is an unfamiliar situation. Do you remember the first time you drove a car, the first time you tried to swim or dive, or the first time you tried to kiss your date? The first time you give a speech you might not feel any more natural than you did then. Nonetheless, physically or artistically skilled people make their actions look easy. A skilled golfer, a talented painter, and a graceful dancer all perform with seeming ease. The beginners are the ones who make a performance look difficult. Apparently, human beings have to work diligently to make physical or artistic feats look easy.

Gestures can clarify and animate your presentations.

What can you do to help yourself gesture naturally when you deliver your speech? The answer lies in feelings and practice. Angry farmers and angry miners appear on television to protest low prices and poor working conditions. These speakers have not spent a lot of time practicing, but they deliver their speeches with gusto and a lot of strong gestures. They also look very natural. The main reason for their natural delivery may be their feelings about the issue they are discussing. They are upset, and they show it in their words and movements. They are mainly concerned with getting their message across. The student of public speaking can also deliver a speech more naturally by concentrating on getting the message across. Self-conscious attention to your gestures is often self-defeating—the gestures look studied, rehearsed, or slightly out of rhythm with your message. Selecting a topic you find involving can have the unexpected benefit of improving your delivery, especially if you concentrate on your audience and your message.

Another way of learning to make appropriate gestures is to practice a speech in front of friends who are willing to make positive suggestions. Indeed, constructive criticism is also one of the benefits you can receive from your speech instructor and your classmates. Actors spend hours rehearsing lines and gestures so they will look spontaneous and unrehearsed on stage. In time, and after many practice sessions, public speakers learn which arm, head, and hand movements seem to help and which seem to hinder their message. You, too, can learn, through practice, to gesture naturally—in a way that reinforces your message instead of detracting from it.

The following are seven suggestions for gesturing effectively:

1. Keep your hands out of your pockets and at your sides when not gesturing.
2. Do not lean on the lectern.
3. Gesture with the hand not holding your notes.
4. Make your gestures deliberate—big and broad enough so that they do not look accidental or timid.
5. Keep your gestures meaningful by using them sparingly and only when they reinforce something you are saying.
6. Practice your gestures just as you do the rest of your speech so you become comfortable with the words and the gestures.
7. Make your gestures appear natural, spontaneous, and unrehearsed.

Facial Expression

A third physical aspect of delivery is facial expression. Your face is the most expressive part of your body. **Facial expression** consists of eyebrows that rise and fall; eyes that twinkle, glare, and cry; lips that pout or smile; cheeks that can dimple or harden; and a chin that can jut out in anger or receded in yielding. Some people's faces are a barometer of their feelings; other people's faces seem to maintain the same appearance whether they are happy or in pain or sorrow. Because you do not ordinarily see your own face when you are speaking, you may not be fully aware of how you appear when you give a speech. In general, speakers are trying to maintain a warm and positive relationship with the audience, and they signal that intent by smiling as they would in conversation with someone they like. However, the topic, the speaker's intent, the situation, and the audience all help determine the appropriate facial expressions in a public speech. You can discover the appropriateness of your facial expressions by having friends, relatives, or classmates tell you how you look when practicing your speech. You can observe how famous people such as Joan Rivers, Rodney Dangerfield, Phil Donahue, and Arsenio Hall use facial expression to communicate.

Eye Contact

Another physical aspect of delivery important to the public speaker is eye contact. **Eye contact** refers to sustained and meaningful contact with the eyes with persons in the audience. Too much eye contact, "staring down the audience," is too much of a good thing, but looking too much at the notes—lack of eye contact—is poor delivery.

Audiences prefer maintenance of good eye contact,[14] and good eye contact improves source credibility.[15] Such conclusions are particularly important since individuals in other cultures may view eye contact differently. The public speaker from another country may be viewed less positively by an American audience than she would be in her native country. Similarly, Americans need to recognize and appreciate cultural differences in eye contact as well as other nonverbal cues.

Eye contact is one of the ways we indicate to others how we feel about them. We are wary of persons who, in conversations, do not look us in the eye. Similarly, in public speaking, eye contact conveys our relationship with our audience. The public speaker who rarely or never looks at the audience may appear disinterested in the audience, and the audience may resent it. The public speaker who looks over the heads of audience members or scans audience members so quickly that eye contact is not established may appear to be afraid of the audience. The proper relationship between audience and speaker is one of purposeful communication. We signal that sense of purpose by treating audience members as individuals with whom we wish to communicate— by looking at them for responses to our message.

How can you learn to maintain eye contact with your audience? One way is to know your speech so well that you have to make only occasional glances at your notes. The speaker who does not know the speech well is manuscript-bound. Delivering an extemporaneous speech from key words or an outline is a way of encouraging yourself to keep an eye on the audience. One of the purposes of extemporaneous delivery is to enable you to adapt to your audience. That adaptation is not possible unless you are continually observing the audience's behavior to see if the individuals understand your message.

Other ways of learning to use eye contact include scanning or continually looking over your entire audience and addressing various sections of the audience as you progress through your speech. Concentrating on the head nodders may also improve your eye contact. In almost every audience, some individuals overtly indicate whether your message is coming across. These individuals usually nod "yes" or "no" with their heads, thus the name *nodders.* Some speakers find it helps their delivery to find friendly faces and positive nodders who signal when the message is getting through.

Movement

A fourth physical aspect of delivery is **bodily movement**—what the speaker does with his or her entire body during a speech presentation. Sometimes, the situation limits movement. The presence of a fixed microphone, a lectern, a pulpit, or some other physical feature of the environment may limit your activity. The length of the speech can also make a difference. A short speech without movement is less difficult for both speaker and audience than a very long speech.

Good movement for the public speaker is appropriate and purposeful movement. The "caged lion" who paces back and forth to work off anxiety is moving inappropriately and purposelessly in relation to the content of the

Evaluation Form for Nonverbal Aspects of Delivery

To summarize the material on vocal and bodily aspects of delivery, you should examine the sample evaluation form below. Use this scale to evaluate each of the following items:

1 = Excellent, 2 = Good, 3 = Average, 4 = Fair, 5 = Weak

Vocal Aspects of Delivery—The Voice

_____ Pitch: Upward and downward inflections
_____ Rate: Speed of delivery
_____ Pause: Appropriate use of silence
_____ Volume: Loudness of the voice
_____ Enunciation: Articulation and pronunciation
_____ Fluency: Smoothness of delivery
_____ Vocal variety: Overall effect of all of the above

Bodily Aspects of Delivery

_____ Gestures: Use of arms and hands
_____ Facial expression: Use of the face
_____ Eye contact: Use of eyes
_____ Movement: Use of legs and feet

speech. You should move for a reason, such as walking a few steps when delivering a transition, thereby literally helping your audience to "follow you" to the next idea. Some speakers move forward on the points they regard as most important.

Because of the importance of eye contact, the speaker should always strive to face the audience, even when moving. Some other suggestions on movement relate to the use of visual aids. Speakers who write on the chalkboard during a speech have to turn their backs on the audience. This can be avoided either by writing information on the board between classes or by using a poster or overhead projector instead.

The college classroom is a laboratory for the student who wants to learn effective movement. By watching professors, lecturers, and fellow students when they deliver speeches, you can learn through observation and practice what works for others and what works for you. Sometimes professors, lecturers, and other students are positive examples; sometimes they provide negative models.

Visual Aids

Do you learn best when you read something, when you see something, or when you do something? Certainly, some skills are best learned by doing. Reading about how to program a VCR or watching another person do it is no substitute for trying it yourself. However, many things we know do not lend themselves to doing. You cannot do economics in the same way you can change a tire. Because so much of public speaking deals with issues and topics that cannot be performed, we must know the most effective methods of communicating for a public speech.

Researchers tried to determine if people remember best through telling alone, through showing alone, or through both showing and telling, by measuring retention three hours and three days after the communication attempt. The results follow:[16]

Method	Retention three hours later	Retention three days later
Telling alone	70%	10%
Showing alone	72%	20%
Showing and telling	85%	65%

Apparently, people retain information longer when they receive it both through their eyes *and* through their ears. Audiences that remember a message because the visual aids helped their comprehension or understanding are more persuaded by the presentation.

Students sometimes gain the impression that public speaking instructors like them to use visual aids, but they will not use visual aids for public speaking outside of the classroom. In fact, the use of visual aids is big business. Can you imagine an architect trying to explain to a board of directors how the new building will look without using models, drawings, and large-scale paintings? Can you sell most products without showing them? Apparently, the skillful use of visual aids is an expectation in the world of business and industry. The place to learn how to use visual aids is in the classroom.

What are **visual aids?** They can be anything from the way you dress, to writing on the chalkboard, to items brought in to show what you are talking about. The student who wears a police uniform when talking about careers in law enforcement, the student who provides a ditto with an outline of her speech for the class, and the student who brings in chemistry equipment are all employing visual aids.

Using Visual Aids

One of the main reasons for using visual aids has already been stated: people tend to learn and retain more when they both see and listen. The effective speaker knows when words will not be sufficient to carry the message. Some messages are more effectively communicated through sight, touch, smell, and taste. In other words, if you are trying to tell an audience about a particularly complex problem in calculus, you might have considerable difficulty communicating that problem with voice only. Complex math problems are more effectively communicated through writing so the problem can be seen. Can audience members compare ten items in their minds? No, but they can if you show the ten items on a bar graph. Can the audience visualize the destruction of a hurricane, tornado, or riot? Perhaps, but some large newspaper photos or slides would result in a more accurate visualization.

Visual aids are not appropriate for all speeches at all times. In fact, because they take preparation and planning, they may not be possible in many impromptu situations. Also, visual aids should not be used for their own sake. There is no virtue in having visual aids unless they help the audience in understanding your message or contribute in some other way to your purpose. Use visual aids when the message is easier to understand visually than orally; use visual aids when they reduce complexity for easier understanding, as when you are explaining many or complex statistics or ideas; and use visual aids when they support your message in ways that cannot be accomplished with words, such as when you display a bar graph showing the increasing costs of home ownership. The use of visual aids demands that you become sensitive to what an audience will be unable to understand only through your words. Finally, visual aids should be visible to the audience only while being referred to and should be out of sight during the rest of the speech. Otherwise, visual aids can become a distraction that steals the focus from you.

Visual aids, like the facts in your speech, may require documentation. You should either show on the visual aid itself, or tell the audience directly where you got the visual aid or the information on it.

Some helpful hints for using visual aids follow:

1. Do not talk to your visual aids. Keep your eyes on your audience. Maintain good eye contact—instead of looking at your visuals.
2. Display visual aids only when you are using them. Before or after they are discussed, they usually become a needless distraction to the audience.
3. Make sure everyone in the room can see your visual aids. Check the visibility of your visual aid before your speech, during practice. If the classroom is twenty-five feet deep, have a friend or family member determine if it can be read from twenty-five feet away. Above all, make sure you are not standing in front of a visual aid.
4. Leave a visual aid in front of the audience long enough for complete assimilation. Few things are more irritating to an audience than to have a half-read visual aid whipped away by a speaker.
5. Use a pointer or your inside arm for pointing to a visual aid. The pointer keeps you from masking the visual, and using your inside arm helps you to avoid closing off your body from the audience.

Be creative in your selection of visual aids.

Types of Visual Aids

What kind of visual aids can you choose from? They are too numerous to cata-
logue here, but some of the main visual aids used by public speakers and
some hints about their use follow.

Chalkboards

Chalkboards are the most readily available visual aid. You can write your
name and the title of your speech on the chalkboard. You can use the chalkboard to write down important or unusual words you employ in your speech.
You can also use the chalkboard to list the items from your speech you want
your audience to remember. Any statistics, facts, or details difficult to convey
orally may be written on the chalkboard. The following are some questions to
ask yourself before using the chalkboard:

1. ***When should the information go on the chalkboard?*** Some public speaking instructors prefer that you place the information on the chalkboard
   before class begins. They dislike the delay caused by writing information
   on the chalkboard between speeches. Other instructors feel just as strongly that having information on the chalkboard before a speech is distracting. Few instructors object to having the speaker's name and the title of
   the speech on the chalkboard.

Figure 15.1 A poster with a written message. (Data from *Consumer Digest* May/June 1984, page 59.)

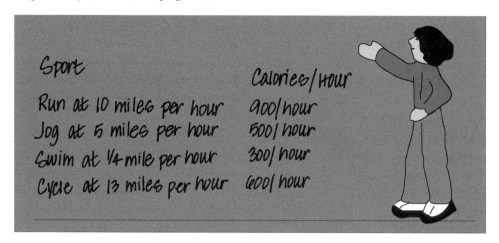

2. *How should you write on the chalkboard?* You should print legibly and large enough so people in the last row can read the information with ease. Also, you can avoid that tooth-shattering squeal by using chalk that has already been used and by angling the chalk so that it makes no noise. As any instructor can tell you, you should practice writing on the chalkboard between classes or when no one else is using the room because it takes some skill. If you don't practice, you might find your words look as if they are misspelled, your letters are too small, and your lines tend to go up or down as you proceed through a sentence.

3. *How should you deliver your speech when you are talking about items you have written on the chalkboard?* You should try to face your audience while you speak. A pointer, yardstick, or even your hand can direct the audience's attention to statements or illustrations on the chalkboard.

A skillful speaker knows when to place the information on the chalkboard, how to write the information on the chalkboard, and how to deliver the speech when using the chalkboard. The effective speaker also knows what kinds of information should be placed on the chalkboard and whether telling, showing, or doing both will help the audience the most. Effective speakers use the chalkboard for "point clinchers," as a way to indicate to the audience the most important points in the speech.[17]

Posters

Posters are another way to present your ideas visually. They are handier than using the chalkboard because they can be prepared ahead of time. The general directions for creating an effective poster are similar to those listed for the chalkboard: the information on the poster should be information that is difficult

Figure 15.2   How much do millionaires give to charity?
Source: Office of Tax Analysis, U.S. Department of Treasury

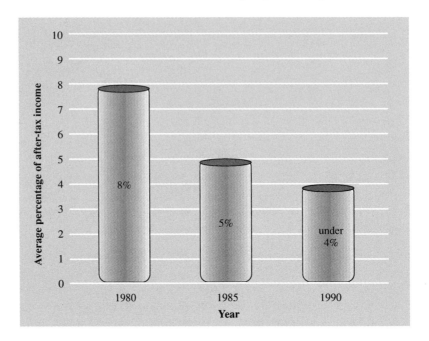

to convey or to understand through listening; the information should be drawn or written in large scale so that people in the back of the room are able to see every word or illustration; the speaker should face the audience while working with the information on the poster; and the visual message should highlight important points.

The message on a poster may be a written message showing the number of calories in hamburgers from fast-food restaurants, stating the three primary reasons why tuition should be raised, or listing the advantages of co-op bookstores. As shown in figure 15.1 posters also can show numbers—for example, percentages, averages, calories per hour, or miles per minute—that might otherwise be difficult to remember. When using numbers, you should remember to round off the numbers for easier understanding.

Three ways to illustrate information on posters are with bar graphs, pie charts, and line graphs. The *bar graph* helps you show an audience how a number of different items compare. For example, the bar graph in figure 15.2 compares the amount of after-tax contributions to charity by American millionaires. As the bar graph clearly indicates, millionaires gave less and less money to charity between 1980 and 1990.

Figure 15.3 A pie chart.

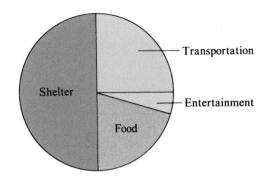

The *pie chart* in figure 15.3 shows what portion of the family budget goes for shelter, food, transportation, and entertainment. Although pie charts show proportions quite well, more people can accurately read a bar graph than a pie chart. What percentage of the family income in the pie chart in figure 15.3 is spent on entertainment? Naturally, the speaker could help by showing the percentages in each slice of the pie.

Figure 15.4 is an example of a *line graph* showing the dramatic decline in the percentage of Americans who earn their living on a farm. The line graph helps the audience visualize the precipitous drop in numbers.

Some suggestions for using posters for visual aids follow:

1. Keep the message simple. A common problem with visual aids is too much clutter. The audience should be able to grasp your point quickly.
2. Use bar graphs rather than circle or pie charts whenever possible because people tend to underestimate the relative area of circles.[18]
3. Use color and artistic talents to make the poster attractive and to gain and maintain attention.
4. Be sure the poster is large enough for everyone to see.
5. Use ready-made posters or pictures, such as travel posters or get hints for your own illustrations from those used on television commercials. Television advertisers tend to use outdoor, daytime shots, with one person but not crowds.[19]
6. Learn to use flip charts—a series of posters. For special effects, uncover each item as you come to it.

Whatever kind of poster you use, keep it in front of the audience as long as you are talking about the subject portrayed. In some cases, it is appropriate to place the used poster on the chalk tray so you can refer to it again in your conclusion as you review the content of your speech.

Figure 15.4 This line graph shows the dramatic decline in the number of farmers in the twentieth century.
(Data from U.S. Census Bureau and U.S. Dept. of Agriculture.)

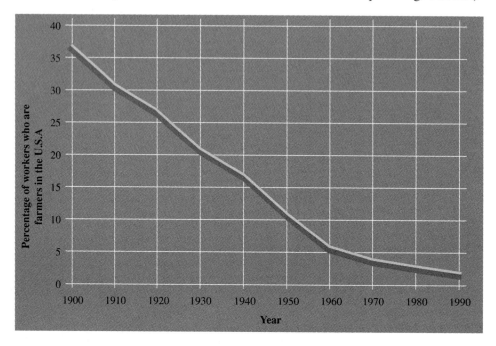

Opaque and Overhead Projectors

Opaque and *overhead projectors* demand special equipment and practice, but they, too, have special advantages in a speech. An opaque projector can project a picture or print from a magazine or book. It can also be used for relatively small, flat objects. Opaque projectors require dim lights and an empty wall or screen. An overhead projector can project transparencies or sheets of clear plastic on which the speaker can write with a special pencil or marker. Transparencies are best prepared ahead of time, but short messages can be printed on them as the speaker talks.

Movies and Slides

Movies and *slides* are good visual supplements to your speech as long as they do not become the speech. Both have the disadvantage of placing the audience and the speaker in the dark, where audience response is hidden. Even so, a one-minute film showing violence on the basketball court or five or six slides showing alternative energy sources can add force to your speech. When you use slides and films, you should check equipment and rehearse. An upside down slide or a jittery film can ruin your speech. You should also arrange for a classmate to turn off the lights, so you do not have to interrupt your speech by asking someone to turn off the lights or by doing it yourself.

Videotapes

Videotapes of movies, homemade videos, and portions of cable and network television recorded by a VCR unit offer the speaker another opportunity to fortify a speech. The downside of videos is that the speaker must supply and set up equipment, prepare the video carefully before presentation, and ensure that the equipment works properly. Resist the temptation to show too much. You should not let the video become the speech; instead, the video is an attention-getter or a form of support or evidence that should not overshadow your contributions to the presentation. The shorter the speech, the shorter the video portion should be. A good example of the powerful impact of a few minutes of video was the Rodney King beating which touched off the Los Angeles riots and made the American people question the justice of their legal process.

Photographs

Another kind of visual aid is the *photograph.* The student who is speaking about Spanish architecture can use photographs of homes and public buildings; the student who is talking about identifying types of trees can have pictures of each type; and the student who is discussing how to do something—such as assembling a bicycle—can have a series of photographs to illustrate and clarify. In figure 15.5, the student speaker used a photograph of a computer "painting" to show the capability of a computer to compose pictures.

A word of warning about photographs: ordinary-size photographs are too small to be easily seen by a classroom full of students. You should consider using ready-made or enlarged, poster-size photographs for all to see. Passing individual photographs is also a questionable practice because the audience will be distracted from your speech as they view the pictures individually. If you have a number of photos, the audience will still be looking at them when the next speaker gets up to speak.

Drawings

Drawings are another type of visual aid useful in public speaking. Most line drawings are simple and are used to clarify. When you draw a map to show your audience how to get to a specific place, when you draw the human foot and name the bones, or when you draw a cartoon character, you are using drawings as visual aids. Figure 15.6 shows a drawing used by a student speaker to illustrate a healthy life-style.

Figure 15.5   Today's graphics can be generated by a computer.

Figure 15.6   A drawing used as a visual aid.

A friend can be a visual aid in a demonstration speech.

Models and Physical Objects

Living models and physical objects can also be used as visual aids. For a speech on fashion design, you can have people model the clothes. For a speech on exercise machines, you can have someone demonstrate the machine.

Physical objects might be the best visual aid if your speech is about something small enough or controllable enough to show but large enough to be seen by everyone without being passed around. Students have brought in model cars, chemistry sets, musical instruments, mountain climbing equipment, weights, and volcanic lava. Live pets, however, can pose special problems for the speaker. Snakes, dogs, cats, hamsters, and monkeys have a unique ability to make fools of their owners. They also are often highly distracting before and during the speech. Finally, some public speaking teachers, or college or university rules, prohibit animals in the classroom.

Handouts

Handouts are an especially effective way to communicate messages difficult to convey orally. One student passed out the American Cancer Society's list of cancer danger signs. Another distributed a handout with the names and call numbers of all of the country-western music stations because he knew the audience was unlikely to remember all the names and numbers. Still another student distributed the contract used when people will parts of their body to a medical center. Such handouts carry the impact of your speech beyond the classroom. They are usually kept, sometimes taken home where they are seen by others, and often discussed later by roommates and spouses.

Handouts have many advantages, but they also have some shortcomings. One shortcoming is that they can be very distracting to the audience and disturbing to the speaker. When distributed during your speech, the handout gets the focus of attention instead of you. The problem is not entirely solved when you distribute handouts at the end of your speech because then they steal the focus from the next speaker. A second disadvantage is that handouts sometimes carry too much of the content of the speech and may become a substitute for the speech. The audience does not have to listen to the speech because they already have it in print.

You as a Visual Aid

Finally, *you* might be the best visual aid for your speech. You can demonstrate karate, show some dance steps, or wear a lead apron. You can wear clothing appropriate for your speech: a suit when telling how to succeed in an interview for a white-collar job, a lab coat when demonstrating chemical reactions, or a uniform when telling why other students should join the ROTC program. One student wore an old flannel shirt, tattered jeans, and a rag tied around his head. He carried a large lantern. His speech was about "steam tunneling," a sport in which students explored the university's steam tunnels. He was faulted for encouraging his audience to participate in an activity strongly discouraged by the university administration, but he certainly was appropriately dressed for his speech.

Helpful Hints for Speech Delivery

This chapter discussed the vocal and bodily aspects of delivery and the use of visual aids. Perhaps how to deliver a speech effectively is obvious. However, the following hints should help you in delivering your speech and in using visual aids:

1. Practice your speech so you can deliver it with only occasional glances at your notes.
2. Keep your eyes on your audience so you can sense whether you are communicating your message.
3. Use facial expressions, gestures, and movements to help communicate your message.
4. Use your voice like a musical instrument to keep the sounds interesting and to affect the audience's response.
5. Speak loudly enough for audience members to hear, slowly enough so they can listen with understanding, and smoothly enough so they do not focus on your faults.

6. Use visual aids to communicate material not easily understood through listening.
7. Make your writing on the chalkboard or on posters large enough for all to see and simple enough for all to understand.
8. Consider using photographs, drawings, live models, objects, slides, films, handouts, and audiovisual equipment to help communicate your message.
9. Sound conversational, look natural, and strive to communicate your message to your listeners.
10. Observe how your classmates, professors, and other speakers deliver their speeches so you can learn from them.

Summary

Four modes of speech delivery are the manuscript mode, the extemporaneous mode, the impromptu mode, and the memorized mode. Each mode has advantages and disadvantages, and appropriate circumstances for its use.

An effective speech requires both vocal and bodily aspects of delivery. Vocal aspects of speech delivery include (1) pitch—the highness or lowness of the speaker's voice; (2) rate—the speed of delivery; (3) pauses—for dramatic effect and for an audience to consider content; (4) volume—the relative loudness of a speaker's voice; (5) enunciation—the pronunciation and articulation of words; (6) fluency—the smoothness of delivery; and (7) vocal variety—voice quality, intonation patterns, inflections of speech, and syllabic duration.

Bodily aspects of speech delivery include (1) gestures—movements of the head, arms, and hands; (2) eye contact—sustained and meaningful contact with the eyes and faces of audience members; (3) facial expression—the varieties of messages the face can convey; and (4) movement—what the speaker does with the entire body during a speech presentation.

Visual aids should be used in speeches when they contribute to or reinforce the message. You should use chalkboards, posters, opaque and overhead projections, movies and slides, photographs, drawings, models and physical objects, handouts, and yourself to help communicate your message. Visual aids should not be used for their own sake, but they should be used when they help clarify your topic. We move next from delivery and visual aids to the informative speech.

Key Terms

articulation   The production of sounds; a component of enunciation.

bodily movement   What the speaker does with his or her entire body during a speech presentation.

delivery   The presentation of the speech by using your voice and body to reinforce your message.

enunciation   The pronunciation and articulation of sounds and words; an aspect of vocal delivery.

extemporaneous mode   A carefully prepared and researched speech with a conversational delivery.

eye contact   The extent to which a speaker looks directly at the audience; an aspect of bodily delivery.

facial expression   The nonverbal cues expressed by the speaker's face.

fluency   The smoothness of delivery, the flow of words, and the absence of vocalized pauses; an aspect of vocal delivery.

gestures   The movements of head, arms, and hands to illustrate, emphasize, or signal ideas in the speech; an aspect of bodily delivery.

impromptu mode   Delivery of a speech without notes, plans, or preparation.

manuscript mode   Delivering a speech from a script of the entire speech.

memorized mode   Delivering a speech that has been committed to memory.

modes of delivery   Four styles of delivery that vary in the amount of preparation required and their degree of spontaneity; includes memorized, impromptu, manuscript, and extemporaneous modes.

pause   The absence of vocal sound used for dramatic effect, transition, or emphasis of ideas; an aspect of vocal delivery.

pitch   The highness or lowness of a speaker's voice; technically, the frequency of sound made by vocal cords; an aspect of vocal delivery.

projection   The body's support of the voice that insures the most distant people in the room can hear what is said.

pronunciation   The conformance of the speaker's production of words with agreed-upon rules about the sounds of vowels and consonants, and for syllabic emphasis.

rate   The speed at which speech is delivered, normally between 125 and 190 words per minute; an aspect of vocal delivery.

visual aids   Any item that can be seen by an audience, for the purpose of reinforcing a message.

vocalized pauses   Breaks in fluency; the use of meaningless words or sounds to fill in silences that negatively affect an audience's perception.

vocal variety   Vocal quality, intonation patterns, inflections of pitch, and syllabic duration; a lack of sameness or repetitious patterns in vocal delivery; an aspect of vocal delivery.

volume   The loudness or softness of a person's voice; an aspect of vocal delivery.

chapter 16

The Informative Speech

What will you learn in this chapter? First, you will discover that the goal of informative speaking is to increase an audience's knowledge or understanding of a topic. Next, we will identify some sample topics for informative speeches as well as the behavioral purposes of them. As we consider presenting information to an audience, topics including information hunger, information relevance, extrinsic motivation, informative content, and information overload are defined and described. How do you organize the content of the informative speech? This chapter will provide the answers. Some of the special skills for informative speaking include defining, describing, explaining, and narrating. An example of an informative speech concludes this chapter. When you complete this material, you will be more competent as an informative public speaker.

What will you learn?

After you have read and thought about this chapter, you will be able to answer the following questions:

1. What is the goal of informative speaking?

2. Name some topics—not listed in the text—that would be appropriate for an informative speech.

3. Can you give some examples of immediate behavioral purposes?

4. How are these concepts related to informative speaking—information hunger, information relevance, extrinsic motivation, informative content, and information overload?

5. Can you explain why defining, describing, explaining, and narrating are "special skills for informative speaking?"

6. Can you state the goal and the immediate behavioral purpose, research and organize your speech, and use some of the special skills in an informative speech of your own?

Nothing is so firmly believed as what we least know.
Michel de Montaigne

Everything has been thought of before; the challenge is to think of it again.
J. W. Goethe

A word to the wise is not sufficient if it doesn't make sense.
James Thurber

As a student, you have already spent the better part of thirteen or fourteen years hearing informative speeches from your teachers. As an employee, you may have to tell others about products, sales goals, and service. As a religious person, you may want to explain scripture, morals, or ideals to others. As a citizen, you may have to speak to others about domestic politics, foreign affairs, or impending legislation. Teachers inform students, priests inform parishioners, and supervisors inform workers. You, like all people, probably will find yourself informing others in oral reports, instructions, and speeches. This chapter focuses on the primary vehicle for informing others—the **informative speech,** a speech intended to increase what an audience knows and understands.

Preparing an Informative Speech

To prepare an informative speech, you should know (1) the intent and the goal of informative speaking, (2) the kinds of topics that best lend themselves to informative speaking, and (3) the kinds of immediate behavioral purposes of informative speaking and how to determine if you have fulfilled them.

The Goal of Informative Speaking

Understanding the goal or intent of informative speaking requires that you understand the "end product" you seek and how to reach that end in ways that enlighten the audience and clarify the topic. The end product of informative speaking is *to increase an audience's knowledge or understanding of a topic.* You accomplish that goal by clarifying your topic in ways that retain the interest of your audience. To *clarify* means "to make clear," coming as it does from Latin, Middle English, and Old French roots denoting "to make clear" or "to make bright." To clarify some concept for an audience, the speaker assumes the audience does not understand the topic clearly until the speaker has an opportunity to explain it. Typically, a majority of audience members have insufficient knowledge or understanding to master or comprehend the informative speech topic. For example, you might know that a set of stereophonic speakers has a "woofer" and a "tweeter," but you might need an informative speech to explain more clearly exactly what those two features mean.

Clarifying a topic for a audience is a primary goal of informative speaking, but a second concern is to make the topic of an informative speech interesting and significant to the audience. We arouse an audience's *interest* in a topic by showing how the subject can be of importance, by relating stories of our own experiences with the subject, and by demonstrating gaps in the audience's knowledge they will want to fill. In fact, if a bit of persuasion is likely to slip into an informative speech, the appropriate place is early in the speech, where you relate the topic to the audience. It is here you quite rightly may reveal why the audience should know more about Wagnerian opera, cross-country

An informative speech should be on a topic that will increase audience knowledge or understanding.

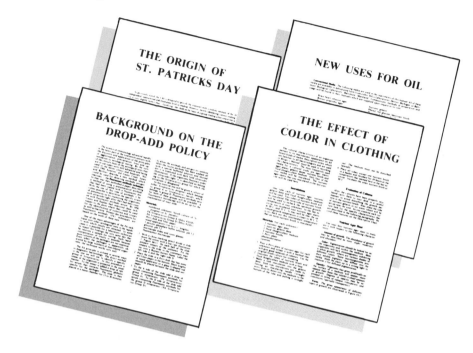

skiing, monetary inflation, or hamster breeding. How to make a topic palatable—literally digestible—to the audience is a continuing concern of the informative speaker.

Besides being interesting, the informative speech should meet the standard of significance. The **significance** of your message is its importance and meaningfulness to, or its consequences for, the audience. The audience, not the speaker, determines significance. For instance, a speech on men who illegally withhold child support is more likely to be both interesting and significant to a roomful of struggling single mothers than a roomful of sophomore fraternity men. A speech on the history of matches might lack interest and significance, and a speech on tax support for emerging nations might be high in significance but low in audience interest.

Topics for Informative Speeches

Selecting a topic for an informative speech and narrowing the topic to the length restrictions of the speech are early concerns for the informative speaker. Chapter 11 provided some general information on topic selection: how to brainstorm for topics and how to conduct personal inventories of your reading

The informative speaker must arouse the interest of the audience and show the significance of the topic.

and viewing habits to determine your interests. Even with that information, you may not know exactly what kinds of topics are most appropriate for informative speeches.

An informative speech is to be predominantly informative; that is, most of the content of the speech should focus on increasing audience knowledge and clarifying concepts for greater understanding. Many informative speeches reveal how to do something, what something is, or how something happens—speeches of exposition, definition, and description, respectively. A list of topics for a number of student-delivered informative speeches follows.

Sample Topics for Informative Speeches

Gun Control	The Best Radio Stations
The Right to Bear Arms	New Software for Writers
Birth Control	Do You Need Fiber Optics?
Investment Strategies	Consumer Guide to Car Phones
The Brief History of Rap	What is Agribusiness?
What is Inflation?	Food Irradiation
What is the Hip-Hop?	Etiquette
Vacation Retreats	Rappelling
What is Recycling?	Genetic Cloning
Why Gangs?	First Aid
The Electric Car	What Coins are Made Of

Sample Topics for Informative Speeches

My Visit to Spain
Communicating with Dress
Underground Homes
College Alcoholics
Automobile Accidents
Chiropractors
The Basics of Interviewing
The Autistic Child
Eye Surgery
Barrel Racing
Unidentified Flying Objects
Exam Anxiety
The Dormitory System
Door-to-Door Sales
Personality Tests
Soft Drinks
What is *Habeas Corpus?*
Who are the Libertarians?
Substance Abuse Centers
Natural Childbirth
The Minimum Wage
The Social Security System
What is a Pacifist?
Pewter
Saltwater Aquariums
Winterizing Your Car
Unique Wood Products
Clear-cutting in Forestry
Ski Boots
What is an Engineer?
Sleep and the College Student
Handling Handguns
Disc-Washers
The Concert Business
Inner-City Living
Adventures of a Bartender
My Tarantula
Generic Labeling
What is Construction Management?
Writing Your Resume´
How Computer Science Makes
   Your Job Easier
Creating Hair Extensions for Rock Stars

What is Active Listening?
Food Preservatives
What is a Finance Major?
Motorcycle Safety
Radiation and Plutonium
What is Political Philosophy?
Police Codes
Volcanoes
Cricket
Simple Automobile Repairs
Hairstyling Made Easy
What is a Couch Potato?
How to Stop Severe Bleeding
What is Mathematical Literacy?
How to Use a Condom
The Flu
Computer Virus
History of Profanity
History of Money
Cryogenics
DNA
Bibliotherapy
The History of Paperback Books
Hormones
Detection of Missing Children
Graphology
Dust
Tears
Secret Service
Peer Pressure
The Homeless and Soup Kitchens
How to Sail
History of La Crosse
Definition of Theology
The Causes of Adrenalin
Halloween
Osteoporosis
Runaway Children
Telemarketing
Alternative Energy Sources
Islam Religion
Adolescent Suicide
Mexican Education

Sample Topics for Informative Speeches

Antilock Brake Systems	Laughter
Foreign Accents	Miss America
Holistic Health	Teen Suicide
Compact Disc Players	Reincarnation
Bull Riding	Dreams
History of Taxation	Cocaine/Opiates
History of Punishment	Ozone
Effects of Steroids	Yoga
Subliminal Advertising	Bermuda Triangle
The Greenhouse Effect	Supreme Court
Chemical Warfare	Bow Hunting
Influences of Television Violence	Tour De France
History of the Saxophone	Witchcraft
The Space Program	Poverty
Hazardous Waste	Government Subsidized Housing
History of Classical Music	Depression
Nuclear Reactors	Calcium
Rodeo Clowns	Whale Beaching
Fire Safety	Resumé Writing
Prayer in Schools	Earthquakes
Career Planning	History of TV
Fetus Rights vs. Maternal Rights	Transportation
Love	Music Types
Suicide	Caffeine
Plastic Surgery	Record Ratings
Stress	Knee Injuries
Political Parties	Word Processing
Nutrition	Total Fitness
United Way	Mickey Mouse
Generic Drugs	Classical Music
Acid Rain	Witchcraft
Hair Replacement	Steroids
Stress	Accounting
Atlantis	Homeless
Andrew Carnegie	Apartheid
Mother's Day	Diabetes
Volleyball	Oil Painting
Cancer	Star Wars
Leisure	Acne
Communism	Barbados
	Farming
	Chocolate

The topics, not necessarily the titles of the speeches, are listed. Therefore, many of the topics look broader than they were when they were delivered as speeches. The speech topic on "Vacation Retreats" was limited to retreats available on the coast of Maine. Nonetheless, this list of topics may give you some ideas for a topic for an informative speech.

Once you have selected and narrowed a topic in a manner appropriate for you, your audience, and the situation, you are ready to specify the behavioral purposes of your informative speech.

Some of the topics are very general and need to be narrowed for the time limits afforded most informative speakers. Other topics are more limited.

Sample Topics for Demonstration Speeches

How to:

Perform Gymnastics	Make a Lamp
Hunt Deer	Write a Resumé
Fish with Flies	Take Shorthand
Climb Mountains	Shoe a Horse
Tame Your Roommate	Defend Yourself
Balance Your Budget	Balance a Checking Account
Jog Correctly for Health	Start a Business
Program Your VCR	Handicap a Horse Race
Press Your Clothes	Fix Food in Your Dorm Room
Use Wrestling Jargon	Change Rooms in the Dorms
Rescue Swimmers in Distress	Play Baseball, Golf, Soccer, Tennis, Darts,
Take Effective Notes	Field Hockey, and Racquetball
Use Your Camera	Use the *Reader's Guide to Periodical*
Win at Poker	*Literature*
Choose a Used Car	Use the Career Planning and Placement
Bungee Jump	Office
Care for Mountain Bikes	Behave in Restaurants
Parasail	Analyze Handwriting
Ride a Jet Ski	Register to Vote
Juggle	Make a Banana Split
Draw	Do First Aid
Fold a Flag	Clean Contact Lenses
Tie a Tie	Make a Piña Colada
Do CPR	Backpack in Europe
Eat Pizza	Change a Baby's Diaper
Play Euchre	Crash Land an Airplane
Make a Pizza	Survive a Natural Disaster
Wrap a Gift	Be a Better Student
Tie Dye	Prevent Rape on Campus
Fold Napkins	'Rush' a Fraternity/Sorority
Make a Salad	Take Your Blood Pressure
Snowboard	Interview for a Job

Sample Topics for Demonstration Speeches

How to:

Choose Ski Equipment	Make Decorative Cakes
Take Good Pictures	Cook with a Hot Pot
Clean a Car	Weatherize Boots
Make Christmas Tree Ornaments	Do a Card Trick
Fill Out a Tax Form	Refinish Furniture
Make Paper Planes and Boats	Cross-Country Ski
Fill out a Time Schedule	Fix a Broken Window
Make Specialty Popcorn	Tune Snow Skis
Clean Tape and Audio Heads	Organize Bolts and Screws
Use the Ohio Lotto	Make a Sock Puppet
Prepare for a Date	Sew on a Button
Test Your Blood Sugar	Load/Unload a Camera
Tape Ankles to Prevent Injury	Make Gift Baskets
Rope Cattle	Groom a Horse
Properly Introduce Someone	Jump Start a Car
Put Out a Grease Fire	Read Body Language
Keep Score in Bowling	Increase Your Metabolism
Make a Nonalcoholic Drink	Give a Back Massage
Make French Bread Pizza	Get Extra Dollars in College
Keep Score in Tennis	Load a Printer
Deal with Beggars	Choose a Mechanic

Behavioral Purposes for Informative Speeches

Two important questions for the informative speaker are (1) "What do I want my audience to know or do as a result of my speech?" and (2) "How will I know if I am successful?" A teacher can teach more effectively if the students know exactly what they are expected to know. Similarly, an audience learns more from an informative speech if the speaker states expectations early in the speech. The effects of an informative speech, however, are unknown unless you make the effects behavioral; that is, your speech should result in behavioral or observable change. A teacher discovers whether students learned from a lecture by giving a quiz or having the students answer questions in class. In the same way, the informative speaker seeks to discover whether or not a message was effectively communicated by seeking overt feedback from the audience. The overt feedback you seek concerns the **immediate behavioral purposes** of your speech, the actions expected during and immediately after the speech.

How will you know if you achieve your behavioral purpose in the informative speech?

The most common immediate behavioral purposes in an informative speech are to encourage audience members to do the following:

1. *Describe differences or similarities among objects, persons, or issues.* For example, after hearing a speech on the subject, audience members can describe an English setter, a person suffering from Down's syndrome, or the Libertarian position on welfare.
2. *Distinguish among different things.* For example, after hearing a speech on the subject, audience members can distinguish between fool's gold and real gold, between a counterfeit dollar and a real dollar, or between a conservative position and a liberal position.
3. *Compare items.* For example, after hearing a speech on the subject, audience members can compare prices on automobiles with the same features and options, a poetic song and a sonnet, or diamonds for cut, clarity, and carats.
4. *Define words, objects, or concepts.* For example, after hearing a speech on the subject, audience members can tell what kerogen is, can describe an English Tudor house, and can explain the concept of macroeconomics.
5. *State what they have learned.* After hearing a speech, audience members can tell you, or can write, your most important points or are able to tell others what you said.

The common behavioral purposes of an informative speech are to describe, distinguish, compare, define, and state. How does a speaker know whether or not these behavioral purposes were accomplished? One method of discovering whether audience members learned anything from your speech is to find out what they know both at the beginning and at the end of the speech. For instance, you could ask at the beginning of your speech, "How many of you have ever taken a personality test?" If you get a small but enthusiastic response, you know you will be informing them about something that is unfamiliar but interesting to them. After you explain the different types of tests and the discrepancies between them, you can ask certain students at the end of the speech to contrast the Thematic Apperception Test and the Myers-Briggs Type Indicator.

Similarly, you may ask your classmates to write down something that indicates whether or not they understood your message. If you explained how to administer CPR, you could ask your classmates to list the steps they would take when they encountered an unconscious man lying on the ground. Likewise, if your topic was to inform them about nutrition, you could ask them to list the foods with the highest or lowest content of cholesterol. In each case, the purpose is stated in such a way that the speaker can determine whether or not the purpose was accomplished.

Once you have decided on specific behavioral purposes for addressing an audience, you must select strategies for achieving those purposes. In other words, you must decide how to adapt your behavioral purposes and the materials of your speech to your particular audience.

Presenting Information to an Audience

If you, as an informative speaker, want to relate to an audience, you should first review the sections in chapter 11 on selecting and narrowing a topic and analyzing an audience. Then, you will be ready to adapt your topic and purposes to your audience. Audience analysis should help you to determine how much audience members already know and how much you will have to tell them to engender understanding. Then, you will have to decide how to generate information hunger, achieve information relevance, employ extrinsic motivation, select content, and avoid information overload in your speech.

Information Hunger

An informative speech is more effective if the speaker can generate **information hunger** in the audience; that is, if the speaker can create a need for information in the audience. Information hunger is easiest to create when a speaker has analyzed the audience and believes hunger for the information can be aroused. Interest in the subject matter of a speech before listening to it is not significantly related to comprehension, but arousal of interest during the speech is related to how much the audience will comprehend.[1] The following

To an audience of prospective parents, an informative speech about birth is relevant.

rhetorical questions could be used to introduce an informative speech and to arouse audience interest: "Are you aware of the number of abused children in your hometown?" "Can you identify five warning signs of cancer?" "Do you know how to get the best college education for your money?" Depending on the audience, these rhetorical questions could be of interest.

Rhetorical questions, questions asked for effect with no answer expected, are just one method of arousing information hunger. Another method is to arouse the audience's curiosity. For example, you might state "I have discovered a way to add 10 years to my life." "The adoption of the following plan will insure world peace." or "There is a secret for achieving marital success." In addition, a brief quiz on your topic early in the speech arouses interest in finding the answers. Unusual clothing is likely to arouse interest in why you are so attired, and an object you created will likely inspire the audience to wonder how you made it. These are just a few ways the public speaker can generate information hunger.

Information Relevance

A second factor relating an informative speech to an audience is **information relevance,** the usefulness of the information to the audience. When selecting a topic for an informative speech, the speaker should carefully consider the relevance of the topic. Skin cancer might be a better topic in the summer when students are sunbathing than in the winter when they are not. An audience might find a speech on tax laws dull. A speech on how present tax laws cost audience members more than they cost the rich might be more relevant, and a speech on three ways to reduce personal taxes might be even more relevant. However, if your audience happens to be composed of eighteen- to twenty-one-year-olds who have never paid taxes, none of the three topics might be relevant. Similarly, a speech on raising racehorses, writing a textbook, or living on a pension might be informative but not relevant because of the financial status, occupation, or age of the listeners. The informative speaker, then, should exercise some care to select a topic that interests the audience.[2]

People expose themselves first to information that is supportive or that fits in with what they already believe or know. People reject less supportive information first, so an audience's predisposition toward a topic can determine whether an audience will come to hear a speech and whether an audience will listen.[3]

Extrinsic Motivation

A third factor in relating an informative speech to an audience is **extrinsic motivation,** the reasons why the audience should listen. An audience is more likely to listen to, and comprehend, a speech if there are reasons outside the speech itself for concentrating on the content of the speech.[4] A teacher who tells students to listen carefully because they will be tested at the end of the hour is using extrinsic motivation. A student can use extrinsic motivation at the beginning of a speech by telling an audience, "Attention to this speech will alert you to ways you can increase energy and creativity", or "After hearing this speech, you will never purchase a poor quality used car again."

Extrinsic motivation is related to the concept of information relevance. The audience member who would ordinarily be disinterested in the topic of fashion might find that topic more relevant when it is linked to job interviews and the kinds of clothing, jewelry, and shoes that employers seem to prefer. The audience member's interest in getting a job makes the interviewer's preferences an extrinsic motivation for listening carefully to the speech.

Any external reasons for why audience members should listen need to be mentioned early in the speech, before the message you want audience members to remember. A statement such as, "You will need this background material for the report due at the end of this week," provides extrinsic motivation for the managers who hear this message from their employer. Similarly, in an informative speech, you may be able to command more attention, comprehension, and action from audience members if they know some reasons outside the speech itself for why they should attend to your message.

The informative speaker can increase audience comprehension through overt audience response.

Informative Content

A fourth factor in relating an informative speech to an audience is the selection of **informative content,** the main and subpoints, the illustrations and examples used to clarify and inform. In chapter 13, we discussed information sources and how to find appropriate supporting materials for the content of your speech. In this chapter, we briefly examine some principles of learning and some research findings that can guide you in selecting your speech content.

First, audiences tend to remember and comprehend generalizations and main ideas better than details and specific facts.[5] The usual advice to speakers—that content should be limited to a relatively small number of main points and generalizations—seems to be well grounded. Specifically, public speakers are well advised to limit themselves to two to five main points or contentions in a speech. Even if the speech is very long, audiences are unlikely to remember a larger number of main points.

Second, relatively simple words and concrete ideas are significantly easier to retain than more complex materials.[6] Long or unusual words may dazzle an audience into thinking you are intellectually gifted or verbally skilled, but they may also reduce understanding of the speech content. It is best to keep the ideas and the words used to express those ideas at an appropriate level.

Humor can make a dull speech more interesting to an audience, but it does not seem to increase information retention. The use of humor also improves the audience's perception of the character of the speaker, and it can increase a speaker's authoritativeness when a speech is dull, although not when the speech is interesting.[7]

Early remarks about how the speech will meet the audience's needs can create anticipation and increase the chances that the audience will listen and understand.[8] Whatever topic you select, you should tell audience members early in your speech how the topic is related to them. Unless you relate the topic to their needs, they may choose not to listen.

Calling for *overt audience response,* or actual behavior, increases comprehension more than repetition. In a study of this subject, the overt responses invited were specific, "programmed" questions to which the appropriate overt responses were anticipated.[9] The results were consistent with other studies that show the virtue of active participation by an audience.

An informative speaker can ask for overt responses from audience members by having them perform the task being demonstrated (for example, two people dance after you explain the technique of the waltz), by having them stand, raise hands, or move chairs to indicate affirmative understanding of the speaker's statements (for example, raise your hand if you are familiar with local building codes), or by having them write answers that will indicate understanding of the informative speech (for example, list four ways to lower your blood pressure). Having an audience go through some overt motion provides feedback to the speaker and can be rewarding and reinforcing for both speaker and listener.

Information Overload

The informative speaker needs to be wary about the amount of information included in a speech. The danger is **information overload,** providing much more information than the audience can absorb either in amount or complexity or both. Information overload comes in two forms. One is when the speaker tells us more than we ever wanted to know about a subject, even when we are interested in it. The speaker tries to cram as much information as possible into the time allowed. Unfortunately, this cramming of information makes the information more difficult to understand.

A second form of information overload is when the speaker uses language or ideas that are beyond the capacity of the audience to understand. The engineer or mathematician who unloads his or her latest formulas on the audience or the philosopher who soars into the ethereal heights of high ideas may leave the audience feeling frustrated and less knowledgeable than before the speech. The solution to information overload is to select a limited number of main points with only the best supporting materials and to keep the message at a level the audience can understand.

Now that you have examined information hunger, information relevance, extrinsic motivation, findings about content, and information overload, you are ready to review some specific suggestions about organizing the informative speech.

Organizing Content

Chapter 14 contained detailed information about the overall organization of speeches. The additional suggestions that follow are based on studies that reveal specific ways the informative speaker can help an audience understand the content of the speech. In general, the research supports the old saying that you should tell audience members what you are going to tell them, tell them, and then tell them what you told them.

Charles R. Petrie, Jr. in his studies of informative speaking, found that the use of transitions can increase an audience's comprehension.[10] That finding underlines the importance of building into the organization of your informative speech transitions between your introduction and body and between your body and conclusion. Other places for transitions include the moves from one main point to another in your speech and into and out of visual aids.

In organizing your informative speech, you should determine which ideas, points, or supporting materials are of greatest importance. Apparently, an audience understands the important points better if the speaker signals their importance by saying, "Now get this," or "This is very important." Some redundancy, or planned repetition, also can increase comprehension.[11] Some of that planned repetition can be included in the previews and reviews in your informative speech.[12] *Advance organizers,* or previews in written work, aid retention by providing the reader with key points prior to their presentation in a meaningful, but unfamiliar, passage.[13] Perhaps it is true in speaking, as well as in writing, that listeners can more easily grasp information when they are invited to anticipate and to review both the organization and the content of a speech.

When you have completed a sentence outline or some other form of outline that includes everything you plan to say, you should check your speech for information overload. Overload is a special problem in the informative speech because speakers have a tendency to inundate listeners with information. Just as some writers believe a longer paper is a better paper, some speakers think the sheer quantity of information they present in a speech makes it better. The most effective public speakers know the quantity of material in a speech makes less difference than the quality of the material. They also know listeners pay more attention to carefully selected material that is well adapted to their needs. In a five-to-eight-minute informative speech, the speaker has only four to six minutes to present supporting materials; the remainder of the time is spent introducing the subject, making transitions, and making internal and final summaries. Your organizational plan should show what material you intend to include in your speech. It can also be your final check on the quantity and quality of the information you intend to present.

Special Skills for Informative Speaking

Public speakers who are highly effective at informative speaking demonstrate certain special skills that lead to their effectiveness. One of these skills is *defining*. Much of what an informative speaker does is revealing to an audience what certain terms, words, and concepts mean. Another skill is *describing*, for the informative speaker often tells an audience how something appears: what it looks, sounds, feels, and even smells like. A third skill is *explaining*, or trying to say what something is in terms or words the audience can understand. A fourth skill is *narrating*, an oral interpretation of a story, event, or description.

Defining

A student who was a model gave a speech in which he talked about *parts modeling;* a student who made his own butter gave an informative speech in which he talked about the *dasher* and the *clabber, bilky* milk, and butter that *gathered;* and an informative speech on aerobics included such terms as *arteriosclerosis, cardiovascular-pulmonary system,* and *cardiorespiratory endurance.* What were these students talking about? In each case, they were using words most persons in the audience did not understand. There is nothing particularly wrong with using terms audience members do not understand as long as you explain the terms in language they *can* understand. You do that by *defining* your terms. Among the most useful methods of defining are the use of comparison, contrast, synonyms, antonyms, etymology, and operational definitions.

The student who told about making butter defined through **comparison,** telling what something is like or similar to, by explaining that the dasher consists of a stick similar to a broom handle. A cross made of two slats, four inches long and two inches wide, is nailed to the end of the handle. The dasher is inserted into the churn, and the churn's opening is covered by a tightly fitted wooden lid with a hole in the middle for the dasher. The student defined a dasher by comparing it to the better-known broomstick and by revealing how it was constructed.

Another method of definition is through **contrast,** which means telling what something is not. In an informative speech, you can contrast between hypochondriasis and psychotic disorders by contrasting the symptoms and effects of each.

A speaker also might define through a **synonym**—a word, term, or concept close or similar in meaning. For example, in an informative speech, the speaker might say depressive psychosis is characterized by loss of interest, dejection, stupor, and silence—a series of words similar to behaviors exhibited by the depressive psychotic patient.

An **antonym** defines by stating the opposite of the term being defined. A hyperactive child is not quiet, immobile, silent, patient, or unexpressive.

Sometimes, you may find it easier to explain a concept or term by revealing the term's **etymology,** or the history and origins of a word. A desk dictionary may give a very brief statement on the origin of a word. More complete origins can be located in specialized such dictionaries as the *Oxford English Dictionary* or the *Etymological Dictionary of Modern English.* A speaker talking about sexual variations might use the term *lesbianism* and could define the term by explaining the Greek poet Sappho wrote poetry about sexual love between women about six hundred years before Christ. Because Sappho lived on the island of Lesbos, "followers of Sappho," or female homosexuals, became known as lesbians. The story about the origin of the word provides a memorable way for the audience to relate to the word.

Another means of defining is the **operational definition,** defining a term by revealing how it works, how it is made, or what it consists of. Chapter 7 on verbal codes discusses this term. The earlier description of a dasher was an operational definition because it defined by revealing how a dasher is constructed. A student delivering an informative speech on rhinoplasty or "a nose job" did so through the following operational definition:

> Modern rhinoplasty is done for both cosmetic and health reasons. It consists of several minioperations. First, if the septum separating the nostrils has become deviated as the result of an injury or some other means, it is straightened with surgical pliers. Then, if the nose is to be remodeled, small incisions are made within each nostril, and working entirely within the nose, the surgeon is able to remove, reshape, or redistribute the bone and cartilage lying underneath the skin. Finally, if the nose is crooked, a chisel is taken to the bones of the upper nose, and they are broken so that they may be straightened and centered.

An operational definition, then, defines by revealing the formula for the thing named: rhinoplasty is the surgery described in the previous sentences; a cake is its recipe; concrete is lime, cement, and water; a secretary is what a secretary does: typing, filing, and answering phones.

Describing

A second special skill of the informative speaker is distinguishing between abstract and concrete words, and between general and specific words. One of the best ways to make an informative speech interesting is by using language forcefully and effectively to describe. You can do that best if you recognize certain differences in words.

For instance, some words refer generally to ideas, qualities, acts, or relationships: these are called **abstract words.** Examples of abstract words might be *freedom* (an idea), *mysterious* (a quality), *altruism* (an act), and *parent-child* (a relationship). Other words are more specific or **concrete** because they refer to definite persons, places, objects, and acts, such as Dr. Bettsey L. Barhorst, the Eiffel Tower, and my economics textbook. Abstract words are useful in theorizing, summarizing, and discussing and are more commonly used by educated persons discussing ideas. Concrete words are most useful in relating your personal experiences, direct observations, and feelings or attitudes. The important point about abstract and concrete, or general and specific, language is to use each where it is most appropriate. The most common error in informative speeches is the use of abstract terms where concrete words would be more forceful and clear. "I have really liked some courses of study here at Oklahoma University," says a student to his classmates and adds, "but others I have disliked." This abstract, general statement has minimal impact. If speaking in concrete and specific terms, the same student might say, "I most enjoyed English, speech, and political science courses, and I disliked courses in chemistry, mathematics, and physics." Descriptions in informative speeches should be specific, accurate, and detailed, rather than general and ambiguous.

Informative speakers should also attempt to use colorful imagery that appeals to the senses. A speaker describing a place might say, "the sun sets in an orange sky against the purple mountain," a victim of shock "appears lifeless, pallid, and feels clammy," or a manufactured meat "tastes like top-grade sirloin."

A valuable exercise for the informative speaker is to carefully review the rough draft of the speech to discover abstract, general, ambiguous words that can be replaced by concrete, specific details.

Explaining

A third special skill for the informative speaker is explaining an idea in terms the audience can understand. An **explanation** is a means of idea development, an alternative way of stating an idea or concept. Often, an explanation simplifies or clarifies an idea while making it interesting to the audience.

An important step in explaining is dissecting, analyzing, or taking something apart so the audience can understand it. Unless you become skilled at disassembling a concept, your explanation may leave audience members more confused than they were before your speech. You have to determine what you can do to make the concept more palatable to the audience and increase audience understanding. John Kenneth Galbraith, a retired professor of economics from Harvard University, wrote many books explaining economics to people who did not know very much about the subject. A close look at one of his explanations is instructive. Galbraith is trying to make the point that politicians and the public often take the voices of a few influential persons as a shift-of-opinion by the majority:

> On the need for tax relief, investment incentives, or a curb on welfare costs, the views of one articulate and affluent banker, businessman, lawyer, or acolyte economist are the equal of those of several thousand welfare mothers. In any recent year, the pleas by Walter Wriston of Citibank or David Rockefeller of Chase Manhattan for relief from oppressive taxation, regulation, or intrusive government have commanded at least as much attention as the expressions of discontent of all the deprived of the South Bronx.[14]

Galbraith is analyzing a situation: Why do the persons of economic advantage have a bigger say in our economy than the millions who live with it? His language is specific and concrete. He is expanding on an idea with descriptive language, and he is doing so by dissecting the concept so we can understand its parts.

Narrating

A fourth special skill for informative speakers is **narration,** the oral presentation and interpretation of a story, description, or event. In a speech, narration includes the dramatic reading of some lines from a play, poem, or other piece of literature; the voice-over on a series of slides or a silent film to illustrate some point in a speech; and even the reading of such information as a letter, a quotation, or a selection from a newspaper or magazine. The person who does the play-by-play account of a ball game is narrating and so is the speaker who explains what a weaver is doing in an informative speech on home crafts.

The person who uses narration in a speech moves just a little closer to oral interpretation of literature, or even acting, because the real cue to narrating is that the narration is highlighted by being more dramatic than the words around it. Sections of your speech that require this kind of special reading also require special practice. If you want a few lines of poetry in your speech to have the desired impact, you will need to rehearse them.

Checklist for an Informative Speech

As you prepare your informative speech, check off each item in the blank on the left to indicate you have taken that item under careful consideration.

Topic

_____ 1. Have you selected a topic about which your content can be predominantly informative?

_____ 2. Have you selected a topic in which you are interested?

_____ 3. Have you selected a topic that the majority of your audience members do not know or understand?

_____ 4. Have you narrowed the topic to fit time limitations?

_____ 5. Have you made it clear to the audience how this topic is important to them?

_____ 6. Have you reviewed the information in chapter 11 on topic selection?

Purpose

_____ 1. Have you determined immediate behavioral purposes for your speech?

_____ 2. Have you included methods of discovering whether or not your immediate behavioral purposes have been achieved?

Content

_____ 1. Have you included ways to arouse information hunger—a need for information in the audience?

_____ 2. Can you use extrinsic motivation to encourage your audience to listen carefully?

_____ 3. Have you selected information that will meet audience needs, reduce complexity, and increase understanding?

_____ 4. Have you used personal experiences, stories, and comparisons to increase audience interest in your information?

_____ 5. Have you reviewed chapter 13 so you know how to find the most effective supporting materials for your informative speech?

Organization

_____1. Have you highlighted your main points by forecasting, repetition, summarizing, and including transitions?

_____2. Have you limited your main points and illustrative materials to improve clarity and to avoid information overload?

_____3. Have you reviewed chapter 14 on speech organization to help you determine which patterns of organization are most appropriate for you, your topic, your situation, and your audience?

Special Skills

_____1. Have you employed your skills in defining, describing, explaining, and narrating?

_____2. Have you tried defining through comparisons, contrasts, synonyms, antonyms, etymologies, or operational definitions?

_____3. Have you used specific, concrete detail and abstract language where they are appropriate?

_____4. Have you tried to be as descriptive as possible by using precise, accurate, and detailed descriptors?

_____5. Have you explained by analyzing or dissecting your concept in ways that invite audience understanding?

_____6. Have you rehearsed any narration in your speech?

Special Features

_____1. Have you reviewed the information in chapter 13 on audience analysis so you know what the audience knows and needs to know?

_____2. Have you reviewed the information in chapter 15 on visual aids so you can employ them where appropriate in your speech?

_____3. Have you reviewed chapter 14 so you know how to indicate your credibility on the topic you select?

_____4. Have you reviewed the information in chapter 15 on delivery so you know how to effectively deliver your informative speech?

An Example of an Informative Speech

So far in this chapter, you have gained additional information on how to select a topic for your **informative speech,** how to determine behavioral purposes and goals for the informative speech, how to present information to an audience, how to organize the informative speech, and how to define, describe, explain, and provide narration for the concepts in your speech. Now we look at an actual informative speech delivered by a student.

Notice how the speaker gains and maintains the audience's attention, relates the topic to himself and to the audience, and forecasts the organization and development of the topic. Notice also how the speaker attempts to clarify the idea with examples high in audience interest, how ideas are translated into language the audience can understand, and how the speaker employs definitions, descriptions, and explanations. The sidenotes will help identify how the speaker is fulfilling the important functions of the introduction, body, and conclusion of an informative speech. The speech that follows is also an example of a speech manuscript.

Speaker gains attention with a very brief tape recording of the opening for a television police show.

Speaker identifies with the audience's lack of knowledge by raising rhetorical questions.

Speaker relates topic to himself and describes his credibility on the topic.

Speaker announces the topic.

Speaker relates topic to the audience.

The Trouble with Codes

I would like you to listen to a very important type of communication (at this point, the speaker plays a few seconds of tape-recorded sound, the introduction to the televised police show called "Adam-12"):

> Adam-12, Adam-12. 211 in progress at 1443 52nd. Handle Code 3.

What you just heard was the beginning of the television show "Adam-12." The voice you heard was the radio dispatcher giving a call to a patrol car. The first time that I heard those words and numbers I could only wonder what in the world she was saying. Who's Adam-12? What's a 211 "in progress," and how do you handle something "code 3"?

Well, you could say that I found out the meaning of the message the hard way. After graduating at the top of my class from the state law enforcement academy and after spending two years on our own city police department, I can tell you what the dispatcher just said. But there are some problems with coding systems like the one you just heard because coding systems are used these days by police, computer scientists, physicians, lawyers, and everyday people. So

Speaker forecasts the development of the speech.

Speaker reminds audience of his credibility.

Speaker raises his first question about the code system.

Speaker defines the police code system.

Speaker raises second issue concerning code.
Speaker relates personal experience to arouse audience interest and attention.

Speaker uses hypothetical example to make his point more specific and concrete.

Speaker employs specific instance.

Speaker compares coded message with its translation.

Speaker employs second specfic example.

Speaker compares coded message with its translation.

today I'd like to explain to you troubles that can arise from the use of coding systems by telling you of some of my personal experiences with them.

At the law enforcement academy, the instructors who taught us the police communication system told us how easy and efficient the system is. At the academy, the system sounded good, but the thought kept running through my mind; how will the system work when the officer is under pressure?

The code system we use is based on numbers. The code contains one hundred entries: 10–1 to 10–100. We learned the codes at the academy, but like things we learn in college, if we don't practice, we forget them.

As I started my career in police work, I found that, at times, the system worked very well. The times I'm talking about are the routine calls we'd receive every day—things like prowler calls and accidents.

For example, if a woman called in and said someone was trying to get into her house, the dispatcher would key the microphone and call the police car designated to be patrolling in that area. It would sound something like this:

Ames 124, 10–14, 1004 West Street, Code 2.

Translated, it would sound like this:

Ames Radio to West area patrol car number 124; 10–14: there is a prowler there now at 1004 West Street; Code 2: get there as soon as possible.

Or another routine call would sound like this:

Ames 124, 10–50 P.I. L-Way and State, Code 3.

Translated, the message would sound like this:

West area patrol car, there is an accident with personal injury involved at the intersection of Lincoln Way and State Avenue; because this is an emergency, use your red light and siren.

Speaker uses specific, concrete language in his description.

Speaker contrasts routine code use with emergency code use.

Speaker uses personal experience to relate stories illustrating the problems with codes.

Speaker uses specific, concrete example.

Speaker's story arouses human interest in the topic.

Speaker employs humor to communicate his message about codes.

Speaker uses descriptive language to depict the situation in his story.

Speakers uses a second narrative to illustrate the problems with the code in actual use.

Speaker uses specific example.

From these examples, you can see that the code system does cut down time and makes the message easier to say. But what about the calls that aren't routine? What about situations in which the adrenaline is flowing?

I discovered how easy it is to forget these codes in a couple of scary ways. I received the following radio transmission from my dispatcher late one night toward the end of a hectic day.

> Ames 124 and 126, 10–94, Happy Chef west, Code 2.

Well, this is what I'd been afraid of! What the heck is a 10–94? So I reached for my handy codebook that I hadn't used for ages—but it wasn't there. I hoped that the backup officer in car 126 would have the answer I needed. As we pulled up to the restaurant, we both got out of our cars and said at the same time to each other: "What the heck is a 10–94?"

We figured the only way to save our pride was to walk in and find out what was wrong. As we walked calmly in, we were met by a very frantic and excited waitress who said that a man had just called to say that he had planted a bomb in the building. Now we knew! A 10–94 was a bomb threat, and we had just walked into the middle of it. So much for the code system.

Another confusing situation happened one night at the scene of a very bad accident, I arrived at the scene of the accident to see a very bloody man running toward my car. Immediately, I picked up my mike and shouted into it:

> 124 Ames, 10–23, 10–50 P.I., 10–56 several injured.

It wasn't until I saw the dispatcher the next day that I realized my mistake. The message I had transmitted was:

> West area car to Ames Radio: I have arrived at the scene of a personal injury accident; send a wrecker to pick up the several injured.

Speaker uses humor to maintain audience interest in the topic.

Speaker signals an impending ending—breaklight function.

Speaker uses an oral footnote to indicate interview.

Speaker uses an outside authoritative source to summarize his information on the police code system.

Speaker is reviewing by repetition.

Speaker uses circular organization to bring us back to his initial attention-getter.

Speaker uses clever ending.

In my excited state, instead of saying 10–57—send an ambulance—I said 10–56—send a wrecker. Fortunately, the dispatcher caught my error and corrected it herself.

You can see the problems that can result with the system. Not understanding messages sent out by dispatchers who use the codes everyday and have them posted by their radios, many police officers have to call back and ask them to repeat the message in English. Last week, I went in to talk with Ann Benson, the head dispatcher and a twelve-year veteran of the Ames Police Department. I confronted her with these problems; this was her reply:

> The code system is designed for speed and efficiency. One problem is that police calls are monitored by everybody from housewives to the press, and there are things that we do not want them to know. So until something better is figured out, we're stuck with it. It's the best we've got, and we'll have to learn to live with it.

Well, that didn't solve my problem—the problem of confusion from forgetfulness or nonuse. I also do not know a better way for an officer to communicate when he or she is under pressure.

I learned the codes the hard way, and I won't forget them, but under pressure I can still slip up. I don't know the answers to the problems of code communication, but I do know what the dispatcher said on the tape that introduced this speech:

> Adam-12 is a police patrol car; the 211 in progress is an armed robbery taking place; and code 3 is an emergency.

So now I thank you for your attention and say: 10–8, 12–24, 10–4.

An Informative Speech Assignment

Deliver a five-to-eight minute informative speech with immediate behavioral purposes that can be checked during or after the speech. Employ visual aids if and where appropriate. Deliver the speech extemporaneously and include oral footnotes and signals that indicate important points in ways that will help the audience remember them. The speech should include an introduction that gains and maintains attention, describes the origins of your credibility on the topic, relates the topic to the audience, reveals what you want the audience to learn, and indicates the organization and development of your speech. The speech should include a conclusion that indicates the end is near, summarizes the main point or points, and that makes the audience pleased that they listened to you.

The immediate purpose of this informative speech was to demonstrate to the audience some problems with the police code system. The primary information the audience should have been able to write down after the speech was two causes of code failure: namely, the inability to use a code when much of it is not routinely used and the chances for error in an emergency situation. The speaker taught the audience parts of the police code by translating specific examples. He demonstrated the problems with the code by citing personal experiences in which he, as a police officer, had made mistakes with the code; and he clarified the code by defining what certain code numbers meant and by explaining how police use the code system. The speaker included a bibliography that cited his term of instruction at the police academy, his interview with the dispatcher, and his use of the police codebook.

Summary

The primary vehicle for informing others is the informative speech. To prepare an informative speech, you should know (1) the intent and the goal of informative speaking, (2) the kinds of topics that lend themselves best to informative speaking, and (3) the kinds of immediate behavioral purposes of informative speaking and how to determine if you have fulfilled them.

In presenting information to an audience, you should strive to generate information hunger (an audience need for the information), achieve information relevance (providing information that is not simply informative), employ extrinsic motivation (reasons outside the speech itself for concentrating on the content of the speech), select informative content (a limited number of main points, generalizations, relatively simple words and concrete ideas, humor, and statements about how the speech will meet audience needs), and avoid information overload (too much information in a speech or information beyond the capacity of the audience to understand).

Key Terms

abstract words   Words or phrases not rooted in physical reality.

antonym   A word that means the opposite of another word.

comparison   A behavioral goal of the informative speech in which the audience weighs the relative values and characteristics of the speech or its uses of objects, events, or issues.

concrete words   Specificity of expression; using words that are not ambiguous or abstract.

contrast   The comparison of unlike things.

etymology   The historical origins of a word.

explanation   A means of idea development that simplifies or clarifies an idea while making it interesting to the audience.

extrinsic motivation   A method of making information relevant by providing the audience with reasons outside the speech itself for listening to the content of the speech.

immediate behavioral purposes   Actions a speaker seeks in an audience during and immediately after a speech.

information hunger   The audience's need for the information contained in the speech.

information overload   Occurs when the quantity or difficulty of the information presented is greater than the audience can assimilate within the given time.

information relevance   The importance, novelty, and usefulness of the topic and the information; a factor in adapting an informative speech to an audience.

informative content   The use of generalizations, simple and concrete words, humor, and statements about how the speech will meet audience needs; the propositions and evidence in a speech.

informative speech   A speech whose purpose is to get audience members to understand or learn.

narration   The oral presentation and interpretation of a story, description, or event; includes dramatic reading of prose or poetry.

operational definition   A definition that consists of stating the process that results in the thing being defined; hence, a cake can be operationally defined by a recipe, a particular house by its blueprints, and a job by its job description.

rhetorical questions   An inquiry asked for effect with no answer expected.

synonym   A word that means approximately the same as another word.

chapter 17

The Persuasive Speech

T his chapter explores persuasive speaking by showing how to prepare a persuasive speech, examining some methods of persuasion, and reviewing some special skills useful to the persuader. An example of a persuasive speech is provided at the end of the chapter. When you complete this chapter, you will be more competent in persuasive public speaking.

Presenting an effective persuasive speech is one of the most practical skills you learn in your communication class. You use persuasion every day in your interpersonal relations: you may try to convince someone to lend you money, you may try to explain to your professor why you missed a class or an examination, or you may try to persuade someone to give you a job. Public persuasion is equally common: coaches try to persuade team members that they can win, managers persuade employees to try a new approach, ministers persuade congregations to obey God, lawyers persuade juries, and people persuade legislators. Public persuasion pervades the mass media through advertising and public relations, and people learn to respond to, and to resist, the appeals.

What will you learn?

After you have read and thought about this chapter, you will be able to answer the following questions:

1. What is persuasive speaking?
2. Can you name the four action goals of a persuasive speech?
3. Can you think of five topics that would be appropriate for a persuasive speech and explain why?
4. What is the relationship between ultimate action goals of your persuasive speech and the behavioral purposes?
5. Can you distinguish among these concepts by explaining each—motivational appeals, speaker credibility, logical appeals, and emotional appeals?
6. What does the research say about these organizational features: placement of best argument, present one or more sides, whether or not to refute counterarguments, and use familiar or novel arguments?
7. Can you explain the four ethical considerations related to persuasive speaking?
8. Can you distinguish among these concepts by defining each—propositions, justification, inferences, deductive argument, evidence, and refutation?
9. What are tests of evidence and why should you know them?
10. Can you deliver an effective persuasive speech using the ideas and information garnered from this book?

You cannot convince a man against his will.

Samuel Johnson

A woman convinced against her will is of the same opinion still.

Leona Hughes

We are more easily persuaded, in general, by the reasons that we ourselves discover than by those which are given to us by others.

Pascal

There are always plenty of people who want to tell you what to do: parents, professors, politicians, sales people, government bureaucrats, and journalists. To function effectively in a free democracy, you need to know both how to persuade and how to be a consumer of persuasion. This chapter is designed to teach you how to both persuade and resist persuasion.

This final chapter builds on all you have learned about yourself as a giver and receiver of stimuli, as a unique perceiver of the world, a person who is self-aware with a self-concept and self-esteem, a critical listener who recognizes fallacious thinking, and a person who understands language and nonverbal communication. Furthermore, your success with this chapter on persuasion depends on your understanding of topic selection, audience analysis, speaker credibility, research skills, organizational patterns, delivery and visual aids. You need to know it all to be a giver and a receiver of persuasion. We begin by discovering what persuasion is and how it is used to shape, reinforce, and change our thoughts and actions.

Preparing a Persuasive Speech

Many people have a mistaken view of what persuasion is and how it works. For instance, some people think persuasion is the skillful manipulation of images to get people to do something they would not otherwise do. To them, persuasion is seduction, getting their way with people by influencing them against their wills. We see persuasion not as seduction or manipulation, but as a more noble pursuit of the best ideas, most workable solutions, and greater support for an idea by the people through effective speaking. The best speakers know how to assemble an argument through their knowledge of critical thinking, and they use the same tools—tests of evidence, inductive and deductive reasoning, and knowledge of fallacies—to analyze what others are saying.

Persuasion and the Goals of Persuasive Speaking

Persuasion is an ongoing process in which verbal and nonverbal messages shape, reinforce, and change people's responses (figure 17.1).[1] Rarely do people change radically as a result of a one-shot persuasive effort. If they change at all, it is because of "an ongoing process" in which they are exposed and respond to messages from speakers, newspapers, magazines, broadcasts, friends, and relatives—to name a few sources.

These multiple messages *shape* our responses by pushing us to respond in some direction.[2] You might in the past have disliked dancing; but because your closest friend loves to dance, you have changed your behavior over time until you now enjoy dancing. A single persuasive speech can start to push an audience in a direction desired by the speaker.

Figure 17.1 Persuasive speaking seeks behavioral effects.

Type of speech	General goal	Action goals	Expected behavior
		Deterrence	Don't do it
	Reinforce	Continuance	Keep doing it
Persuasion	Shape		
	Change	Adoption	Start doing it
		Discontinuance	Stop doing it

Persuasive messages can also *reinforce* past behavior, that is, reward the person for persisting in some action or for avoiding some action. In persuasive speaking, we call the general goal of reinforcing **continuance** or **deterrence.** By continuance we mean that you encourage the audience to keep doing what they are doing, such as using seat belts, going to synagogue, or eating low-fat foods. By deterrence we mean that you encourage the audience to avoid some behavior, such as using drugs, smoking, or joining a gang.

Persuasive messages can *change* people's actions. Under this general goal of changing an audience's behavior are the action goals of persuasive speaking called **adoption** and **discontinuance.** By adoption we mean that the audience is asked to start some behavior untried in the past, such as driving at or below the speed limit, starting a daily exercise program, or eating low-cholesterol foods. By discontinuance we mean that the audience is encouraged to stop some current activity, such as voting Republican, eating junk foods, and drinking alcoholic beverages.

You can improve your chances of persuading an audience if you write out your ultimate goal and your immediate behavioral purposes. For example, a student delivering a persuasive speech against jogging might state the following for an ultimate goal:

> The ultimate goal of my persuasive speech is to convince people who jog that they should quit (discontinuance) and to convince people who do not jog that they should never start (deterrence).

The same speaker also might state the following immediate behavioral purposes:

> One of my immediate behavioral purposes is to have the audience write down at the conclusion of my speech the three harmful effects that jogging has on the body: shin splints, bone bruises, and knee problems. A second immediate behavioral purpose of my speech is to have the joggers in the audience start reducing their workout times to avoid problems encouraged by fatigue.

The persuasive speaker need not reveal the ultimate purpose of the speech itself but, ordinarily, should reveal the immediate behavioral purposes of the speech. Audience members are more likely to write down the harmful effects of jogging if they are told early in the speech of that expectation. They may resist the persuasive speaker, however, if they know the ultimate goal of the speech.

Many speech communication professors will want you to use the general goals of shaping and changing and the action goals of adoption and discontinuance. They may even discourage speeches with the goal of reinforcing and the action goals of deterrence and continuance. One of the reasons for encouraging you to give persuasive speeches with adoption and discontinuance action goals is that you and the teacher will be better able to observe change in the audience. With deterrence and continuance action goals, the audience's behavior may remain the same, but it would be risky to attribute that lack of change to the effect of your speech.

Topics for Persuasive Speeches

Some topics are more appropriate for persuasive speeches than others. For instance, current and controversial topics lend themselves to persuasion better than topics that are outdated and accepted by nearly everyone. Some public speaking instructors believe the best topics for persuasive speeches are those that place the speaker at odds with the majority of audience members. However, that position disregards speeches with a continuance or deterrence goal.

Chapter 11 focused on selecting a speech topic through brainstorming and personal inventories. Another method is to look through newspapers and magazines and listen to radio talk shows to discover what issues people are currently concerned about. Even letters to the editor in your campus, local, or regional paper can provide ideas for a persuasive speech.

You may also find it helpful to survey topics used previously in persuasive speeches, such as the persuasive speech topics in the list that follows. As you read over the list of topics for persuasive speeches, you should recognize that what is current and controversial at one college may be bland and dated at another. Many topics and titles are broader than their treatment in the speech, and other excellent topics emerge every day.

Topics for Persuasive Speeches

More Prisons?
Improve Race Relations
Rebuild the Inner City
Register to Vote
Should News Be Entertaining?
The Folly of Dieting
Parking
The Megavitamin Myth
The Trouble with Christianity
Equal Pay for Women
Vegetarianism
Political Apathy
Bilingualism
Buy a Home Computer!
Youth Gangs are Dangerous
Affirmative Action for All
Adopting a Child
Cured Meats and Cancer
The Truth about Pesticides
Less Money for Defense
Improve Your Nutrition
You Should be a Parent
The Power of Nonviolence
Add Fiber to Your Diet
Getting Involved in Government
We Need Trade Unions
Television Violence
Misbehavior at Games
Be Assertive
Volunteer Your Time
Buy Generic Drugs
Against Jogging
Motorcycle Safety
"Crack"
AIDS Can be Cured
Divestiture in South Africa
Obese Children
Corporate Funding of Higher Education
Recycling
Media Exploitation (and Deception) of
  AIDS
Juvenile Justice System
Governmental Interference in Third
  World Development

Mandatory AIDS Testing for a Marriage
  License
"Diplomatic Immunity"
Medical Device Flaws
Anorexia Nervosa
Effects of Alcohol
Chemical Warfare
Don't Procrastinate!
Abortion or Adoption?
Do You Have Dyslexia?
Tanning Booths and Skin Cancer
Support Nuclear Power
Become a Vegetarian
Don't Drink and Drive
End Hazing
Apply for Credit
Legalize Euthanasia
AIDS Victims Rights
Anti-Intimacy
Fraternity Hazing
Surrogate Mothers
Animal Experimentation
Eat a Good Breakfast
Project Literacy
Dental Health
Forest Fires
Electroshock Therapy
Don't Use Sexist Language
Listen to Alternative Music
Creative Writing Is for Everyone
Create Your Own Buttons/Banners
Donate to Ronald McDonald
Participate in Aerobics
Support the Humane Society
Negotiation with Terrorists
Insurance and Malpractice
Tariffs on Foreign Imports
Censor Rock & Roll Music/Ratings
Juvenile Justice Reform
Increase U.S. Submarines
Fast Food Is Dangerous to Your Health
Support a Political Candidate or Issue

Topics for Persuasive Speeches (continued)

Take Philosophy 101, a Yoga Class (or Any Class You are Convinced Every Student Should Take)

Join the Food and Hunger Coalition, Performing Arts Series, PBS, Forensics Team, Hall Government (or Any Other Organization, Club, Movement)

Reform the Suburbs

Divorce

Child Support

Lower the Drinking Age

Sex Bias on the Job

Against the Minimum Wage

Hauling Nuclear Waste

Strengthening Our Defense

Vacationing in Florida

Drugs Are Dangerous

Advantages of ROTC

Why You Shouldn't Vote

Celibacy for You

Male Chauvinism

Against Football

The Campus Food Service

Hire the Handicapped

Legalize Drugs

Buy Real Estate

Try Effective Listening

Watch Less Television

Student Drinking Can Kill You

Cohabitation Is Not for Everyone

Stop Sexual Assaults

Appreciate Modern Art

X Rays Are Dangerous

Legalize Gambling

Is Cocaine for You?

Leaded Gasoline ,

AIDS/Drug Testing

Eat a Balanced Diet

Federal Deficit

Ride a Bicycle

Drive Safely

Stop Littering

Water Pollution

Abortion

Steroid Use

Star Wars

Unionization

Stop Smoking

Pit Bulls

Pro/Communism

Time Management

Discrimination

Make Out a Will

Don't Waste Food

Gun Control

Drug War

· Acid Rain

Human Rights

Gay Adoption

Castrate Rapists

Premarital Sex

Lower Cholesterol

Gambling

Pro/Terrorism

Socialism

Elvis is Alive

Big Brothers/Sisters

Autism

Read the Newspaper

Space Exploration

Reporting Child Abuse

Pro/Condoms in High Schools

Get Involved in Student Politics

Donate Blood, Plasma, Organs

Read the New Testament

Learn Life-Saving Techniques

Rodeo-Sport or Animal Cruelty

Learn a Foreign Language, How to Speed-Read, How to Use a Word Processor, CPR, etc.

Wear a Motorcycle Helmet

Rechannel Aggression

Topics for Persuasive Speeches (continued)

Wear Seat Belts	National Health Plan
Eliminate Pigeons	National Education Agenda
Don't Use Birth Control	Minimum Wage Increase
Buy American Products	Increase Voting Percent
Join the Peace Corps	Integrated Marriages
Stop Nail-Biting	Pornography Legislation
Stop Liability Suits	Use of Lie Detectors

These topics, like those in chapter 16 on informative speeches, vary in their specificity. Many of them need to be narrowed for a typical persuasive speech assignment.

Persuading an Audience

Audiences may be persuaded in a variety of ways. Researchers Marvin Karlins and Herbert I. Abelson observed, "Information by itself almost never changes attitudes."[3] You can persuade an audience, however, by using motivational appeals, employing source credibility, using logical or emotional appeals, organizing your materials effectively, and observing ethical guidelines for persuasion. We will discuss each of these methods in this section. You are also encouraged to review the material in chapter 5 on critical thinking.

Motivational Appeals

The word **motivation** is based on a Latin term that means "to move," and that is how we use the term in everyday conversations: "What was his motive in buying that expensive car?" "She had plenty of motivation for getting a job outside of the home"; or "His motive was to act just like the other firefighters." If we boil motivation down to its essential ingredients, three forces motivate or move people to behave in one way or another.[4]

One motivating force is *what our body tells us to do.* This physical basis of motivation explains our need for air, water, and food. We can get along without air for less than three minutes, without water for a couple of days, and without food for a week. Having unpolluted air to breathe, clean water to drink, and desirable food to eat takes much human energy, but our basic bodily needs motivate us to do what is necessary to preserve these resources.

The second motivating force is *what our minds tell us to do.* This psychological basis of motivation is based on our sense of rationality, as well as on our emotions, feelings, and perceptions. We are moved to do some things because it is reasonable in our minds to do so. We do other things because we feel good about doing them. We avoid still other activities because they make us feel bad about ourselves. The human mind motivates us to act in ways that comfort it.

The third motivating force is *what other people want us to do.* This third force is a powerful social motivator that encourages us to conform to roles and norms. You may act like a student because your fellow students reinforce you when you do and punish you when you do not. You may attend classes because that is what students are to do. You might find yourself doing any number of things because family, friends, and co-workers expect and reward them.

Human behavior is very complicated. No explanation of why human beings behave the way they do is entirely satisfactory. Knowing the three kinds of motivational forces will not permit you to manipulate an audience to elicit the behavior you seek. Nonetheless, the most effective persuasive speakers—advertisers, politicians, and lawyers—have learned how to analyze their audiences—consumers, voters, and juries—so they are more often successful than unsuccessful in reaching their objectives.

Speaker Credibility

Who and what you are can make a powerful difference in persuasion. In chapter 12, we explored the concept of speaker credibility and what audiences look for in a speaker: competence, trustworthiness, dynamism, and co-orientation. A highly credible speaker has more impact on an audience than a speaker with low credibility. A persuasive speaker who is seen as similar to the audience is more likely to be effective than one who is perceived as dissimilar. Sometimes, a highly credible speaker can attain more attitude change when he or she asks for more.[5]

All speakers need to avoid asking for too much lest they get a **boomerang effect,** an unintended situation in which the speaker and the message get the opposite of what is asked. The speaker wants the audience to vote Republican, but they find he and his message so repugnant that they are less likely than before to vote Republican.

An example of how speaker credibility works occurred when Harvard University sent a recruiter to a large midwestern university in an effort to secure more first-rate students from that part of the country. The pre-law students gathered in a room to meet the recruiter, who turned out to be a second-year law student from Harvard. The all-white audience of pre-law students seemed quite surprised when the recruiter turned out to be black. They showed their skepticism with their initial questions. "What was your grade point average as an undergraduate?" asked one member of the audience. "3.9 on a 4.0 scale," answered the recruiter. "Well," inquired another student, who apparently was not suitably impressed with the grade point average, "what did you earn on the LSAT?" "Seven hundred seventy," replied the recruiter. The pre-law students asked no more questions. The speaker was of a different race and from a different part of the country, but his grade point average and his

Who and what you are can make a powerful difference in persuasion.

LSAT score (800 was top) were higher than anyone's in the room. The audience listened with respect to his speech on how to get into one of the best law schools in the country.

You can signal the origins of your credibility to your audience by describing how you earned the right to speak on the topic. Perhaps your major will help: A nuclear engineer has the authority to speak on nuclear energy; a business major is a credible source on buying stocks and bonds; and a physical education major can speak with authority on exercise programs. Maybe your experience is the key to your credibility: your years in the military may have given you some insights into military waste; your years as a mother and homemaker may have given you authority to speak on time efficiency, raising children, or relating to a spouse; or your part-time job at a fast-food establishment may permit you to speak with some authority on management-labor relations.

Whatever the origins of your credibility, remember to reveal them early in the speech. Your authority may very well provide a reason for the audience to listen. If you reveal your credibility late in the speech, audience members may have paid little attention because they did not know you spoke with authority on the topic.

Another caution is also in order. While you must demonstrate your credibility to the audience, you can go too far in self-disclosing. Psychologists Burger and Vartabedian showed that as the speaker's prestige increases, the appropriateness of self-disclosure, as determined by the audience, decreases.

People who are high in prestige, such as those in Congress, are well advised to avoid high levels of personal revelations.[6] Some personal information can be offered by anyone; but perhaps no speaker should "tell all."

Logical Appeals

Motivational appeals and speaker credibility are just two ways to persuade an audience; a third important method is the use of reasoning or logic to convince an audience. The main ingredients of **logical appeals** are propositions and proofs. Professor John C. Reinard, of Arizona State University, has summarized the research done on evidence in the last half-century. He demonstrates the importance and the consistency of this research. Evidence is central to the persuasive process.[7]

A *proposition* is a statement that asserts or proposes something: "The United States should have uniform regulations for child support"; "The city should reduce the fines for traffic offenses"; or "The college should change its definition of 'a student in good standing.' " Notice that a proposition always recommends a change in the status quo, the way things are right now. The primary method of persuading an audience a current policy should be changed and another policy should be adopted is through the use of proof or evidence.

The persuasive speaker can use a wide array of evidence to demonstrate the wisdom of retaining present practices or changing current policies, such as: quotations from authoritative persons, conclusions from studies and reports, or experiences of individuals injured or helped by current policies. The underlying principle in logical appeals is that the audience should accept the side that presents the most convincing or the "best" evidence to support itself. In other words, our behavior should be based on the best evidence; it should be consistent with the persuasive speaker who provides the most effective proof or evidence.

Logical appeals can also be refuted; that is, they can be attacked. Another persuasive speaker can analyze the situation suggested in the proposition and find the analysis faulty. The opposing persuasive speaker may find the authorities who were quoted were biased, the reports and studies were flawed, or better evidence would invite a different conclusion.

Finally, it is important to recognize the world does not run by logic or evidence alone; sometimes beliefs are irrational or not based on evidence. A persuasive speaker might present considerable evidence on why you should eat legumes and cheese instead of meat without changing your behavior or beliefs on that subject. The persuasive speaker is always faced with the disconcerting fact that even the best evidence or proof in support of a persuasive proposition might not alter audience behavior.

Emotional Appeals

Although logical and **emotional appeals** are often seen as diametrically opposed concepts, most of our behavior is based on a mixture of emotional and rational "reasons." A speaker may persuade an audience to accept his or her immediate behavioral purposes for emotional, rather than logical, reasons. A story about one person's bad experience with the campus bookstore may inspire many persons in the audience to take their business to another store. It matters little that the experience may have been a one-in-a-thousand situation, that it may have been as much the customer's fault as the manager's, or that it had never happened before. Such is the power of our emotions that they can persuade us to defy the law, fight another nation, or ignore evidence. As one writer put it:

> The creature man is best persuaded
> When heart, not mind, is inundated;
> Affect is what drives the will;
> Rationality keeps it still.

(Reprinted from Marvin Karlins and Herbert I. Abelson, *Persuasion, How Opinions and Attitudes are Changed,* Copyright © 1970 by Springer Publishing Company, Inc., New York. Used by permission.)

The emotional appeal that has received the most attention from researchers is the *fear appeal.* Janis and Feshbach examined three levels of fear appeals in communication on dental hygiene and found the weak threat worked better than the moderate threat, which worked better than the strong threat.[8] Powell used strong and weak fear appeals in a civil defense message that threatened loved ones. His research found more opinion change when the fear appeal was strong.[9] These results may appear contradictory, but the research on reassurance with fear appeals is not. Your fear appeals are likely to work better if you reveal to the audience how they can avoid the fearsome consequences. For example, you could say, "Not brushing your teeth can lead to gum disease and tooth loss, so listen to my tips on oral hygiene."

Omitting reassurance does not influence the audience's ability to recall facts from the speech, but a speech with reassurance results in greater shifts of opinion than one without reassurance. Also, the speaker who includes reassurance is regarded by the audience as a better speaker than the one who does not.[10]

Fear appeals are not the only emotional appeals. Many unethical speakers use race, religion, nationality, sexual preference, jealousy, and anger to inspire their audience to action. The only protection against such speakers is your own rationality, powers of analysis, and good sense.

Special Organizational Considerations

Chapter 14 surveyed the basic organizational types. The patterns used most often in persuasive speaking are problem-and-solution, cause-and-effect, and topical-sequence. In the first two patterns, you have to carefully gauge how much time to spend on the problem or cause and how much time to spend on the solution or effect. The key to deciding is how much the audience needs to know and which part contains your most important persuasive effort. The topical-sequence pattern is highly versatile and is used in providing three reasons why you should use fishing scents, five characteristics of quality clothing, or some evidence for using fetal tissue to help victims of Parkinson's disease.

Besides choosing a basic pattern of organization, you need to consider how much to say in your introduction. In informative speaking, you usually say exactly what you want your audience to learn from your speech. In persuasive speaking, you may not want to say your immediate behavioral purpose because the audience is unlikely to accept your point of view until you have made your arguments. You might, therefore, omit your purpose until the audience is ready for it, and you might have to increase your audience's readiness to accept your position on the issue.

Other organizational considerations in persuasive speaking concern placement of your arguments, presenting one or more sides of the issue, whether or not to include counterarguments, and using familiar or novel arguments in your speech.

1. *Should my best arguments come first, in the middle, or last in my persuasive speech?* Arguments include information that support your stated proposition. Arguments presented first or early in the body of the speech seem to have more impact in speeches on controversial issues, on topics with which the audience is uninvolved, on topics the audience perceives as interesting, and on topics highly familiar to the audience. On the other hand, arguments seem to have more impact on an audience later in the persuasive speech when audience members are involved in the issue, when the topic is likely to be less interesting, and when the issue is moderately unfamiliar to the audience.[11] No research to date indicates the most important arguments should be presented in the middle of the speech. The middle is the place where attention is likely to wane, so the effective speaker usually builds in human interest stories and interesting supporting materials to maintain audience attention.

2. *Should I present one side of the issue, or both, or many?* A persuasive speaker should present one side of an issue when the audience is friendly, when the speaker's position is the only one the audience is likely to hear, and when the speaker is seeking immediate but temporary change of opinion. A persuasive speaker should present both sides or many sides of an issue when the audience initially disagrees with the speaker or

when it is likely the audience will hear other sides from other people.[12] Presenting both sides or multiple sides to a hostile audience may make the speaker seem more open-minded or less rigid to the audience. Also, presenting the other sides of the issue reduces the impact of counterarguments.

3. *Should I refute counterarguments?* When you deliver your persuasive speech, you are likely to employ a number of arguments with supporting materials to encourage your audience to accept your persuasive proposition. The arguments against your stated position are called **counterarguments.** In a both- or multi-sided persuasive speech, you reveal arguments that might be against your position. The best advice based on current research is to refute counterarguments before proceeding to your own position on the issue, especially when the audience is likely to already know the counterarguments.[13] If you favor freedom of choice on the abortion issue and your audience is familiar with the pro-life (anti-abortion) side of the issue, then you should refute those known counterarguments—point out their relative weaknesses or flaws—before you reveal your own position on the issue.

4. *Should I use familiar or novel arguments in my persuasive speech?* On most topics, you will have to recognize familiar arguments even if it is for the purpose of refuting them. However, research indicates *novel* arguments, or new arguments the audience has not heard before, have more impact than familiar ones.[14] A student who delivered a persuasive speech in favor of gun control pointed out a common counterargument from anti-control forces was that gun registration would provide national enemies with a ready-made list of gun owners. The student who favored gun control pointed out the membership list of the National Rifle Association already provided an extensive list of gun owners that could be used by national enemies. The argument was novel and served to nullify the claim made by the anticontrol side on the issue. You, too, should seek new, novel, or original arguments in support of your own case and against the positions of others. Old and familiar arguments may be useful in your persuasive speech, but the ones the audience has not heard before have greater impact.

The **Monroe motivated sequence,** developed originally by the late Professor Alan Monroe, has been widely acclaimed for its usefulness in organizing speeches.[15] The sequence has five steps:

1. *Attention.* You must gain and maintain audience attention, and you must determine a way to focus audience attention on the content of your speech.

2. *Need.* Once you have the audience's attention, you must show audience members how the speech is relevant to them. You must arouse a need for your information in an informative speech and for the change you suggest in a persuasive speech.

3. *Satisfaction.* Your speech presents the information the audience needs or is a solution to their needs. You satisfy the audience by meeting needs with your plan.
4. *Visualization.* You reinforce your idea in the audience's collective mind by getting audience members to *see* how your information or ideas will help them.
5. *Action.* Once the audience has visualized your idea, you plead for action. The audience might remember your main points in an informative speech and state them to others, or the audience may go out and do what you ask in a persuasive speech.

The Monroe motivated sequence is a kind of problem-solving format that encourages an audience to get concerned about an issue. It is an appropriate organizational pattern for persuasive speeches, especially when the audience is reluctant to change or accept the proposed action.

Ethical Considerations

Ethics or standards of moral conduct are written and unwritten rules of conduct. Many of our standards for ethical behavior are codified into law: we may not slander in speech or libel in writing someone who is not a public figure; we may not start a panic that can endanger the lives of others; we may not advocate the overthrow of our form of government.

Many of the ethics of persuasion are not matters of law, but violations of these unwritten or uncodified rules do have consequences. There is no law against showing a picture of a fetus at the bottom of a wastebasket in your speech against abortion, pointing out acne sufferers in your speech on dermatology, or having your audience unknowingly eat cooked rat meat, but audience members may find your methods so distasteful that they reject you and your persuasive message.

In chapter 12, you learned of some ethical considerations in speaker credibility. The following are some of the generally accepted rules, or ethical standards, that govern the preparation and delivery of persuasive speeches:

1. *Accurate citation of sources.* When you are preparing and delivering your speech, you should be very careful to gather your information and to state it accurately. Specifically, you should reveal where or from whom you received information if it was not your own idea or information. Oral footnotes, written footnotes, and bibliographies should be a continuing reminder to speakers of who said something or where the information was found is important. Making up quotations, attributing an idea to someone who never said it, omitting important qualifiers, quoting out of context, and distorting the information from others are all examples of ethical violations that spring from this rule.

2. *Respect for sources of information.* Have you ever gone to the library to do research for a paper or speech only to find that some inconsiderate individual has already cut out the information you seek? Removing or defacing information meant for everyone is a serious violation of ethics punishable in most colleges and universities. Unfortunately, few of the offenders are caught, but the idea of "doing unto others as you would have them do unto you" is in operation here. Unless all students respect public sources of information, everyone suffers. This rule extends to respect for persons you interview. These people are willing to share information with you, so it behooves you to treat them and their information with respect in person and in your speech.

3. *Respect for your audience.* Persuasion is a process that works most effectively when there is mutual respect between speaker and audience. Attempts to trick the audience into believing something, lying to the audience, distorting the views of your opposition, or exaggerating claims for your own position are all ethically questionable acts. It helps if you already accept the idea that a speaker should speak truthfully and accurately, that the persuasive speaker is best if he or she can accurately portray the opposing arguments and still win with arguments and evidence. If you do not believe that truth works better than the alternatives, then perhaps the fact may sway you that audiences can be very hostile to a person who has tricked them or who has lied, distorted, or exaggerated information simply to meet an immediate behavioral purpose or an ultimate goal.

4. *Respect for your opponent.* Persuasive speeches invite rebuttal. There is nearly always someone inside or outside your audience who thinks your ideas or positions are wrong. A good rule of thumb is to respect your opponent, not only because he or she may be right, but also because an effective persuasive speaker can take the best the opposition has to offer and still convince the audience he or she should be believed. The idea that you should respect your opponent means you should not indulge in name-calling or in bringing up past behaviors that are irrelevant to the issue. It means you should attack the other person's evidence, sources, or logic—not the person. Practical reasons for observing this rule of ethics are that few of the issues about which we persuade are settled, that you may find in time that your opponent's position is better in many respects than your own, and that you will have to live with many issues not resolved in the manner you most desire.

You may get the impression from these four ethical guidelines that every persuasive speaker must be part angel. Not quite. The ethical rules for persuasive speaking allow for considerable verbal combat, for devastating the arguments of others with better or more persuasive evidence, for finding new supporting materials your opposition has not found, and for majority acceptance of your ideas. Persuasive speaking is not for the fainthearted, but it is much cleaner verbal combat if you obey the ethical guidelines that call for accurate citation of sources, respect for written and human sources of information, respect for your audience, and respect for your opponent.

Special Skills for Persuasive Speaking

Just as the informative speaker must learn special skills in defining, describing, explaining, and narrating, the persuasive speaker must learn special skills in arguing, providing evidence, and rebutting the arguments of others. In this section, you discover what an argument is, what tests of evidence are, and how to counter the arguments of others.

Arguments, Evidence, and Critical Thinking

In chapter 5, you learned about critical thinking, observations and **inferences,** arguments, propositions, proofs, inductive and **deductive arguments, enthymemes,** and fallacies. Since persuasive speaking includes the use of reasoning, you should review the critical thinking portion of that chapter to prepare yourself for composing your own speeches and analyzing the persuasive speeches of others.

Remember that an **argument** consists of a proposition and its justification.[16] In persuasive speaking, the proposition embodies what you want the audience to believe or do, for example, communication classes should be required; physicians' fees should be competitive; or welfare payments should be increased. **Evidence** is proof intended to get the audience to accept the proposition, the reasons for acceptance.[17] To add to what you already know about critical thinking, we will now add two criteria that evidence must meet if it is to be persuasive. These two criteria are tests of evidence and believability.

The first criterion is that your proof must meet the **tests of evidence.** The following are some of the questions you can use to test evidence in your speeches or the speeches of others:

1. Is the evidence consistent with other known facts? Did the speaker look at a relatively large number of student co-ops to determine that student co-ops are successful? Have any student co-op stores failed?
2. Would another observer draw the same conclusions? Has anyone other than the speaker determined that other student co-ops are successful? What does the speaker mean by "success"?
3. Does the evidence come from unbiased sources? Does the vice president for student affairs have anything to gain by favoring student co-op bookstores? Who made the claim that students will get better value for their used books? Who said other schools have established successful student co-ops?

The presentation of evidence, both verbal and visual, can help persuade an audience.

4. Is the source of the information qualified by education and/or experience to make a statement about the issue? The vice president may be well educated, but what does he or she know about co-op bookstores? What about the qualifications of the sources for the information on used books or successful co-ops?

5. If the evidence is based on personal experience, how typical was that personal experience? Unless the personal experience was typical, generalizable, realistic, and relevant, it is questionable as evidence.

6. If statistics were used as evidence, were they from a reliable source, comparable with other known information, current, applicable, and interpreted so the audience could understand them?

7. If studies and surveys were employed, were they authoritative, valid, reliable, objective, and generalizable? A study done by persons who favor student co-op bookstores, for instance, would be questionable because the source of the study is biased.

8. Were the speaker's inferences appropriate to the data presented? Did the speaker go too far beyond the evidence in reaching the conclusion that students should establish their own co-op bookstore?

Checklist for a Persuasive Speech

Topic

_____ 1. Have you selected a topic about which your content can be predominantly persuasive?

_____ 2. Have you selected a topic about which your audience is not already persuaded?

_____ 3. Is your topic current?

_____ 4. Have you made it clear to the audience how the topic is important to them?

Purpose

_____ 1. Have you determined a specific persuasive goal for your speech?

_____ 2. Is your speech purpose aimed at adoption, discontinuance, deterrence, or continuance?

_____ 3. Have you determined immediate behavioral purposes for your speech?

_____ 4. How are you going to be able to tell the degree to which you have achieved your purposes?

Content

_____ 1. Have you found physical, psychological, or social motives to which you can appeal?

_____ 2. Have you included information about yourself that can improve your speaker credibility?

_____ 3. Have you used logical appeals that allow reasoning to persuade?

_____ 4. Have you used emotional appeals that might persuade your audience?

_____ 5. Have you used evidence to support your claims?

_____ 6. Have you selected language that is unbiased, clear, and powerful?

9. Was important counterevidence overlooked? Often, in our haste to make a positive case, counterevidence is ignored or omitted. What evidence against student co-ops was left out?

10. What is the speaker's credibility on the topic? Did the speaker earn the right to speak on the topic through research, interviews, and a thorough examination of the issue? Has the speaker had experience related to the issue?

The answers to these ten questions are important. Evidence that meets these tests has met the first requirement of good evidence.

Organization

_____ 1. Where have you placed your best information or argument and why?
_____ 2. Are you presenting one side of the issue or more and why?
_____ 3. Can you refute potential counterarguments?
_____ 4. Have you thought of any new or novel arguments?

Ethics

_____ 1. Do you feel what you are advocating is in the best interests of your audience?
_____ 2. Have you cited sources accurately throughout your speech?
_____ 3. Have you avoided misrepresentation, distortion, exaggeration, and deception by sticking to a high standard of truthfulness?
_____ 4. Have you planned anything in your speech you would not want others to do to you in a persuasive speech?

Special Skills

_____ 1. Have you employed inferences or deductive arguments in your speech?
_____ 2. Have you used tests of evidence and believability to ensure you have the best evidence?
_____ 3. Can you refute opposing arguments in a way that avoids fallacies or highlights the fallacies used by an opponent?

The second requirement of good evidence is that the audience believe in the evidence, trust it, and accept it—**believability.** Finding evidence that meets the tests of evidence is difficult enough, but at least the speaker has some guidelines. Why an audience will not believe evidence is more mysterious. The effective persuasive speaker knows all of the major arguments for, and against, the persuasive proposition. The evidence selected to be used in the speech is chosen from a multitude of arguments both because the evidence meets the tests of evidence and because the speaker's audience analysis indicates this evidence is most likely to be believed. A speaker addressing a group of fundamentalist Christians may know that supporting materials from scripture will fall on friendly ears; that same evidence may not be believed by groups who do not accept the authority of the Bible. The effective persuasive speaker chooses evidence both because it meets the tests of evidence and because it meets audience requirements for believability.

An Example of a Persuasive Speech

The following persuasive speech was presented by the principal of a private school who was the keynote speaker for an African-American Alumni Reunion at a university. The scene was a large room with four hundred guests, returning African-American alumni, and their spouses. The speaker was African American as were all but about twenty white administrators and professors who were invited guests. Can you determine how the speaker was shaping her audience, what action goals she was trying to achieve? Can you tell how the speech was adapted to the particular audience? Can you find her main arguments, and logical and emotional appeals?

Why We Can't Wait

Oh, what a night! An Ohio University Black Alumni Reunion. A delightful idea to get us together in this way. Congratulations to George Reid, Assistant Director of the Office of Alumni Relations, the O. U. Alumni Association, and the wonderful network of Black Alumni chapter leaders who envisioned this occasion. It really has been very special.

Such a special group: highly educated black folks with degrees. Each of us left a part of ourselves here in Athens. Where is your degree from O. U.? Does it hang proudly from your home or office wall? Did you have it mounted and metal engraved? Or is it gathering dust in a corner, a drawer, or hidden in a forgotten box in your basement? Is it lost? Whatever the case, your degree from Ohio University distinguishes you among African Americans. Each year, attainment of that degree becomes more extraordinary.

While the percentage of African Americans who graduate from historically black institutions approximates 50 percent or better, considerably fewer blacks (between 10 percent and 30 percent) graduate from predominantly white colleges and universities. Ohio University is no exception. In a recent study conducted by *Black Issues in Higher Education* to identify the top fifty producers of black graduates, O. U. made only one of the many lists. As an English major, I was pleased to know that "letters" was the category in which our alma mater distinguished itself and that the inhabitants of Ellis Hall are still holding forth. Grouping the results according to types of degrees, these lists were dominated by the historically black colleges and universities. Howard University was first on the undergraduate list and among the top five on several others. The findings of this study simply reaffirm what we already know: Our graduation from O. U. was an extraordinary achievement whenever it occurred, and we still feel good about it.

Because of the dismal truth about blacks in America today, our destiny is inextricably linked to that of our less educated brothers and sisters. Our success is qualified and relative to the overall attainments of our people. It is both a mirror and a lens. A mirror of our incredible history of perseverance against all sorts of odds; a lens through which our race is viewed by others. While the mirror image may be somewhat flattering, the lens is cracked and cloudy.

We are a lot of things, but one thing is sure, we are not examples of how successful the American higher education system can be. In truth and in fact, we are outstanding examples of the system's failure. We did not succeed because of the system; we succeeded in spite of it. Our ebony life stories acquired new meanings upon graduation. We are either maximizing, minimizing or still trying to get a handle on our potential.

Historically, we represent the "Talented Tenth" that W. E. B. DuBois celebrated in the *Souls of Black Folks.* Writing in 1903 he stated:

Fifty years ago the ability of Negro students in any appreciable numbers to master a modern college course would have been difficult to prove. Today it is proved by the fact that 400 Negroes, many of whom have been reported as brilliant students, have received the bachelor's degree from Harvard, Yale, Oberlin and seventy other leading colleges.

Presumably, this four hundred predated John Newton Templeton who was the first African American to graduate from Ohio University in 1828 but was the fourth African-American college graduate in the U. S. Nor would it account for Edward James Roye, the second African American who enrolled at O. U. in 1833 but graduated from Oberlin.

Nevertheless, DuBois, himself a graduate of Harvard, documented the disparity between the number of African-American college and university graduates in the North as compared to the South. He argued eloquently for expanded opportunities for African Americans in higher education, especially in the South. Of course, this argument was the centerpiece of his legendary disagreement with Booker T. Washington, founder of Tuskegee Institute, who promoted vocational training for the masses of black people. DuBois maintained, however, that:

We ought not to forget that despite the pressure of poverty, and despite the active discouragement and even ridicule of friends, the demand for higher training steadily increases among Negro youth: there were, in the years from 1875 to 1880, 22 Negro graduates from Northern colleges; from 1885 to 1890 there were 43, and from 1895 to 1900, nearly 100 graduates. Here, then is the plain thirst for training; by refusing to give this Talented Tenth the key to knowledge, can any sane man imagine that they will lightly lay aside their yearning and contentedly become hewers of wood and drawers of water?

Obviously, DuBois was making a case for **why we can't wait** at the start of this century. His records may have included Joseph Carter Corbin, the third African American to attend O. U., who earned a B. A. in 1853. Corbin was elected Superintendent of Public Education in the state of Arkansas during the Reconstruction period and served as President of the University of Arkansas at Pine Bluff from 1873 to 1890. The first African-American woman to graduate from O. U. did so in 1916, at least thirteen years after publication of the *Souls of Black Folks.* Mrs. Blackburn, who eventually chaired the Home Economics Department at Central State and later taught in West Virginia, is honored with a portrait which hangs in the Alumni Lounge on the second floor of Baker Center.

But, we are the "children of the dream". (And if you have not read the new book so entitled and authored by Audrey Edwards and Dr. Craig Polite, get it ASAP.) What dream? The dream of integration, equality, and equity for all Americans. Collectively, we are the fulfillment of our parents' deepest desires and testimony to their sacrifice. We are the realization of Martin Luther King's dream for America. We're it. The black middle class. What have we accomplished since leaving Athens?

Personal gain notwithstanding, recognized and appreciated, what differences have we made? Creating a better way of life for our own families and our own children is truly meaningful, praiseworthy. But what are we doing for our people? How many brothers and sisters are we preparing to follow in our footsteps? Who are we mentoring, inspiring, cloning, to take our places in the next century? (Hm! Guess we won't be doing what we're doing forever.)

Have you really thought about that and all its implications? To whom will you bequeath your membership in the elite "Talented Tenth?" If we are not planning for that, and most of us aren't, you now know **why we can't wait.** While it is slightly larger at present, the so-called "Talented Tenth" is in danger of shrinking. From where I sit, it can easily become the "Talented Twelfth or Sixteenth or Twentieth." Remember, I work with students at risk of failure and dropping out of a suburban high school. A place like where most of us now live. For me, their failure to achieve is frightening and dangerous. They are not hungry, homeless, or helpless. In fact, they have everything they need and too much of what they want. Virtually all African-American children attend school in only 400 of the 15,700 odd public school districts in America. If the most advantaged among them are in danger of not making it, where does that leave us as a people?

For African Americans, progress has occurred in only the last 130 of the 400 years since slavery began. Of course, some of our ancestors were on this continent long before then. In fact, when Christopher Columbus got lost and drifted in this direction, it's ludicrous to think he called himself discovering anybody, especially us! Other people are free to believe he discovered them if they want to, but the guy was late by a few hundred years! By then, brothers and sisters who look like me and you had been here so long, our kinfolks in mother Africa had written them off as prodigals. But I digress!

When we look back at what has happened in the past fifty years to African Americans, we know that we live in a world to which most black people do not, cannot, and will not have access. Despite Roosevelt's New Deal, World War II, the G.I. Bill, ***Brown vs. the Topeka Board of Education,*** the Civil Rights movement, Johnson's Great Society, Vietnam, affirmative action, Reaganomics, and "education presidents," something far short of phenomenal progress has occurred among most of our people.

The truth is:

- That black students are considered by anyone and everyone to be "at risk" for underachievement, dropping out, unemployment, poverty, chemical addiction, incarceration, murder, and parenthood without the benefit of marriage.

- That black student achievement consistently falls below national norms on nearly every measure in all categories year after year.

- That black students are three times more likely to be labeled mentally handicapped and enrolled in special education classes (Between 1976 and 1982, enrollment in the learning disability category in public schools increased by 125 percent).

- That black students are three times more represented in the 25 percent of students who drop out of high school after grade nine or higher.

- That less than 25 percent of this year's black high school graduates will enter college in September, as compared to nearly 60 percent in 1979.

- That nearly a third of those who enter college will require remediation in computation, comprehension, and writing skill development.

- That only 12 percent of black students who enter college in September are likely to graduate; only 4 percent of those will go to graduate school.

- That the public schools continue to get blacker (and browner), while the ranks of black educators has declined from more than 8 percent of the total force in 1979 to less than 5 percent today.

   At the same time, however, the new black upper class to which we belong came into fruition.

- In 1967, less than 5 percent of black families were counted in the middle class with household incomes of $15,000 or more. By 1987, 36 percent of African Americans had middle class incomes of $25,000 or more.

- In 1970, only 6.9 percent of African Americans had such incomes; but by 1989, that figure had grown to 11.5 percent. Between 1970 and 1989, the percentage of blacks who had upper middle-class incomes of $50,000 grew by 182 percent.

- In 1988, the median net worth of black households in the top 20 percent of the income distribution was $47,160, while the net worth of all black households in 1988 was only $4,169, and 29 percent of black households had a zero or negative net worth.

By contrast with white America the discrepancy is glaring:

- In the top 20 percent of the incomes distribution, white households' median net worth was $119,000 compared to $47,000 for African-American households.

In the face of these truths, we should be doing more than celebrating ourselves. Be honest. Great as this reunion is, weekends like this are made for egomaniacs. Only those who consider themselves successful really attend. Isn't that why you have been spending time asking about "so and so" or wondering "whatever happened to. . . ?"

Black people are still largely miseducated in this country. That includes graduates of Ohio University. None of the degree programs here, save Black studies, are teaching African Americans "how to get over." We had to learn, or are learning, that for ourselves, from one another—our peers, our elders; and it isn't easy. For black folks, having a degree signifies the skills and competencies you may possess. But the opportunity to utilize those competencies to your own benefit is related directly to behaviors—how we act and interact in the dominant society. Knowing what to do means nothing if we don't know how to act.

Because most of us do not work for ourselves, we are dependent upon white America for the opportunity to succeed. Regrettably, racism is alive and well. In America, it still does not matter how much you know or where you went to school. If you are black, white America still thinks you have "your place." That place may not be the one you are seeking.

Based upon our marginal success as educated professionals, many in the dominant society now believe wrongly that too many blacks have found their way to the middle class. Until Rodney King and the L.A. riots, they formulated their beliefs about African Americans mostly on the blacks readily seen employed in low-end, high-visibility jobs in banks, airports, hotels, restaurants, department stores, and reception areas throughout corporate America. Of course, many of these jobs are changing complexion as downsizing, glass ceilings, and retrenchment strategies are being implemented. But the cosmetic truth about placing spooks by the door never enters their minds. But some of us have sat, will sit, or are sitting by those doors trying to get over. But I don't knock it. Being inside these diminishing doors looking out makes inordinately more sense than what's happening outside of them.

A new underclass has been growing which finds more and more blacks illiterate, unemployed, underemployed, impoverished, and/or chemically dependent. Fewer and fewer of them will achieve our success in the first half of the next century. They are disenfranchised and disillusioned with the system as well as with us. We have abandoned the inner cities in favor of suburbia. Our attempts at "do-gooderism" ring hollow to our brothers and sisters with less. What alienates us from our own people is not race or color, but class.

For our part, some of us don't make matters any better. Despite our education, it is a fact that some of us still do not know how to wear success. I have been black three times. I know us. Sometimes the more educated we are, the worse we are. We get carried away. We get full of ourselves. We ego trip and look down on others. We outgrow our parents and neighbors and childhood friends. We become intolerant of the lesser educated. We become fools!

White America is unimpressed with how impressed we are with ourselves. White America is unfazed by the number of degrees we can earn or honors we attain. White America is undaunted by how well we dress, the types of cars we prefer to drive; unless, of course, we are buying our clothes and cars from them or selling for them. They know that we do not support black business and that we spend 96 cents of every dollar in our collective $200 billion dollar annual income with them. They know better than we how vulnerable we are as a people; and they make book on it. They get rich on it. They know what we've been taught; but they also know how little we may have learned. They know that our education was largely devoid of information about the behaviors that account for *their* success.

DuBois reminds us that:

the function of the university is not simply to teach bread winning, or to furnish teachers for the public schools or to be a center of polite society; it is, above all, to be the organ of that fine adjustment between real life and the growing knowledge of life, an adjustment which forms the secret of civilization.

Without a concentrated effort to recruit our replacements, our accomplishments will be pivotal in African-American history, but incidental, like Reconstruction. You recall that all this really neat stuff happened to emancipated blacks and freedmen for a brief period in the nineteenth century, only to be followed by an extensive and sustained era of retrenchment. Save what has happened to us and others like us from the 1960s till now, the twentieth century will likely end pretty much like it began for most African Americans.

So, it's simply not enough to be a "credit" to our race; we must do more. The uniqueness of our place in black history requires that we protect and promote whatever gains we think we've made. For me, assuming this responsibility is an imperative. As this portion of our history is being written, I want to be on the right side of it. I want to know that, in my own limited way, I fully understood and accepted the responsibility to perpetuate the legacy. It is a legacy of accomplishment which qualified all of us for inclusion in DuBois' famous fraction.

We're running out of time—another reason **why we can't wait.** We have something really important to do and little time to get it done. Or how much longer are we going to wait for somebody else to get us moving, for somebody else to notify us and unify us? While we are here in Athens, we have a great opportunity to plan for the perpetuation of our legacy. There is so much that we could do if we put our minds to it. Those minds that were nurtured in the Hocking Valley, between the rolling hills and sloping greens of the most beautiful campus in Ohio.

Now, I know what I'm asking. I'm asking you to think about making a commitment. Preservation of our legacy at Ohio University can take many forms. Let me suggest a few.

First and foremost, we should join our local or regional O. U. Black Alumni Chapter. All of us are gainfully employed, so we can afford the dues. But, there are other "dos" (D-O-S). These will require us to share our most precious possession—time. Our time should be spent in traditional and nontraditional ways. Do fund scholarships, do recruit prospective students, do mentor and hire Ohio University graduates. Such alumni activities fall into the traditional category.

But this not an either/or proposition. We must engage in both traditional and nontraditional initiatives. What about creating something new? What would it mean to establish an endowed chair which could rotate biannually among the colleges of the university we all represent? And what if that chair were dedicated to the perpetuation of black scholarship in each field we represent? And what if such a chair were responsible to conduct research and disseminate findings which would not only expand the body of knowledge in each area but infuse it with culturally relevant information? Not to your liking?

Well, what about a lecture series featuring distinguished African Americans in each field we represent and some that we don't? Such a series could be sponsored annually in any month other than February so as to dispel the myth that that is the only appropriate time to celebrate African-American excellence. These are just a couple of ideas rolling around in my head. If we would put our minds to it, we could create something significant—something that the university would fall over itself trying to promote.

Both of these ideas require much more than substantial amounts of money. They would require all of the human and material resources we could muster. Another reason **why we can't wait.**

In the gap between what is and what ought to be stands the "waiting room" of life. That room is bursting at the seams with people who cannot find the time to be involved. Each of us know people who cram themselves into that space for life. Some of them are our professional colleagues, neighbors, family members, and friends. But not us; we are different. Most of us are busy for real, but we know that only busy people take time and make time to do the right thing. It's something to think about.

Our coming together to socialize and reminisce is great. But partying and "remembering when" will not impact our people. Our coming together, of necessity, must be purposeful in the long term. It must be meaningful in ways that make a difference. Our togetherness should anticipate the twenty-first century. And if coming together in this way is the most effective means to focus our attention upon our responsibility, then so be it.

Finally, we are the missing pages of this document. (Black History of O. U. and Athens.) I want us to finish writing it. It should be a book, not a booklet. It should be a multivolume series of books about the legacy of excellence among African Americans who passed through Ohio University. The new alumni directory is a start. It can be the source for developing the countless success stories we are writing with our lives. The story of how we came, saw, and conquered should not only become a lasting part of the university's more recent history, but evidence of our commitment to perpetuate a remarkable legacy of excellence.

In the words of British poet Edwin Markham:

There is a destiny that makes us brothers. None goes his way alone. For what we put into the lives of others, comes back into our own.

But in the less familiar but still memorable words of the late Dr. Benjamin E. Mays, long-time president of Morehouse:

I have only just a minute,

Only sixty seconds in it,

Forced upon me—can't refuse it,

Didn't seek it, didn't choose it.

But it's up to me to use it.

I must suffer if I lose it.

Give account if I abuse it,

Just a tiny little minute—

But eternity is in it.

Resisting Persuasion

At the beginning of this chapter, we promised to tell you how to persuade and how to be a consumer of persuasion. In this section, we suggest some measures you can take to resist persuasion, not only in public speaking, but as you face it on the telephone, from salespeople, and in advertising.

1. *Your best form of resistance is avoidance.* You do not have to watch or read advertising, go into stores where you do not intend to buy, listen to telemarketers, or watch half-hour television advertisements posing as programs.

2. *You should exercise healthy skepticism about all messages.* Persuaders who are seeking easy prey look for the uneducated, the desperate, the angry, and the unsuspecting. They avoid people who are educated, articulate, cautious, and careful. You should use your knowledge of argumentation, evidence, and proof to analyze claims.

3. *You should on serious matters check claims with other unbiased sources.* A good rule is to verify any persuasive claims with at least two other sources of information. A politician tells you that lower taxes will be good for you. What do the editorials, the political commentators, and the opposition say about that plan? Consumer magazines, especially those that take no advertising, are less likely to be biased as are news sources that embrace objectivity.

4. *You should check out the credibility of the source.* Be suspicious if a salesperson will not reveal the phone numbers of satisfied customers, if a business is new or changes location often, and if a speaker has a questionable reputation for truth or reliability. Credible sources have people, institutions, and satisfied audiences who can vouch for them. Con artists typically do not. Two major television evangelists have been discredited in recent years over verifiable charges that they violated ethical codes.

5. *You should not be in a hurry to accept a persuasive appeal.* Most states have laws that allow even a signed contract to be rejected by the customer in the first twenty-four to forty-eight hours—in case you have second thoughts. Accepting claims on impulse is a dangerous practice that you can avoid by never making an important decision in the context of a sales pitch. Have you ever heard of a business person who refuses to take the money the next day?

6. *You should question the ethical basis of proposed actions.* Angry people are easy to turn to violence; desperate people will willingly turn to desperate measures; and frustrated people can be easily convinced to undermine. You need to ask if the proposed action is self-serving, if it is based on pitting one group against another, and if it is going to be good for you when viewed in retrospect.

7. *You should use your knowledge and experience to analyze persuasive claims.* If a claim sounds too good to be true, it probably is too good to be true. If you have a "gut feeling" that a claim seems wrong, you should find out why. You should use all you know about logic, evidence, and proof to see if the persuader is drawing a sound conclusion or making an inferential leap that is justified by the evidence. Finally, all evidence should be open to scrutiny. Check it out.

8. *You should use your own values as a check against fraudulent claims.* If someone is trying to get you to do something that runs counter to what you learned in your religion, in your home, from your knowledge of the law, or from your friends, you should be wary. Sales always enrich the seller, but infrequently enrich the buyer. You can choose to sacrifice, but you should not sacrifice unwittingly. Your values are good protection

against those who would cheat you. It is all right to ask the question, "What would my parents, my friends, my neighbors, my professor, or the church think of this decision?"

9. ***Check what persuaders say against what they do.*** You might add: judge them more by what they do than by what they say. Talk may not be cheap but it costs less than deeds, and the proof of what a person says is in their behavior. Our environmental President [Bush] looked a bit silly when he refused to sign an international environmental agreement, and many an "education governor" has cut the budget for education. You learn to trust someone who does what they say; you learn to distrust those who say one thing and do another.

10. ***Use your freedom of expression and freedom of choice as protection against unethical persuaders.*** In the United States, you can hear competing ideas and the choice is yours. You can educate yourself about issues and ideas by reading, watching, and listening. Education and learning are powerful protection against persuaders who would take advantage of you. Use your freedoms to help you defend yourself.

As this chapter was being written, a hapless telemarketer called, this time during breakfast instead of during dinner. He offered me "one million dollars in the *Time* magazine sweepstakes to add my name to the list—with no obligation to buy." "Wouldn't I like to be a millionaire?" he inquired. Whoow. Hold on. What is happening here? First, the million dollars was to get my attention. Second, entering my name in a sweepstakes is at best a lotto ticket with a better chance of death by lightening than of winning. Third, by asking if I want to be a millionaire, he expects a "yes" response, to which he will add a series of other "yes" responses until he gets you to say "yes" to a trial subscription—for some minimal payment—to the magazine. Following the first recommendation for resisting persuasion, I told him I was ***not*** interested in becoming a millionaire, thanked him, and hung up the phone. That is resisting unwanted persuasion. Now that you know ten suggestions for resisting persuasion, you too can practice the strategies for keeping others from manipulating your mind and your pocketbook.

Summary

Preparing a persuasive speech requires that we classify our ultimate purpose in behavioral terms as a speech of adoption, discontinuance, deterrence, or continuance; we find an appropriate topic; and we write an ultimate goal and immediate behavioral purposes for persuasion.

Audience members may be persuaded through motivational appeals (physical, psychological, and social), speaker credibility, logical appeals, and emotional appeals. The organization of a persuasive speech includes the placement of arguments and evidence, the number of sides presented to different kinds of audiences, the use of refutation, and the use of familiar and novel arguments.

Learn to use persuasion and to resist it by being skeptical, cautious, ethical, analytical, and intelligent. Take advantage of your freedom to speak, listen, and learn, so no one can take advantage of you through persuasion, a skill that can be used for good or for ill. Above all, practice what you have learned in this text so you can enrich your own life.

Persuasive Speech Performance

Deliver an eight-to-ten-minute persuasive speech in which you try to achieve immediate behavioral purposes consistent with an ultimate action goal, such as adoption or discontinuance. The speech should fulfill the functions of an introduction (see chapter 14), with special emphasis on establishing your credibility (see chapter 12). The speech should also fulfill the functions of a conclusion (see chapter 14). The body of the speech should consist of at least three major arguments with supporting materials (evidence) selected because of their appropriateness for your audience. Include oral footnotes and, if appropriate, visual aids (see chapter 15). Deliver the speech extemporaneously with as much eye contact and as little attention to notes as possible.

Persuasive Speech Document

Put the title of your persuasive speech and your name at the top of a sheet of paper. State your ultimate action goal and your immediate behavioral purposes. Then compose a manuscript of your persuasive speech, with sidenotes to indicate what functions you are fulfilling in the introduction and conclusion, what your main and subpoints are, and what kinds of evidence you are using. Conclude with endnotes or footnotes and a bibliography in proper form.

Key Terms

adoption Inducing an audience to accept a new idea, attitude, belief, or product and to demonstrate that acceptance by behavioral change; an action goal of the persuasive speech.

arguments Propositions and justifications or evidence used to persuade.

believability The idea an argument has to go beyond logic and common sense; it must also be acceptable to an audience before it will be effective in a speech.

boomerang effect Occurs when the audience's attitudes toward the speaker's position on a topic become more negative during the speech.

continuance Persuading an audience to continue present behavior; an action goal of the persuasive speech.

counterarguments Rebuttals to an argument.

deductive arguments Arguments based on a major premise, a minor premise, and a conclusion, rather than on evidence.

deterrence Persuading an audience to avoid some activity; an action goal of the persuasive speech.

discontinuance Inducing an audience to stop doing something; an action goal of the persuasive speech.

emotional appeals Persuading audience members to change an attitude or behavior through an appeal—usually in a narrative form—to their emotions.

enthymeme A deductive argument with a missing premise.

evidence Anything that constitutes proof of a proposition.

inference Conclusions drawn from observation.

justification All of the evidence that can be gathered in support of a proposition.

logical appeals Use of propositions and proofs to persuade an audience.

Monroe motivated sequence A problem-solving format that encourages an audience to become concerned about an issue; especially appropriate for a persuasive speech.

persuasion An ongoing process in which verbal and nonverbal messages shape, reinforce, and change people's responses.

tests of evidence Questions used to test evidence in a speech.

Appendix

Interviewing for a Job

The job interview is a specialized form of interpersonal communication. College students are likely to have experienced job interviews, and older students may have experienced many. Because the stakes are high in most job interviews, everyone needs to learn how to improve their performance. This appendix is provided so you can learn what an interview is, how it works, and how you can do your best.

What is a Job Interview?

A **job interview** is a dyadic exchange in which the interviewer asks most of the questions, the interviewee provides the answers, and the participants proceed in a purposeful manner toward a predetermined goal. The interview is dyadic because it usually consists of two people; it is an exchange because it is highly interactive; it is a question-and-answer format because the interviewer uses about 30 percent of the time, and the interviewee uses about 70 percent of the time;[1] it is purposeful because the interviewer and the interviewee have an agenda; and it has a predetermined goal because the interviewer is seeking an employee and the interviewee is seeking a job.

How Do You Prepare for an Interview?

As in public speaking, audience analysis is a very useful skill in interviewing. In this case, the company and the interviewer are your audience, and your task is to discover as much as possible about the company and the interviewer as you can. The following five steps outline how you can gather this information:

1. *Be highly aware of every detail of the job description.* You need to match your qualifications with the company's needs. If the position description says you need "communication skills," then you need to reveal or demonstrate your skills. If the position description says you are expected to have experience, you need to explain how your experience would help the company.
2. *Find out as much as you can about the company, firm, or business that is doing the hiring.* An inside informant, such as an alumn who already works for the company, is very valuable. Another source of information is

any information the public relations people say about the company, its employees, its products, and even its pictures. The photos often reveal the company's culture, the kind of clothing the employees wear, the importance of machines and technology, the quantity and quality of their products. The company's annual report, directories that name the officers and their job titles, and business and industrial magazines and trade journals can provide valuable information about the firm.

3. *Anticipate questions.* What are the most likely lines of inquiry? How will you answer such questions as "Why are you interested in a sales position? How will your major, your experience, or your interests help in this position? Why are you interested in this particular company?" Having prepared, but not rehearsed answers, will allow you to be concise and fluent.

4. *Decide what to bring to the interview and how to make an impression on the interviewer.* A cover letter explaining your interest in the position and a resumé are appropriate if the interviewer does not already have these items. Depending on the type of job, other items may be of interest, such as a few examples of your work, a portfolio of your best work, or a video of your best productions. While it is better to overdress than to underdress, it is best to dress the way people dress in that job for that company.

    You should figure out before the interview any way that you are special. Do you speak more than one language? Have you traveled more than most people or lived in more parts of the country? Are you particularly good at something that most people are not? Were you an Eagle scout, a concert pianist, an actress or something else that might make you stand out from the other applicants?

5. *Come to the interview prepared with some questions that you have about the company or the position for which you are applying.* Do you know what you expect to be paid? Do you know if the company provides benefits, such as preventive health care, disability, pension, major medical, dental, eye, or recreational opportunities? Do employees get commissions, bonuses, paid or unpaid vacations, opportunities for advancement, or relocations? How long do people ordinarily stay in entry-level positions? What kind of activities and accomplishments are rewarded? Intelligent questions can demonstrate serious interest in the job.

What Happens in the Interview?

The interview opens with introductions and handshakes. You should remember that in interviews the interviewer is making judgments about you, and first impressions are important.[2] Do you seem confident, poised, and knowledgeable? Do you look and act like people who already work for the company? Do you seem like someone who will fit in with the "culture" of the company? Similarly, you can start making judgments about the interviewer and the company he or she represents.

The interviewer usually controls the amount of time spent on each portion of the interview. If the interviewer wants a casual opening with "small talk" about the interviewing room, the weather, and your university, then the interviewee should "go with the flow." Both parties are just getting acquainted, but both are making judgments about the other.

As the interview moves into the main portion, the interviewer will begin to ask substantive questions about your qualifications. The twelve questions asked most frequently by interviewers in an employment agency follow:

1. What brings you to this agency?
2. What sort of a job are you looking for?
3. What other efforts have you made to find a job?
4. Why do you want to leave your present job?
5. What percentage of your college expenses did you earn yourself?
6. What do you think of your present job?
7. What makes you think you would be good at the new job?
8. This question is unspoken. The interviewer simply falls silent, a device to test the applicant. Some applicants feel that they must keep the ball rolling.
9. What sort of money are you looking for?
10. What do your parents do?
11. What are your best qualities?
12. Since no one is perfect, what are your worst qualities?[3]
    The last question and question number 8 are examples of what are called "stress questions," questions that are purposely difficult to answer.

The following are examples of other stress questions:

• What will you do with your first paycheck?

• What skeletons do you have in your closet?

• If I asked your friends what they liked least about you, what would they say?

Whatever your answers to these questions, you should understand that they—like many of the others—are intended to discover if you are ambitious, disciplined, personable, poised, and dedicated. If you are a skillful interviewee you can answer the stress questions by discerning what the real question is. For instance, the question about your first paycheck could be answered by "I would start to pay off my student loans," "I would need it to set up an apartment," or "I would get a car that I could use for my job." One student disarmed the interviewer by saying, "I would buy a Bible for my mother."

What do you have to be careful about in the substantive part of the interview? Watch your attitude. Be careful not to come across as arrogant, insincere, prejudiced, cynical, immature, impolite, self-centered, unfocused, uninterested, or materialistic.[4] Instead, try to concentrate on what the company wants and how you can contribute. Work on discerning what they are looking for and showing how you can fit.

Be careful not to give overly long answers to the questions, and be careful not to be too brief. A lot of "yes" and "no" answers is unsatisfactory, and an answer that lasts over a minute or two is usually too much.

After you have given the interviewer ample time to find out what she wants to know about you, you should make sure you have time to ask a few questions of your own. You should not have an entire grocery list of questions, just a few important ones about the company's expectations, opportunities, and prospects. As much as possible, the questions should be posed as company-centered, and not self-centered. For example, instead of saying, "How much will I earn?" you can say, "What do people who are already in this position like most and least about it?" or "Do people make a career out of this kind of work, or do they tend to move up or over to other positions?"

The end of the interview is a good place to clear up any misconceptions about you or your qualifications. It is also a good time to summarize your best points about your qualifications and special interests in the position. It ends with thanks for the interview and any last expressions of your desire to have the position. Make sure you get the interviewer's business card if you have not done so already.

After the interview, it is a good idea to follow up with a brief letter to the interviewer, reminding him or her of who you are and how interested you are in the position. Since interviewers often talk with dozens of people per day, it is wise to include something in the letter about what happened in the interview as a reminder.

What Do Interviewers Criticize?

You might find useful the behaviors that interviewers criticize most often. What exactly do interviewers mean when they say that interviewees have poor communication skills, seem ill-prepared for the interview, show a lack of interest or motivation, and have unrealistic expectations?

What interviewers see as *poor communication skills* are long, rambling responses; too little specificity, concreteness, and descriptiveness; nonverbal and verbal signs of nervousness; poor command of the language; and signs of dishonesty. One study showed that interviewees who used short answers, long pauses, vagueness, constant smiling, shifting posture, and grooming behavior (fixing hair, brushing off lapels, adjusting clothing) were perceived as dishonest.[5] Experienced interviewers become highly skilled at spotting evasive answers, nonverbal indicators of uneasiness, and cues of dishonesty. You will have fewer problems as an interviewee if you talk neither too little nor too much, if you give complete but not necessarily comprehensive answers, and if you answer all questions truthfully.

When interviewers say that an interviewee is *ill-prepared for the interview,* they usually mean that the interviewee does not know the position description, the company, or the product. Another sign of an ill-prepared interviewee is a lack of intelligent questions during the interview. An interviewee who has prepared carefully for the interview, who has practiced for the interview, and who has prepared possible answers for potential questions is more likely to impress the interviewer. Still another sign of an ill-prepared interviewee is one who does not know how to dress appropriately for the interview.

What do interviewers mean by *lack of interest or motivation?* A lack of interest is indicated if the interviewee does not know how this particular job fits into his or her career goals. Lack of interest is indicated also if the interviewee seems unenthusiastic about the interview or the prospect of employment. An interviewee who too often answers, "I don't know" may be signaling a lack of forethought or interest. An interviewee who is afraid of the interview to the point of self-consciousness may be unable to think beyond the self to the concerns of the interviewer.

A lack of motivation might be signaled by the interviewee who is too agreeable or too disagreeable. You do not have to be delighted by everything a job has to offer, but you do have to show some verbal and nonverbal signs that you want to do the job. One college graduate was asked by the interviewer why she liked her part-time job in college. Her answer: "Because the job was close to home, and it started late in the day. It was easy to get to and didn't interrupt my sleep." The interviewer understood her message to be that her personal schedule was more important than her work schedule. On the other hand, you do not have to be a wimp who willingly accepts low pay, poor hours, no benefits, and no job security. The interviewer could be trying to find out how little the company can get by with in hiring you.

When an interviewer says that an interviewee has *unrealistic expectations,* that judgment usually means that the interviewee wants too much pay, too many perks, or wants to start too high on the organizational ladder. New employees usually do not get the fancy offices, private secretaries, and a company car. They often do get weekend and night shifts, long hours, more travel, and less privacy. In a deep recession, college graduates take jobs that used to go to high school graduates. During an economic boom, salaries and benefits soar, and college graduates get the best jobs. In good times and bad, college graduates often overestimate their starting place, their time in the entry-level position, and their prospects for advancement. Sometimes, too, college graduates have a negative attitude about the very jobs that many companies use to start their employees. A serious talk with alumni who have been out for a year or two will help you begin with realistic expectations.

How to Cope with Rejection

You will not get every job for which you apply. Even if you have faced rejection before, the failure to secure a job that you really wanted is a bitter pill to swallow. Some people liken it to being rejected by a lover because it seems like such a personal rejection. What can you do to improve your chances and retain your positive self-esteem?

One idea is to learn from every interview. After you complete an interview, think over everything that you remember that went well—or didn't go well. If some of your answers were less than satisfactory, think of a different way to answer them. If you felt uncomfortable in the situation, unduly nervous for instance, you had better role play with a friend or relative, go to more interviews, or prepare more carefully so you are not caught unaware. You can improve your interviewing performance by regarding every interview as a learning experience.

Another approach is to be inventive about your audience analysis. Have you ever gone to the company that you want to work for to see what they do and how they do it? Have you gone to the alumni association to see if any graduates from your school work for the company? Alumni are usually very willing to talk with you on the phone or in person about the firm, and they might even become an advocate on your behalf. Have you written to the company for additional information about them? Most companies are more than willing to share information with a prospective employee.

Key Term

job interview   Dyadic exchange in which the interviewer asks most of the questions, the interviewee provides the answers, and the participants proceed in a purposeful manner toward a predetermined goal.

Notes

Chapter 1

1. See, for example, Paul T. Rankin, "Measurements of the Ability to Understand the Spoken Language" (Ph.D. diss., University of Michigan, 1926); Paul T. Rankin, "Listening Ability: Its Importance, Measurement, and Development," *Chicago Schools Journal* 12 (1930): 177; and J. Donald Weinrauch and John R. Swanda, Jr., "Examining the Significance of Listening: An Exploratory Study of Contemporary Management," *Journal of Business Communication* 13 (Fall 1975): 25–32.

2. See, for example, Ritch L. Sorenson and Judy C. Pearson, "Alumni Perspectives on Speech Communication Training: Implications for Communication Faculty," *Communication Education* 30 (1981): 299–307; Vincent Di Salvo, David C. Larsen, and William J. Seiler, "Communication Skills Needed by Persons in Business Organizations," *Communication Education* 25 (1976): 69–75; and Dan H. Swensen, "Relative Importance of Business Communication Skills for the Next Ten Years," *Journal of Business Communication* 17 (Winter 1980): 41–49.

3. *Bladerunner* is a 1982 film produced in the U.S.A. and directed by Ridley Scott.

4. John Grisham, *Pelican Brief* (New York: Doubleday, 1992).

5. Robert N. Bellah, et al., *The Good Society* (New York: Knoff, 1991).

6. David K. Berlo, *The Process of Communication* (New York: Holt, Rinehart & Winston, 1960).

7. Carl R. Rogers, *On Becoming A Person* (Boston: Houghton Mifflin, 1961), 18.

8. Students who wish to learn more about non-human communication systems are directed to Jane Goodall, *The Chimpanzees of Gombe* (Cambridge, MA: Belknap-Harvard, 1986).

9. Carl R. Rogers, *Client-Centered Therapy* (Boston: Houghton Mifflin, 1951), 483.

10. Dean C. Barnlund, "A Transactional Model of Communication," in *Foundations of Communication Theory,* eds. Kenneth K. Sereno and C. David Mortensen (New York: Harper & Row, 1970), 98–101.

11. George Herbert Mead, quoted in *Sociology: Human Society* by Melvin De Fleur et al. (Glenview, IL: Scott, Foresman, 1977), 138.

12. Blaine Goss, *Processing Communication* (Belmont, CA: Wadsworth, 1982).

Chapter 2

1. See, for example, C. R. Berger and R. J. Calabrese, "Some Explorations in Initial Interaction and Beyond: Toward a Developmental Theory of Interpersonal Communication," *Human Communication Research* 1 (1975): 99–112.

2. Richard Restak, *The Brain* (New York: Bantam Books, 1984), 244.

3. Marshall R. Singer, "Culture: A Perceptual Approach." In *Intercultural Communication: A Reader,* 4th ed., ed. Larry A. Samovar and Richard E. Porter (Belmont, CA: Wadsworth, 1985), 63.

4. V. P. Richmond and D. Robertson, "Communication Apprehension as a Function of Being Raised in an Urban or Rural Environment" (Monograph, West Virginia Northern Community College, 1976).

5. Judy C. Pearson, *Gender and Communication* (Dubuque, IA: Wm. C. Brown Publishers, 1985).

6. Alistair B. Fraser, "Fata Morgana—The Grand Illusion," *Psychology Today* 9 (January 1976): 22.

Chapter 3

1. William Schultz, *Here Comes Everybody.* 2d ed. (New York: Irvington, 1982).

2. Jane Anderson, "Discover Yourself: Go Hiking Alone," Fort Wayne *Journal Gazette* (21 March 1976).

3. Abraham H. Maslow, "Hierarchy of Needs," in *Motivation and Personality,* 2d ed. (New York: Harper & Row, 1970): 35–72.

4. Paul Watzlawick, Janet Helmick Beavin, and Don D. Jackson, *Pragmatics of Human Communication: A Study of Interactional Patterns, Pathologies, and Paradoxes* (New York: W. W. Norton, 1967).

5. See, for example, Anthony G. Greenwald, Francis S. Bellezza, and Mahzarin R. Banaji, "Is Self-Esteem a Central Ingredient of the Self-Concept?" *Personality and Social Psychology Bulletin* 14 (1988): 34–45.

6. Michael Argyle, *Social Interaction* (New York: Atherton, 1969), 133.

7. Ann H. Baumgardner and Paul E. Levy, "Role of Self-Esteem in Perceptions of Ability and Effort: Illogic or Insight?" *Personality and Social Psychology Bulletin* 14 (1988): 429–38.

8. Robert Rosenthal and Lenore Jacobson, *Pygmalion in the Classroom: Teacher Expectation and Pupils' Intellectual Development* (New York: Holt, Rinehart & Winston, 1968), vii.

9. Walker Percy, *Lost in the Cosmos: The Last Self-Help Book* (New York: Farrar, Straus and Giroux, 1983), 39–40.

10. Nancy J. Bell and William Carver, "A Reevaluation of Gender Label Effects: Expectant Mothers' Responses to Infants," *Child Development* 51 (1980): 925–27.

11. J. Condry and S. Condry, "Sex Differences: A Study of the Eye of the Beholder," *Child Development* 47 (1976): 812–19.

12. Bonni R. Seegmiller, "Sex-Typed Behavior in Pre-Schoolers: Sex, Age, and Social Class Effects," *Journal of Psychology* 104 (1980): 31–33.

13. S. Tibbits, "Sex-Role Stereotyping in the Lower Grades: Part of a Solution," *Journal of Vocational Behavior* 6 (1975): 255–61.

14. A. B. Heilbrun, "Measurement of Masculine and Feminine Sex Role Identities as Independent Dimensions," *Journal of Consulting and Clinical Psychology* 44 (1976): 183–90.

15. Sandra L. Bem, "The Measurement of Psychological Androgyny," *Journal of Consulting and Clinical Psychology* 42 (1974): 155–62.

16. See, for example, Diana M. Zuckerman, "Self-Esteem, Self-Concept and the Life Goals and Sex-Role Attitudes of College Students," *Journal of Personality* 48 (1980): 149–62.

17. See, for example, Alice Ross Gold, Lorelei R. Brush, and Eve R. Sprotzer, "Developmental Changes in Self-Perceptions of Intelligence and Self-Confidence," *Psychology of Women Quarterly* 5 (1980): 231–39.

18. Susan Pomerantz and Robert C. House, "Liberated versus Traditional Women's Performance Satisfaction and Perceptions of Ability," *The Journal of Psychology* 95 (1977): 205–11.

19. Lynn L. Gigy, "Self-Concept of Single Women," *Psychology of Women Quarterly* 5 (1980): 321–40.

20. Constance J. Seidner, "Interaction of Sex and Locus of Control in Predicting Self-Esteem," *Psychological Reports* (1978): 895–98.

21. Judy C. Pearson, "Academic Women: How to Succeed in the University" (Paper presented to the Speech Communication Association, Chicago, Illinois, 1986).

Chapter 4

1. Robert N. Bostrom and Carol L. Bryant, "Factors in the Retention of Information Presented Orally: The Role of Short-Term Listening," *Western Journal of Speech Communication* 44 (1980): 137–45.

2. Some of the complexities of the memory of both auditory and visual stimuli are explored in Frank R. Schab and Robert G. Crowder's, "Accuracy of Temporal Coding: Auditory-Visual Comparisons," *Memory and Cognition* 17 (1989): 384–97.

3. Ralph G. Nichols and Leonard A. Stevens, "Listening to People," *Harvard Business Review* 35 (1957): 85–92.

4. Larry R. Smeltzner and Kittie W. Watson, "Listening: An Empirical Comparison of Discussion Length and Level of Incentive," *Central States Speech Journal* 35 (Fall 1984): 166–70.

5. P. T. Rankin, "The Measurement of the Ability to Understand Spoken Language," *Dissertation Abstracts* 12 (1926): 847.

6. J. Donald Weinrauch and John R. Swanda, Jr., "Examining the Significance of Listening: An Exploratory Study of Contemporary Management," *Journal of Business Communication* 13 (February 1975): 25–32.

7. Elyse K. Werner, "A Study of Communication Time" (Master's thesis, University of Maryland, 1975).

8. See, for example, Miriam E. Wilt, "A Study of Teacher Awareness of Listening as a Factor in Elementary Education," *Journal of Educational Research* 43 (1950): 626; D. Bird, "Have You Tried Listening?" *Journal of the American Dietetic Association* 30 (1954): 225–30; and B. Markgraf, "An Observational Study Determining the Amount of Time That Students in the Tenth and Twelfth Grades Are Expected to Listen in the Classroom" (Master's thesis, University of Wisconsin, 1957).

9. L. Barker, R. Edwards, C. Gaines, K. Gladney, and F. Holley, "An Investigation of Proportional Time Spent in Various Communication Activities by College Students," *Journal of Applied Communication Research* 8 (1981): 101–9.

10. Andrew D. Wolvin and Carolyn G. Coakley, *Listening* (Dubuque, IA: Wm. C. Brown Publishers, 1982); and Florence I. Wolff, Nadine C. Marsnik, William S. Tacey, and Ralph G. Nichols, *Perceptive Listening* (New York: Holt, Rinehart & Winston, 1983).

11. Larry L. Barker, *Listening Behavior* (Englewood Cliffs, NJ: Prentice-Hall, 1971): 10.

12. D. Barbara, "On Listening–the Role of the Ear in Psychic Life," *Today's Speech* 5 (1957): 12.

13. Kenneth B. Clark, "Empathy: A Neglected Topic in Psychological Research," *American Psychologist* 35 (February 1980): 188.

14. Arthur P. Bochner and Clifford W. Kelly, "Interpersonal Competence: Rationale, Philosophy, and Implementation of a Conceptual Framework," *Speech Teacher* 23 (1974): 289.

15. William S. Howell, *The Empathic Communicator* (Belmont, CA: Wadsworth, 1982), 3.

16. Ibid.

17. Carl R. Rogers, *Freedom to Learn* (Columbus, OH: Charles E. Merrill, 1969), 237.

18. Joseph N. Capella, "Interpersonal Communication: Definitions and Fundamental Questions," in *Handbook of Communication Science,* ed. Charles R. Berger and Steven H. Chaffee (Newbury Park, CA: Sage Publications, Inc., 1987), 216–17.

Chapter 5

1. Carolyn J. Mooney, "Professors Are Upbeat about Profession but Uneasy about Students Standards," *The Chronicle of Higher Education* 36 (November 8, 1989): 1, 18–21.

2. Larry L. Barker, *Listening Behavior* (Englewood Cliffs, NJ: Prentice-Hall, 1971), 10.

3. H. Rowe, *Problem Solving and Intelligence* (Hillsdale, NJ: Erlbaum, 1985).

4. Robert H. Ennis, "A Concept of Critical Thinking," *Harvard Educational Review* 32 (1962): 83–84.

5. Robert H. Ennis, "Goals for a Critical Thinking Curriculum," in *Developing Minds: A Resource Book for Teaching Thinking,* ed. A. Costa (Alexandria, VA: Association for Supervision and Curriculum Development, 1985), 54.

6. R. J. Marzano, R. S. Brandt, C. S. Hughes, B. F. Jones, B. Z. Presseisen, S. C. Rankin, and C. Suhor. *Dimensions of Thinking: A Framework for Curriculum and Instruction.* (Alexandria, VA: Association for Supervision and Curriculum Development, 1988).

7. T. G. Devine, "Can We Teach Critical Thinking?" *Elementary English* 41 (1964): 154.

8. Benjamin Bloom, *Taxonomy of Educational Objectives. Handbook 1: Cognitive Domain* (New York: Longmans, Green, & Co., 1954).

9. J. Piaget, *To Understand Is to Invent: The Future of Education* (New York: Viking, 1948/1974).

10. Lauren B. Resnick and Leopold E. Klopfer, *Toward the Thinking Curriculum: Current Cognitive Research.* (Washington, DC: USA Association for Supervision and Curriculum Development, 1989), 3–4.

11. L. C. Plunkett and G. A. Hale, *The Proactive Manager: A Complete Book of Problem Solving and Decision Making* (New York: John Wiley and Sons, Inc., 1982).

12. E. D'Angelo, *The Teaching of Critical Thinking* (Amsterdam, the Netherlands: B. R. Gruner, 1971), 7.

13. Robert H. Ennis, " A Taxonomy of Critical Thinking Dispositions and Abilities," In *Teaching Thinking Skills: Theory and Practice,* eds. J. Baron and R. Sternberg. (New York: Freeman, 1987).

14. R. J. Marzano, R. S. Brandt, C. S. Hughes, B. F. Jones, B. Z. Presseisen, S. C. Rankin, and C. Suhor. *Dimensions of Thinking: A Framework for Curriculum and Instruction.* (Alexandria, VA: Association for Supervision and Curriculum Development, 1988): 23.

15. R. J. Marzano, R. S. Brandt, C. S. Hughes, B. F. Jones, B. Z. Presseisen, S. C. Rankin, and C. Suhor. *Dimensions of Thinking: A Framework for Curriculum and*

Instruction. (Alexandria, VA: Association for Supervision and Curriculum Development, 1988), 23.

16. See William D. Brooks and Robert W. Heath, *Speech Communication,* 6th ed. (Dubuque, IA: Wm. C. Brown Publishers, 1989), 36–38.

17. For additional information on the uses and limits of argument, see Douglas Ehninger's, "Argument as Method: Its Nature, Its Limitations, and Its Uses," *Speech Monographs* 37 (1970): 101–10.

18. Anita Taylor, Arthur Meyer, Teresa Rosegrant, and B. Thomas Samples, *Communicating,* 5th ed. (Englewood Cliffs, NJ: Prentice-Hall, 1989), 128.

Chapter 6

1. Ray L. Birdwhistell, *Kinesics and Context* (Philadelphia: University of Pennsylvania Press, 1970), 128–43; Albert Mehrabian and Susan R. Kerris, "Inference of Attitude from Nonverbal Communication in Two Channels," *Journal of Consulting Psychology* 31 (1967): 248–52; Timothy G. Hegstrom, "Message Impact: What Percentage Is Nonverbal?" *Western Journal of Speech Communication* 43 (1979): 134–42; and Miles L. Patterson, "Nonverbal Exchange: Past, Present, and Future," *Journal of Nonverbal Behavior* 8 (1984): 350–59.

2. Loretta A. Malandro, Larry Barker, and Deborah Ann Barker, *Nonverbal Communication* (New York: Random House, 1989), 10–12.

3. Albert Mehrabian, *Silent Messages* (Belmont, CA: Wadsworth, 1971), 113–18.

4. Paul Ekman and Wallace V. Friesen, "The Repertoire of Nonverbal Behavior: Categories, Origins, Usage, and Coding," *Semiotica* 1 (1969): 49–98.

5. Paul Ekman and Wallace V. Friesen, "Head and Body Cues in the Judgment of Emotion: A Reformulation," *Perceptual and Motor Skills* 24 (1967): 711–24.

6. Edward J. J. Kramer and Thomas R. Lewis, "Comparison of Visual and Nonvisual Listening," *Journal of Communication* 1 (1951): 16–20.

7. See, for example, Carol M. Werner, "Home Interiors: A Time and Place for Interpersonal Relationships," *Environment and Behavior* 19 (1987): 169–79.

8. Edward T. Hall, *The Hidden Dimension* (New York: Doubleday, 1966).

9. James R. Graves and John D. Robinson, II, "Proxemic Behavior as a Function of Inconsistent Verbal and Nonverbal Messages," *Journal of Counseling Psychology* 23 (1976): 333–38; and Judee K. Burgoon, "A Communication Model of Personal Space Violations: Explication and an Initial Test," *Human Communication Research* 4 (1978): 129–42.

10. Michael Argyle and Janet Dean, "Eye-Contact, Distance, and Affiliation," *Sociometry* 28 (1965): 289–304.

11. B. R. Addis, "The Relationship of Physical Interpersonal Distance to Sex, Race, and Age" (Master's thesis, University of Oklahoma, 1966); Gloria Leventhal and Michelle Matturro, "Differential Effects of Spatial Crowding and Sex on Behavior," *Perceptual and Motor Skills* 51 (1980): 111–19; and C. R. Snyder and Janet R. Endelman, "Effects of Degree of Interpersonal Similarity on Physical Distance and Self-Reinforcement Theory Predictions," *Journal of Personality* 47 (1979): 492–505.

12. Carol J. Guardo, "Personal Space in Children," *Child Development* 40 (1969): 143–51.

13. Robert Sommer, "The Distance for Comfortable Conversation: A Further Study," *Sociometry* 25 (1962): 111–16.

14. Edward T. Hall, "Proxemics: The Study of Man's Spatial Relations and Boundaries," *Man's Image in Medicine and Anthropology* (New York: International Universities Press, 1963), 422–45.

15. William C. Schutz, *Here Comes Everybody* (New York: Harper & Row, 1971), 16.

16. Ashley Montagu, *Touching: The Human Significance of the Skin* (New York: Harper & Row, 1971), 82; J. L. Desper, "Emotional Aspects of Speech and Language Development," *International Journal of Psychiatry and Neurology* 105 (1941): 193–222; John Bowlby, *Maternal Care and Mental Health* (Geneva: World Health Organization, 1951), 15–29; and Ronald Adler and Neil Towne, *Looking Out/Looking In* (San Francisco: Rinehart Press, 1975), 225–26.

17. Donald K. Fromme, William E. Jaynes, Deborah K. Taylor, Elaine G. Hanold, Jennifer Daniell, J. Richard Rountree, and Marie L. Fromme, "Nonverbal Behavior and Attitudes toward Touch," *Journal of Nonverbal Behavior* 13 (1989): 3–14.

18. Bernie S. Siegal, *Peace, Love and Healing: Bodymind Communication and the Path to Self-Healing* (New York: Harper Perennial, 1990), 134.

19. J. D. Fisher, M. Rytting, and R. Heslin, "Hands Touching Hands: Affective and Evaluative Effects of Interpersonal Touch," *Sociometry* 3 (1976): 416–21; Donald K. Fromme, William E. Jaynes, Deborah K. Taylor, Elaine G. Hanold, Jennifer Daniell, J. Richard Rountree, and Marie L. Fromme, "Nonverbal Behavior and Attitudes toward Touch," *Journal of Nonverbal Behavior* 13 (1989): 3–14.

20. V. S. Clay, "The Effect of Culture on Mother-Child Tactile Communication," *Family Coordinator* 17 (1968): 204–10; and S. Goldberg and M. Lewis, "Play Behavior in the Year-Old Infant: Early Sex Differences," *Child Development* 40 (1969): 21–31.

21. Sidney Jourard and J. E. Rubin, "Self-Disclosure and Touching: A Study of Two Modes of Interpersonal Encounter and Their Inter-Relation," *Journal of Humanistic Psychology* 8 (1968): 39–48.

22. Sidney Jourard, "An Exploratory Study of Body Accessibility," *British Journal of Social and Clinical Psychology* 5 (1966): 221–31.

23. Nancy Henley, "Power, Sex, and Nonverbal Communication," *Berkeley Journal of Sociology* 18 (1973–1974): 10–11.

24. S. M. Jourard, *Disclosing Man to Himself* (Princeton, NJ: Van Nostrand, 1968).

25. D. C. Barnlund, "Communicative Styles of Two Cultures: Public and Private Self in Japan and the United States," in *Organization of Behavior in Face-to-Face Interaction,* eds. A. Kendon, R.M. Harris, and M.R. Key (The Hague: Mouton, 1975).

26. Ernest Kramer, "The Judgment of Personal Characteristics and Emotions from Nonverbal Properties of Speech," *Psychological Bulletin* 60 (1963): 408–20.

27. James C. McCroskey, Carl E. Larson, and Mark L. Knapp, *An Introduction to Interpersonal Communication* (Englewood Cliffs, NJ: Prentice-Hall, 1971), 116–18.

28. Kramer, "Judgement of Personal Characteristics," pp. 408–20.

29. Gregory Bateson, D. D. Jackson, J. Haley, and J. H. Weakland, "Toward a Theory of Schizophrenia," *Behavioral Science* 1 (1956): 251–64.

30. Barbara Westbrook Eakins and R. Gene Eakins, *Sex Differences in Human Communication* (Boston: Houghton Mifflin, 1978): 99–103; and Teresa J. Rosegrant and James C. McCroskey, "The Effect of Race and Sex on Proxemic Behavior in an Interview Setting," *Southern Speech Communication Journal* 40 (1975): 408–20.

31. Reprinted from "Every Human Being Is a Separate Language" by Pat Hardman in *The Salt Lake Tribune* 3 September 1971.

32. Seymour Fisher, "Body Decoration and Camouflage," in *Dimensions of Dress and Adornment: A Book of Readings,* eds. Lois M. Gurel and Marianne S. Beeson (Dubuque, IA: Kendall/Hunt, 1975).

33. Lynn Procter, *Fashion and Anti-Fashion* (London: Cox and Wyman, 1978).

34. Marilyn J. Horn, "Carrying It Off in Style," in *Dimensions of Dress and Adornment: A Book of Readings,* eds. Lois M. Gurel and Marianne S. Beeson (Dubuque, IA: Kendall/Hunt, 1975).

35. M. O. Perry, H. G. Schutz, and M. H. Rucker, "Clothing Interest, Self-Actualization and Demographic Variables," *Home Economics Research Journal* 11 (1983): 280–88.

36. L. R. Aiken, "The Relationship of Dress to Selected Measures of Personality in Undergraduate Women," *Journal of Social Psychology* 59 (1963): 119–28.

37. L. C. Taylor and N. H. Compton, "Personality Correlates of Dress Conformity," *Journal of Home Economics* 60 (1968): 653–56.

38. S. H. Hendricks, E. A. Kelley, and J. B. Eicher, "Senior Girls' Appearance and Social Acceptance," *Journal of Home Economics* 60 (1968): 167–72.

39. H. I. Douty, "Influence of Clothing on Perception of Persons," *Journal of Home Economics* 55 (1963): 197–202.

40. M. C. Williams and J. B. Eicher, "Teenagers' Appearance and Social Acceptance," *Journal of Home Economics* 58 (1966): 457–61.

41. P. N. Hamid, "Some Effects of Dress Cues on Observational Accuracy, Perceptual Estimate and Impression Formation," *Journal of Social Psychology* 86 (1972): 279–89.

Chapter 7

1. "Quayle's 'Cultural Elites': 'They Know Who They Are,'" *Athens Messenger,* 12 June 1992, p. 1.

2. Benjamin Lee Whorf, "Science and Linguistics," in *Language, Thought and Reality,* ed. John B. Carroll (Cambridge, MA: M.I.T. Press, 1956), 207–19.

3. John Barbour, "Edwin Newman Talks to Himself, But for a Good Reason," *Des Moines Sunday Register,* 5 June 1977.

Chapter 8

1. Charles R. Berger and Richard J. Calabrese, "Some Explorations in Initial Interactions and Beyond: Toward a Developmental Theory of Interpersonal Communication," *Human Communication Research* 1 (1975): 98–112.

2. William Schutz, *The Interpersonal Underworld* (Palo Alto, CA: Science and Behavior Books, 1976).

3. J. W. Thibaut and H. H. Kelley, *The Social Psychology of Groups* (New York: Wiley, 1959); and G. C. Homans, *Social Behavior: Its Elementary Forms* (New York: Harcourt Brace Jovanovich, 1961).

4. Morton Deusch and Robert M. Kraus, "Studies of Interpersonal Bargaining," *Journal of Conflict Resolution* 6 (1962): 52.

5. Thibaut and Kelley, *The Social Psychology of Groups.*

6. Gerald R. Miller, *Explorations in Interpersonal Communication* (Beverly Hills, CA: Sage Publications, 1976).

7. I. Altman and D. A. Taylor, *Social Penetration: The Development of Interpersonal Relationships* (New York: Holt, Rinehart & Winston, 1973).

8. See, for example, Leslie Baxter, "Self-Disclosure as a Relationship Disengagement Strategy: An Exploratory Investigation," *Human Communication Research* 5 (1979): 212–22; Leslie Baxter, "Strategies for Ending Relationships: Two Studies," *Western Journal of Speech Communication* 46 (1982): 223–41; Leslie Baxter, "Relationship Disengagement: An Examination of the Reversal Hypothesis," *Western Journal of Speech Communication* 47 (1983): 85–98; and Leslie Baxter, "Trajectories of Relationship Disengagement," *Journal of Social and Personal Relationships* 1 (1984): 29–48.

9. Mark L. Knapp, *Social Intercourse: From Greeting to Goodbye* (Boston: Allyn & Bacon, 1978).

10. Ronald M. Sabatelli and Michal Rubin, "Nonverbal Expressiveness and Physical Attractiveness as Mediators of Interpersonal Perceptions," *Journal of Nonverbal Behavior* 10 (1986): 120–33; and Howard S. Friedman, Ronald E. Riggio, and Daniel F. Casella, "Nonverbal Skill, Personal Charisma, and Initial Attraction," *Personality and Social Psychology Bulletin* 14 (1988): 203–11.

11. William W. Wilmot, *Dyadic Communication,* 2nd ed. (Reading, MA: Addison-Wesley, 1980).

12. Elizabeth M. Perse and Rebecca B. Rubin, "Attribution in Social and Parasocial Relationships," *Communication Research* 16 (1989): 59–77; C. R. Berger and R. Calabrese, "Some Explorations in Initial Interaction and Beyond: Toward a Developmental Theory of Interpersonal Communication," *Human Communication Research* 1 (1975): 98–112; and C. R. Berger, R. R. Gardner, G. W. Clatterbuck, and L. S. Schulman, "Perceptions of Information Sequencing in Relationship Development," *Human Communication Research* 3 (1976): 29–46.

13. Charles R. Berger and Kathy Kellermann, "Personal Opacity and Social Information Gathering," *Communication Research* 16 (1989): 314–51.

14. Mark H. Davis and H. Alan Oathout, "Maintenance of Satisfaction in Romantic Relationships: Empathy and Relational Competence," *Journal of Personality and Social Psychology* 53 (1987): 397–410.

15. David A. Kenny and Thomas E. Malloy, "Partner Effects in Social Interaction," *Journal of Nonverbal Behavior* 12 (1988): 34–57.

16. Ben R. Slugoski and William Turnbull, "Cruel to be Kind and Kind to be Cruel: Sarcasm, Banter and Social Relations," *Journal of Language and Social Psychology* 7 (1988): 101–21.

17. Steve Duck, "Social and Personal Relationships," in *Handbook of Interpersonal Communication,* eds. Mark L. Knapp and Gerald R. Miller (Beverly Hills, CA: Sage Publications, 1985), 672–73.

18. Malcolm R. Parks, "Ideology in Interpersonal Communication: Off the Couch and Into the World," in *Communication Yearbook,* 5 ed. M. Burgoon (New Brunswick, NJ: Transaction Books, 1982).

19. See, for example, Joe Ayres, "Strategies to Maintain Relationships: Their Identification and Perceived Usage," *Communication Quarterly* 31 (1983):

62–67; J. G. Delia, "Some Tentative Thoughts Concerning the Study of Interpersonal Relationships and Their Development," *Western Journal of Speech Communication* 44 (1980): 97–103; and Julia T. Wood, "Communication and Relational Culture: Bases for the Study of Human Relationships," *Communication Quarterly* 30 (1982): 75–83.

20. Melvin Lee, Philip G. Zimbardo, and Minerva Bertholf, "Shy Murderers," *Psychology Today* 11 (November 1977): 148.

21. Reprinted by permission of William Morrow & Company, Inc. from *The Shoes of the Fisherman* by Morris L. West. Copyright © 1963 by Morris L. West.

22. John Powell, *Why Am I Afraid to Tell You Who I Am?* (Niles, IL: Argus, 1969): 12.

23. L. B. Rosenfeld, "Self-Disclosure Avoidance: Why I Am Afraid to Tell You Who I Am," *Communication Monographs* 46 (1979): 63–74.

24. Joseph Stokes, Ann Fuehrer, and Lawrence Childs, "Gender Differences in Self-Disclosure to Various Target Persons," *Journal of Counseling Psychology* 27 (1980): 192–98.

25. Jack R. Gibb, "Defensive Communication," *The Journal of Communication* 11 (1961): 141–48.

26. J. C. McCroskey and T. A. McCain, "The Measurement of Interpersonal Attraction," *Speech Monographs* 41 (1974): 267–76.

27. Judy C. Pearson and Brian H. Spitzberg, *Interpersonal Communication: Concepts, Components, and Contexts* (Dubuque, Iowa: Wm. C. Brown Publishers, 1990), 56.

28. B. J. Palisi and H. E. Ransford, "Friendships as a Voluntary Relationship: Evidence from National Surveys," *Journal of Social and Personal Relationships* 4 (1987): 143–59; J. P. Wiseman, "Friendship: Bonds and Binds in a Voluntary Relationship," *Journal of Social and Personal Relationships* 3 (1986): 191–211.

29. Pearson and Spitzberg, *Interpersonal Communication* 303–8.

30. Ibid., 308.

31. Judy C. Pearson, *Interpersonal Communication: Clarity, Confidence, Concern* (Glenview, IL: Scott, Foresman, 1983).

32. Gail Sheehy, *Passages: Predictable Crises of Adult Life* (E. P. Dutton, Inc., 1976), 24–25.

Chapter 9

1. "The Lowdown on Hip-Hop: Kids Talk about the Music," *Newsweek,* 29 June 1992, 50.

2. "The Lowdown on Hip-Hop," 51.

3. Larry A. Samovar and Richard E. Porter, *Communication Between Cultures* (Belmont, CA: Wadsworth Publishing Company, 1991).

4. W. Henry, "Beyond the Melting Pot," *Time,* 9 April 1990, 28–31.

5. Samovar and Richard, *Communication Between Cultures.*

6. Larry A. Samovar and Richard E. Porter, *Intercultural Communication: A Reader* (Belmont, CA: Wadsworth Publishing Company, 1991).

7. Deborah Tannen, *You Just Don't Understand: Women and Men in Conversation* (New York: William Morrow & Company, Inc., 1990).

8. Leda M. Cooks and Mark P. Orbe, "Beyond the Satire: Selective Exposure and Selective Perception in 'In Living Color'" (Paper presented at the annual meeting of the International Communication Association Convention, Miami, Florida, 1992).

9. O. L. Taylor, "Clinical Practice as a Social Occasion," in *Communication Disorders in Multicultural Populations,* ed. L. Code and V. R. Deal (Rockville, MD: American Speech-Language-Hearing Association, in press).

10. John Leland, "Rap and Race," *Newsweek,* 29 June 1992, 47.

11. Leland, "Rap and Race," 47.

12. Lorene Cary, "As Plain as Black and White," *Newsweek,* 29 June 1992, 53.

13. Thomas Kochman, *Black and White: Styles in Conflict* (Chicago, IL: University of Chicago Press).

Chapter 10

1. Louis Cassels, "You Can Be a Better Leader," *Nation's Business* (June 1960.)

2. Cecil A. Gibb, "The Principles and Traits of Leadership," in *Small Groups: Studies in Social Interaction,* ed. A. Paul Hare, E. F. Borgatta, and R. F. Bales, rev. ed. (New York: Alfred A. Knopf, 1965), 87–95.

3. Paul Hersey and Kenneth Blanchard, *Management of Organizational Behavior: Utilizing Human Resources,* 4th ed. (Englewood Cliffs, NJ: Prentice-Hall, 1982).

4. Gerald M. Goldhaber, *Organizational Communication,* 2nd ed. (Dubuque, IA: Wm. C. Brown Publishers, 1979), 236.

5. Judy C. Pearson, Ritch L. Sorenson, and Paul E. Nelson, "How Students and Alumni Perceive the Basic Course," *Communication Education* 30 (1981): 299–307.

6. John K. Brilhart, *Effective Group Discussion,* 3rd ed. (Dubuque, IA: Wm. C. Brown Publishers, 1978), 20–21.

7. Randy Y. Hirokawa, "Group Communication and Decision-Making Performance: A Continued Test of the Functional Perspective," *Human Communication Research* 14 (1988): 487–515.

8. Susan Jarboe, "A Comparison of Input-Output, Process-Output, and Input-Process-Output Models of Small Group Problem-Solving Effectiveness," *Communication Monographs* 55 (1988): 121–42.

9. Ibid.

10. Marvin E. Shaw, "Communication Networks," in *Advances in Experimental Social Psychology,* ed. Leonard Berkowitz, vol. 1 (New York: Academic Press, 1964): 111–47.

11. The information that follows is based on Judy C. Pearson, *Gender and Communication* (Dubuque, IA: Wm. C. Brown Publishers, 1985), 316–19. The reader is encouraged to consult that source or a summary provided by John E. Baird, "Sex Differences in Group Communication: A Review of Relevant Research," *Quarterly Journal of Speech* 62 (1976): 179–92.

12. Dennis S. Gouran, "Variables Related to Consensus in Group Discussions of Questions of Policy," *Speech Monographs* 36 (1968): 387–91.

13. Jerold W. Young, "Willingness to Disclose Symptoms to a Male Physician: Effects of the Physician's Physical Attractiveness, Body Area of Symptom and the Patient's Self-Esteem, Locus of Control and Sex" (Paper presented to the International Communication Association Convention, Acapulco, Mexico, May, 1980).

14. Earl Bennett South, "Some Psychological Aspects of Committee Work," *Journal of Applied Psychology* 11 (1927): 348–68.

15. Richard L. Hoffman and Norman K. V. Maier, "Quality and Acceptance of Problem Solutions by Members of

Homogeneous and Heterogeneous Groups," *Journal of Abnormal and Social Psychology* 62 (1961): 401–7.

16. B. F. Meeker and P. A. Weitzel-O-Neill, "Sex Roles and Interpersonal Behavior in Task-Oriented Groups," *American Sociological Review* 42 (1977): 91–105.

17. Patricia Hayes Bradley, "Sex, Competence and Opinion Deviation: An Expectation States Approach," *Communication Monographs* 47 (1980): 105–10.

18. See, for example, Richard Bauer and James H. Turner, "Betting Behavior in Sexually Homogeneous and Heterogeneous Groups," *Psychological Reports* 34 (1974): 251–58.

19. R. Harper, "The Effects of Sex and Levels of Acquaintance on Risk-Taking in Groups" (Ph.D. diss., University of North Dakota, 1970).

20. See, for example, Alan H. Benton, "Reactions to Demands to Win from an Opposite Sex Opponent," *Journal of Personality* 41 (1973): 430–42.

21. See, for example, Joseph H. Hattes and Arnold Kahn, "Sex Differences in a Mixed-Motive Conflict Situation," *Journal of Personality* 42 (1974): 260–75.

22. See, for example, Monroe M. Lefkowitz, Leonard D. Eron, Leopold O. Walder, and L. Rowell Huesmann, *Growing up to Be Violent: A Longitudinal Study of the Development of Aggression* (New York: Pergamon Press, Inc., 1977).

23. See, for example, H. L. Kaplowitz, "Machiavellianism and Forming Impressions of Others," in *Contemporary Social Psychology: Representative Readings,* ed. Thomas Blass (Itasca, IL: F. E. Peacock, 1976).

24. Michael E. Roloff, "The Impact of Socialization on Sex Differences in Conflict Resolution" (Paper presented at the Annual Convention of the International Communication Association, Acapulco, Mexico, May, 1980).

25. Sidney M. Jourard, *Self-Disclosure: An Experimental Analysis of the Transparent Self* (New York: John Wiley, 1971).

26. J. Bond and W. Vinacke, "Coalition in Mixed Sex Triads," *Sociometry* 24 (1961): 61–75.

27. Thomas K. Uesugi and W. Edgar Vinacke, "Strategy in a Feminine Game," *Sociometry* 26 (1963): 75–88.

28. I. Mat Amidjaja and W. Edgar Vinacke, "Achievement, Nurturance, and Competition in Male and Female Triads," *Journal of Personality and Social Psychology* 2 (1965): 447–51.

29. Ibid.

30. Joan E. Marshall and Richard Heslin, "Boys and Girls Together: Sex Composition and the Effect of Density and Group Size on Cohesiveness," *Journal of Personality and Social Psychology* 31 (1975): 952–61.

31. B. Aubrey Fisher, "Differential Effects of Sexual Composition and Interactional Context on Interaction Patterns in Dyads," *Human Communication Research* 9 (1983): 225–38; and Elaine M. Yamada, Dean Tjosvold, and Juris G. Draguns, "Effects of Sex-Linked Situations and Sex Composition on Cooperation and Style of Interaction," *Sex Roles* 9 (1983): 541–54.

32. Donald G. Ellis and Linda McCallister, "Relational Control in Sex-Typed and Androgynous Groups," *Western Journal of Speech Communication* 44 (1980): 35–49.

33. Alex F. Osborn, *Applied Imagination: Principles and Procedures of Creative Thinking* (New York: Scribner's, 1953), 300–301.

34. Roy F. Baumeister, Stuart P. Chesner, Pamela S. Senders, and Dianne M. Tice, "Who's in Charge Here? Group Leaders

Do Lend Help in Emergencies," *Personality and Social Psychology Bulletin* 14 (1988): 17–22.

35. Connie S. Hellman, "An Investigation of the Communication Behavior of Emergent and Appointed Leaders in Small Group Discussion" (Ph.D. diss., Indiana University, 1974).

36. Morris Aderman and Carol A. Johnson, "Leadership Style and Personal History Information," *Journal of Psychology* 102 (1979): 243–50.

37. R. White and R. Lippit, "Leader Behavior and Member Reaction in Three 'Social Climates'," in *Group Dynamics: Research and Theory,* ed. Dorwin Cartwright and Alvin Zander, 2nd ed. (New York: Harper & Row, 1960): 527–53; L. P. Bradford and R. Lippit, "Building a Democratic Work Group," *Personnel* 22 (1945): 142–52; and William M. Fox, "Group Reaction to Two Types of Conference Leadership," *Human Relations* 10 (1957): 279–89.

38. See, for example, L. L. Rosenbaum and W. B. Rosenbaum, "Morale and Productivity Consequences of Group Leadership Styles, Stress, and Type of Task," *Journal of Applied Psychology* 55 (1971): 343–58; and Paul Hersey and Kenneth Blanchard, *Management of Organizational Behavior: Utilizing Human Resources,* 4th ed. (Englewood Cliffs, NJ: Prentice-Hall, 1982).

39. Dorothy M. Haccoun, Robert P. Haccoun, and George Sallay, "Sex Differences in the Appropriateness of Supervisory Styles: A Nonmanagement View," *Journal of Applied Psychology* 63 (1978): 124–27.

40. John K. Brilhart, *Effective Group Discussion,* 3rd ed. (Dubuque, IA: Wm. C. Brown Publishers, 1978): 170–82.

Chapter 12

1. "What Are Americans Afraid of?" *Bruskin Report* 53 (1973).

2. Much of the following information concerning communication apprehension comes from James C. McCroskey and Lawrence R. Wheeless, "The Nature and Effects of Communication Apprehension," *Introduction to Human Communication* (Boston: Allyn & Bacon, 1976), 81–90.

3. Judy C. Pearson and Donald D. Yoder, "Public Speaking or Interpersonal Communication: The Perspective of the High Communication Apprehensive Student," Educational Resources Information Center (ERIC), ED 173870, May 1979.

4. Alan Feingold, "Correlates of Public Speaking Attitude," *The Journal of Social Psychology* 120 (1983): 285–86.

5. Ibid.

6. John A. Daly, Anita L. Vangelisti, Heather L. Neel, and P. Daniel Cavanaugh, "Pre-Performance Concerns Associated with Public Speaking Anxiety," *Communication Quarterly* 37 (1989): 39–53.

7. Teri Kwal Gamble and Michael Gamble, *Communication Works,* 2nd ed. (New York: Random House, 1987), 401.

8. Adapted from two exercises provided by Teri Kwal Gamble and Michael Gamble, *Communication Works,* 2nd ed. (New York: Random House, 1987), 401–2.

9. Everett L. Worthington, Jr., Robert M. Tipton, Janet S. Comley, Thomas Richards, and Robert H. Janke, "Speech and Coping Skills Training and Paradox as Treatment for College Students Anxious about Public Speaking," *Perceptual and Motor Skills* 59 (1984): 394.

10. G. D. Hemsley and A. M. Doob, "The Effect of Looking Behavior on Perceptions of a Communicator's Credibility," *Journal of Applied Social Psychology* 8 (1978): 136–44.

11. E. A. Lind and W. M. O'Barr, "The Social Significance of Speech in the Courtroom," in *Language and Social Psychology,* ed. H. Giles and R. St. Clair (Oxford, England: Blackwells, 1979).

12. N. Miller, G. Maruyama, R. J. Beaber, and K. Valone, "Speed of Speech and Persuasion," *Journal of Personality and Social Psychology* 34 (1976): 615–25.

13. Aristotle, "Rhetoric," in *The Basic Works of Aristotle,* trans. W. Rhys Roberts and ed. by Richard McKeon (New York: Random House, 1941), 1, 1356a, LL. 12–14.

14. Ralph L. Rosnow and Edward J. Robinson, eds., *Experiments in Persuasion* (New York: Academic Press, 1967), 18.

15. Wendy Wood and Carl A. Kallgren, "Communicator Attributes and Persuasion: Recipients' Access to Attitude-Relevant Information in Memory," *Personality and Social Psychology Bulletin* 14 (1988): 172–82.

16. Kenneth G. DeBono and Richard J. Harnish, "Source Expertise, Source Attractiveness, and the Processing of Persuasive Information: A Functional Approach," *Journal of Personality and Social Psychology* 55 (1988): 541–46.

17. Derived from a study by Christopher J. S. Tuppen, "Dimensions of Communicator Credibility: An Oblique Solution," *Speech Monographs* 41 (1974): 253–60.

18. Ibid.

19. Rosnow and Robinson, *Experiments in Persuasion,* 8. *See also,* Kenneth Andersen and Theodore Clevenger, Jr., "A Summary of Experimental Research in Ethos," *Speech Monographs* 30 (1963): 59–78.

20. Marvin Karlins and Herbert I. Abelson, *Persuasion* (New York: Springer, 1970), 113–14.

21. Carl I. Hovland and Walter Weiss, "The Influence of Source Credibility on Communicator Effectiveness," in *Experiments in Persuasion* (New York: Academic Press, 1967), 21.

22. Wayne N. Thompson, *Quantitative Research in Public Address and Communication* (New York: Random House, 1967), 54.

23. Andersen and Clevenger, "A Summary," 59–78.

24. L. S. Harms, "Listener Judgments of Status Cues in Speech," *Quarterly Journal of Speech* 47 (1961): 168.

25. Harry Sharp, Jr. and Thomas McClung, "Effects of Organization on the Speaker's Ethos," *Speech Monographs* 33 (1966): 182–83.

26. Thompson, *Quantitative Research,* p. 56.

27. Ibid.

28. Stephen E. Lucas, *The Art of Public Speaking,* 3rd ed. (New York: Random House, 1989), 21.

Chapter 13

1. Erwin P. Bettinghaus, *The Nature of Proof* (New York: Bobbs-Merrill, 1972), v.

2. Ibid.

3. Ibid.

4. William Safire, "When a Mistake Becomes Correct, and Vice Versa," *Des Moines Sunday Register,* 30 November 1980, p. 3C.

Chapter 14

1. "Bones Found in Kenya May Be from Apes' Progenitor," *Chronicle of Higher Education,* 7 December 1983, 1.

2. "Research Notes," *Chronicle of Higher Education,* 7 (December 1983): 1–2.

3. James J. Kilpatrick, "Death Sentence as Gun Control?" *Des Moines Tribune,* 12 December 1980, p. 18.

4. "The Killing Goes On," *Des Moines Tribune,* 11 December 1980, p. 18.

5. Ibid.

6. "Research Notes," 1–2.

7. Tom Wicker, "You, Me and Handguns," *Ames Daily Tribune,* 18 December 1980, p. A4.

8. Ibid.

9. Ibid.

10. Ibid.

11. "Research Notes," 1–2.

12. The examples of incorrect and correct parallel form are derived from U.S. Education Secretary T. H. Bell's announcement in 1984 concerning figures from 1982 and before, "State School Official Pleased by Ohio's Grade," *Athens Messenger,* 6 January 1984, p. 13.

13. From a fictional account based on historical facts: James A. Michener, *The Covenant,* 2 vols. (New York: Random House, 1980).

Chapter 15

1. Ernest H. Henrikson, "An Analysis of the Characteristics of Some 'Good' and 'Poor' Speakers," *Speech Monographs* 11 (1944): 120–24.

2. Roland J. Hard and Bruce L. Brown, "Interpersonal Information Conveyed by the Content and Vocal Aspects of Speech," *Speech Monographs* 41 (1974): 371–80; and D. F. Gundersen and Robert Hopper, "Relationships between Speech Delivery and Speech Effectiveness," *Speech Monographs* 43 (1976): 158–65.

3. Charles R. Petrie, Jr., "Informative Speaking: A Summary and Bibliography of Related Research," *Speech Monographs* 30 (1963): 81.

4. Herbert W. Hildebrandt and Walter Stephens, "Manuscript and Extemporaneous Delivery in Communicating Information," *Speech Monographs* 30 (1963): 369–72.

5. Erwin Bettinghaus, "The Operation of Congruity in an Oral Communication Situation," *Speech Monographs* 28 (1961): 131–42.

6. Henrikson, "An Analysis of the Characteristics of Some 'Good' and 'Poor' Speakers," 120–24.

7. Howard Gilkinson and Franklin H. Knower, "Individual Differences among Students of Speech as Revealed by Psychological Test—I," *Journal of Educational Psychology* 32 (1941): 161–75.

8. John L. Vohs, "An Empirical Approach to the Concept of Attention," *Speech Monographs* 31 (1964): 355–60.

9. Charles Woolbert, "The Effects of Various Modes of Public Reading," *Journal of Applied Psychology* 4 (1920): 162–85.

10. John W. Black, "A Study of Voice Merit," *Quarterly Journal of Speech* 28 (1942): 67–74.

11. Donald Hayworth, "A Search for Facts on the Teaching of Public Speaking," *Quarterly Journal of Speech* 28 (1942): 247–54.

12. Charles Woolbert, "The Effects of Various Modes of Public Reading," *Journal of Applied Psychology* 4 (1920): 162–85; George M. Glasgow, "A Semantic Index of Vocal Pitch," *Speech Monographs* 19 (1952): 64–68; Kenneth C. Beighley, "An Experimental Study of the Effect of Four Speech Variables on Listener Comprehension," *Speech Monographs* 19 (1952): 249–58; and Black, *Study of Voice Merit,* 67–74.

13. Edward J. J. Kramer and Thomas R. Lewis, "Comparison of Visual and Nonvisual Listening," *Journal of Communication* I (1931): 16–20.

14. Martin Cobin, "Response to Eye Contact," *Quarterly Journal of Speech* 48 (1962): 415–18.

15. Steven A. Beebe, "Eye Contact: A Nonverbal Determinant of Speaker Credibility," *Speech Teacher* 23 (1974): 21–25.

16. Elena P. Zayas-Baya, "Instructional Media in the Total Language Picture," *International Journal of Instructional Media* 5 (1977–1978): 145–50.

17. Kenneth B. Haas and Harry Q. Packer, *Preparation and Use of Audiovisual Aids* (New York: Prentice-Hall, 1955), 163–68.

18. Michael MacDonald-Ross, "How Numbers Are Shown: A Review of Research on the Presentation of Quantitative Data in Texts," *AV Communication Review* 25 (Winter 1977): 359–409.

19. Isbrabim M. Hebyallah and W. Paul Maloney, "Content Analysis of T.V. Commercials," *International Journal of Instructional Media* 5 (1977–1978): 9–16.

Chapter 16

1. Charles R. Petrie, Jr., "Informative Speaking: A Summary and Bibliography of Related Research," *Speech Monographs* 30 (1963): 79–91.

2. See N. C. Cofer, *Verbal Learning and Verbal Behavior* (New York: McGraw-Hill, 1961).

3. Lawrence R. Wheeless, "The Effects of Attitude, Credibility, and Homophily on Selective Exposure to Information," *Speech Monographs* 41 (1974): 329–38.

4. Charles R. Petrie, Jr. and Susan D. Carrel, "The Relationship of Motivation, Listening Capability, Initial Information, and Verbal Organization Ability to Lecture Comprehension and Retention," *Speech Monographs* 43 (1976): 187–94.

5. Petrie, "Informative Speaking," 80.

6. Carole Ernest, "Listening Comprehension as a Function of Type of Material and Rate of Presentation," *Speech Monographs* 35 (1968): 154–58. See also, John A. Baird, "The Effects of Speech Summaries upon Audience Comprehension of Expository Speeches of Varying Quality and Complexity," *Central States Speech Journal* 25 (1974): 119–27.

7. Charles R. Gruner, "The Effect of Humor in Dull and Interesting Informative Speeches," *Central States Speech Journal* 21 (1970): 160–66.

8. Petrie, "Informative Speaking," 84.

9. Charles O. Tucker, "An Application of Programmed Learning to Informative Speech," *Speech Monographs* 31 (1964): 142–52.

10. Petrie, "Informative Speaking," 81.

11. See O. L. Pence, "Emotionally Loaded Argument: Its Effectiveness in Stimulating Recall," *Quarterly Journal of Speech* 40 (1954): 272–76.

12. Baird, "Effect of Speech Summaries," 119–27.

13. David Ausubel, "The Use of Advance Organizers in the Learning and Retention of Meaningful Material," *Journal of Educational Psychology* 51 (1960): 267–72.

14. John Kenneth Galbraith, "The Three Attacks on Social and Economic Consensus," *Des Moines Sunday Register,* 4 January 1981. Reprinted from an article in the *New York Review of Books.* Reprinted with permission.

Chapter 17

1. Marvin Karlins and Herbert I. Abelson, *Persuasion: How Opinions and Attitudes Are Changed,* 2nd ed. (New York: Springer, 1970).

2. Based on Gerald R. Miller, "On Being Persuaded: Some Basic Distinctions," in *Persuasion: New Directions in Theory*

and *Research,* ed. Michael E. Roloff and Gerald R. Miller (Beverly Hills, CA: Sage, 1980).

3. Adapted from Wallace Fotheringham, *Perspectives on Persuasion* (Boston: Allyn & Bacon, 1966), 33.

4. Based on James V. McConnell, *Understanding Human Behavior: An Introduction to Psychology* (New York: Holt, Rinehart & Winston, 1977): 243–51.

5. C. Hovland and H. Pritzker, "Extent of Opinion Change as a Function of Amount of Change Advocated," *Journal of Abnormal and Social Psychology* 54 (1957): 257–61.

6. Jerry M. Burger and Robert A. Vartabedian, "Public Self-Disclosure and Speaker Persuasiveness," *Journal of Applied Social Psychology* 15 (1985): 153–65.

7. John C. Reinard, "The Empirical Study of the Persuasive Effects of Evidence: The Status After Fifty Years of Research," *Human Communication Research* 15 (1988): 3–59.

8. I. S. Janis and S. Feshbach, "Effects of Fear-Arousing Communications," *Journal of Abnormal and Social Psychology* 48 (1953): 78–92.

9. Fredric A. Powell, "The Effects of Anxiety-Arousing Messages When Related to Personal, Familial, and Impersonal Referents," *Speech Monographs* 32 (1965): 102–6.

10. Frances Cope and Don Richardson, "The Effects of Measuring Recommendations in a Fear-Arousing Speech," *Speech Monographs* 39 (1972): 148–50.

11. R. L. Rosnow and E. Robinson, *Experiment in Persuasion* (New York: Academic Press, 1967): 99–104.

12. Karlins and Abelson, *Persuasion,* 22–26.

13. Ibid.

14. D. Sears and J. Freedman, "Effects of Expected Familiarity with Arguments upon Opinion Change and Selective Exposure," *Journal of Personality and Social Psychology* 2 (1965): 420–26.

15. For additional information on the uses and limits of argument, see Douglas Ehninger, "Argument as Method: Its Nature, Its Limitations, and Its Uses," *Speech Monographs* 37 (1970): 101–10.

16. Gerald R. Miller, "Evidence and Argument," in *Perspectives on Argument,* edited by Gerald R. Miller and Thomas R. Nilsen (Chicago: Scott, Foresman, 1966): 25. See also Robert P. Newman and Dale R. Newman, *Evidence* (Boston: Houghton Mifflin, 1969).

17. Douglas Ehninger, Bruce E. Gronbeck, and Alan H. Monroe, *Principles of Speech Communication,* 9th brief ed. (Glenview, IL: Scott, Foresman, 1984): 249.

Appendix

1. Charles J. Stewart and William B. Cash, Jr., *Interviewing Principles and Practices,* 3rd ed. (Dubuque, Iowa: W. C. Brown Publishers, 1982), 10.

2. R. D. Avey and J. E. Campion, "The Employment Interview: A Summary and Review of Recent Research," *Personal Psychology* 35 (1982): 290, 303.

3. John T. Hopkins, "The Top Twelve Questions for Employment Agency Interviews," *Personnel Journal* 59 (May 1980): 209–13.

4. Based on Charles S. Goetzinger, Jr., "An Analysis of Irritating Factors in Initial Employment Interviews of Male College Graduates" (Ph.D. Purdue University, 1954).

5. Robert E. Kraut, "Verbal and Nonverbal Cues in the Perception of Lying," *Journal of Personality and Social Psychology* 36 (1978): 380–91.

Credits

Photo Credits

Chapter 1

Opener: ©Jim Weiner/Photo Researchers, Inc.; p. 6: ©Bill Bachmann/The Image Works; p. 7: ©Jim Weiner/Photo Researchers, Inc.; p. 15: ©Cleo Freelance Photography

Chapter 2

Opener: ©Kolvoord/The Image Works; p. 32: ©1992 Lawrence Migdale; p. 40: ©Bob Coyle

Chapter 3

Opener, p. 46, p. 51: ©Bob Coyle

Chapter 4

Opener: ©Richard Anderson; p. 62: ©James L. Shaffer; p. 68: ©Richard Anderson; p. 72: ©Ulrike Welsch/Photo Researchers, Inc.

Chapter 5

Opener, p. 93, p. 99: ©Joseph Nettis/Photo Researchers, Inc.; p. 377: ©1992 G. Cloyd/Martin M. Rotker Photography

Chapter 6

Opener, p. 123: ©Richard Anderson; p. 128: ©Anea Vohra/Unicorn Stock Photos

Chapter 7

Opener: ©Bob Coyle; 7.1: ©Tim Davis/Photo Researchers, Inc. ©Bob Coyle

Chapter 8

Opener: ©Bob Daemmrich/The Image Works; p. 159: ©Richard Anderson; p. 161: ©Bob Daemmrich/The Image Works; p. 163: © Michael A. DiSpezio; p. 173: ©Cleo Freelance Photography; p. 179: ©Michael A. DiSpezio

Chapter 9

Opener, p. 189: ©Day Williams/Photo Researchers, Inc.; p. 192: © Bob Daemmrich/The Image Works; p. 196: ©Fujifotos/The Image Works

Chapter 10

Opener: ©James Shaffer; p. 214: ©Richard Luria/Photo Researchers, Inc.; p. 223: ©Bob Daemmrich/The Image Works; p. 226: ©Catherine Allport/The Image Works

Chapter 11

Opener: ©James Shaffer; p. 239: ©Alan Carey/The Image Works; p. 245: ©James Shaffer; p. 253: ©Holt Confer/The Image Works; p. 258: ©James L. Shaffer

Chapter 12

Opener: ©T. Savino/The Image Works; p. 271: ©James L. Shaffer; p. 276: ©T. Savino/The Image Works; p. 277: AP/Wide World Photos

Chapter 13

Opener, p. 288: ©Martha McBride/Unicorn Stock Photos; p. 295: ©James Shaffer; p. 300: ©Nancy Anne Dawe

Chapter 14

Opener: ©Karen Holsinger Mullen/Unicorn Stock Photos; p. 319: ©James Shaffer; p. 330: ©Chris Boylan/Unicorn Stock Photos; p. 337: ©Karen Holsinger Mullen/Unicorn Stock Photos

Chapter 15

Opener, p. 358: ©AP/Wide
World Photos; p. 364:
©Joseph Nettis/Photo
Researchers, Inc.; p. 370:
©Michael A. DiSpezio; 15.5:
©Bryce Flynn/Picture Group,
Inc.

Chapter 16

Opener: ©Bob Daemmrich/The
Image Works; p. 386, p. 391:
©Mary E. Messenger; p. 393:
©William Hopkins, Jr.; p. 395:
©Bob Coyle

Chapter 17

Opener: ©T. Savino/The Image
Works; p. 419: ©Michael Siluk;
p. 427: ©James G. White

Index

Intercultural communication,
186–205, 206
accommodation and,
189–190, 205
advertising and, 199
assimilation and, 189–190,
205
assumed similarity and, 200
code sensitivity and, 203
defined, 188, 206
denial of differences and,
200
descriptive feedback and,
204
diversity and, 203
early termination and, 201
examples of, 188
frustration and, 201
hasty generalizations and,
203
melting pot theory and,
189–190
misinterpretation of codes in,
200–201
open communication chan-
nels and, 204
personal self-assessment and,
203
potential problems in,
198–202
stereotyping and, 203
strategies to improve, 203
supportive communication
and, 203
Internal locus of control, 54–56,
57
Interpersonal communication,
16–18, 21, 155
dyadic, 18
friends and, 176
small group, 18
*Interpersonal Communication
and Human
Relationships,* 166
Interpersonal relationships,
156–182, 183
coping through, 162
definition of, 158
friends and, 176
fulfilling needs through, 162
importance of, 159
improving communication
in, 178–179
interacting over time in, 159
interdependence in, 158
nature of, 158–164
number of people in, 158
patterns of interaction in, 158
positive experiences through,
163

stages in, 164
understanding others
through, 160–161
understanding ourselves
through, 159–160
understanding our world,
161
Interpretation, 29, 34–35, 37
Interviewing for a job, 441–446
communication skills and,
444
definition of, 441
expectations and, 445
interest in, 445
motivation for, 445
preparing for, 441, 445
process of, 442–444
questions asked in, 443
rejection and, 446
Interviewing people, 296
conducting the interview,
296
Intimate distance, 121–122
Intrapersonal communication,
15–16, 21
critical thinking and, 101
Introduction, 316–317, 347
Involvement, 238, 261
Irrelevant conclusion, 108, 111

J

Janis, I. S., and S. Feshbach, 419
Jargon, 143, 154
Joarbut, Joseph, 91
Job interview, 441–446
Johari Window, 42–44, 57, 160
blind self, 43, 57, 160
hidden self, 43, 57, 160
open self, 42–43, 57, 160
unknown self, 43–44, 57, 160
Johnson, Lyndon B., 91
Johnson, Magic, 8
Johnson, Samuel, 409
Jones, Franklin P., 157
Jourard, Sidney M., 3, 125
Justification, 102, 112, 439

K

Karlins, Marvin, and Herbert I.
Abelson, 415
Kennedy, Florynce R., 315
Kennedy, John F., 343
Key word outline, 331–333, 347
Kinesics, 118, 130
King, Rodney, 8, 432
Knapp, Mark L., 165
Knapp, Mark L., and Ania L.
Vangelish, 166

Knowledge of topic, 238–239
Korzybski, Count Alfred, 135
Kubler-Ross, Elisabeth, 157

L

Landman, Theodore, 41
Language, 134–153
as personal, 135–137
as verbal code, 134
culture and, 137
distortion in, 144
metaphor and, 145
race and, 201
setting and, 140–141
situation and, 140–141
unconventional usage in, 141
words as obstacles in,
141–144
Laissez-faire leadership,
224–225, 232
Leadership, 208, 223–225, 232
appointed leader, 216, 231
creative thinking and, 227
critical thinking and, 227
developing the group in, 227
emergent leader, 216, 232
facilitating understanding in,
227
initiating in, 225–226
organizing in, 226
participation in, 225–226
promoting relationships in,
227
small groups and, 223
spreading participation in,
226
styles-of-leadership, 223
Lee, Melvin, Philip G. Zimbardo,
and Minerva Bertholf, 170
Library exercise, 293
Liking, 119
Line graph, 371
Listening, 60, 87
active, 64–66
barriers to, 72–73
behaviors associated with,
78–83
checklist for, 79
critical, 90–110, 111
defensiveness in, 64, 87
illustration of, 61
improving our, 77–78
interference with, 69
long-term memory in, 60
to mass media, 63
noise and, 69–73
nonverbal skills of, 83
overcoming distractions to,
77–78

process of, 60–63
recall after, 60–61
response styles in, 70–71
short-term memory in, 60
thinking and, 90–110
time spent, 62
types of, 63–69
verbal demonstrations of, 82
verbal skills of, 78–83
Loaded terms, 65
Logical appeals, 418, 439
Logical proof, 102, 112
Long-range goal, 258–259, 324, 347
Lost in the Cosmos: The Last Self-Help Book, 48

M

MacMillan, Donald, 28
Major premise, 106
Mann, Thomas, 3, 315
Manuscript mode, 353, 378
Maslow, Abraham, 41
Mays, Dr. Benjamin E., 435
McLuhan, Marshall, 188–189
Mean, 302, 311
Meaning, 8, 21
Median, 302, 311
Medicine and nonverbal communication, 124
Mehrabian, Albert, 119
Melting pot theory, 189, 206
Member satisfaction, 215, 232
Memorized mode, 353–354, 378
Mental distractions, 72, 87
Message, 12, 21
Metatalk, 142, 154
Minor premise, 106
Misinterpretation of codes, 200–201, 206
example of, 202
MLA Handbook for Writers of Research Papers, 292, 341
Mode, 302, 311
Models, 375
Modes of delivery, 352–354, 378
Modern Quotations for Ready Reference, 289
Monroe motivated sequence, 421–422, 439
Morris, Charles, 41
Moses, Grandma, 43
Movement, 364–365
Movies, 372–373

N

Narrating, 399, 407
Narrowing the topic, 240
Neologisms, 140, 154
Neutrality, 174
Newman, Edwin, 147
New York Times, 289
Nin, Anais, 115
1984, 5
Noise, 14, 21, 69–73
factual distractions as, 72, 87
mental distractions as, 72, 87
physical distractions as, 72, 87
semantic distractions as, 73, 87
Nonassertiveness, 173, 183
Nonverbal codes, 14, 21, 114–130
bodily movement in, 118–120
cues and meanings in, 116–117
definition of, 118–129
identification of, 118–129
intentionality and, 117–118
kinesics and, 118
liking in, 119
motives and, 117–118
problems in interpreting, 116–118
responsiveness and, 119
status and, 119
unintentional cues and, 117–118
Nonverbal communication, adaptors, 120
affect displays in, 120
artifacts in, 127–128, 130
emblems in, 119
evaluating, 365
illustrators in, 119
improving your, 129–130
medicine and, 124
negative feedback in, 64
objectics and, 127–128, 131
regulators in, 120
religion and, 124
space in, 120–122
touch and, 123–126
vocal cues in, 125–127
Normal communication apprehension, 266–268
Norms, 212–213, 232

Notetaking, 94–95
applying standards in, 95
capturing information, 94–95
establishing standards for, 95
exercise in effective, 96–97
Novel arguments, 421

O

Objectics, 127–128, 131
Objective reception, 24, 37
Observation, 106, 112, 250–251, 261
Opaque projectors, 372
Open self, 42–43, 57
Operational definitions, 148, 154, 397, 407
Oral footnote, 311
Orbe, Mark, xxii, 186–206
Organization, 29, 37
closure in, 31–32, 37
figure and ground, 30–31, 37
proximity and, 32–33, 37
similarity in, 32–33, 37
Organizational patterns, 333–339, 347
causal-sequence, 336–337
problem-and-solution, 337–338
spatial-sequence, 335–336
time-sequence, 334, 348
topical-sequence, 338–339
Organizing your speech, 314–347
Orwell, George, 5
Out of the Barrio: Toward a New Politics of Hispanic Assimilation, 303
Outlining, 323–348
main points in, 325–347
principles of, 324–327, 347
subpoints, 325, 348
sub-subpoints, 325, 348
Overhead projectors, 372
Oxford English Dictionary, 140–141, 397

P

Pacino, Al, 48–49
Panel, 218
Paralinguistic features, 125, 131
Parallel form, 326, 347
Paraphrasing, 148, 151, 154
Parks, Malcolm, 169
Pascal, 409
Passages: Predictable Crises of Adult Life, 181

Vocalized pauses, 357, 378
Vocal variety, 360–361, 378
Volume, 125, 357–358, 378
Voluntary audience, 244–245, 261

W

Warhol, Andy, 263
Washington, Booker T., 429
Watzalawick, Beavin and Jackson, 44

Weinrauch, J. Donald, and Johan R. Swanda, 62
West, Morris L., 172
Whorf, Benjamin Lee, 146
Who's Who in America, 289
Why Am I Afraid to Tell You Who I Am?, 172
"Why We Can't Wait," 428–435
Wilde, Oscar, 39
Williams, Mason, 54
Wilmont, William, 168
Women and touch, 124
Words as verbal symbols, 134

World Almanac, 288
Writings, 62
Written and visual resources, 287–291, 312

Y

You Just Don't Understand: Women and Men in Conversation, 193